THE MISUSE OF PERSONS
Analyzing Pathological Dependency

THE MISUSE OF PERSONS
Analyzing Pathological Dependency

Stanley J. Coen

THE ANALYTIC PRESS

1992   Hillsdale, NJ   London

Published by The Analytic Press, Inc.
365 Broadway, Hillsdale, NJ 07642

This book incorporates, in thoroughly revised form, material previously published elsewhere. Grateful acknowledgment is made to the *Journal of the American Psychoanalytic Association* for permission to adapt and revise portions of the following articles: "Intolerance of responsibility for internal conflict" (1989) 37:943-964; "Perversion as a solution to intraspychic conflict" (1985) 33(suppl.):17-57; "The sense of defect" (1986) 34:47-65; "Superego aspects of entitlement (in rigid characters)" (1988) 36:409-426; "Sexualization as a predominant mode of defense" (1981) 29; "Twin transference as a compromise formation" (with permission also of coauthor P. Bradlow) (1982) 30:599-620; the *International Journal of Psycho-Analysis* for permission to adapt a portion of "Pathological jealousy" (1987) 68:99-108; Gardner Press, Inc. for permission to adapt portions of the following chapter: "The analyst's uses and misuses of clinical theory: Interpretation" *The Yearbook of Psychoanalysis and Psychotherapy* (1987) 2.

Library of Congress Cataloging in Publication Data

Coen, Stanley J.
The misuse of persons : analyzing pathological dependency / Stanley J. Coen.
p. cm.
Includes bibliographic references and index.
ISBN 0-88163-139-6
1. Dependency (Psychology) 2. Personality Disorders.
3. Psychoanalysis. I. Title
[dnlm: 1. Dependency (Psychology) 2. Personality Disorders. BF
575.D34 C672m]
RC569.5.D47C64   1991
616.85'8--dc20
DNLM/DLC
for Library of Congress   91--47096
                                                              CIP

Printed in the United States of America
10 9 8 7 6 5 4 3 2 1

For Ruth
And for Gwen, Jennifer, Michael, Debbie, and David
With Love and Appreciation

CONTENTS

Part IV
The Pathological Need for the Other

Part V
Conclusion

PREFACE

This book is the product of nearly 20 years of exploration, thought, and writing. It represents an integration of my perspective on the psychopathology and psychoanalysis of certain forms of pathological object relations that are expressed as varieties of pathological dependency. Pathological dependency becomes the cornerstone for understanding attempts to avoid destructiveness through sexualization, sadomasochism, perversion, and repetitive dependent enactments. I emphasize the maintenance of defensive illusions through the misuse of others. Problems of analyzing patients who are content—indeed determined—to preserve such pathological object relations, with the analyst as well as with others, are addressed. These are patients who do not seem very sick in their daily lives but who have considerable difficulty with the analytic process. They avoid responsibility for what is wrong within themselves and tend to attribute their problems to others.

How to motivate such patients to confront their own internal conflicts (and to feel safe enough to do so) becomes crucial for the progress of their psychoanalysis (or intensive psychoanalytic psychotherapy). My focus is on how to help such patients to move forward, out of pathological dependency toward autonomy and self-management. I especially emphasize how to assist patients ameliorate their terror of their rage and destructiveness; this terror has driven them backward into dependency. What I (Coen, 1981, 1985a, 1986, 1987a, 1987b, 1988a, 1989; Coen and Sarno, 1989) have written previously, I have rethought, modified, and integrated within my current perspective.

The reader who would like further background on the development of the concepts of repetition, sexualization, perversion, and
perverse object relations as these apply to pathological dependency
will find it in the appendix, although this book can certainly be read
without consulting the appendix. Indeed, the reader is encouraged to
immerse himself or herself in the main clinical arguments of this book
before reading the appendix. However, the appendix will help to
clarify some of the routes I have followed in integrating my views of
pathological dependency. I invite the reader to share this psychoanalytic journey with me.

A number of people have significantly helped me to investigate
and write my views of these psychoanalytic problems. Foremost is
my wife, Dr. Ruth Imber, who has not only supported my writing
with love and patience, but who has also been a helpful critic of my
psychoanalytic positions and encouraged me to clarify and simplify.
I thank my children for their tolerance of my writing passion and for
their loving acceptance and help. If not for Michael's sharing with me
his love of computer science and his help, this book could not have
been completed. Gwen, Jennifer, and Debbie helped with bibliographic research, and Debbie also assisted with word processing.
David, thank you for your patience.

The Columbia University Psychoanalytic Center has been especially encouraging of my psychoanalytic development and my writing.
I am appreciative of their having awarded me the Alexander Beller
Memorial Prize for Psychoanalytic Writing in 1982. Two close friends
and colleagues, Paul Bradlow, M.D., and Arnold Rothstein, M.D.,
helped me to begin writing psychoanalytic papers. First my teacher
and psychoanalytic supervisor, Paul became my collaborator, coauthor and friend. Arnold ("Chuck"), as friend, model, fond critic, and
supporter has consistently inspired me and my writing. Among the
other colleagues who encouraged me and offered useful criticism as I
began to write psychoanalytic articles, I want to thank Drs. Arnold
Cooper, Helen and Donald Meyers, Robert Michels, Ethel Person, and
Daniel Shapiro. Harold Blum, M. D., as editor of the *Journal of the
American Psychoanalytic Association*, contributed to the clarification and
development of my ideas. Theodore Shapiro, M.D., continued this
editorial assistance. I am grateful to have had the opportunity to
present some of this material at meetings of the American Psychoanalytic Association and the Association for Psychoanalytic Medicine.
Such discussions of my work have been invaluable.

Other colleagues and friends have helped to sustain my psychoanalytic writing, especially Drs. John Gedo, Robert Gillman, James
Hamilton, Leo Loomie, Patrick Mahony, Anna and Paul Ornstein,

Harry Penn, Eleanor Schuker, and Martin Silverman. I want to thank my patients for what they have taught me, which should be abundantly evident throughout this book. It should be some satisfaction to my patients that I have learned most from the difficulties we encountered in helping them to move forward. The psychoanalytic candidates at the Columbia University Psychoanalytic Center, to whom I have taught psychopathology for many years, have repeatedly asked questions that opened new areas for me to explore. Finally, I want to thank my editor, John Kerr, for his thoughtful, wise, and constructively critical readings of my manuscript, which helped me to organize and present my ideas more clearly and coherently. I am grateful to my copy editor, Carol Lucas, for helping me to express what I meant to say, and to Eleanor Starke Kobrin and Paul Stepansky for their help in producing this book.

December 1991

Part I

BACKGROUND FOR THE STUDY OF PATHOLOGICAL DEPENDENCY

1

INTRODUCTION

In the course of writing a number of clinical psychoanalytic papers, I realized that there was a relatively coherent focus to the problems I had been addressing. A group of analytic patients had relative difficulty with using the analytic process productively so as to face their internal conflicts, resolve them, change, and terminate their analyses or intensive psychotherapies. They tended to protect themselves from responsibility for their own internal conflicts through the use of stable relationships with others. These pathological object relationships were highly resistant to change since they served as a predominant mode of defense against the patient's own internal conflicts. I came to view these defensive, pathological relationships as varieties of pathological dependency, as a feared inability and avoidance of assuming emotional responsibility for themselves. Much of this difficulty centered on the dread of confronting rage and destructiveness in themselves and in their vitally needed objects. This difficulty led to terror of separateness and of the loss of the vitally needed relationship and to an exaggerated sense of the danger of rage and destructiveness, which could obliterate the needed other. Various defensive illusions (sometimes quasi-delusions) about the protective functions of the object relationship led the patient to idealize and cling to it. This behavior separated him further from his hostile aggression, his own autonomous abilities, and his perceptions of how crippling and unsatisfying this pathological relationship really was.

A central contention of this work is that the defensive uses of others could be understood within a traditional psychoanalytic perspective on intrapsychic conflict. I find no difficulty with integrating

3

such interpersonal defensive operations ("the misuse of others") with an emphasis on understanding the analysand's attempts to manage and to avoid his own intrapsychic conflicts. A major purpose of this book is to describe the workings of such interpersonal defensive operations in relation to management and avoidance of intrapsychic conflict.

Pathological dependency is analyzable only insofar as these important defensive needs can be acknowledged and engaged within the treatment. This book focuses on dependent patients who tend not to change in psychoanalysis or psychoanalytic psychotherapy and on how to help them to move forward. Such patients may feel good within the treatment, want very much to continue it, or may chronically complain that they are not being helped, that they should see another analyst, or that they should be out of treatment. But, of course, they do nothing of the sort. An endless, supportive, or complaining treatment relationship may be what certain patients, consciously or unconsciously, feel they need. Is this relationship really the most such patients can obtain from treatment? If not, what prevents them from going further and how can we help them change?

We need to differentiate between analyzable and unanalyzable patients with pathological dependency; that is, we must decide whom we can and cannot help. This distinction may not be clear until there has been a trial of analytic treatment. The first step is for the analyst to face the impasse clearly in his own mind and then with the patient as well. Close attention to the protective illusions derived from the dependent relationship and to the dangers feared on one's own assists the patient's attempts at growth and individuation. These dangers largely refer to loss of the illusion of being cared for and protected, with the accompanying helpless, powerless, dependent submission that screens the patient's terror of his own rage and destructiveness. Although much of the patient's rage is focused at the parents he feels have not cared for him adequately, have encouraged his dependent adaptation and psychological disability, or both, this background need not be the whole story; that is, murderous rage is easier to tolerate if it can be justified. Much of it cannot be so easily attributed to others; invariably that fact is what is most painful to bear. For dependent patients, it is, indeed, dangerous to feel like murdering the vitally needed parental object. If analyst and patient can strip away the seductive appeal of regressive dependency so that the patient can face his rage and destructiveness on his own, then he can move forward.

The psychoanalytic literature on difficult patients tends to focus on two areas: problems of suitability for analysis and the "unanalyzable" patient and problems of severe psychopathology, such as serious narcissistic or impulsive acting out, infantile character disorders, the borderline, and the psychotic. The people described in this book cannot easily be classified under these diagnostic categories. In certain respects they do not seem to be very sick. Most of them would be regarded not as borderline but as neurotic character disorders. Their daily functioning can be quite good, even superior and successful. It is on the couch that they seem "sick," in their difficulty with the analytic process, with concentrating in an ongoing, integrative way on what is wrong within themselves, and with working seriously to change that. They easily become stuck or seem stuck right from the beginning of treatment. This book describes such psychopathology, explains it, and describes techniques of working with such patients toward change and away from stasis.

Surprisingly little has been written about such inability to change in analysis; the exceptions are noted later. Psychoanalytic authors have been too hesitant to discuss their difficult cases or their failures. We need to clarify why we have had difficulty helping certain people, and who both we and they expect will benefit from psychoanalysis. My claim is that close attention to such problems will enable the analyst to help such patients better. We discuss conflicts in the analyst and in the patient that contribute to the dependent stalemate. To a degree, each partner has been willing or has needed to become enmeshed in a pathological relationship, which has subverted the analytic task. Careful consideration of the transference–countertransference interplay between patient and analyst usually allows both parties to move out of this impasse. That goal is the task of this book.

Equally surprising is how little has been written in the psychoanalytic literature about pathological dependency. It certainly has not been subjected to extensive psychoanalytic investigation. My view is that systematic analysis of pathological dependency in the patients described here is the only way to end the therapeutic stalemate. To do so, the analyst needs a clear understanding of the almost irresistible pull of such dependent attachment for his patient, as well as potentially for himself. If the analyst cannot tolerate his own reverberating with the patient's wishes for dependent enmeshment, just as if such wishes are so strong that they lead to mutual enactment, he will be unable to analyze this dependency successfully in his patient. This book is intended to help the analyst to bear and then to reject such regressive wishes a little more comfortably.

Patients with pathological dependency fear being left alone with themselves and with what is inside themselves. They thus cling to others, even if this clinging is denied, reversed, or transformed into something erotic, perverse, or sadistic. The presence of others is felt to be necessary to regulate, contain, and manage oneself. Such pathological dependency may appear as just that, or as sexualization, sadomasochistic object relations, or perversion. To analyze sexualization, sadomasochism, and perversion successfully, the analyst must resolve the underlying pathological dependency.

Certain types of interactive defenses, which involve another person, tend further to tie the patient in with that person. Such interactive defensive modes and these forms of pathological dependency are interconnected. Their maintenance is felt to be essential by such patients; change is to be avoided. This book describes various genetic contributions to the adoption of such defenses, as well as the dynamic operation of such interactive defensive modes within pathological object relations. Emphasis is on how to engage patients about the stalemate in the treatment, how to motivate them to face, more fully, what terrifies them, and how to help them to integrate and manage such frightening affects and wishes. Most crucial is helping the patient to develop the motivation consistently to face what is wrong and to take pride in this difficult, new task. For such patients, this becomes a new, more mature ideal, very different from their prior ego and superego identifications. These internal parental imagoes have encouraged avoidance of responsibility for internal conflict, as if this were too much to bear. The patient has come to believe his inner voices, which have largely told him that he lacks the strength and ability to tolerate facing his conflicts. He must become capable of destroying/relinquishing these undermining parental imagoes and bearing his own rage and destructiveness. He needs to consolidate an identification with healthier aspects of the parents and with the analyst's work ego, which emphasizes that facing and tolerating what is most painful within are necessary to become fully separate. The patient will need to value such responsible psychic management, so that he can become convinced that he can regulate himself on his own, without parent or analyst. Such analytic change is to be accomplished primarily by systematic analysis of the patient's avoidance of responsibility for what is wrong within, rather than by identification with the analyst.

For these patients, the need for the object and the need for interactive defenses, to a degree, tend to become one and the same. Such defenses are both intrapsychic and interpersonal; they operate both within a person's own mind and between him and another. They tend to be learned in childhood by identification with a parent(s) who uses such interactive defensive modes. This defensive mode tends to be built into a style of relatedness between parent and child.

Parents who need to protect themselves by using others will, of course, do the same with their children. To the degree that a person is unable to take responsibility for what is troublesome within himself, he will need to find other ways to cope with this. What the parent cannot tolerate and manage within himself, he will, most likely, be unable to tolerate within the child. Then the parent will be unable to help the child gradually to learn to tolerate and manage within himself such troublesome feelings and wishes, so that the child cannot accomplish the essential maturational task of affect tolerance and management.

Of course, any feelings or wishes can be found troublesome by the parent and then by the child. What seems to cause the most trouble, however, are various shadings of angry, destructive feelings. By trouble, I mean difficulty with tolerating, managing, and integrating these feelings, so that one can become comfortable with their existence within oneself. Without some resolution of these problems, a person continues to struggle to get away from what is troublesome and frightening inside himself. For the mother to assist her child with affect tolerance and management of destructive feelings, she must be able to tolerate and manage her own destructiveness and her hatred of her child. The mother must rely on her own ability to integrate and manage hostile aggression so that she can gradually assist her young child with this task. If she cannot do this for herself, she will also be unable to withstand her child's aggression toward her. Certainly, she will be unable to help her child to learn to integrate aggression. Of course, more than assistance with managing aggression is needed from the parent for the child to feel comforted, loved, valued, and understood. The young child needs the mother's protection so that he feels neither overstimulated by libidinal wishes nor overwhelmed by aggressive urges.

Since parents do not simply mold their children, what is wrong in our patients cannot simply be blamed on the parents. But certain recurrent factors tend to set the stage in childhood for the development of interactive defensive modes and for the clinging to pathological ways of relating. Many other factors, as we shall see, contribute to their maintenance during childhood and adulthood.

Difficulty with handling angry feelings ordinarily involves aspects of id, ego, and superego functioning. These people are angry, whether or not they show or acknowledge this anger. Superego standards and enforcement are harsh, restraining, and inflexible. In part, they have been needed to manage the overload of anger, to keep it inside, away from the core of the feelings. In part, the superego harshness derives from identification with similar hostile, restrictive qualities in the parental superego and ego attitudes. Further, the child will identify with the parents' attitudes toward themselves as well as toward the child; these identifications will also be built into the superego standards and regulatory functioning, as well as into the ego attitudes that interact with these. Typically, the child as a whole will be insecure about his acceptability and about his capacity to manage this burden of anger. As a result and through identification with parental modes of defense and adaptation (here in relation to angry feelings), the ego will seek to avoid, ignore, get rid of, or magically transform into their opposite such threatening angry feelings. As a result, the ego cannot gain a sense of confidence and mastery that it can tolerate, survive, live with, and integrate intense anger.

Infantile attitudes in the parents breed infantile attitudes in their offspring. Rarely do these infantile attitudes occur in isolated sectors of personality functioning; more often, this is widespread, to be found in multiple areas of the personality. Similarly, we cannot easily isolate the ego's defensive mechanisms from the rest of the personality. Brenner (1982) has reminded us that there are no specialized defense mechanisms, that any ego function can be used for defense, as well as, and even simultaneously, for other purposes. I emphasize the interrelations between defense and the ways in which people use or, rather, misuse each other. Such misuse of persons differs from the ordinary use of others in relationships that tends to be both more reciprocal, considerate, and loving and less destructive, extractive, and entitled. Infantile parents who feel they cannot manage what is frightening within themselves will be unable to assist their children with learning to manage their dangerous affects and wishes. These parents will envy and resent the child's new potential for managing his life better than the parents can do. They will tend to use the child to assist them with their own needs for defense and survival. Such parents tend to be afraid of being on their own, of managing themselves, as if such autonomy were unbearable. Fears of abandonment–separation, unacceptability, mutilation, and guilt tend to lead such parents into enmeshment with at least some of their children. Incomplete separation-individuation during development intersects with incomplete ego, superego, and id development and integration.

Furman (1985) points out dynamic factors in not remembering good aspects of a parent and the mental representation of the absent parent. I believe that we need to be careful not to ascribe undue metapsychological or developmental significance to our clinical findings. Thus Furman reports that her child patient's primitive rage at the absent mother felt overwhelming and killed her love for her mother. Furman describes her patients' defensive use of their difficulty with drive fusion. Not to love and not to remember being loved serve to justify aggression, to lessen restraint and guilt. Willick (1987) criticizes Adler (1985) similarly and notes that a patient's difficulty with remembering the analyst need not mean (regressive) failure of evocative memory but can derive from the patient's anger and needs to protect himself.

I do not mean to dismiss problems of developmental arrest; however, before we assume developmental arrest, we need to consider how such psychological disability functions dynamically for the patient. I am very cautious about assuming actual psychological deficiency. I prefer to consider the multiple, dynamic uses served by the apparent disability. A major theme of this book is that regressive functioning is highly motivated, overly determined. Because of the protections it offers and the dangers it avoids, it is not at all easily relinquished.

Incomplete separation-individuation tends to be exploited defensively. Parent and child, afraid of loss and destruction, will tend to form object relationships that are narcissistic in one of their aspects. By a narcissistic object relationship, we mean that self and other are not clearly and separately perceived; nor are self and other acknowledged to have equally legitimate and separate needs. That is, self and other will be defensively confused, mixed up to lessen the fear of losing or destroying someone who is fully differentiated from oneself. Differences between self and other will be denied or blurred so as to capture the other within one's own psychic orbit. Such blurring of differences involves magic, grandiosity, omnipotence, and playing at merger. One either becomes a god in a world of one's own creation or else shares in the parental omnipotence by trading roles with the parent with regard to who is the god and who is the worshiper—or both. If one is a god or the parent is a god, one can undo destruction and maintain the illusion of safety, permanence, and protection. This protective play is not psychosis but a fantasy world of omnipotent illusions, that protect against loss and destruction. The appeal and excitement of mixing and merging are defensively heightened, as by sexualization or sadomasochism. The danger of destruction of a hated object is attenuated by the excited longing for special, forbidden, sexual, or sexualized merger with this object. This mixing and merging leads to an intense enmeshment between self and object, from which the patient has been unable (terrified) to extricate himself.

Such defensive narcissistic object relations in pathological dependency link with defensive analization. This defensive mixing and merging of self and object can be regarded as an anal defensive mode.

As in one's object relations, one attempts similarly to manage painful, frightening affects by mixing and merging feelings, destroying differences between feelings, so as to make them (everything) meaningless. These regressive anal defenses first, in object relations and second, in the management of affects are aimed especially against fears of destructiveness. The first alters the representation of the object, so that some aspect of the self is, in effect, pasted onto it or some aspect of the object is pasted onto the self. The second attempts to alter one's affective experience, so that dangerous feelings (and wishes) need not be fully faced, because they are made meaningless.

Some important disclaimers are in order. First, I wish to point out that my aim here is not neo-Kleinian. It is a pragmatic issue that defense against destructiveness is a central task for the patients under consideration. In this sense, the Kleinians and neo-Kleinians have been helpful. Influential traditional psychoanalysts have also needed, from time to time, to remind us of the difficulty we all have tolerating the most intensely troublesome of our human feelings and wishes, which can be or are destructive. It is a relief for psychoanalysts, just as for our patients, to shift the emphasis away to less destructive issues such as narcissistic injury, fragility, depletion, deprivation, and needs of others to support self-esteem and self-cohesion. These issues are all important in their own right; they should not be minimized. On the other hand, they also need to be understood in connection with destructive affects and wishes. Of course, frustration and narcissistic injury can lead to rage, but once it has come into existence, the rage must nonetheless be managed; it is not of secondary importance. When I refer to rage and destructiveness, I mean by the former the affect and by the latter the linked wish or intention. Destructiveness refers not to behavior alone but to wishes and intentions. Sometimes the affect will be either more prominent or more obscured; sometimes, the wish. But they are invariably connected.

The second disclaimer is that the focus here on the use or misuse of people and on the connections between defense and object relationship is not intended to be an interpersonal one. That is, our psychoanalytic focus is on internal (intrapsychic) reality, rather than what we may assume transpires between two people. I am interested in how elements of object relationships are built into bits of psychic structure as wishes, expectations, and promises. How the developing child constructs his own internal experience of external reality will depend on much more than what is observable to an outsider. Wish, need, affect, defense, restraint, and punishment all will shape the construction of internal experience, which will then affect external (and internal) object relationships. Thus, interpersonal is to be understood in relation to intrapsychic. To a degree, they cannot be separated and must at the same time be separated; that is, what goes on within our minds and between ourselves and others are parts of a whole. Consideration here of interactive defensive modes, as used in pathological object relations, is intended to be understood within a traditional intrapsychic psychoanalytic perspective. Unlike some others, I have no trouble integrating an object relations perspective within traditional psychoanalytic conflict theory. Hence, drive and object relations easily fit together for me.

There has been a trend in psychoanalysis of emphasizing interaction between analyst and analysand. For example, projective identification has been described (Ogden, 1979; Porder, 1987) as actually involving an intended effect on the analyst, so that something is induced in the analyst. More broadly, the analytic process is now conceived of as a dynamic interaction that, to a degree, involves unconscious attempts on the part of the analysand to actualize an internal scenario (object relations, drive, defense, punishment, and so on). The analyst must allow himself to become immersed in this scenario, to feel the varied roles that are imposed on him. Whatever is difficult for the analyst to bear in himself, he will, of course, have trouble bearing in his patient. The analyst thus must maintain both an interpersonal and an intrapsychic focus for himself and especially for his analysand. It is not an either/or choice; both are necessary. The analyst's access to intense feelings in himself and in his patient is the precondition for interpretation of conflict.

My final disclaimer can be only a partial one. This book should not be viewed as a revisionist erosion of traditional psychoanalysis. The intention here is not to replace the intrapsychic with the interpersonal nor to replace the dual drive theory with an exclusive emphasis on aggression. The concepts espoused here are solidly within the best of contemporary traditional psychoanalysis. Of course, I have my own personal biases, preferences, and needs, which affect both how I understand and practice psychoanalysis and how I write about it. I expect that awareness and tolerance of this in myself, as is my theme, will allow me to keep to the task at hand.

Probably what most determines whether the patients under consideration here will change is the capacity of the analyst to focus on and to bear both the patient's hatred and his own hatred toward the patient. Heretofore, the patient has been unable to do this. Just as the mother needs to assist the child with modulating and integrating his affects, so, too, does the analyst need to assist the patient. Especially with these patients, the analyst needs to help them to acknowledge, tolerate, integrate, and manage what they most wish to disown. The analyst does not become a substitute parent as he assists the patient to enhance his affect tolerance. The analyst uses his capacity for managing his own passions to assist the patient; he does so by interpretation of the patient's excessive fearfulness of the consequences of processing his feelings. The psychoanalytic literature from Winnicott and Racker to Bird and Kernberg has been helpful in encouraging analysts to own and to bear their hatred for patients as a crucial factor toward change. Yet countertransference hatred, since it is so difficult, is not readily discussed or described in our literature. Attention to countertransference hatred is also an important aim in my writing this book. The difficulty of tolerating and integrating rage, destructiveness, hatred, and sadism is an endless task. It is so for our patients, just as it is for ourselves. The better we can acknowledge and bear this in ourselves, the better we can help our patients to do the same. That path is the one we must follow to help our patients out of dependency toward autonomy and self-management.

WHAT IS
PATHOLOGICAL
DEPENDENCY?

We all remain dependent, to some degree, throughout the entire course of our lives. We turn to others for certain functions we feel unable, at times, to provide for ourselves. Pathological dependency is different. It refers to the felt inability to manage on one's own and to be alone. Lacking the confidence and willingness to manage his own emotional life, both within his mind and to varying degrees in his actual behavior, the pathologically dependent person has to be overly involved with other people. Emotional knowledge of this dependency may be covered over and disguised.

Let me introduce you briefly to such pathological dependency. To do so, let us turn to Sigmund Freud as he struggled to create psychoanalysis, by drawing on what he could perceive as conflicted within himself. He needed another person with whom to share his discoveries, another person who would encourage him in his bold explorations. Wilhelm Fliess, otolaryngologist of Berlin, assumed this long-distance role for Freud. Initially, Freud idealized his colleague, imagined that they would solve major puzzles of life in tandem, and obscured Fliess's deficiencies. (For an extended discussion of these issues, see Coen, 1985b, 1988b.) In the Freud–Fliess correspondence (Coen, 1985b), Freud repeatedly insists that he needs Fliess's continued presence and encouragement to counteract his depression, loneliness, flagging self-confidence, and hesitation with his ideas and their written expression. This dependent Freud seductively pleads with Fliess to respond to him:

> I feel very isolated, scientifically blunted, stagnant and resigned. When I talked to you, and saw that you thought something of

13

me, I actually started thinking something of myself, and the picture of confident energy which you offered me was not without its effect . . . . For years now I have been without anyone who could teach me anything [Freud, Letter 6, 1954, p. 60].

People like you should not die out, my dear friend; we others need the like of you too much. How much have I to thank you in consolation, understanding, stimulation in my loneliness, in the meaning of life you have given me, and lastly in health which no one else could have brought back to me. It is essentially your example that has enabled me to gain the intellectual strength to trust my own judgment . . . and to face with deliberate resignation, as you do, all the hardships the future may have in store. For all that accept my simple thanks. [Letter of New Year's Day, 1896, cited in Jones, 1953, pp. 298-299].

I am in a rather gloomy state, and all I can say is that I am looking forward to our congress as to a slaking of hunger and thirst. I shall bring with me nothing but a pair of open ears, and shall be all agape [Freud, Letter 48, 1954, pp. 168-169].

So you see what happens. I live gloomily and in darkness until you come, and then I pour out all my grumbles to you, kindle my flickering light at your steady flame and feel well again; and after your departure I have eyes to see again, and what I look upon is good [Freud, Letter 101, 1954, p. 272].

You can have no idea how much your last visit raised my spirits. I am still living on it. The light has not gone out since; little bits of new knowledge glimmer now here, now there, which is truly refreshing after the comfortlessness of last year. . . . I need you as my audience [Freud, Letter 103, 1954, pp. 274-275].

Through his self-analysis and through the success of his creative work, this first psychoanalyst was able, to a degree, to relinquish some of his dependency.

Let me introduce you briefly to Mrs. J (see chapter 10), who actually wanted me to become the mother, father, and lover of whom she felt so deprived. She intended that I sustain her, reassure her, and love her rather than analyze her. She would feel very hurt, indignant, and outraged if I attempted to interpret anything she found unacceptable within herself. Given the trauma of her early life (mother developed tuberculosis when Mrs. J was one year old and died when the patient was two and a half years old; she was raised by various uncaring relatives until father remarried and brought her to his home during her early adolescence), her difficulties were understandable. The dilemma was that she quickly became content to live out her dependent wishes with me rather than to seek to understand and resolve them. This case is an extreme version of pathological dependency, is highly erotized, and is supported by a profound sense of entitlement and denial. But there are similarities to other patients with pathological dependency who are content to remain in analysis or feel that all they really want is support and kindness from the analyst.

Mr. E (chapter 7) with his profound sense of defectiveness (born with multiple physical defects and a mother who humiliated him), argued for years that he needed me to be the interested, supportive parent he had never had. He insisted that he could not feel anger on his own unless I first emphasized in every session how awful his childhood had been. Of course, I would help him try to feel the awfulness of his early life. He would deny and avoid his attachment to me and want me, instead, simply to provide him with caring. Mr. E became content to remain in analysis with me but felt hopeless that I would ever really give him what he needed. He could feel some anger and dissatisfaction with me as the deficient parent in the transference. But he needed even more to cling to me and to deny the awfulness of being with a parent/analyst who not only did not love and care for him but hated and resented him. To interrupt this stalemate, he had to acknowledge how awful his dependency on a hateful, sadistic mother was and how it had impeded his autonomy, self-sufficiency, and strength. That is, he had to bear sustained sadness and rage in the analytic transference over time and struggle to relinquish his wish to be attached to the analyst at any cost to himself.

Pathological dependency can be considered usefully from multiple interrelated perspectives: incomplete separation–individuation; developmental arrest and disability; pathological narcissism, with continued narcissistic needs for others, other than narcissistic needs of objects. Nonnarcissistic needs of others include need satisfaction; maintenance of psychological balance; protection against vulnerability and overstimulation; assistance with drive management and affect tolerance; and assistance with a variety of other ego functions, such as accurate perception and evaluation of oneself and others, judgment, memory, and thinking. In what follows I draw on these perspectives of separation-individuation, uncompleted psychological development, pathological narcissism, and object need. In doing so, however, I place the analytic focus on dependency, which offers a better approach to analyzing such patients. This focus will lead us to key questions in attempting to analyze dependency: why does the patient need to hold on so tightly to another person, and what is he afraid of in being on his own? Keeping these questions in mind between analyst and patient facilitates the analysis of pathological dependency. This perspective highlights how and why the other person is being drawn upon by the patient. By pathological dependency, I mean an intense (life-or-death) clinging to another, with literal terror of examining, in an ongoing, responsible way, the underside of the patient's psyche. The patient's defensive uses of his apparent or real disability, through misuse of another person (pathological dependency) so as to avoid internal conflict, organize the analytic focus around conflict rather than around presumed psychic defects. This emphasis on conflict advances the cause of the patient's analysis.

My concern here is with helping patients to acknowledge their pathological dependency, in whatever form it may take, and to become troubled about it so as to develop the motivation to work their way out of it. The problem is often that such patients are not disturbed by their pathological dependency because it feels so gratifying, so vital to their very existence. This problem will keep patients stuck, craving more of the same, repeating the same defensive patterns, avoiding facing and integrating what has frightened them all of their lives. Ordinary dependency is easier to analyze, to modify, to change. In ordinary dependency, patients are not so terrified of letting go of another and of being on their own. We all turn to others for certain of our needs throughout the entire course of our lives, even after termination of successful analysis. We regard someone who cannot rely on others comfortably as pathologically detached and schizoid, as having substantial narcissistic defenses against object need. Patients with ordinary dependency are more flexible, less rigid, more willing and able to bear responsibility for some of what is wrong within themselves, without such incessant need for another to manage conflict for them.

A key heuristic point in the analysis of pathological dependency is that rage and destructiveness have been regarded as too dangerous to assimilate within the core of one's ego. The value of this heuristic point, which in some ways entails oversimplification, is that it shifts the focus from other aspects of dependent needs outlined above to what has here become the core danger—destructiveness and its avoidance. When destructiveness has been too frightening to integrate during development, regressive, defensive, narcissistic object relationships tend to be established. The patient defensively confuses self and other, and mixes them up so as to protect against loss and destruction. Illusions of invulnerability are sought in magical, omnipotent merger, so that destructiveness can be denied and undone. That is, if the other's differentiation from oneself is denied, then the patient's fear of losing or destroying the other is lessened. Aspects of incomplete separation-individuation are exploited defensively to undo the dangers of destruction and loss of the vitally needed other.

Hence, in cases of pathological dependency, separateness and autonomy will inevitably be impaired, with the patient terrified of being alone or of feeling unloved. When he feels loved, he feels safe from his own and the other's destructive hatred, which remains intolerably frightening. He will run from hatred in himself and in the other, toward the reassurance of loving and feeling loved. This pattern becomes compulsive, addictive, insatiable, and endless. To the degree that destructiveness remains terrifying, the other is clung to for reassurance and protection. The patient cannot be alone with his own destructive hatred. Instead, he needs the continual evidence that he is loved (lovable) rather than hateful. This constant input of "loving" soothes his rage, guilt, and impaired self-esteem; it gets him away from intolerable feelings of destructive anger. Of course, such patients are temporarily able to bear their anger. But at some point they have to undo it and extract reassurance that they are loved and loving.

Freud tells us and shows us, in his letters to Fliess (Freud, 1985) and in parts of "The Interpretation of Dreams" (1900), how his increasing self-confidence and partial ability to relinquish the need for a Fliess derive from his newfound tolerance of his own dark side. Freud tells us about his struggles with his ambition, death wishes, rivalry and hatred, incestuous longings. As he became able to tolerate the intensity of such painful, negative feelings in himself, he was able to shift the focus in his work and in his writings to the centrality of one's (his own, his patient's, the reader's, everyone's) affective life. This book is not the place for an assessment of how well Freud succeeded in working through his dependency. I cite the foregoing to call attention to his own personal recognition that relinquishment of dependency is connected with the ability to tolerate the full extent of one's destructiveness. Freud did indeed struggle in his relationship with Fliess between surrender and submission to an idealized, aggrandized, encouraging, and protective other; he also frankly struggled with the wish to take over more of this power and ability for himself, to compete with, outdo, and destroy the other.

Because of the dangers of separation and destruction of the object, fantasied merger with the object is used for defense in pathological dependency. Bak (1956) described the concept of "overflowing" between self and object and emphasized defensive confusion between self and other to protect against the danger of destruction of the object. Aspects of self and object are mixed together, using identification and projection. Concomitantly, there is a magical, omnipotent denial of the outside world. In my view, one can be reassured against destruction of a vitally needed object if he can merge somewhat with the object, so that the object is no longer fully separate (able to be lost or destroyed). Such partial, reversible, fantasied merger is used by neurotics, especially in pathological dependency; it contrasts with the fixed, delusional merger of psychotics. Nevertheless, such defensive merger (exploiting incomplete separation-individuation) impairs separateness, reality sense, and confidence in one's ability to manage destructive affects and wishes. In this regressive defense, one is reassured against destruction by illusions of magical, grandiose, omnipotent merger with, and control of, the world (one's vitally needed object). This regressive defense is a central aspect of pathological dependency.

Magic and illusion characterize the defensive style of patients with pathological dependency. They rely on magical techniques of riddance, elimination, denial, and undoing so as to avoid pain and danger. Linking these defensive activities with anal fantasies helps to illuminate their mechanisms and aims. This link is to be understood metaphorically as the self-protective effort to get rid of threatening feelings, perceptions, and ideas. It connects with isolation of affect and repression. Pathologically dependent patients do not want to know what is wrong in a focused, ongoing way. They cling to a dependent relationship with the analyst, as if that will be sufficient to cure them, without the continued, painful need to face and integrate their own internal conflicts. On the contrary, what is wrong is not fully allowed to register affectively. Within a few sessions it is gone, the patient having returned to the safety of not knowing and not wanting to know what is wrong. The affective meaning of what is wrong has been eliminated. Defensive analization has been described by Bach and Schwartz (1972) and by Chasseguet-Smirgel (1978, 1983) as protecting against narcissistic injury by attempting to make what is painful not count, by denying differences and differentiation (as between self and other, male and female, child and parent) by making everything the same, so that differences are made meaningless. Differences are to be destroyed, rendering everything homogenized, as if it had been magically transmuted into feces. This view of defensive analization, although helpful, tends to minimize the need for defense against rage and destructiveness, by focusing only on narcissistic injury (Shengold, 1988, makes a similar criticism of Chasseguet-Smirgel). Ordinarily, defensive analization refers to a defense against fully experiencing affects and wishes. This has most recently been explicated by Shengold (1988), who emphasized the patient's attempt to shut off murderous and cannibalistic feelings, much as one would try to squeeze the anal sphincter fully shut.

Defense against affect and defense against separateness of the object are complementary when considered from the point of view of the internal object world. Clearly, affects and internal object relations are interrelated. Traditionally, the concept of defensive anality has emphasized defense against destructive affects rather than the danger of destruction (loss) of the vitally needed other. These defensive aims are complementary to the degree that the subject is not fully autonomous. Denial of difference also aims to rob the powerful object of its distinctive attributes, which now become shared property. In this view, anxieties about destruction of the object and the self (castration, robbery, envy, bodily attacks, murder, cannibalism) lead to, and are managed by, defensive analization, with its omnipotent illusions, denial of reality, destruction of meaning, and avoidance of feeling. Such defensive techniques significantly interfere with growth and autonomy and encourage pathological dependency.

We need to emphasize the intractability of pathological dependency. Symbiotic illusions of magical protection are seductive, convincing, and difficult to relinquish. In pathological dependency, patients cling to another for such protection and feel unduly frightened of relinquishing it. Interactive defensive modes encourage children/patients to rely on someone else for their psychological management. A climate is established that to be alone psychologically is tantamount to death, that no one can manage this autonomy. Instead of the child/patient increasingly being helped to tolerate and integrate his intense affects and wishes, so as to become an autonomous person, he becomes more frightened of his world, inside and outside. Self-doubting and self-undermining originally served to obscure angry criticism of parents. They then continue to erode the patient's confidence in his feelings and judgments, so that he must look to others for answers. But the symbiotic illusion of reassurance, that everything will be all right so long as the couple is together, becomes too appealing to set aside, so as to feel one's dark side. This symbiotic illusion of reassurance becomes the (usually unconscious) basis for the emotional setup in the analysis. The patient is primarily motivated by the desire "to be in analysis," and he only *seems* to work diligently at solving problems. This underlying setup will usually be clearest at times of separation, when the patient feels panicky. Or it can be seen when the patient seems content with himself and the analysis because of the illusion of the analyst's magical protection, in the patient's not feeling motivated to work out further what is wrong within himself, even when the patient takes a complaining stance toward the analyst. Such a complaining stance may still preserve the illusion of protection, through the patient's remaining in treatment. It is easy for the analyst to become impatient, critical, and angry with the patient about the latter's lack of motivation for change. That is precisely the problem. The patient with pathological dependency is terrified to let go of the illusion of magical protection. He is afraid to face, in a consistent way, his rage and destructiveness, which he has denied and reversed for so long. He has sought to turn the other from an object of hatred into a powerful savior.

SOME BACKGROUND: A LACUNA IN THE LITERATURE

Pathological dependency, although very common, certainly in my practice, is rarely written about. It may seem that dependency is so old hat that it need not be considered further. Another possible explanation for the dearth of writings on the topic is that similar phenomena are subsumed under the headings of sadomasochism, pathological narcissism, anxiety, separation-individuation, or developmental arrest. Yet though all these phenomena may be encountered in pathological dependency, the syndrome is fully explicated by none of them. The classic psychoanalytic text *Dependence in Man* by Parens and Saul (1971) explains certain aspects of dependence and defenses against it but does not deal with the analysis of pathological dependency. Not all patients with pathological dependency exhibit sadomasochism. It is also true that separation-individuation tends to be incomplete in pathological dependency, but it tends to be exploited defensively. As for the role of anxiety, it, too, constitutes an incomplete descriptive rubric. When destructiveness has been too frightening to integrate during development, regressive, defensive, narcissistic object relationships tend to be established. That is, if the other's differentiation from oneself can be denied in magical, omnipotent merger, then the patient's fear of losing or destroying the other is lessened. Aspects of incomplete separation-individuation are exploited defensively to undo the dangers of destruction and loss of the vitally needed other. Issues relating to narcissistic vulnerability, typically experienced by the patient as a long-standing sense of defect, may also play a role in pathological dependence. But here, too, these issues do not tell the whole story. The analyst must also recognize the defensive uses of the apparent or real disability and the accompanying misuse of another person (pathological dependency) so as to avoid internal conflict; a focus on the use of the defect organizes the analytic approach around conflict rather than on presumed psychic deficits. In sum, I contend that a focus on dependency provides a better psychoanalytic approach to understanding and analyzing patients than the perspectives of sadomasochism, pathological narcissism, separation-individuation, or anxiety. Such a focus as I have in mind presupposes an integration of object relations theory with traditional conflict models in psychoanalysis so that the dependency can be interpreted not only in terms of the willingness to cling to an object but also in terms of the conflicts that are thereby escaped.

In certain respects, the approach taken in this work is not wholly new. Dependency has been traditionally understood as narcissistic reassurance from others because of guilt derived from conflict (e.g., Freud, 1909; Jones, 1929; Fenichel, 1945; Kernberg, 1988). Indeed, Freud (1909) tells us that the Rat Man tried to manage himself in this way in relation to male friends, his mother, his "lady," and Freud, his analyst. Using the Rat Man as his exemplar, Fenichel (1945) then subsequently described the obsessional's use of witnesses against his superego. Fenichel's term referred to the obsessional's attempt to avoid his own internal superego judgments by substituting other people as auxiliary superegos, who will either praise or condemn the patient. The mechanism informs the obsessional's real relations with others: "Various attempts, real and magical, are made to influence the testimony of these 'witnesses'" (Fenichel, 1945, p. 293). By listening to the other person's opinion of him and by seeking to influence him in various directions, the patient attempts to bypass his own conscience. The Rat Man used others to reassure himself that he was not bad. Unfortunately, Freud was not able to work with this enactment in the analytic transference, wherein much of the dependent, sadomasochistic transference sought to avoid the patient's own self-assessments (cf. Kanzer, 1952; Muslin, 1979; Langs, 1980; Mahony, 1986). It is implied that the Rat Man invited a willing Freud to penetrate his body and mind, so as to become responsible for the Rat Man's psychic regulation; this invitation was mainly because of the patient's fear of his own destructiveness.

Similarly trenchant formulations bearing on the topic of pathological dependency can be found scattered throughout the literature on narcissistic dependency and masochism. Jones (1929) especially understood the core of narcissistic dependency to be reassurance against guilt (derived from oedipal conflict). Similarly, Kernberg (1988) describes the dependency of the (neurotic) depressive-masochistic character as involving excessive guilt because of unconscious ambivalence and excessive reaction to frustration of his expectations. Such patients have an abnormal vulnerability to disappointment by others; they make intense efforts to get sympathy and love or, at least, to provoke others to feel guilty. Their demandingness, especially when they feel hurt and aggrieved, and their guilt provoking lead to angry rejection from others, so that they feel depressed and unloved. The core conflict is postulated to be oedipal guilt, which is defended against in these interpersonal and intrapsychic ways.

Fenichel (1935) insisted that narcissistic dependency is more complicated than conflict over oedipal guilt; he suggested it involves a primitive mechanism of self-esteem regulation with oral determinants, as well as oral fixation. External narcissistic supplies (being loved) are required from others to maintain self-esteem. Fairbairn (1940, 1941, 1943, 1944), emphasizing oral contributions to more severe psychopathology, described conflicts about expressing needs to be loved. When patients feel that their love is bad and destructive or that they are unlovable because of their hatred, they both want loving reassurance against this and fear risking further rejection and humiliation. In Fairbairn's view, such patients' sense of themselves as bad is largely derived from the internalization of bad aspects of the parents. The child, in Fairbairn's conception, thereby seeks to preserve a good external relationship with the parents or, at least, to preserve the illusion of hope, protection, and trust in the good parental images. Fairbairn implies that masochistic surrender to an idealized parental imago, with the patient's taking on himself the burden of badness, protects against the hopelessness and despair of the child's destructive rage at the inadequate or bad parent.

Unlike narcissistic dependency and masochism, pathological dependency has barely been described in the psychoanalytic literature. Of course, dependency often involves sadomasochism, although it is broader and need not be masochistic. Beginning in the late 1940s, an object relations perspective began to influence psychoanalytic writing on masochism and emphasized pathological early object relations (including terror of abandonment and clinging to the object), intense threatening aggression, inadequate regulatory structures for ego defense and superego judgment and containment, deprivation, and search for love in a pain-dependent mode (Rado, 1945–1955; Berliner,

1947, 1958; Brenman, 1952; Menaker, 1953; Loewenstein, 1957; Bergler, 1961; Rubinfine, 1965; Ferber and Gray, 1966). Separation-individuation theory has modified this perspective, with emphasis on uncompleted individuation, inability to relinquish the vitally needed parental object, and terror of destroying it (Cooper, 1973; Asch, 1976; Grossman, 1986; Novick and Novick, 1987). Patients with beating fantasies are reported to have histories in which the parents were unable to contain the child's aggression, tended to feel overwhelmed and to surrender to the child, and thereby intensified the child's feelings of danger and monstrousness, with a quasi-delusion of omnipotent destructiveness (Rubinfine, 1965; Ferber and Gray, 1966; Novick and Novick, 1987). The child's sense of destructiveness is intensified by parental externalization (and blaming) of hostile aggression onto the child and by intrusiveness and interference with separateness and autonomy (Novick and Novick, 1987). To retain the vulnerable, destructive mother, the child accepts her externalizations. The Novicks report impaired ego defense against destructiveness (mainly anal sadism), reliance on primitive defense (denial and projection), and absence of a structured superego in their children with fixed beating fantasies. They suggest that the beating fantasy functions in place of the absent superego and that aggression is disguised as libidinal pleasure.

In pathological dependency, objects, external and internal, are exploited in attempts to avoid responsibility for one's internal conflicts. This idea goes beyond Fenichel's (1945) view of the obsessional's using other people as witnesses against the superego. A focus on this exploitation of others as developmental failure, although correct, tends to miss the dynamic gains of such repeated misuse of other people. Dependent wishes for love and acceptance become a way of life and lead to interminable treatment. Deprivation becomes an excuse for what is wrong within the patient.

DEFENSE AND THE MISUSE OF OBJECTS

This book emphasizes the variety of ways in which others are used to protect against internal conflict for which the patient cannot accept responsibility. Emphasis on defense in one's needs of objects helps to avoid unwarranted assumptions about ego defects or developmental failures. Sandler and A. Freud (1985) discuss externalization as the result of difficulty tolerating internal conflict. Sandler suggests that the apparent projection of guilt in such cases is actually an externalization of responsibility. Sandler posits as a developmental task the increasing acceptance of responsibility for internal conflict. Despite the difficulty with tolerating responsibility for themselves, not all such patients have an arrest in superego development. Sandler (p. 419) especially emphasizes patients' difficulties with responsibility for intense aggression. Very severe guilt leads to externalization of responsibility for such aggression. Aggressive behavior toward others may serve partly as externalized superego attack. Partial acceptance of guilt and responsibility for one's own aggression may coexist with such externalization and attacks on others. I fully agree with Sandler's focus on problems of intense aggression and severe guilt as central factors in patients' inability to tolerate responsibility for their own conflicts. I would add the factors of intense fear of loss and dread of autonomy, together with illusions of magical protection through a regressive, dependent relationship.

Giovacchini (1967) reports externalization in the analytic transference, especially with more disturbed patients, as aiming to establish a familiar environment, within which the patient can use his "adaptive techniques" (p. 117). Illusions of safety and magical protection may be implicit in this view of externalization.

Winnicott (1956) describes, as the "anti-social tendency," behavior that involves both object seeking and the danger of destruction, where there is inability to preserve a good maternal imago. He considers that such patients, unlike psychotics, know that the fault lies in the environment rather than in themselves. Their claims on others thus make sense. Khan (1962, 1964, 1965a, 1969) elaborates Winnicott's idea into a theory about perversion. Although it need not be the case, there is the risk here of overemphasis on interpersonal needs without sufficient attention to how and why the patient uses his current objects.

Modell (1961, 1965, 1971, 1976) posits magical illusions of safety and protection in what he regards as transitional object relatedness. He connects denial with denial of separateness and belief in a protective object. Modell postulates that patients with narcissistic personality disorder seek such protective objects to shield them from reality, frustration, pain, and work. Incomplete separation-individuation and dangerous feelings of vulnerability are present. Modell emphasizes separation guilt, besides separation anxiety, as contributing to difficulty with using and benefiting from psychoanalysis. Such separation guilt derives partly from sadistic wishes to destroy or rob the other and partly from unconscious fantasies that one's own separate existence means the unwished-for death of the other. Modell makes clear (1984, pp. 75–80) his view that such guilt comes about not only because of instinctual sources (oral sadism) but also because of external reality. One feels guilty at having one's own good, separate existence, because of what has actually happened to others in one's family. Modell regards fantasies that what one possesses has been stolen from others as "primal fantasies." Rather than regard such "separation guilt" as based on external reality or on primal fantasies, I would relate it to the complexities of the object relationship, which cannot be relinquished, and to the affects, which cannot be integrated.

The traditional view has been that defense was only an intrapsychic process, separate from the object world (A. Freud, in J. Sandler with A. Freud, 1985, p. 190). We now acknowledge that object relations influence and participate in defensive activities. This view is especially true for the regressive modes of object relating here considered. Modell's (1984) clarification (elaborating on Balint's, 1950, point) that defense needs to be understood within both an intrapsychic context and a two-person context was helpful. Where internalization is predominant, emphasis on the intrapsychic and on intrapsychic defense is largely sufficient. To the degree that we all need others to help regulate ourselves, however, we also need to pay attention to defense in our relations with others. Sandler (with A. Freud, 1985, p. 192) clarifies that the perspective on defense as only an intrapsychic process separate from the object world applies only to the actual mechanisms of defense; in contrast, the motives for defense do involve the object. Symbolic aspects of defensive activities, Sandler notes, involve unconscious fantasies of objects. Dorpat (1987) emphasizes the role of object relations in both the formation and the maintenance of defenses. Interactive defensive maneuvers as implicated in pathological modes of object relating have been described by Modell (1984), Balint (1950), Ogden (1979, 1983) Dorpat (1985), Räkköläinen and Alanen (1982). I believe that all defensive activity involves action on one's own affects, wishes, internalized objects, and, to varying degrees, the external environment and external objects.

Recently, Porder (1987) has argued that projective identification does not accurately describe the repetitive parent–child behavioral enactments that occur. Porder emphasizes that vignettes of projective identification reveal enactments in which affects are actually induced in the other (analyst) rather than projected. He regards these as chronic repetitions of a parent–child interaction, with the patient primarily identified with the aggressor (parent), while the analyst plays the child role. Porder also notes that such patients use "the same defensive armamentarium" (p. 450) that had been used by the pathological parent(s). I fully agree with Porder that these defensive constellations need not reflect experiences of earliest infancy and that they can be used for defense against any psychic content. Porder offers three suggestions why the defensive parental identification remains unconscious: requirement by the pathological parent for extreme submission of the patient/child; a propensity for action because of limitation in verbal expression; and guilt about the identification with the hated/feared aspects of the parent. His view of projective identification, as turning passive into active and as a compromise formation serving each psychic agency, is unobjectionable. Still, I would prefer an exclusive emphasis on defense when we consider defense mechanisms rather than to regard defense as a compromise formation. What is missing, however, is fuller consideration of the reasons for the persistent defensive repetition. Porder is certainly correct that such patients act in the treatment and repeat the pathological behavior of a parent. Similarly, Porder's discussion of Ogden's (1979) patient does not sufficiently emphasize the affects and impulses that the patient could not tolerate in himself so that he "projected" them and had to act in the transference.

Porder (1987) does not acknowledge that Ogden (1979, 1983) had already described action within an object relationship as a hallmark of projective identification. To a variable degree, in projective identification, affect and identification are *induced* in the other. Ogden viewed the complex of projection and reintrojection in projective identification as offering possibilities for change. He did, however, briefly contrast projective identification with other defensive operations. The former involves attempts to "avoid, get rid of, deny, or forget feelings and ideas" (p. 360). This contrasts with attempts at mastery and integration, living with and containing aspects of oneself without disavowal (cf. Klein, 1976b). Still, Ogden took an optimistic developmental approach to projective identification, which focused on the possibility for processing unacceptable psychic content through an interactive object relationship. As Porder noted, defensive transference repetition and identification with parental defensive style warranted greater emphasis. For example, Ogden (1979) might have considered that his patient's mother used disowning, blaming, and projective identification in the mother–child relationship. Ogden did not discuss integrative versus nonintegrative defensive repetition (see chapter 6), although this subject is implicit in his work.

In this book, attempts to resolve and integrate conflict are contrasted with defensive, repetitive avoidance of facing and mastering conflict through perpetuation of pathological dependency. This general defensive style focuses on the wish not to know what is wrong, to avoid facing and struggling with it, and to preserve the status quo within the illusion of safety offered by a dependent relationship. This defensive aim contrasts with the defensive activities of other patients, which are more focused within specific areas of conflict and allow the rest of the ego to preserve adaptive and autonomous functioning.

Pathological dependency is not a diagnosis that necessarily determines the level of the patient's psychic organization. When we assess pathological dependency, we assume that the patient has felt the need to exploit his lack of full autonomy and independence for varied defensive purposes. Within this book, we especially attempt to understand pathological dependency as it describes the patient's treatment behavior. It is especially in analysis that pathologically dependent patients seem sick because of their considerable difficulty with becoming analytic patients. During the initial consultations the analyst can assess pathological dependency. Not until a trial of analysis, however, can the analyst gauge how much it will impede a constructive analytic process. Even within a trial of analysis, we take for granted that pathologically dependent patients will become stuck.

We describe pathological dependency as a form of endless, unconstructive engagement between analyst and patient. Analyst and patient need to explore whether the patient can move beyond this impasse. Both the pathologically dependent patient's character defenses and his object relations contribute to his seeming so impaired as an analysand, that is, his defensive organization attempts not to know and not to feel what is wrong throughout his psyche. In relation to the analyst, he wants to feel protected and contained, rather than analyzed. To attach himself to the analyst, he believes, usually unconsciously, that he must offer himself up as helpless and disabled and submit to the greater wisdom and authority of the analyst. Hence, the pathologically dependent patient tends to be paralyzed initially as an effective psychoanalytic collaborator. This book describes analysis of pathologically dependent patients and emphasizes those conflicts in the patient, as well as in the analyst, that tend to perpetuate the dependent impasse. This book addresses how to help such patients to release the stranglehold of their dependency so as to move forward toward autonomy and independence. The crucial step toward such responsible self-management, which this book elaborates, involves aiding the pathologically dependent patient to become a constructive collaborator in his analysis.

Most, but not all, pathologically dependent patients tend to enjoy feeling dependent. Dependency feels good, safe, and familiar, something they can relax with and allow themselves to treasure. In pathological dependency, patients need even more to exaggerate the pleasures of dependency so as to cover over rage, hatred, and dissatisfaction with their dependent submission to the other. Certain more rigid dependent patients (see chapters 14 and 15) who are especially afraid of loss of control of regressive (merger/surrender), sexual, and destructive wishes will be unable to relax and enjoy such dependent wishes. The first step in analyzing pathological dependency involves the patient's being able to feel with conviction his own intense dependent *desires.* Only then can the patient become troubled about what he himself wants. That is, the pathologically dependent patient needs to take responsibility for dependency's having become his own choice before he can become troubled about what he has done to himself. Analytic sequences in the analysis of pathological dependency are described in chapter 15.

3

WHAT IS DESTRUCTIVENESS AND WHY IS IT SO FRIGHTENING IN DEPENDENCY?

Since the pathologically dependent patient's fears of rage and destructiveness in himself and in his vitally needed other are so central to his conflicts, this chapter clarifies some differences among rage, hatred, destructiveness, and sadism. For a successful analysis of a pathologically dependent patient, analyst and patient need access to as much of the patient's hidden violence as possible, which needs to be kept out in the open between the analytic couple. This book emphasizes that the analyst needs to facilitate such passionate analysis in order for pathologically dependent patients to achieve lasting change (see chapter 15). Hence, we need to pay close attention to the vicissitudes of the dependent patient's rage and destructiveness, which the patient will continually attempt to obscure and evade.

Let us be clear that rage refers to affective experience while destructiveness refers to the associated wish or intention. Thus rage and destructiveness are linked aspects of affect and wish. This view elaborates Feiner's (1977) differentiation, except that in considering destructiveness, I prefer not to make a sharp distinction between wish and action. Multiple feelings and wishes are subsumed under rage and destructiveness, including varying intensities of angry feelings and hurtful wishes. The most frightening of these usually are those that most threaten to destroy the other or the relationship with the other. The more vitally one needs the other, the more dangerous rage and destructiveness become. One cannot wish to devour, murder, or castrate the other, if one cannot tolerate being alone (with one's feelings and impulses). Thus, destructive wishes (such as cannibalism, evisceration, murder, robbery, castration, humiliation, rejection, disconnection, dehumanization, abandonment, contempt, belittling, spoiling, scorn, domination, and so on) are all frightening in themselves, but even more frightening to the degree that one fears loss of the other. Inherent in this fear are the patient's fantasies that even allowing himself to feel his destructiveness will endanger the relation with the other. This imagined danger refers to fears of loss of control of the patient's fantasied, omnipotent power, together with a sense of vulnerability and weakness in the other, so that the other must succumb to expressions of the patient's violence. When a parent has been unable to tolerate and withstand expressions of the child/ patient's violence, the latter becomes frightened of the combination of omnipotent power in the self coupled with weakness and vulnerability in the other. Defensively these images tend to be reversed, with the patient's emphasizing his own weakness and vulnerability compared with the powerful other, a reversal that is an important contributor to pathological dependency. Hatred and wishes to destroy the other contribute to the patient's fear of his own destructive violence. Of course, the hatred derives from multiple psychic levels and varied conflicts, as we would expect with any patient. In pathological dependency it is especially compounded by the patient's feeling that he has had to sacrifice his own autonomy and independence to preserve the relationship with the vitally needed other.

The patient needs to repeat such potentially dangerous, violent confrontations between self and other in the analytic transference to become convinced that his destructiveness can be felt, managed, and contained. Indeed it is reassuring when the patient finally tries out this confrontation, with relative loss of control toward the analyst, who neither crumbles nor counterattacks. Of course, patients vary in how they fear they will damage the analyst; this fear correlates significantly but not only with the patient's intention toward the analyst, even with wishes to rob, mutilate, or murder. Pathologically dependent patients tend to fear that the analyst (parent) will be unable to listen to their wishes for separateness and destruction of the other and the pathological bond with the other, including wishes to demean, supersede, and discard the other. Rage and hatred are further intensified in pathological dependency because of the patient's fury about his life-and-death need of the other. Rage leads to wishes to get rid of the other and is followed by terror and rage at separateness, leading to intensified bonding, followed by more rage at the stranglehold the patient feels the other has over him. The analyst must facilitate the patient's feeling and expression of this rage, hatred, and destructiveness toward the analyst, so that the patient can become convinced that both can survive the patient's hatred, the analyst's counterhatred, and the patient's wishes to destroy the analyst and the bond with him. In doing so, the patient wishes to rob the analyst of his good and strong attributes, so as to become a capable person in his own right.

Chronic hatred and pathological dependency intersect. Patients attempt to manage the immediate destructiveness of intense rage toward a vitally needed object by the containment of chronic hatred and chronically hateful relationships. This adaptive and defensive transformation of rage in the attempt to contain it within an object relationship is a central function of pathological dependency. Pao (1965) pointed out that a relationship "perpetuated" by hatred differs from a sadomasochistic relationship, in that there is less libido tempering the hate. He suggested that hatred involves the ego's assimilation and attempted mastery of rage. Intense rage and destructiveness need to be justified and externalized, leading to repetition of frustrating situations and the need to create "bad" objects (Nacht, 1948; Grotstein, 1982). Bollas (1984–1985) reports that one genetic contributor in the stable, chronic need to hate and be hated is the attempt to engage a distant, unavailable parent through what was emotionally intense in the parent—the latter's hatred of the child. Better to be hated and thus cared about than to be disregarded and abandoned. Although this hateful bonding seems similar to sadomasochistic object relating, Bollas, like Pao, claims to be describing something less sexualized and less exciting, altogether a purer form of hating.

I suggest that there is a spectrum in the management and metabolism of rage and destructiveness. This metabolism has to do with how well the ego and superego are able to accept and tolerate such rage and destructiveness. When rage and destructiveness become too frightening to bear, various emergency solutions may be required: regression of varying degrees, even psychotic disorganization; efforts to deny, undo, and justify the anger so that one can tolerate oneself (to the superego) and not fear overwhelming retaliation both as punishment and as expected response from (internal and external) objects; efforts to master and use the anger in the form of chronic hatred and chronically hateful relationships; illusory efforts to transform destructiveness into something exciting, sexual, or good, as in sexualization. In these terms, sadism may be regarded as an effort to manage rage and destructiveness by illusory transformation into an exciting sexual game (sexualization). This illusion does not necessarily mean that destructive affect has been changed (fused, neutralized, transformed) into something that is no longer threatening. Only in illusion is the rage no longer present in sadism. On the other hand, to a degree, sadism is easier for some to manage than less attenuated destructiveness, and so it is adaptive.

Hatred and a focus on murdering the object one denies needing can partly serve as defense against dependency (especially wishes to be cared for and loved), passivity, and helplessness (Hill, 1938; Pao, 1965; Bollas, 1984–1985). In certain respects, it is less humiliating to view oneself as hateful, cruel, or thoroughly perverse than to acknowledge one's childlike, irresistible hunger for others' care and concern (Margolis, 1977). Intense sexual or angry feelings in the self or in the other serve to counter the danger that one has ceased to exist. This enhancement and animation of the self is one function of sexualization and of aggressivization. Rage and hatred then help to define boundaries between self and other (Epstein, 1977), just as they help to energize the self rather than yield to despair and immobilization. The pathologically dependent patient cannot dispense with a relation with a powerful other, who is to be responsible for him, even though he may play at reversing who is who in this game. When he feels most impotent and insignificant or when he fears he will uncontrollably destroy his world, he is tempted by the wish to surrender to an idealized/aggrandized other. Passive, masochistic surrender offers the promise of a comforting, protective, containing parent, who will totally take over one's care and responsibility for one's global destructiveness. Note that passive, masochistic surrender is not the same as despair in human relations, immobilization, and giving up. Rather, it is another way to defend against these greater dangers.

I view sadism as a partially organized and sexualized defense against destruction and object need, rather than a failure of defense that would lead to disorganization, despair, and immobilization. Sadism involves defensive organization and management of dangerous need and global destructiveness. The vitally needed but intensely hated object (mother) must be preserved from the wish to annihilate her. Both tender longings (between mother and child) and primitive destructiveness are managed by placing the object under the subject's total control. In sadism, sexualization is exploited for the *illusion* that intense destructive rage has been tamed and transmuted into pleasurable excitement. The sadistic, entitled attitude of domination and extractiveness preserves object relations and self-esteem regulation. It counters depressive tendencies toward despair and giving up by insisting that one has the right to use others for one's own needs.

Patients with pathological dependency vary in the degree of

mature superego structuralization with higher level guilt in contrast to the preservation of harsh, poorly integrated, unreliable, and inconsistent superego forerunners. To a significant degree, however, guilt and fears of destructiveness are managed largely by the manipulation of the other person (cf. Glover, 1933, 1964; Gillespie, 1952, 1956). Externalization, magical riddance, denial, and providing justification for one's "badness" avoid facing and integrating one's conflicts. Certain pathologically dependent patients tend to avoid the dictates of their fairly well-structured superego by varied defensive techniques (see chapter 9). I suggest that primitive guilt is linked with the need for containment and control of dangerously destructive wishes (Novick and Novick, 1987, on the fixed beating fantasy). Where there is incomplete and unsatisfactory superego structuralization, wishes to be punished, beaten, and stopped have to serve a (relatively unsatisfactory) regulatory function. What there is of a beginning superego is drawn on and drawn into such libidinized attempts to manage oneself. A predominant motivation in the sadist's disguised pathological dependency is this need for another to regulate and contain his destructiveness, so that he and his object world can survive.

I do not believe that destructiveness is primarily a problem only for the more disturbed patient. At all levels, with all patients, and with all psychic contents, it is difficult to face and integrate intense, hostile aggression. I do not intend to skew hostile aggression so as to overemphasize a preoedipal origin or determination. But early (primitive) destructiveness, involving murder and cannibalism, must be reckoned with. It infiltrates every developmental level and requires intense defense. Shengold (1988) has recently elaborated this point well. At the oedipal level, too, integration of destructiveness (murder and murderous competition, envy, robbing and taking, castration, and so on) is a central psychoanalytic task. My impression is that analysis of this oedipal destructiveness is, at times, avoided by interpretative focus on castration anxiety, retaliation, punishment, and guilt (Coen, 1987). That is, some of the analysand's destructiveness does not become sufficiently focused within the analysis and within the transference because of defensive displacement or projection, either outside the transference or onto the fantasied other (parent/analyst). For example, displaced destructiveness may occur in cross-gender analysis, if the competitive destructiveness within the transference (to the analyst as parent of the sex opposite to the analyst's actual gender) is allowed to remain displaced onto the patient's actual (same-sex) parent. Similarly, in clinical practice, interpretation of castration anxiety may tend to keep the aggression on the side of the object, rather than to enable the patient to take full responsibility for his own castrative wishes.

The analyst's problems in attempting to engage the dependent patient's dreaded violence are considered in chapters 11, 12, and 15. Remember that the analytic task in the analysis of pathological dependency is to assist the patient to tolerate and work with as much of his rage and destructiveness as he and the analyst can stand. Whatever tends to impede the patient's full ownership of his violence will limit the ultimate therapeutic effectiveness of the analysis. Hence, we consider how the analyst can best facilitate a passionate analysis of the pathologically dependent patient so as to help him to achieve lasting change (see especially chapter 15). The goal to achieve change is the reason for our persistent search for the patient's own destructiveness, which is hidden behind his anxiety, guilt, and endless wishes to be punished and contained within a dependent relationship. The pathologically dependent patient has learned to tolerate and ultimately to ignore the signals of anxiety and guilt that he experiences. This avoidant attitude has become preferable to facing seriously the dangerous psychic content that leads to such signals of anxiety and guilt. The analytic task thus involves consistent attention to the patient's fears of hating and loving passionately.

Part II

THE INABILITY TO MANAGE ONESELF

4

RESPONSIBILITY FOR CONFLICT AND THE INCAPACITY TO BEAR IT

We all have some difficulty acknowledging what is wrong within us. This difficulty is a basic postulate of conflict theory and is a crucial aspect of every psychoanalysis. With the ordinary analyzable patient, however, appropriate interpretation of defense and resistance eventually enables the patient to get at his own internal conflicts. How long this task may take varies, of course, but eventually the ordinary patient is able to hold still long enough with his own conflicts so that some attempt at resolving them can be made. Pathologically dependent patients continue to avoid responsibility for what is wrong within themselves by turning to others for illusory solutions. What is wrong feels too objectionable for the patient to bear within himself so as to face and attempt to integrate these conflicts. Instead, defensive repetition (especially with sadomasochistic object relating), externalization, denial, and blaming keep the focus of what is wrong outside of the patient himself. As a result, such patients become stuck in treatment, since they have such great difficulty with facing what is wrong within themselves. Instead, they attempt to put the problem and the solution outside of themselves. This chapter explores the difficulty such patients have with accepting responsibility for managing their own internal conflicts.

The patients under consideration have rigid characters, that is, intrapsychic rigidity, rather than merely external character style. Not all of these patients may seem so rigid in their dealings with others outside of the psychoanalytic situation. Their rigidity is manifest in the constricted way in which they respond to interpretation of their conflicts within the analytic situation. They do not take in the

37

analyst's interpretation of their conflicts and open these further so as to explore the underlying feelings and wishes. On the contrary, they close off the analyst's words as well as their awareness of the objectionable aspects of themselves. I want to elaborate Shapiro's (1981) concept of character rigidity, which I have found very helpful. The more insecure a patient is, in the sense of terror of unacceptability and abandonment/rejection, the more he will need to restrict awareness and expression of anything negative in himself (and in the other). Otherwise, the other and one's own conscience threaten permanent rejection. Thus he must live in a state of vigilance, toward himself and toward the other, to remain constantly alert to the life-and-death dangers of loss and destruction. He must continually attempt to rid himself of his own "badness" so that he will be kept around. Either the patient must avoid his "badness" or else repetitively justify it. He is so terrified of his own intense affects, wishes, and impulses that he does not want to experience these. Honest self-examination is intolerable. These patients cling defensively and repetitively to relationships that make them feel safer. They relate by supplicating, complaining, provoking, fighting, or blaming. The other is to be responsible for oneself and for what is present within oneself. Within such a relationship, the patient feels protected, cared for and loved, and safe from his own superego condemnation of his own "badness." Either the other becomes the bad one, or else the other will spare him the role of the bad one.

The patient repeats with others a parent–child relationship wherein separateness and autonomy were felt as terrifying and the other was invested with the promise of special, magical protection. In his current relationships, the patient exploits others in order to avoid responsibility for his own internal conflicts. Just as a parent has done this with the child, so the child–patient continues to repeat this with others, including the analyst. Responsibility for oneself and for what is within oneself is held to be more than anyone can stand on his own. The patient especially fears examining his own destructiveness, just as he fears facing the parent's destructiveness.

These patients are very angry. Some of the time they can acknowledge how angry they feel. The problem is not just that they defend against feeling angry, as, at times, of course, they do. They have enormous difficulty with taking responsibility for their own destructiveness so that they can face it, work with it analytically, and integrate it. For the patient to become separate and responsible for himself, like an ordinary analysand, the patient must relinquish a pathological, defensive identification with a destructively undermining parent. The terrors of confronting the destructive collusion with such a parent will be considered.

The problem is not just that such patients are terrified of their intense feelings and wishes; we all are, at times. More damaging is the collusive belief (with the parent) that separateness is death, that neither can survive facing what exists within himself. If this destructive illusion/delusion can be confronted, then the patient may become able to accept responsibility for his own conflicts.

We connect intolerance of responsibility for internal conflict with defensive repetition and with pathological object relations. Such inability to face one's internal conflicts is a cornerstone of pathological dependency. Unless this intolerance of responsibility for internal conflict can be modified, it will lead to interminable analysis and perpetuation of the patient's pathological dependency.

In the following clinical vignettes, I focus on impasses in each patient's treatment that illustrate how intolerance for what was wrong within the patient came into the treatment situation between patient and analyst.

CLINICAL VIGNETTES

Mr. A

Mr. A was content to be in analysis so long as the analyst was reasonably supportive and interpreted his conflicts as largely derived from deprivation and trauma during childhood, especially his relationship with a domineering, intrusive, and rejecting mother. With interpretation of defense, he was able to attach to the analyst his urgent, hungry wishes for caring. Some of the time he became able to recognize and to tolerate his angry demandingness that he, not someone else, be the one attended to. But Mr. A had great difficulty with ongoing acknowledgment and integration of his angry hunger.

Mr. A began his session, as he usually did, by telling the analyst the latest news of his life. He certainly knew that he craved the analyst's interest and wanted the analyst to sympathize with his plight. He knew, too, that his attempts to actualize his intense hungry desires, to feel cared for and protected, were a central problem for him. But he felt as if he could not do otherwise. The analyst's interpretations of this problem would make him feel hurt, criticized, and angry.

Mr. A pleaded that he needed the analyst to listen to his most recent experience. He felt angry that he had been mistreated, humiliated at a business dinner. The way he had been aggressively questioned about his ability to finance the deal was outrageous. In fact, Mr. A could not put down enough cash to consummate the deal. He felt that he had been humiliated by the implications in the questioning that he could not afford the purchase and that he was not to be "trusted" with the financial details unless a deal were imminent. Mr. A was well aware that he could antagonize others by his angry responses, and he struggled to keep himself under control. But in response to the questioning he became sarcastic, and argumentative and felt enraged. Realistically, he knew it did not matter whether he behaved himself or not; the deal would never occur.

In telling this story, the patient wanted sympathy for how badly he had been treated. The analyst commented that it was very difficult for Mr. A to feel helpless with others. The patient readily agreed and went on about how he had been mistreated. The analyst pointed out that Mr. A was not making the obvious connection with his rage, that this situation was similar to his feeling helpless with his mother, who could so easily humiliate him and make him feel puny and insignificant. In her intrusive and domineering way, his mother had treated him as if he did not count. Yes, of course, that was so. Mr. A became silent, seemingly angry with the analyst for not being on his side. Unable to take responsibility for either his rage or his vulnerability, Mr. A remained in a paranoid stance, of justifying his anger and seeking comfort from others (analyst).

With 10 minutes left in the session, he rather casually mentioned a dream of the night before that had frightened him. A war was spreading in Asia and began to include more and more countries: Cambodia, Vietnam, Thailand. It was becoming clear that this war would be a major nuclear war, that everyone would become involved in it. U.S., and that Soviet leaders were talking on the hotline, but there seemed little chance to avert nuclear disaster. Mr. A and his wife were then on a cruise ship with others, including a well-known, controversial political figure. Everyone was discussing the imminence of nuclear disaster. Then it was as if the war were raging and the patient and his wife were in a lifeboat. He was worried about his daughter, who was in New York. Another scene followed—as if the day after a nuclear attack, in which the patient and his wife were surveying and recovering from what had happened.

Mr. A told the dream in his typically exhibitionistic style, and tried to impress and engage the analyst. The dream had been frightening, but, of course, it all turned out fine in the end. He referred to the dream as a movie and enjoyed thinking about the political figures depicted. The analyst suggested that the dream was related to the predominant feeling of the session, anger. Mr. A did not connect the dream with his own angry feelings but, instead, mused further about the excitement of the dream. The analyst interpreted that Mr. A felt the need to dissociate himself from his own destructive fury, to experience himself as an innocent bystander to this scene of world destruction. He replied that, sure, he was angry at these guys but not that angry. The analyst told him that, on the contrary, he was so frightened of his own angry impulses that he kept wanting reassurance and comforting from the analyst and others that everything would be fine. Yes, Mr. A countered, he knew how furious he could be, and he understood what the analyst meant, but he was not sure that he was so frightened of his anger.

Why could Mr. A not take responsibility for his own angry destructiveness? Why did he need repetitively to externalize the conflict so that he was the victim of others' aggression and to seek sympathy for his mistreatment? Why was it so difficult for him to address his own internal conflicts rather than repetitively to seek attention and caring from others? An attempt at analysis had to be interrupted because of the persistence and intensity of his insistence that the analyst be supportive. When the analyst (or life) frustrated him too much and he felt dangerously enraged, he would fall asleep in the sessions. Homosexual wishes for physical contact with the analyst, as well as longings to be cared for, to sleep at the analyst's breast, and to have the analyst eliminate all difficulties contributed to his somnolence. He fully believed that sufficient warm concern from the analyst or his wife would not only make him feel better but protect and spare him the exigencies of life. Having him sit up and providing him with more contact helped some of the time. Psychotherapy replaced psychoanalysis as the treatment modality. But even with more support and contact, it was still not possible for Mr. A really to confront consistently what was wrong within himself.

Ms. D

Despite her mistrust and guardedness, manifest in her conscious withholding and suppression of certain fantasy material, Ms. D's analysis was relatively productive for some time. To a degree, she could acknowledge that she felt bitterly deprived, envious of others, greedily wanting more for herself. With sufficient interpretation of the defenses against her transference longings, she could feel how much she wanted the analyst to love her.

Once, however, she had become painfully aware of the intensity of her angry hunger and of the difficulties this caused her with others, Ms. D consciously resolved to change her behavior; she decided that she would be less angrily demanding, exhibitionistic, and competitive with others. Simultaneously, she attempted to get rid of her enraged, destructive, and hungry feelings and impulses. She especially attempted to control herself at the advertising agency where she worked. She judged herself bad and feared being gotten rid of. It became increasingly difficult for her to hold still with what troubled her within herself. She would quickly repress, suppress, or disown what she acknowledged about herself and often projected the critical attitude onto the analyst. Her earlier belligerent stance now became more frankly sadomasochistic; she wanted to feel connected with the analyst by fighting with him.

Ms. D knew very well how much she wanted a father to love and protect her. Transiently and in dreams, the analyst would appear as the adoring father who would love her, impregnate her, and bestow his penis on her. Then she would feel good, strong, and powerful as a woman with a penis. She could easily fantasize provoking the analyst into showing that he really did love her enough to set limits with her, unlike her parents. But she seemed unable to take such fantasies seriously.

The analyst told her repeatedly that she wished to be locked into an endless relationship with him in which he would forever pursue her and try to help her to change while she would spurn and defeat his efforts. In this sadomasochistic engagement, she could avoid her terror of being on her own and of having to feel responsible for what she dreaded inside herself, especially her anger and her wanting to be loved. The sadomasochistic struggle was a kind of negative love (forever), in which she simultaneously expressed and contained her hatred, while justifying it as a reaction to the frustrations imposed by the analyst and the analysis. But such interpretations were only sometimes useful. Sometimes she would grasp what the analyst meant; at other times she would protest she did not understand, or she would justify herself instead. Ms. D felt that accurate self-evaluation was more than she could stand. Moreover, she felt that she had good reason to feel enraged and envious; equally, she felt justified in maintaining her defensive attempts to be good (loved) rather than bad (unloved). In this respect, the sadomasochistic relationship with the analyst, despite her denial, continued the mother–child bond; however upsetting, blaming and accusing the mother-analyst of mistreatment and neglect were still preferable to moving outside of the magically protective orbit of mother.

With repeated interpretation of Ms. D's insistence on retaining the position of feeling cheated, abused, and deprived and of her unwillingness to relinquish a fighting relationship with the analyst, eventually a change occurred. She began to acknowledge with conviction how safe she had felt in her struggle with the analyst. Indeed, her envy and bitterness were not justified by present reality. She began to accept responsibility for her self-absorption, her exploitation of others, and her rejection of their needs. Some of the time, she allowed herself to feel loving and loved, especially with the analyst. She again became painfully aware of how frightened she felt to be separate and to confront her own destructiveness.

Nevertheless, Ms. D continued to dissociate herself from her (transient) acknowledgment of destructiveness, greed, and envy in herself, as well as in those around her. She did not want to believe that such "badness" could really be in herself or in others she needed so vitally. She minimized, got rid of, or forgot such perceptions of herself and of others. For example, despite the pain these behaviors caused her, she needed to deny destructive competitiveness and domination by certain art directors at her agency. Rather than feel enraged with them, she surrendered to their hostile criticism and felt hopelessly defective. She could only agree with her supervisor's petty carping about trivial aspects of her work and believe that this did, indeed, mean she would never succeed. She could not sustain rage at this competitive undermining. With repeated interpretation of her denial of the destructiveness of others and her wishes to be protected and cared for by them, she could recognize what was wrong and not feel worthless. But sometimes she could not understand, even intellectually, why someone would want to be destructive to others. Telling her that she was terrified of hating someone who wanted to demean, dominate, or use her, as she had felt her mother had tried to do when she was a child, did not help much. To acknowledge real destructiveness in others and in herself in an ongoing and integrative way would become too dangerous. She was, however, now well aware of the protection she felt in submitting to others' attacks on her as justified. She understood the analyst's interpretation that she could then further contain and restrain her rage and destructiveness, punish herself for her badness, and feel magically protected under someone else's tutelage. Still, the longing persisted to be contained by a dominant other. Ms. D continued to fear loss of control of her violence unless she was protected or dominated by another person.

Consistent interpretation of her sadomasochistic, vindictive attempts to ruin the analysis (see further description in chapter 6) caught her attention sufficiently. She became frightened that, indeed, despite

her best efforts not to feel angry, she could not escape her destructiveness. Before this point, Ms. D had been relatively untroubled by
the analyst's focus on the sadomasochism she was enacting. That, at
least, had reassured her that her rage was not leaking out. She again
was able to feel her violent rage, although usually directed at the
analyst's wall rather than his person; but she could feel how much she
wanted to smash her fist through the wall, to tear his office to pieces.
Although she again opened up such angry feelings more freely, at
some point she would become terrified and need to dissociate herself
from them, as she feared violent action or disorganization into psychosis. Now, however, she was again confronted by her angry, hungry passions, especially with the analyst. She could feel anew, now
more strongly, how much she wanted him to be her loving father, to
fill her up with good things, so that she would never feel envious,
deficient, and unloved again. Fantasies that the analyst would reject
or frustrate her led to intense rage. Bearing her greed and envy with
the analyst was very painful; she felt insatiable. She feared how much
she wanted to extract everything good from the analyst's body, inside
and outside, and she feared she would actually do so.

The analyst helped to tame her exaggerated sense of power by
questioning her fantasy that he would be helpless to protect himself
against her violence. She could connect her exaggerated sense of
power now, with more conviction, to her own sense of terror in
relation to parental violence and to her consequent identification with
the aggressor. She became able to grasp that she had wanted to feel
like a powerful, uncontrolled person who could do whatever she
pleased so as not to feel so helpless and that her own controls were
much better than her parents'. As a result, she began to feel safer.

Mr. L

Mr. L was a very bright, capable, successful executive. Although he
was thoughtful and reflective about his work, he found it difficult to
be so about himself. In his sessions, he would feel angry, disappointed, and cheated, constantly preoccupied with some current
"deprivation," as though he preferred to cling to such feelings rather
than to work with them. Often it did not seem as if he were primarily
seeking comfort or reassurance from the analyst in telling this
material. Rather, Mr. L seemed to be involved in a chronic war with
the world, in which he accused others of incompetence, stupidity,
self-absorption, and neglect.

Sometimes, Mr. L would fall silent. If asked about his silence, he would respond that he had again become preoccupied with work problems, which meant that he was once more nursing his sense of being slighted. Although he easily felt deprived, Mr. L had great difficulty allowing himself to need others and to want them to care about him (unless it was absolutely clear that this care was forthcoming from the other). He found it difficult to commit himself to his wife. He continued to feel preoccupied, resentful, and hurt about the end of his last love affair. So, too, he seemed to want nothing from, and showed no personal interest in, the analyst. He resented the burdens of his treatment, and its time and money, adding to his already difficult life. The analyst was not helping him enough and was not making his life better or changing his relationship with his wife. He had difficulty allowing himself really to care about himself or about others. He was not sure that, as an adult, he had really loved anyone. As a child he had loved his father; he felt he had had little relationship with his depressed, anxious mother. He had always felt lonely, on his own. He had idealized his father and what he and his father had shared. This idealization provided him with a feeling of belonging.

Usually what was wrong for Mr. L was his frustration and outrage about the stupidity of the senior executives at work, in effect, their not valuing him sufficiently, or about his wife's being preoccupied or demanding. He refused to let go of his outrage at not having been promoted at work on schedule. Even after he received the promotion, he continued to rail against those responsible. He seemed like an entitled, lonely, unhappy, chronically angry boy. He now realized how deprived he had felt as a child. He had not known that he had had any feelings about his mother's emotional unavailability or her anxious, critical, spoiling way of relating. In the course of treatment, Mr. L came, very reluctantly, to acknowledge that his father's narcissistic self-absorption and illnesses had disappointed him, that he had missed having a consistent relationship with his father, as well as with his mother. But it remained very difficult for Mr. L to take responsibility for what was wrong in terms of his own conflicts. He blamed the world while he denied his difficulties. He had come to realize that he had felt so impotent as a child to express anger and dissatisfaction to either parent. Neither parent could accept his spoken or implied complaints or help him with his loneliness and unhappiness. Mr. L certainly understood the analyst's interpretations that his chronically angry, cheated, "paranoid" attitude derived from his felt deprivations of childhood. He could remember how lonely he had felt as a child and how easily he had felt wronged. He could even agree with the analyst that the arguments he had had with both parents over sweets were expressions of his feeling angry at his parents for not providing him with more love and caring. Nevertheless, Mr. L found it very difficult to do much more than complain about his current mistreatment. At times, he could let himself be touched and feel very sad and hungry about others' generosity or love. But he seemed afraid to reveal his own tremendous hunger to be loved. His angry, dissatisfied stance certainly protected him from more clearly facing his own wishes. He found it difficult to confront his rage and disappointment with both parents or to admit that his continual faultfinding with others was a continuation of a childhood wish to show someone what was wrong and to receive redress.

The analyst repeatedly interpreted that Mr. L's continued unhappiness largely derived from his wanting to attack the parents in his mind for current (and past) frustration. He was told, in many different ways, that he wanted to remain connected to the parents in his mind in this angry, dissatisfied, vengeful way. He was told that in his "paranoid" and schizoid way, he did not allow himself to be close to, and gratified by, others. Such interpretations did not have much effect on Mr. L. He seemed to dismiss them, as, indeed, he tried to put out of his mind most of what transpired between himself and the analyst. It was as if the analyst could not derail Mr. L from his ongoing, bitter complaints of current mistreatment. Nor could Mr. L develop sufficient awareness of his need to attack and devalue others so that he could modify this pattern. There was a bitter seriousness, which seemed to brook no interference, to Mr. L's dismissing and rejecting everyone else from sharing in his world. Mr. L could understand the analyst's interpretation that he was now reversing roles and rejecting everyone else and his needs of them, as he had felt rejected as a child. But he did not feel moved when the analyst interpreted that the analyst's feeling lonely, isolated, and helpless in Mr. L's world brought to life feelings that Mr. L was afraid to experience for himself. Indeed, the analyst largely felt unable to be of much help to Mr. L.

On the other hand, as the treatment progressed, Mr. L eventually became more aware of how much he enjoyed certain solitary, self-comforting behaviors, which gave him the illusion of another's caring presence. Lying in a bed of leaves on a crisp fall afternoon now reminded him of his crawling under the bed when he felt he had needed someone to comfort him as a child. He could now connect emotionally his hoarding of precious possessions with wanting to feel loved in a safe way. He loved his collection of fine broadcloth shirts from a distinguished men's clothier. Mr. L could remember some times when he had felt touched by warmth and generosity in others, although he struggled not to give in too much to his wishes for caring. He was particularly struck with the memory of a poor, schizoid man, Jason, who would talk with him near his summer home. At the end of one summer, Jason gave the patient his own prized Indian ring. It seemed both to Mr. L and to me that Jason was recognizing himself as a child in Mr. L and trying to help him. As Mr. L was saying good-bye after a weekend visit in another city, he "accidentally," as he put it, reached up to kiss the other man goodbye. He felt puzzled by this gesture. But he smiled broadly when the analyst interpreted his hungry wish to feel close to this man. Transiently, he could allow others in, including the analyst. Despite his denial that he felt anything for the analyst, with repeated interpretation of his need to distance and magically pretend he could get rid of others (analyst), he increasingly enjoyed evidence of the analyst's understanding of him. Although this enjoyment seemed clear to both patient and analyst, Mr. L would not overtly acknowledge this. He continued to insist that he neither sought nor expected that he would ever achieve closeness with others, that he would remain as he was, which was better than he had been.

DISCUSSION

All three of these patients had great difficulty taking responsibility for their own internal conflicts. Despite intellectual and sometimes even emotional knowledge of what was wrong and of what needed to be addressed, each patient continued to complain about frustration and mistreatment by others. Interpretation of the repetitive, defensive functions involved did not help much; neither did interpretation of the style of relationship that was being repeated in relation to the analyst and to the world more generally. The patients could grasp that their attitudes were unrealistic and overly demanding for an adult. They could then restrain their behavior. But they found it very difficult to take seriously, in an ongoing, integrative way, what troubled them about themselves. This dangerous psychic content referred especially to angry, destructive feelings and envious, greedy, acquisitive impulses. Their terror of the intensity of their aggressive and destructive wishes involved harsh superego judgments of themselves as bad and unworthy, deserving of being gotten rid of.

Warding off the judgments of a harsh superego (see chapter 9) involved justifying one's present rage as caused by current reality; one was entitled to feel and want what one did, in fact, feel and want. Someone else was the bad one, not oneself, and someone else deserved punishment. The patient was only reacting to, and defending himself against, the aggression and mistreatment of others. To the degree that a person grows up feeling unloved and fearful of neglect, rejection, and abandonment, he may need to restrict, as best he can, what he feels and what he wants (character rigidity). He will continually need to convince his harsh conscience that he deserves to be kept around by demonstrating that he is good, not bad. He feels terrified that if "badness" is discovered within him, he will be gotten rid of.

To feel acceptable in the face of such external (and internal) danger, a person may submit to the hostile caretaker and view himself, rather than the other, as the "bad one." The child accepts the role of the "bad one" in order to be loved by the hostile parent, but he needs to convince the parental introject that he, the child, does not hate the parent, because awareness of hatred would endanger the relationship. So the child needs to be the "bad one," who, nevertheless, is not angry about his situation. Initially, the angry ones, who deserve to be gotten rid of, are the siblings or other children. Later, the child blames, sometimes consciously, sometimes unconsciously, the external parent as responsible for the child's own anger. Eventually, roles are traded frequently as to who is the good one and who is the bad one. As a result, the patient never takes seriously his charges against the other or against himself.

A negative parental introject serves to contain and comfort angry destructiveness. Fear of one's impulses and of others' aggression and rejection intensifies dependency and interferes with autonomy. None of the patients could manage emotionally on their own; a dependent relationship was felt to be necessary for survival. While they were able to analyze certain aspects of their dependency, they needed to reenact a complaining relationship with the analyst and emphasize their victimization, mistreatment, and neglect by the analyst as well as by everyone else. They remained unhappy, lonely, neglected, mistreated children. They felt entitled to obtain what they had missed and to be absolved from guilt for their rage and demandingness.

Let us be clear that the rage and destructiveness that these patients had difficulty tolerating did not just relate to bad parenting. Of course, they did feel enraged with their parents' failures with them. Dangerous feelings from every stage of development, contaminated by destructiveness, were subsumed under the category of intolerable "badness." Intense hostility had infiltrated every psychic content, even loving and sexual wishes, so as to exaggerate the danger. Aspects of phallic oedipal rivalry mixed with preoedipal conflict. Oedipal-phase progression was, however, incomplete in each of these patients.

The patients consciously sought attention, admiration, and encouragement, which they protested were their due. This dependent turning to others interfered with taking responsibility for themselves. On the contrary, rather than manage themselves, they wanted more from others. In part, they refused to assume responsibility for themselves, insisting with angry hunger and vengeful blaming that this was the responsibility of others. That this avoidance of responsibility would lead to an interminable treatment or to an endless, unsatisfying mode of relating to others did not matter much. Rather, because of the terror of abandonment, endless relationships were desired. Change was frightening; sameness and repetition were reassuring. Therefore, they wanted to remain as they were.

Internalization of reasonable expectations and standards conflicted with the wish to have others continue to be responsible for oneself. Learning and change were thus to be avoided. The patients had not progressed developmentally so as to have a smoothly functioning, well-integrated superego. Superego functioning was uneven; harsh superego forerunners and superego corruption existed simultaneously. The patients preferred to think that they were simply unable to manage their own self-esteem regulation. To a degree, this inability was, of course, true. But all patients remained and wanted to remain locked into using others as auxiliary superegos, as responsible for regulating them. Others were to help them feel good, to catch them at their transgressions, to punish them, to contain and restrain them, and so to love them. They had once established this pattern with a parent.

The patients continued both to feel bad and to try to point an accusing finger at others as the bad ones. They had difficulty grasping that they were willing to remain bad in relation to a parental imago, which would protect and care for them. To take responsibility for oneself by really confronting one's sense of badness and seeking to change it meant to let go of a symbiotic relatedness with others. This mode of relatedness perpetuated the magically protective illusion that one was safe, that everything would be all right. Clinging to the parent guaranteed safety; the dangers could then be regarded as external to the enmeshed couple. Neither hated the other or wanted to destroy and leave the other, and feelings of badness, the price paid for this mutual denial, became merely a means of increasing the enmeshment.

To a degree, everyone needs to justify those impulses and wishes that make him feel guilty and anxious. With the ordinary analyzable patient, interpretation of the patient's defensive, self-justifying, and entitled attitudes toward such conflicted impulses and wishes eventually allows further analysis, which does not happen with the patients described here. Instead, a kind of defensive confusion ensues. The patient attempts, consciously and unconsciously, to conceal the impulses and wishes about which he feels guilty. The entitled defense is intensified. Or else a frenzy of self-criticism obscures what the patient feels guilty about. He cannot hold still, in an ongoing, integrative way, with what he feels guilty about, so as to attempt to resolve his conflict. For example, in attempting to analyze Ms. D's greed and envy, sometimes she could face them in herself and make sense of them. At other times, however, she would become threatened and fight with the analyst and with herself. Now she was being good; she was no longer feeling such angry hunger as before. Why was the analyst condemning her? Did she, indeed, still feel such greed and envy? She did not know, nor did she want to know. If she was still so angry and hungry, better that this fact remain hidden, as at the start of her analysis.

By way of rationalizing her defensive confusion, Ms. D described her fear of becoming overwhelmed with rage; when she felt angry, she wanted to smash the analyst's wall and the analyst. It might really happen that she would go out of control, as had certain family members, and attack others. She had actually smashed her hand against a wall when she felt furious. Her rage was too dangerous; she must be inherently evil and unlovable. And she did not want to know the truth.

Ms. D's inability to tolerate her own rage was intimately linked to her inability to connect it meaningfully and realistically to a sense of actual injustice. In this respect, she was, indeed, her parents' child. Both of Ms. D's parents had attempted to adjust reality so as to fit their own extractive needs, without much consideration of what was fair between parent and child. Neither parent could hold still and respond reasonably to Ms. D's questioning of their selfishness. On the contrary, they would turn this questioning back on Ms. D, as if she were being unappreciative of all she had received from them. They exaggeratedly distorted how generous they had been with her, while substantially depriving her and using her for their own needs. Indeed, Ms. D was confused about what was fair and who was the greedy one. To preserve the parent–child relationship from her rage, she accepted the role of the selfish one, without, however, really having connected this role with her own greed and envy, which remained dissociated.

The other two patients also shared some of this confusion about what is fair between self and other, confusion derived from relationships with extractive parents who denied their misuse of the child and who, by projective identification, attempted to put their own greed into the child. Their parents had failed to help them as children to learn to face, tolerate, and manage their own age-appropriate needs and feelings, so that they could be clear about what existed within themselves. The same applied to their attempts as children to discern the parents' excesses; their parents, unable to face and integrate what really existed within themselves, could not assist the child with clarifying parental impingement on the child.

DEFENSE AND LEVEL OF PSYCHIC ORGANIZATION

The pathologically dependent patient may be able temporarily to acknowledge feelings and attitudes about which he feels guilty. Superego fears of abandonment and loss of love (and castration), together with terror about the strength of his destructive impulses, lead him to run away from his conflicted feelings quickly. Thus, he will believe he has (quickly) resolved what is wrong and will feel relieved. The very painful emotional knowledge about his conflicted impulses may soon disappear. What is wrong will soon become externalized again. The patient remains confused about what is wrong and where (in whom) it is located. The patient's "badnesses" remain isolated or compartmentalized rather than integrated within the ego's core. Simply to view what is described here as developmental failure, although correct, tends to miss the dynamic gains of such repeated misuse of other people. Dependent wishes for love and acceptance become a way of life and lead to interminable treatment. Deprivation becomes an excuse for what is wrong within the patient.

In chapter 6, I outline a hierarchy (following Rapaport, 1953; Gill, 1963; Valenstein, 1971; and Klein, 1976b) of defensive aims and modes. The ego's defensive aims range from avoidance, riddance, or isolation to efforts at organization and integration of what had been previously regarded as intolerable. Dorpat (1987) contrasts denial, isolation, and disclaiming of responsibility with responsibility for avowed action, integration, and constructive adaptation. In a very schematic way, we can posit that the ordinary neurotic patient is relatively able to express and synthesize conflict in fantasy, to handle it within his own mind. When patients are unable to handle conflict within fantasy, then they are impelled to enact it repetitively so as to manage the associated anxiety. Although the tendency to act is generally regarded as characteristic of lower level character integration (narcissistic and infantile characters, borderlines, perverts, and so on), this book emphasizes that certain pathologically dependent patients, who can be regarded as within the range of neurotic character disorders, tend to resemble sicker patients in their defensive reliance on repetitive enactments that involve others. Most of the patients I describe as pathologically dependent are not borderline. Some may have identified with a parent's borderline functioning in the effort to preserve intrapsychically a fragile or dangerous parent–child relationship. Such patients will have to relinquish this pathological identification, but they are not organized intrapsychically as borderline.

Chiefly in the analytic setting does the pathologically dependent patient seems "sick" in that he has such difficulty with using the analytic process to face and integrate what is wrong within. Also, some of these patients may seem sick because of their defensive need to view themselves as incapable, unable to manage alone, clinging to another for psychic regulation. Action and the use of other people aim to manage what the patient feels unable to manage for himself. When compromise formation in fantasy is insufficient to allay anxiety, other, more powerful (interactive, behavioral) defensive modes are utilized. The overriding aim is then not mastery and integration of what is threatening within oneself, but avoidance and protection against this. The patient seeks the illusion that he has rid himself of the internal danger because he is too threatened to attempt to face and integrate his conflict. The other person (external and internal object) is then used, to a degree, for the patient's imperative needs.

The analyst's interpretive strategy should address itself to the defensive purposes being served. Emphasis on defense in one's needs of objects helps to avoid unwarranted assumptions about ego defects or developmental failures. Dependency and transference repetitions in analysis can most usefully be explored in terms of how and why the object is being used by the patient. This focus leads to questioning what the patient is afraid to take responsibility for in himself, so as to be able to synthesize and integrate internal conflict.

Just as children tend to identify with, and to adopt, parents' defensive styles, so, too, do they identify with parents' defensive aims. When parents have avoided responsibility for their "badnesses" by intense denial, projective defenses, and interactive defensive modes (such as dependency, sadomasochism, sexualization, or perversion), the child will tend to identify with this avoidant style. The ordinary neurotic patient and his parents, of course, defend themselves, as we all do, but such defensive activities tend to be more circumscribed, encroach less on reality and object relations, and usually allow for more responsible guilt and autonomy. By contrast, the aim of repetitive behavioral enactments is to repeat and thereby avoid, rather than to face, synthesize, integrate, and change.

The analyst must be well aware of the countertransference potential of judging the patient as infantile and irresponsible out of his own envy of the patient's entitled defensive position. It helps to remain well aware of how terrified such patients are of facing, in an ongoing, integrative way, their own "badness." The analyst may also resent the patient's unrelenting demands to make him (and everything else) better, rather than to analyze conflict. The patient's chronic externalization (the analyst is bad, deficient, impotent, ineffectual) may be especially provocative. The patient's inability to become an ordinary analysand, able to assume some responsibility for his problems, makes the analyst feel helpless, angry, and dissatisfied with himself and reinforces the patient's feeling of being a failure, deficient, and unlovable. This development in the treatment repeats experiences with a parent in which the patient could not and would not satisfy the parent so as to feel lovable and good. Interpretation of this transference and countertransference repetition may be very helpful.

The potential for an escalating interlocking spiral of transference and countertransference hatred makes the analytic field ripe for a defensive collusion between patient and analyst that is designed to forestall this threat. Analyst and patient may act as if they have a helpful, caring relationship that should continue forever, without acknowledging the mutual anger and dissatisfaction. Analyst and patient need to confront being stuck and feeling resentful about a relationship that is unsatisfactory, despite illusions to the contrary. Such repeated interpretations with Mr. L and Ms. D, but not with Mr. A, were helpful indeed. The analyst has to get underneath his "objective" frustration and anger with these difficult patients, to bear his role as the hateful, rejecting, dissatisfied parent who is fearfully hated by the patient. It is easier and safer for both analyst and patient superficially to tolerate feeling frustrated that the patient does not make more progress. Unless the intense hatred, back and forth, between analyst and patient, between parent and child, is engaged, the patient will remain stuck.

At times, I have found myself involved in a partial denial of these patients' willingness to persist in a regressive, dependent, sadomasochistic transference relationship. Then I would tend to feel helpless, frustrated, and angry, temporarily losing my focus on the patient's dread of relinquishing this transference mode. At other times, I could feel the appeal of the patient's offer of specialness, as he attempted to re-create an intense parent–child bond, or I overly protected myself from awareness of such temptation by impatience with this transference repetition. My awareness of such countertransference feeling alerted me to focus more clearly on the patients' wishes to remain stuck in their pathological dependency. I needed to allow myself to reverberate with such regressive wishes in these patients, while continuing to analyze these wishes in them. Ms. D and Mr. L were able partially to relinquish this pathological mode of relating with the analyst. Note, however, that all three patients, to a degree, persisted with this (predominantly internalized) sadomasochistic bonding. The analyst's countertransference was not the primary problem here. That is, even when the analyst, through his own self-analysis, could refrain from contributing to the patients' needs to perpetuate a sadomasochistic bond within the analytic setting, such wishes continued in these patients. What is important to acknowledge, for analyst and for patient, is what the patient seems unable to change. Persistent analytic focus on this did, indeed, help each patient.

In part, this kind of transference repetition protects patient and analyst from experiencing each other as caring and loving because of the dangers for both of feeling loving. Vengefulness, spite, destructive spoiling, negativism, and stubbornness are used defensively to keep the patient from feeling grateful and appreciative of what is good in what he receives. One-sided emphasis on anger and rejection is safer than the danger of something good and loving that may not last.

The genetic background in these cases, as reconstructed from the transference, together with memories and information from relatives, has been an alternation of deprivation and indulgence, in which parent and child take turns at caring for the other. Indulgence, like provocativeness or excitement, is proffered and sought as a defensive comfort when a parent cannot be genuinely loving. The alternation between the promise of indulgence and chronic deprivation intensifies rage, demandingness, and the entitled attitude. This dependent, exploitative mode of relating had been the pattern of the parent–child relationship. A parent had exploited the child as a way of avoiding responsibility for internal conflict. To a degree, the child was related to as a part-object, viewed through projective identification and externalization, with a partial denial of his own autonomy and identity. There was an implied promise that if the child accepted this relationship, he would share in a special, protected, magical relationship with the parent. The promise of specialness is seriously frustrated, or, at best, it is inconsistently gratified.

For certain of these patients, this specialness was highly sexualized, overly tempting the patient with incestuous gratification, victory, and grandiosity. These exciting expectations led to repetitive re-creation of, and clinging to, the sexualized specialness, as well as to intense guilt at such repeated oedipal enactment. Such oedipal guilt (erotic, destructive, grandiose) was handled by defensive focus on repetitive excitement and on surrender and clinging in the parent–child relationship. Oscillation between such sexualized specialness and the parents' relative emotional unavailability much of the time intensified the patients' feelings of rage and their entitlement to reexperience the intensely exciting connection. At a deeper level, the patients know they were being used and were using the parents. These oedipal games transgressed the ordinary boundaries between parent and child, caused intense pleasure and intense pain, and addicted the patients to a parent–child relationship that interfered with separateness and responsibility.

Is growing up with such troubled parents largely the cause of the patients' seeming to be so sick? In many aspects of life, these patients do not seem sick, in contrast to their functioning in the psychoanalytic situation. My impression is that trauma is a significant but not exclusive factor. These patients experienced substantial neglect, abandonment, exploitation, cruelty, and, for some, terror in relation to parental violence. This experience is sufficient to explain one major contribution to the patient's rage. Equally significant, however, is the seductive invitation to share a pathological object relationship with a disturbed parent and to share the parent's primitive, interactive defensive mode. The patients were terrified that their hatred would disrupt the precarious but vital relationship with the parent. This terror interfered both with their ability to own up to their feelings and with full individuation. Within this framework, conflicts from every developmental level become embedded and avoided.

To get at the underlying rage, such patients need to acknowledge how neglected and misused they have felt by a parent(s) and how they have repeated this pattern with others. Renunciation of the entitled defense against acknowledgment of one's neglect and misuse of others leads to painful acknowledgment of one's angry wishes to hurt others, who do not deserve this hurt. The most malignant forms of entitlement (see chapter 9) occur in the context of patients' feeling that they have been misused and exploited by a parent(s); as a result they now feel free to take what they want from others, who deserve their exploitation. Chronic vengefulness and exploitation involve a wished-for, but reversed, exploitative parent–child relationship.

The rapid reversal of roles from victimized child to the powerful (parental) avenger and abuser avoids the hatred associated with each role and the patients' acknowledgment of how crippled they have felt. To varying degrees, in the patients reported, the parent–child relationship was predicated on the attempt to destroy the child's confident responsibility for himself as a separate, autonomous person. To accept responsibility now for himself, the patient must confront how very much the parent(s) has not wanted him to do so and how much he has surrendered and colluded in this pressure. Parents who are terrified of taking responsibility for themselves as separate persons establish an emotional atmosphere of danger and helplessness. This attitude may be covered over with defensively grandiose and omnipotent attitudes. More terrifying than specific fearfulness of one's instinctual life is the shared childhood "delusion" that separateness is deadly. The emotional climate established by such a parent—of terror of abandonment, starvation, destitution, and destruction—leads the child (as the parent, indeed, wishes) to cling ever more tightly to the parent. The child perceives and denies the parent's own destructive envy, hatred, and wishes to be rid of the child. Parental hatred intensifies the child's own sense of danger and his rage. With such a vulnerable parent, the child's rage feels dangerously destructive. Because the parent feels endangered by the child's autonomy, the parent undermines the child's attempts to act on his own initiative: competitively, by ridicule or humiliation, by guilt provoking or withdrawal. To preserve the precarious parent–child relationship, which the child now feels is lifesaving, the child surrenders further, doubting his own mind, discrediting his own abilities, idealizing the parent as savior. Once the child feels so undermined in his ability to manage on his own, he will become frightened of whatever tends to move him in the direction of experiencing his own separate wishes. Thus, he will doubt and undermine his own feelings, wishes, and perceptions. He will forever be unclear about his own separate position.

Patients who have endured such a childhood unconsciously come to believe that to face their darkest urges on their own will be catastrophic to themselves and to their loved ones. Indeed, this belief has been communicated to them by their own parents. It is not just that taking responsibility for oneself is tantamount to killing the parents (Loewald, 1979). The patient must face his terror of confronting the illusion that no one is strong enough to tolerate his feelings on his own, especially his deep hatred of the parent(s) who has contributed to his emotional crippling. Although pathologically dependent patients may fear loss of control over their violence, the danger is not usually in their behavior, which tends to be inhibited, but in the hate-filled intensity of their feelings and wishes. On the contrary, the patient prefers a quick, angry discharge in action, as he hopes to be done with his anger, to the therapeutic need to hold still with his violence and to face it over time. If the patient is, indeed, strong enough to survive examination of his own feelings and wishes, the "delusional" system will be relinquished/destroyed, the parent–child relationship will terminate, and the child/patient will go on as a separate and confident adult. As the patient feels safer with his own destructiveness, he relinquishes the hostile parental introject and tolerates responsibility for his feelings and wishes. Then he can become an ordinary analysand and proceed with his analysis.

5

DEPENDENCY AND THE SUPEREGO

This chapter explores interrelations between dependency and superego functioning. Freud (1923, 1939) described the dependency of the ego upon the superego in two broad directions: the fear of hostile criticism and the need for love, protection, and approval. We expect the mature, well-integrated superego to help provide autonomous self-regulation in the absence of the parents or their representatives. In this sense, formation of the superego is an enormous developmental step toward self-sufficiency and independence. Dependency between internal psychic imagoes or psychic structures or in relation to other people runs counter to this mature goal. That is, people behave dependently in relation to other people as well as in relation to aspects of their own internal psyche. These parts of the psyche on which people depend may be structured and depersonalized and function as reasonable guides for balancing one's inner needs against those of others as well as against the possibilities and limitations of external reality. Then we refer to these aspects of the psyche as relatively mature ego and superego. Or aspects of parental imagoes that have been built into one's psyche persist without taming of harsh, destructive, primitive attitudes. It then seems as if the person continues to relate to these aspects of his psyche as he once did to either an actual parent or an exaggerated and distorted fantasy version of that parent. "Object-cathexes" are to be transformed into "structures," Freud tells us (1923, p. 55).

I have differentiated patients with pathological dependency, who cannot assume responsibility for their own conflicts, from those who can do so more readily. Here I especially emphasize aspects of superego functioning that seem to distinguish these patients. The paradigmatic patient I write about was surprising in his ability, despite his severe, dependent psychopathology, to use the analytic process constructively. My task here is to differentiate his ability to make such good use of the analytic process from the inability of other very dependent patients to do so. I suggest that an essential factor for relinquishment of pathological dependency is superego identification with a parent/analyst, who confidently encourages and admires the patient in his attempts at responsible psychic integration and regulation. This parental attitude, of course, must become the patient's own motivation for the dependency to be resolved. To the degree that such healthy identification has been lacking, the patient must destroy and relinquish those parental imagoes, which have quashed the patient's independence and autonomy. This process includes shedding ego and superego identifications with aspects of a parent who *avoids* facing conflict by interpersonal defensive maneuvers and *encourages* an immature, dependent, irresponsible, entitled attitude. To shed these identifications, the patient must become capable of tolerating on his own all that he dreads most within himself, especially his own murderous rage and destructiveness.

The principal superego aim in pathological dependency is to avoid integration of conflict and management of destructive feelings and to preserve a pathological parent–child relationship. In this sense, the superego and ego in pathological dependency are highly corrupt and irresponsible. Much of this irresponsibility derives from an identification with an infantile, irresponsible parent and satisfies the need to preserve the idealized aspect of the parent–child bond. Self-hatred does not lead the patient to responsible, guilty concern about his "crimes." Instead, dependent, sadomasochistic submission of the ego to the superego perpetuates the pathological object relationship without allowing for integration and change. This pattern contrasts with the ordinary superego goals of enhancing autonomy, maturation, and growth by renunciation/restraint of drive impulses, so as to feel approved of by parental imagoes.

When the parent–child relationship has become overridden by destructiveness, psychic disability, and emotional misuse of the other person, ego and superego identifications and functioning are contaminated. In analysis, the patient must begin to value responsible psychic management, so that he can become convinced that he can regulate himself on his own, without parent or analyst. The pathologically dependent patient's terrors and considerable difficulties in approaching this position are explored. The analysis must consider how to help to motivate such patients to want to work out their own internal conflicts rather than to continue to settle for a dependent relationship in which they are reassured of their safety and accept-ability. I want to stress that I am not advocating an "active" tech-nique, in which we exhort dependent patients to identify with us in boldly facing their internal terrors. What I am discussing is standard psychoanalytic technique. The emphasis is, however, on what is necessary to help patients who are stuck at pathological dependency to move forward. The passion you may hear in my writing refers to what is required to engage the patient about his contentment with the status quo and his terror of the conflicts he is avoiding. Otherwise, no change will occur. Infantile, irresponsible patients need to learn a model of responsible facing and integrating of conflict. I do not advocate substituting the analyst's superego for the patient's or encouraging an imitative identification with the analyst's functioning. Change is accomplished primarily by systematic analysis of the patient's avoidance of responsibility for what is wrong within, rather than by identification with the analyst.

Transference and countertransference wishes for closeness, shar-ing, and similarity must be resolved for separateness and autonomy to be established. Ultimately, superego standards and aims change by relinquishment of infantile values derived from pathological parental models and relationships, once the patient has become capable of responsibly bearing his own destructiveness. The wish to be like and to be liked by the analyst may initially assist the analytic process, but it, of course, eventually becomes a resistance to the patient's progres-sive integration of what is wrong within. On the other hand, for patients who have not had a sufficiently well-developed ego and superego model of facing and integrating conflict, some identification with the analyst's model of psychic functioning will be necessary. These valued attributes, as well as all the rest of the analyst's treasures (as seen through the child/patient's eyes), will eventually become the focus of envious and rivalrous conflict, as the patient becomes engrossed in wanting to rob and destroy the analyst, so as finally to make these attributes his own.

Trying to explain what will lead to change and what will perpetuate the dependency can easily become muddled, reflecting the opposing uses the patient makes of the analyst, to preserve dependency as well as to reach for change and independence. The goal in the analysis of pathological dependency is *not* ultimately to foster identification with the analyst's superego. The patient needs help to relinquish his wish to substitute for his own superego that of the analyst; he then attempts to influence the analyst's superego by manipulating the analyst's responses. To develop the willingness and ability to rely on one's own superego rather than that of another person, a primary goal in the analysis of pathological dependency, requires letting go of the pathological relationship with another person. A number of steps are required to accomplish this goal. First, the pathologically dependent patient, as his defenses against attachment to the analyst lessen, will indeed want to model himself after the analyst. Early in treatment, the pathologically dependent patient has to be helped to connect his dependent wishes to the person of the analyst for the ultimate purpose of resolving his dependency. Indeed, it is useful to tell patients who are afraid of becoming dependent on the analyst that the analytic goal is not dependency but independence via the route of analyzing their dependent wishes toward the analyst. Second, a central analytic task in the analysis of pathological dependency is to assist the patient to move to the level of wishes for dependency rather than continuing to believe that he must actually behave dependently. We emphasize this shift soon in the vignette of Dr. S. Third, patients whose ego and superego have not encouraged facing and integrating conflict need to come to value this mature psychic goal. Initially, they will do so by identification with what they perceive as the analyst's superego. What has to be worked through here are the varied wishes to rely on the analyst rather than ultimately to rely on oneself. Such wishes include wanting the analyst to remain the custodian of the patient's feelings and desires and wanting to please the analyst, to change for the sake of the analyst, to be the analyst's favorite, and so on. At some point the analysis must address the pathologically dependent patient's fears and wishes not to follow the dictates of his own conscience but to rely, instead, on that of the analyst. Reliance on one's own conscience requires the ability to tolerate in an ongoing way what is most frightening and objectionable within oneself.

I have come to the same conclusion as Schafer (1960), who suggested that the parents' attitudes toward the child's identifications significantly affect superego functioning:

If the child's tendencies in this regard are not ignored, shamed, competed against and suppressed, but rather recognized and, within appropriate limits and with appropriate exceptions, encouraged and rewarded, then these favorable *evaluations* will be taken up in the superego identifications, and the child, and later the adult, will be free to feel that it is good to try to meet the ego ideal, that one can love oneself for making the attempt (pp. 180–181, italics added).

Schafer implied that the whole complex interaction between child and parents affects superego formation. In pathological parent–child interaction, Schafer reports exaggerated intensification of (oedipal) drive conflict and a "faulty model" for managing it. Healthier parents manage their own (oedipal) conflicts better and help to manage the child's aggressive expressions more consistently, firmly, and reasonably. When the parents have been unable to provide affective management and there is inadequate superego formation in the child (and in the parent), superego functioning will need to be excessively severe.

Affect tolerance and management develop, in large part, out of the child–parent relationship. Children need to be helped by their parents to integrate stimuli and, eventually, affects. Furman (1985) describes the mother's role as auxiliary ego and mediator between the young child's drives and the developing ego. Elaborating from Anna Freud and Winnicott, Furman refers to the mother as needing to shield the young child from excesses of libidinal and aggressive stimulation, so that the child can begin to integrate these. Furman's argument becomes awkward when she tries, in overly concrete, energic terms, to account for sexually overstimulated and seduced children's having sufficient libidinal endowment and input, yet having inadequate drive fusion. The problem here is not just the quality of libido or even traumatic, overwhelming, or uncontrollable sexual excitement. Sexually overstimulated or seduced children must also struggle with intense rage at their abuse by the parent (adult) who misuses them. Such a parent cannot provide adequate loving regulation, comforting, and assistance with ego integration.

Interpersonal defensive operations tend to be learned in childhood by identification with a parent who uses such interactive defensive modes. This defensive pattern tends to be built into a style of relatedness between parent and child. Parents who are unable to take responsibility for what is troublesome within themselves will tend to protect themselves by involving others (including their children) in their conflicts. What the parent cannot tolerate within himself, he will, most likely, be unable to tolerate within the child. Then the parent will be unable to help the child to learn gradually to tolerate and manage within himself such troublesome feelings and wishes. Ordinarily, parents move from managing painful feelings for their very young children by comforting, holding, and responding to bodily and emotional needs to assisting their older children to modulate and integrate their feelings. A parent who cannot tolerate and manage his own affects will be unable to help his child with this essential maturational task. My aim here is to contrast superego identifications, standards, and values, that encourage responsible affective integration and management, as well as mature adaptation, from those that hopelessly give up on the prospect of independent affective management and, instead, substitute some variety of pathological dependency.

CLINICAL VIGNETTE

Dr. S sought treatment because of anxiety, depression, and continual pressure to find others to care for him, often to the neglect of his work. He felt alone, bereft of family, insecure, wanting very much to feel cared about and connected with the analyst. Counterphobically, he began to arrange multiple trips and emphasized his pleasure in traveling. Surprisingly, he did not appreciate how difficult it was for him to be on his own.

When he traveled, he feared that he would again have to seek out a woman to care for him sexually, as he had done in the past, or else go through prolonged masturbation with fantasies of a woman enjoying stimulating him, masturbating him, or sucking his penis. He would invariably be passive in his fantasies and sexual preferences. He felt anxious that he could not sustain himself emotionally or write his lectures, research reports, or articles. At the start of a new project, he felt anxious that he could not do it, that others would be angry and dissatisfied with him. His colleagues resented his unwillingness to share in the ordinary work of his medical school department. Despite his anxiety, he would become interested in only the more difficult, challenging projects. Once he had gotten past his initial anxiety, procrastination, and temptation (often acted upon) to escape to more exciting activities, he would work very well. He was regarded as bright, capable, and industrious. His own narcissistic needs, however, would often take over his work, so that he did too much work on a project, at too great an expense in time and money, to exhibit himself for others' admiration. Once involved in a project, he could not let go of it, even to sleep or to attend to the rest of his life. He hungered for more exciting involvement, which, indeed, is how he lived his life.

Dr. S quickly indicated that he wanted an analysis. Given his history of depression and considerable regressive potential, the analyst felt uneasy. In effect, Dr. S put himself on the couch. When he soon began to talk about not wanting to go to work, not wanting to face the problems of life, wanting to stay in bed, the analyst feared

Dr. S would disorganize. The analyst attempted to interpret this apparent regression as a driven wish: to be cared for as a child by a parent. To the analyst's surprise, this interpretation made sense to Dr. S, and, to a degree, he was able to shift to the level of talking about wishes instead of acting. But acting on what he felt, rather than holding still and experiencing it, was a major problem for Dr. S. Showing him the identifications with both parents' avoidance of facing and managing their feelings, in effect their running away from these feelings, helped him. Mother would withdraw and regress, sulk, and torture everyone else with her bad feelings. Father would leave—probably run off to other women or travel. Once Dr. S could see that his father had not helped him with his mother's depression and his own feelings, but, instead, encouraged in him activities like father's, he began to feel angry at his deprivation. This anger had initially been hidden under his insistence about how much each of his parents had loved him. The initial truth seemed to be, rather, that he had been very much neglected by both parents. Mother at times could narcissistically connect with him in a kind of seductive duet. He loved his father and missed him; father had been more consistently available than mother, at least to participate in activities with him. But he and the analyst could now see, in his behavior with his family and in the transference, how little sense he had had of someone's really being concerned with his feelings.

As soon as Dr. S began to use the couch, his loneliness and hunger for contact became more intense. In his fourth session on the couch he reported a dream from the previous night:

> I was watching advertisements of women in lingerie. They seemed to be exposing as much of themselves as they could get away with. They were exposing their breasts and vaginas, which I was touching; they were very wet. One of the girls had her legs spread. I was touching her vagina on the inside. It was very wet and moist. The exciting thing was having someone be so overtly seductive about their sex.

He described his mother as having been pretty but noted that she had seemed so uncomfortable with hugging and touching. He said he felt sad, lonely, left out. The analyst asked, "Do you want physical contact and closeness with me, too?" He replied:

> Physical contact is not something I want with you. Closeness, I do—in the sense of getting to know more about you, what you think about analysis. I'd like to get a better sense of you as a

human being. You're very good at maintaining the objectivity required for this process. I often feel I'd like to pierce through some of that. You know I feel it's a little too clinical.

Later the analyst said, "It's unclear, just as with your mother, how close can you feel with me? What can you and I tolerate?" The next day Dr. S commented:

It feels good to be here today. It almost feels like I could need this place for my protection. I think one of the things I want from you more that I don't get is an occasional good word: "Good work"; "You're doing well." I did have a dream last week about Dr. X, who I did have a closer relationship with. I don't think he maintained that distance. I don't know that that was any good. We were talking to each other in his office. The session ended. He went into his other office, which was an imaginary office, where he took care of his academic responsibilities. A nurse and secretary were there. He was busy but said that I could talk for a moment more with him.

Dr. S said he felt a desire to expand the treatment, to get to know the analyst more. He commented that in the dream he felt he needed more support. The analyst interpreted: "It certainly sounds like you're saying through the dreams and in the sessions that you want much more closeness with me, that you want to move in more closely, more personally." He answered:

I guess I do. It's just hard to acknowledge those feelings, when it's clear they can't be reciprocated. It's kind of like my feelings with my mother. I was saying yesterday that I didn't feel physically attracted to my mother because it seemed like such an impermissible thing, like I was more concerned with pleasing her, sharing with her, but never feeling any physical desire for her, though I admired her beauty, so there must've been something about it that made it so impermissible.

In the next session, he reported a dream from the night before:

I went back to my old medical school department. I saw one of the senior professors. He told me of all the people in the department, he was most sorry I'd left and he really loved me, like he was exalting me. He was very close, our faces were very close, almost like he was hugging me, saying how sorry he was that I'd left, how I was the most special junior faculty member, that he loved me. [He tells how difficult it is for him to feel left out. Analyst: "Is that how you feel on days when you and I don't meet?"] A little bit. Sometimes I'm afraid this whole process is feeding my desire to be special. When I'm not here, I don't have much tolerance for not being special.

The analyst asked him how he wanted to be special with the analyst and later told him that when he was left on his own, he wanted someone to be warm and loving with him.

A week later he reported the dream:

I was with a woman who was doing gymnastics or calisthenics. Then another woman came in, and it wasn't exciting. I wanted her to leave to be alone with the first woman. The first woman was standing on her head. I could see her vagina and her behind. She was completely naked. I was being distracted by the other woman. She left. I was sucking the woman's breasts. They didn't taste very good. Then something came out of them, like milk or sperm, more like sperm. I jerked back like it was a little disgusting. It came out of her breast, but it was sticky. It made me feel repulsed. I've had dreams before of a woman who was pretty; I was involved with her sexually, then her genital area turned out to have a penis. Here there was no penis but there seemed to be sperm coming out of it.

The analyst interpreted, "You want to feel closer and to suck, but you're not quite sure what this is you're sucking, a breast or a penis, a woman or a man." Later the analyst added that his wanting to feel closer and suck with the analyst made the patient uncomfortable.

The next day he narrated the dream:

I was at a retreat or a convention. I'd driven there poorly, swerving around on the road, making others nervous and critical of how I was driving. I was by the ocean. Huge waves were coming up; they were scary. I saw one wave which was really huge but much further out. I went out a little way to the beach. I thought it was good I didn't go out further; I could've been drowned. There was a seawall there. I was afraid I could've been knocked into the seawall. I wasn't. One wave came up to my chest. These other waves were scary. I got close enough to be in danger. Even though I was with other people in the dream, I was feeling alone and isolated in the face of all this danger. I'm not at all sure what my relation with you is like or should be like. This whole transference thing is very confusing. I'm not really sure I understand the rules. I feel not in control, which, I guess, is a scary feeling. I think I'm trying to keep myself in control even here. Part of it might be that I'm going away. I was thinking yesterday when I left that I was constructing rules in here about how I should relate to you that were keeping me at a distance. I remember when I first called you up and I got your tape message, I felt good that your message had an inviting, friendly ring to it. I guess I find being assertive and aggressive, work. It doesn't come naturally to me. Sucking a breast is not really assertive; it feels more comforting. Even in my work I always feel I'm fighting a desire to give up, not have to be always fighting, aggressive, working out problems.

Dr. S struggled with his fears that, like his parents, neither he nor the analyst would be able to tolerate his devouring wishes and destructive rage. He easily became furious, attacking, and demanding when he felt overly frustrated. He dreamed of himself as molten lava or as maggots devouring and destroying whatever was in his path. Dr. S experienced both parents as too fragile and troubled to stand what he felt. The analyst was surprised how tolerant Dr. S was of being shown the ugly sides of his character pathology, his selfishness, greed, extractiveness, lack of generosity and concern for others' needs. Almost always, he seemed genuinely appreciative of what the analyst told him, no matter how painful. He experienced this as if the analyst were a concerned father taking him in hand, teaching him how to grow up. If he felt hurt and angry at clarifications of his character pathology, it would usually be because the analyst was about to leave him for a holiday or vacation.

To a degree, Dr. S was devoted to chasing after excitement, pleasure, satisfaction, and admiration and constantly keeping himself filled up with external supplies. It was relatively easy to show him that because of his fears of loss he hesitated to love others. Several times when a relative was ill, the analyst interpreted Dr. S's self-involved focus on how he was missing out on some enjoyable activities. He was told that if he let himself feel that this relative was someone he loved and valued, he would then feel sad and afraid. He quickly connected danger with the earlier losses of his parents; he was now able to feel how much he loved his sick relative. Dr. S then had little difficulty setting aside his own activities so as to be more available. Such changes were dramatic but short-lived. Over and over again, Dr. S would be impressed with his difficulty with being empathic, caring, loving, and vulnerable in allowing himself really to feel close to others. He would resolve to be different, not to put his own needs first, but, of course, this change was very difficult for him to accomplish.

Dr. S found it very difficult to tolerate the demands of his wife's academic career. He would also become very angry at his daughter and would yell at her or, at times, hit her when he could no longer tolerate being the parent and he urgently and anxiously felt he needed a parent. Initially, it was difficult for him to try to identify with his child's feelings, even to think about how she was feeling and what she needed. Instead, he had identified with attitudes to her, from both parents, that children's needs and feelings are in the way of the parents' needs. He mourned and raged about what was missing in his parents' attitudes toward him. He showed surprise and delight that the analyst did not seem put off by how much he wanted from him. He now felt much more conflict about balancing his hunger for external supplies against his new-found pleasure in generously and lovingly providing for his family. Yet his envy of his wife and daughter for receiving what he wanted was extremely strong, and since it usually operated out of his awareness, it often interfered with his developing capacities as a husband and father.

It gradually became clear in the analysis that alongside Dr. S's deprivation were intense experiences of indulgence. Mother and child, at times, would play at enacting scenes imbued with a mutually seductive, narcissistic specialness, in which the couple would view themselves as being specially creative and attractive. This play encouraged Dr. S's grandiose longings to be mother's favorite, her lover and rescuer. The overindulgence was also present in the relation with father as Dr. S was able to manipulate father's guilt about ignoring him, so as easily to extract money from him. Dr. S defensively maintained the conviction that he could and should have what he wanted; alongside this was the hopeless terror that he would be neglected and abandoned, unable to influence his caretakers. That he could not control how and when the analyst was with him surprised him—and then frightened and enraged him. He expected that the analyst would accommodate him so that all his hours in analysis were convenient and that the analyst would respond much of the time in a warm and supportive manner. The combination of deprivation and indulgence, more tilted toward the former, seemed to fix Dr. S on the promise that he should and would have what he felt he had missed. If only his next scientific paper were brilliant enough, then he would be loved and admired forever. Of course, intellectually he knew better. But when these expectations were frustrated, he felt enormous, murderous rage, which terrified him because of the danger of destroying/losing his vitally needed objects.

Dr. S wanted very much to be loved and admired by the analyst, whom he both envied and admired like a little boy with his father. The phallic aspects of this attitude were clear and interpretable. So, too, was his wish that the analyst be the father who protects him from the depressed, burdensome mother by taking him in hand and raising him. Part of his desire was loving, and part involved envy, destruction, and robbery of what he perceived to be the analyst's reasonableness and maturity. Along with this attitude, from the first, was a wish to identify with the analyst/father as a reasonable, mature man, to become like him in this respect. That is, he wanted more than to be the passive child who is fed by and entitled to rob the endowed parent. He seemed to have felt encouraged by his father to model himself after the father. Father expected that the patient would follow in father's footsteps in becoming as successful as father had been. His father seemed genuinely to want the patient to lead his life well and to use the father's attitudes, experience, and money to accomplish this goal. In the analytic transference, for both partners, there was also a confident sense that by facing, tolerating, and integrating what was worst in himself, Dr. S could ultimately identify with what he perceived as the analyst's mature attitudes. Thus, from the first, he could tolerate being shown his character defects with little loss of self-esteem and with a hopefulness and confidence that the analyst/ father welcomed his growth and change. Nevertheless, integrating his considerable rage and destructiveness was terrifying for Dr. S. Given the severity of his psychopathology and the analyst's initial apprehension about analyzing him, his ability to use the analytic process constructively was impressive. The analyst was especially intrigued by his erroneous initial appraisal of Dr. S and about the strong, healthy ego and superego identifications, attitudes, and values that contributed to Dr. S's analytic growth.

For example, here is a glimpse of Dr. S later in the analysis, before an extended separation. He reported a dream in the context of talking about wanting people to open up to him:

> I was coming down the platform like at the subway, coming for an appointment with you, for which I was late. The door closed. Before I could get upset about it, the door opened again and I could get on. I no longer felt shut out by the door. I experienced it as a personal opening up of the subway door so I could get to see you on time. I want to get to my appointment on time; the

doors open up and connect me to you. Then I was home with Barbara [wife]. She was washing the dishes at the sink. I could see a big opening by her behind, where her asshole was. It was not like she was beckoning me; she was going through her normal routine. But she was welcoming me to enter her from behind while she was doing dishes. In each dream it was like no holds barred.

The next day he discussed the dream further:

Maybe that's why I feel such an urgent need for sex at times. Two people can't be very far apart if they're having sex. They have to rub up against each other or be inside each other. They have to tear down the walls between them. I suppose there is some level at which I want to hold you and you hold me so we don't separate. Now I know I'm uncomfortable feeling like a little boy who wants his father to hug him, but the father isn't comfortable with touching, hugging, being physically close. He'd come bowling with me, but he wouldn't touch me. I always was attracted to families where people were physically close. My parents almost never touched each other. Maybe I'm afraid to fantasize about being physically close with you because you'll reject me like they did. Why did I need to masturbate so much in order to feel close? I missed out on physical closeness in my family. You have your own needs and family like my father. My father left, wasn't around much when I needed him. I wish he'd just shown some love, felt some love. I couldn't really feel close to him. My father and mother both had walls. I rubbed up against a lot of walls. [The analyst intervened, "But now you don't want walls, but an inviting space, an entrance."] I guess you put up walls, too, the wall of the session ending, the wall of your long August vacation, the wall of not revealing anything about yourself. How do I get close to you that way? I'd like to be as close to you as to George [adolescent best friend]. I could talk to him for hours. He was what was missing in my family. I'd like you to be like that. Maybe when I can't sleep at night, I should think about you rather than masturbate.

DISCUSSION

Dr. S's regressive, dependent wishes were profound and threatening. His fears of being overwhelmed by dependent longings were a significant feature of the early resistance to the development of the transference. Once the analyst became assured that Dr. S would not disorganize, he could more comfortably invite the patient to use him emotionally as fully as possible. The analyst's safety and confidence that Dr. S's intense neediness could be worked with analytically helped the patient to tolerate, face, and manage these terrifying desires. Had the analyst continued to worry that the patient would disorganize or had he feared Dr. S's consuming hunger for attachment, nurturance, and strength, the analytic process probably would have derailed (as had happened to Dr. S before). Despite his dread of needing the analyst so fully, he came to feel safer, protected, and contained the more he was able to attach these dependent wishes to the analyst. Alongside Dr. S's powerful wishes to be cared for were also progressive wishes for autonomy and a confidence that he could grow and ultimately resolve his intense dependency. In contrast, other patients with pathological dependency tend to accept dependency and disability as a way of life in which they will be stuck forever.

Dr. S differed from many other patients in whom the hatred and destructiveness between child and parent, recapitulated between patient and analyst, had infiltrated learning, change, and growth. Where parent and child have attempted to block change, to keep the child/patient fixed on his infantile disabilities, dependent, subservient, unable to go his own way without the parent, the scenario is very different. Dr. S could also be destructively self-punitive or ignore his conscience, but he could, more easily than many, identify with the analyst's intent to help him grow. Beyond (interpretable) wishes thereby to please and seduce the analyst, there was a hopeful, confident sense that the analyst wished to see him mature and that he could accomplish this goal.

I am impressed with how different this patient's attitudes are from those of other patients, who seem much healthier but who tend, to varying degrees, to remain stuck in their pathologically dependent relationship, intrapsychically, with loved ones, and with the analyst. In these patients, the defensive and offensive fighting, attacking, and self-justifying remain the vehicle for connectedness with the needed other. The patient seems unable to face fully, in an integrative way, what is wrong within, so as to be able to change. This inability applies both to the drive contents, especially intense destructiveness, rage, and hunger that cannot be tolerated, as well as to the object relationship that cannot be relinquished. Feeling like an angry, excluded child, the patient continues to clamor for more and remains perennially dissatisfied and discontented, no matter how much he acquires. The angry fight continues with the rejecting, unloving parental imago. Somehow the patient needs to get the sense that he can really become a mature adult in his own right, separate and apart from a parent or an analyst. The conviction that the parent/analyst welcomes his growth and selective partial identification with the latter's good, mature attitudes makes it easier to relinquish the infantile struggle and move forward. Beyond the wish to join the other must be the belief and respect, in both partners, in the child/patient's ultimate growth and separateness. Most of these patients do not have this conviction. To attain it, they will need to relinquish wishes toward, and identifications with, destructive parents encouraging symbiosis.

To the degree that parent and child have sought to block such growth, so that they remained bound together, the patient will tend to feel humiliated and shown up by the analyst's interventions. Internally, the (destructive) superego intends not to help the patient but to rub in his disability/badness. Hence, it becomes difficult to master what is wrong in a constructive way. One source for the patient's negative feelings is this destructive parental voice within the superego, to which he defensively surrenders instead of disregarding it or railing against it. The patient will have to integrate his rage at the crippling parent and at his own collusion, so as to relinquish the bond and his sense of disability.

Of course, in each analysis of pathological dependency, the balance of destructiveness between child and parent will vary. These patients tend to resist accurate perception and integration of who has hurt whom and in analysis are equally inclined to exaggerate in either direction. Defensive emphasis on their hatred of a monstrous parent may block full integration of themselves as monstrous. Or the monstrous self may shield the monstrous parent. For analysis to succeed, the patient must tolerate and integrate the full extent of rage and destructiveness as these exist both within himself and within the other.

"THE FAULTY MODEL" FOR MANAGING CONFLICT

Recall Schafer's (1960, pp. 180–181) remark that a "faulty model" for managing (oedipal) drive conflict may result from pathological parent–child interaction. Schafer's usage and my elaboration of this concept of faulty model begin with our reconstructed versions of the actual parent–child relationship. The focus here is on how parents teach children to tolerate affects and to address and to manage conflicts. Of course, this faulty model is internalized and then tends to be exaggerated and exploited within the psyche. In pathological dependency, the faulty model includes parental inability and avoidance of management of conflict, preoedipal as well as oedipal, in which what is wrong within is not confronted and resolved. Conflict is especially avoided by techniques of riddance and through interpersonal defensive operations. What is wrong is obfuscated and wrongly attributed to the other (child), who is invited to become the repository of badness/wrongness. Responsible self-awareness, self-management, and integrity are lacking. Dependency between parent and child, as well as with others, aims to protect against internal dangers that cannot be integrated. This faulty model becomes essential to the child's survival; it is a seductive and easy mode for avoiding what is wrong. So, too, is the parental invitation to share a grandiose specialness, in which each becomes indispensable to the other. When sexually tinged, this becomes even harder to resist; all that is wrong in the relationship can be hidden by defensive emphasis on exciting specialness. This is so different from parental encouragement of the child's attempts to tolerate and manage his own painful feelings, integrate them, be responsible for them, and balance his needs and feelings against what is reasonable with his loved ones. The faulty model encourages misuse of others, selfishness, and disrespect; lack of empathy, love, and generosity; hypocrisy, deceit, and enormous emotional disability.

Where parent and child have been locked into a fight against separateness and autonomy and used the other to manage one's own dependent needs and (interpersonal) defensive operations, fear and rage intensify and infiltrate the psychic apparatus. The war between parent and child is built into the psyche. Evaluative, defensive, containing, protecting, judging, restraining, and punitive functions are contaminated and subverted by rage and fear and by identifications with parental imagoes who avoid responsible integration of their own feelings and undermine and attack the child's attempts to do so. To the degree that separateness cannot be tolerated between parent and child, responsible. autonomous psychic functioning will be undermined. The child will come to feel that he is incapable of managing his feelings and wishes on his own, without the external regulation of a parent. Rage, destructiveness, envy, and greed are regarded as too dangerous to bear, for both the child and the parent, and so must be avoided. This belief exaggerates the child's sense of needing external regulation to manage what is dangerous within. Whatever threatens to destroy the pathologically dependent parent–

child relationship and lead toward separateness is exaggeratedly regarded as catastrophic.

Such parents tend to envy and resent the child's autonomy, abilities, and valuable attributes, which contrast with their own sense of disability and dissatisfaction. Unconsciously they attack and undermine these abilities. The parent also hates the child for the child's differences from the parent, because they imply the potential to lose the child. Thus the child is encouraged to be only a copy of the parent, to identify with the pathological aspects of the parent. The child's hatred of the parent intersects with the parent's hatred of the child, which contributes to the child's sense of being resented, unwanted, and rejectable. Because of the mutual dependency, the hatred must continually be undone. The child's fears of losing and destroying the needed parent intensify the child's identification with the parent and further interfere with individuation.

In this model, dangers stem both from the id and from pathological object relations; the two sources are, of course, inextricably intertwined. The patient fears his rage and destructiveness and also the loss of a relationship with another, which is felt to be vital for survival. These dangers merge. To face his own murderousness means to get rid of, to let go of parental imagoes. To become responsible for oneself means to face what is most awful within, ultimately one's own murderousness, and to feel capable of bearing this on one's own. Such patients may well have previously tolerated murderous impulses briefly and then quickly undone them by resurrecting the image of the parent whom they need for protection. Penance, expiation, guilt (at least in part), and reparation aim to undo such destructiveness and to reinstate the submissive, dependent child–parent relationship. Ego and superego, in part, now enact this relationship of pathological dependency, often contaminated by sadomasochism.[1] From this perspective, the superego aims not only to keep dangerous impulses and wishes in check but also to preserve and maintain a needed object relationship. The regulation of ego and id by the superego aims to preserve the child's infantile dependence on parental authority, as actually played out in their interrelationship. The danger is not just the feared liberation of threatening feelings and impulses but the equally alarming burden of having to bear them on one's own. The patient fears that he will lose control of himself and

---

[1] Schafer (1960) wrote "Ego and superego each represent parent and child in a continuing hostile interplay" (p. 167). Schafer was emphasizing the superego's attack on the ego because of the latter's (forbidden) identification with the parent. He noted that masochism intensifies this interplay.

actually become destructive; equally, the patient also fears that he can manage such destructiveness on his own and so go his own way.

What is wrong is shifted away from the actual internal, guilty conflict, whatever the psychosexual level from which it derives, onto the external relationship with one's judge and regulator. Once one has been punished or absolved and at least temporarily reinstated and reassured, all is well, at least for now. What the patient fears and feels guilty about within himself is avoided in this cat-and-mouse game. The relationship with the other person reassures the patient that his feared wishes and impulses are safely contained within his surrender to the strong critic/judge, who can then be seduced and manipulated (cf. Loewenstein's, 1957 "seduction of the aggressor"). The patient maintains the comforting illusion that the other one is forever on the lookout for signs of the patient's emergent badness, which will be stopped before it gets dangerously out of hand. The badness itself is never confronted in a responsible enough way to allow for integration of the feared impulses and wishes. So long as another person remains responsible for the patient and appears satisfied or indicates how such satisfaction is yet to be won, the patient's own self-judgments cannot mean much to him. We are describing a pathological, dependent method of avoidance of one's own superego judgments, of self-esteem regulation, and of affect and drive control. Intrapsychically as well, the patient wants a parental imago to regulate, control, punish, forgive, and also love him. That is, his dependency is both intrapsychic and interpersonal. Externalization of superego judgments and of internal conflict here intersects with the actualization of a pathologically dependent internal object relationship.

On the other hand, some patients *seem* not to feel sufficiently guilty about what is wrong within them. Angry, hungry, exploitative, these patients are not able to stop themselves, to be reasonable and respectful of the rights of others. Despite self-torture and temporary depression, their guilt is quickly washed away in entitled rationalizations, so that they justify themselves in extracting what they feel they need from others (Coen, 1988a). At another level, these patients do, indeed, feel guilt, which they experience as feeling depressed and self-critical. The problem is that they manage to avoid connecting such guilt with their extractiveness. Such extractiveness, of course, intersects with an urgent, driven sense of need, an expectation that they must be filled up in order to function, a hunger to be loved, and an intolerance of frustration. Concern about extractiveness is compounded by anxieties about destruction and loss, which derive from earlier fears of abandonment, loss of love, castration, and guilt. Now the superego threatens the patient with such dangers of destruction and loss. That is, fears of destruction and loss, which abound per se in patients afraid of being on their own, are further exploited by the superego. Such patients now want someone else to take them in hand as tutor, guide, and loving and concerned parent, in effect to bring them up again. They both cannot take responsibility for what is wrong within themselves and do not want to. Their available superego identifications tend to be with aspects of the parents' defensive avoidance of responsible integration of conflict and of parental superego pathology. They need to temper their immoderate hunger for what they feel they have missed, to change their expectations of what is reasonable and possible with others, and to become concerned about their own tragedies and the damage they cause their loved ones. That is, these patients need to identify with a reasonable, loving, mature parent—toward themselves and toward their loved ones. This attitude requires relinquishment of the angry, deprived, insatiable, entitled posture and of the identification with exploitative, relatively unconcerned and/or overindulgent, infantile parents. Dr. S needed to make this shift from identification with the infantile, exploitative aspects of both parents to a predominant identification with the healthier aspects of his father's more mature and generous attitudes. It was especially helpful in his treatment to interpret repeatedly that treating his daughter the way he felt he had been treated avoided and justified his parents' previous neglect and disregard of him and thus muted his rage and hurt.

EGO AND SUPEREGO IN PATHOLOGICAL DEPENDENCY

Ordinarily, superego functions include observing and evaluating, caring, judging, censoring and punishing, guiding, containing, protecting, correcting, and restraining. The superego aims to preserve positive ties to both parents by restraining/renouncing direct instinctual aims. The ego accepts the superego's hostile restraint in order to feel accepted and loved, initially by the actual parents and then by the internalized parental imagoes within the superego, which are later depersonalized. There is a vital forward movement through superego formation so that the child becomes capable of regulating himself actively in the absence of the parents. We expect the superego to offer signals of anxiety and guilt, which are heeded, so that the patient has some recognition of his conflicts and their dangers. He can then live reasonably comfortably and flexibly within his compromise formations. In this model, the superego serves as a guide to the patient's ego, which is able to effect a reasonable balance among the various vectors pressing on it (Waelder, 1930). The superego's excessive and unreasonable harshness is not taken literally but is understood in its infantile derivatives and is considered in relation to current reality, wishes, object relations, and reasonable needs for defense. The ego then functions in its executive capacity, taking responsibility for managing its various functions in the best ways that it can. Superego signals are helpful indications that one's wishes and impulses are getting out of hand. Such a patient does not want to abdicate responsibility for what is wrong within himself. On the contrary, he feels pride and satisfaction in his ability to feel his conflicts and to struggle to manage these as best he can.

In contrast, the dependent ego needs to avoid facing what is wrong and feels too terrified of the underlying wishes and feelings to attempt to integrate them. This ego does not relate to the superego as a potentially helpful monitor/guide. Rather, the ego wishes to surrender to the superego as punisher/regulator/God or to an external person who is representative of such a relationship and who will be responsible for what is wrong and manage this. The goal is not to exercise the ego's executive functions in relation to its various vectors in as mature and responsible a way as possible. Self-knowledge is to be avoided in favor of indications of goodness or badness, signs like red or green traffic lights, which do not really connect with deeper conflict but merely hint whether danger is near. The focus shifts from the danger of internal destruction and loss of the vitally needed internal parental imago, to the more easily observable current status of an external object relationship. The patient fears either that he will destroy his needed internal object or that he will lose it because of the condemnation of his superego, wherein sits this critical parental imago.

Instead of viewing superego functioning in pathological dependency as involving a regressively sexualized and aggressivized morality, as of course, it does, I suggest we consider the superego's aims. In pathological dependency, the superego and ego identifications do not admire and encourage autonomous functioning, responsibility for internal conflict, or movement toward mature integration. Instead, they interdict them. To a degree, to feel connected with the parental imagoes requires dependency, subservience, and disability. Such superego identifications do not aim to restrain the child's instinctual desires, so that he can be admired and loved by the parents and their intrapsychic representatives as he matures and manages himself better. On the contrary, the superego identifications encourage

immature, dependent, irresponsible, and avoidant psychic functioning. The aim is to preserve the dependent pathological relationship
with the troubled parent by subverting a realistic perception and
accurate evaluation of what is wrong between the couple and within
each of them and by vigorous defensive efforts at avoidance of rage
and destructiveness. To the degree that there are not other, more
positive, encouraging parental identifications, growth means abandonment and loss. Until such patients can tolerate being on their
own, at some point, they will have to run from their hatred and from
their wishes to be rid of the pathological parent–child relationship
back to the safety and security of parental protection. Although
hatred in oneself and in the parent can be acknowledged transiently,
eventually the patient will need to obscure such recognition.

A whole set of magically protective illusions is attributed to the
dependent relationship. It is expected to keep each partner safe from
the vicissitudes of life. When one lives under the constant terror of life
and death, loss and destruction, such magical bonding becomes
appealing indeed. The external interpersonal relationship parallels
the intrapsychic relationship. What needs to be emphasized is the
patient's willingness, intrapsychically and interpersonally, to live in a
subservient, dependent, regulated, tortured mode that offers the
illusion of safety, protection, and love. Thus, the patient believes that
being in analysis (forever) protects him from disaster coming both
from outside himself and from inside himself. For example, another
patient, Mr. I, described his family's conscious belief that if they all
remained together in relative harmony, they were safe from all the
dangers existing in the outside world. Together they could fight
against dirt, disease, contamination, and the badness of others. One
family member's enemy had to be the enemy of all, as they bonded
loyally together, with each ready to share the pain of the other. Mr. I
needed to deny that his mother had used him to manage her
considerable difficulties, that the family ideal of equal sharing was a
myth. Similarly, it was very hard for him to integrate his rage at his
mother's controlling and infantilizing bodily intrusions. He preferred
to idealize them as bestowing a glorious specialness as a reward for
his passivity and dependency. Mr. I continued to desire and expect
such total caring and consciously believed that it represented paradise. To tolerate and integrate his rage at the mother who had
disabled and crippled him emotionally was too frightening. With the
analyst, too, he simply wanted harmonious coexistence and acceptance, which would comfort him and protect him from his rage,
destructiveness, and guilt. As quickly as he could, Mr. I would put
out of his mind what was wrong, as if he were finished with it, and

attempt to reassure himself that he was now good. Similarly, his mother would praise him as a child for listening to her complaints of unhappiness and mistreatment. Then he would feel special, valued, no longer angry, hurt, used, or neglected; once he was accepted by mother, nothing else counted. In the analysis, Mr. I was addicted to repetitively seeking such states of acceptance in which, indeed, nothing else had any meaning and in which he succeeded in erasing what had been painful.

The underside is the patient's rage that he has sacrificed himself, that he and the parent have dependently exploited the other, and that he has given up his autonomy and confidence to preserve a relationship with a troubled, destructive parent. To manage this rage, the patient has had to doubt and undermine himself and to remain fixed at infantile levels of expectation and illusion. To the degree that parent and child share the illusion that separateness is death, the child/patient cannot tolerate growth toward maturity.

To a degree, such patients feel overly powerful with regard to their dependent parent, who cannot tolerate rage and separateness. Some of these parents surrender to the child's aggression because of the parent's vulnerability (to loss and destruction) and make the child feel that, indeed, he can destroy the parent (Rubinfine, 1965; Novick and Novick, 1987). Such children/patients become so terrified of their power to manipulate, take from, and destroy others (parents) that they continually need to feel the illusion of someone else's protective presence. They run away from full ownership of their rage and destructiveness to the protective illusion of themselves as weak, vulnerable, and victimized by a powerfully destructive other, onto whom is projected the patient's destructiveness. Denial, projection, blaming, self-justification, provocation, undoing, reaction formation, idealization, and surrender all aim to avoid integration of murderous rage. A number of my patients turned out to have emphasized their own weakness and vulnerability, in part, as a defense against the terrifying conviction that they could too easily destroy a fragile parent. It was safer to view themselves as weak than to realize the extent of the parent's weakness and vulnerability to their criticism, rejection, and hatred.

In the absence of a pathological need for the other, destructiveness does not become so unbearable; ordinary defenses and superego judgments are sufficient to modulate it. If the patient can give up the parental object, then murderous wishes become tolerable. Relinquishing such dependent need for the other reduces terror and rage at abandonment and frustration so that, paradoxically, affect management becomes easier. To the degree that the predominant parental imagoes sanction and enjoy the patient's confident autonomy, it is easier to move forward toward pride in mature functioning. The parental imagoes, which are destructive of separateness, beckon toward regressed, dependent disability. They can be relinquished if the patient can gain conviction that he can manage his hatred and destructiveness on his own and that he can largely provide for his needs.

6

REPETITION VERSUS CHANGE

Defensive repetition in pathological dependency especially aims to undo destructiveness and to preserve the distorted parent–child relationship. A patient's behavioral repetitions include those actually enacted with another person and those enacted within one's own psyche that connect with an internal psychic imago. That is, behavior includes not only action easily observable in relation to other people but also fantasy, thought, and actions performed in private. Clinically, the analyst begins to think about repetition with dependent patients when they seem not to change but, instead, to repeat the same old patterns. The analyst may easily feel frustrated, helpless, and angry that he seems so unable to help such patients to move forward. This feeling, of course, becomes the signal to reflect on the meanings of repetition and lack of change. The ordinary patient becomes alarmed when he becomes aware that he is repeating rather than progressing. The pathologically dependent patient, instead, feels reassured that everything remains the same.

Repetition has had two contrasting meanings in psychoanalysis. On the one hand, we have regarded repetition as a conservative tendency to maintain the status quo or to revert to earlier times. This meaning is the more important one in pathological dependency. On the other hand, we have viewed repetition as progressive, as aiming toward change. Thus transference repetition in psychoanalysis offers the possibility of insight and change, which is why we welcome the establishment of a transference neurosis during psychoanalysis. Alternatively, transference repetition maintains what is safe and familiar and serves as a defense against hidden dangers and change.

This chapter concentrates on those repetitions that aim to preclude change.

This chapter intentionally overemphasizes repetition as a defense against destructiveness. At the same time, such repetition is also viewed as a kind of destructiveness, not as a death instinct but as a rageful, vindictive refusal to change, separate, and manage on one's own. Movement toward autonomy contrasts with endlessly attacking and clinging to unsatisfying parents. Careful attention to, and interpretation of, the destructiveness in such refusal to change must complement interpretation of defensive avoidance in endless repetition within a pathological object relationship. Patients tend to be less troubled by their wishes to cling and to make contact (benign dependency), even in sadomasochistic fighting, than by their wishes endlessly to destroy/torture and extract from parents/analyst (malignant dependency). These two sides of pathological dependency must be integrated to relinquish such endless defensive repetition and exploitation within a pathological object relationship. It is less terrifying to perpetuate a connection with an unsatisfactory parental imago than to feel with conviction how intensely one wishes to destroy, kill, and permanently get rid of this parent. Other motives for repeating and for holding on to old defensive patterns and to old modes of relating to others are, necessarily, not attended to in detail here.

Clinically we can, indeed, distinguish stable, chronic defensive repetitions that aim to preclude change, and these differ from ordinary repetitions, which are more easily analyzed. I emphasize the difficulty of interrupting this former group of defensive repetitions, which implicate pathological modes of object relating and interactive defensive maneuvers (cf. Balint, 1950; Ogden, 1979, 1983; Räkkö-läinen and Alanen, 1982; Modell, 1984; Dorpat, 1985; Sander, 1989). Other people tend to become much more tied into these repetitions, for defense and adaptation, so that the patient fears intensely that he cannot manage himself alone or let go of his vitally needed object. In these forms of pathological dependency, because of terror of loss and destruction, the patient must cling to his object and avoid responsibility for what is threatening within himself. Change is to be avoided; instead, sameness and repetition are sought for the reassurance they provide. The patients here considered can only transiently tolerate their dark side, with little ability to integrate this. Persistent analytic focus on their wish for endless, defensive repetition within a pathological object relationship is essential if structural change is to occur.

Within this clinical context, I differentiate between repetition that aims to avoid integration and repetition that allows for integration and change. Ordinarily, repetition allows both for stasis and for change. In his repetitions, the ordinary patient struggles between attempting to integrate and attempting to dissociate himself from aspects of his conflicts. Patients can, in repeating, experiment with mastery, integration, and change, that is, with the possibility of relinquishing the repetition and moving to a higher level of integration. In the type of defensive repetition here emphasized, the defensive aim is predominantly avoidance, riddance, and denial of danger by not acknowledging and integrating threatening psychic contents. The dangers of destruction and loss of what is regarded as a vitally needed object relationship are judged as too great to allow for such integration. Mastery and change are thereby precluded. This process is, indeed, different from ordinary defense analysis in the ordinary neurotic patient with his ordinary defensive repetitions, however resistant he may seem at the moment.

In the defensive organizations considered here, repetition, in fantasy and in action, aims especially at undoing of intense destructiveness by perpetuating a dependent relationship with another. Another person is used to contain and manage what one fears one cannot handle alone. Of course, object relationships do not function only for defense or only for defense against hatred. That view would be much too simplistic and would miss the major contributions of contemporary child development and object relations theory. Heuristically, however, I believe that for clinical practice, it is worth highlighting the magical role of repetition in fantasy and in action for undoing destructiveness within a pathological object relationship. Given the difficulty of analyzing (i.e., changing) such defensive repetition within pathological modes of object relating, such emphasis and differentiation are warranted and helpful.

Let us contrast defensive repetition in a patient who was able to interrupt it and to face the conflict embedded and avoided by it with defensive repetitions that were much more difficult to alter. Recall Dr. S (from chapter 5), who, when overly frustrated, would yell at or hit his daughter. Early in the analysis it seemed that Dr. S needed ongoing contact with someone whom he unconsciously viewed as a supportive parent. When he felt left on his own too long, he would feel depressed, weak, and unable to work and would long for someone to touch him. When he felt that way in his daughter's presence, he would become angry and impatient and lash out at her. He was told by the analyst that he then wanted to trade roles with his daughter, so that she would become the parent and he would become the cared-for child. But it also became clear to the analyst, and with interpretation also clear to Dr. S, that he was repeating something with his daughter. He felt especially pained when the analyst interpreted that by attacking his daughter, he identified and agreed with both his parents that the parents' needs are more important than the child's and that it is all right for parents to hate and resent their child. Dr. S was told that by repeating his parents' (especially mother's) resentment of, and attack on, his needs via his attacks on his daughter, he avoided fully feeling his rage at both parents. He was then able to feel with much more conviction how much each parent had resented and wished to be rid of him. As he could now identify with his parents' rejection and hatred of him, he felt freer to hate and rage against them. His empathy for his daughter's emotional needs increased considerably as he mourned his own childhood neglect. He resolved to be a better parent for his daughter than either of his own parents had been for him.

Now let us consider two constellations of defensive repetitions that could not be so easily interrupted.

Let me introduce you to Mr. X, whom I later (see chapter 8) describe as using sexualization as a predominant mode of defense. In the termination phase, Mr. X seductively tried to engage the analyst and to enact displaced transference wishes to seduce the analyst. This termination was initiated and planned by the patient. Then (and now in retrospect) I did not feel the patient was ready to terminate. We certainly did work on his hurt and outrage, even though he wanted to leave, that I would tolerate his leaving. I did explain to him my assessment of what he still needed to resolve within the analysis. But I am sure that I was not as forceful then (this was a control case) as I would be now about his continued need for analysis. Nor could I then have been as comfortable as I would be now with engaging his sense of me as the rejecting analyst/parent and drawing out fully his hatred of me.

Notice how sexualized episodes aim to manage the patient's dependency on the analyst, especially feelings of loss, rejection, hurt, humiliation, and rage. For example, in a Monday session he reported that the previous weekend he had made a call from a telephone booth to a male model whose telephone number he remembered from several years before. Using a fictitious name, he arranged a date. He then masturbated twice, with the fantasy of meeting this man and seducing him homosexually. The previous Friday he had reported masturbating, with the fantasy of seducing a male student into having mutual masturbation with him. In the fantasy, he invites the "kid" to his apartment, gets him drunk, and talks to him about sexual experiences with women and then with men, all the while observing how he is arousing the student; they then perform mutual masturbation. To the Friday masturbation fantasy, he immediately associated; "Maybe you'll think less of yourself as a competent analyst. How can I talk about leaving when I'm having homosexual fantasies?" On Monday, he commented: "C [wife] has to be taught how to make love more comfortably; she needs a lesson, she's a dud, she just lies there passively, everything has to be done to her. If I can't control her, I strike! . . . How can you let me go with these problems! Don't let me go! If I'm still homosexual, then you stink as an analyst." He later added: "I've got to be in control. Nobody's an individual; they're all extensions of me!"

In the first year of the analysis, when Mr. X experienced the analyst as unresponsive, he engaged in similar perverse behavior. He would call up a male photographic model who had advertised in a newspaper, it being clear that this was a vehicle for homosexual contact. Mr. X would talk with the man about arranging a meeting (date), and sometimes he would talk to the man about the size of the latter's penis. While arranging the appointment, which he had no intention of keeping, he would masturbate to orgasm and hang up. Usually he played it straight on the telephone and "deceived" the other person, although it was certainly clear that the call was a seductive game both would play while simultaneously denying it. I understood and interpreted the telephone call as an acting out of the transference, in which Mr. X sought to demonstrate that the analyst was responding intensely to him. Mr. X was proclaiming that the analyst-wife was at the other end of the telephone, as if to say, "I got you to respond to me in that you're the excited listener, or I'm the excited listener to your phallic exhibitionism!" Alternatively, he would claim in fantasy: "It doesn't matter if you don't love and value me. I can seduce a total stranger; no man can resist me!" If the analyst had not cured him of his homosexuality, then he was stronger than the impotent analyst, who would have to pursue him endlessly to prove his effectiveness. He wished that he could be the only child the analyst would ever need and that nobody could supplant him. He boasted seductively that the analyst would never again find a patient so adept at elaborating fantasies at the drop of a hat, at producing such richly symbolic dreams. He revived wishes from earlier in the analysis to seduce the narcissistic, self-absorbed analyst-mother with offers to make the analyst famous and great; analyst and patient could be Gepetto and Pinocchio, a traveling road show, to serve the analyst-mother's glory and keep the two together.

It was clear at the end of Mr. X's analysis that, although he had changed considerably, he had not achieved full separation-individuation and full ownership of his hatred and destructiveness.

Many important meanings were worked on in the above material in relation to narcissism, object relations, rage, and sexuality (homosexuality, heterosexuality, and autoerotism). What now needs to be emphasized, however, is the persistence of the sexualized interactive defense as protection against separation and separateness and denial of rage, hurt, and humiliation, especially at being left and left out. Although this was shown to him repeatedly, the persistent repetition of this defensive pattern was both not sufficiently appreciated and simultaneously regarded as the limits of Mr. X's analyzability. Mr. X did not fully assimilate and integrate his rage, especially in relation to his mother's oscillating involvement with him, either directly in relation to his mother or in the analytic transference to me as the analyst/mother. This maternal imago would shift from seeming depressed and emotionally unavailable to appearing overly seductive, close, inviting him to be her twin. To a degree, he did not fully integrate these two aspects of his mother so as to face his rage at the limitations of the mother–child relationship. His sexually seductive behavior and fantasies continued magically to transform his rage at the unavailable object into excitement at the response he could omnipotently extract from the other. Although this was interpreted, the overall repetitive enactment was not sufficiently focused as a major defensive effort to avoid separateness and full ownership of his destructiveness. It would have been better to focus more consistently on Mr. X's failure to integrate and work through his rage, by his use of repetitive defensive activities, especially sexualization, which aimed to avoid such integration. In retrospect, I think we both spared ourselves the full force of his hatred.

We did not work sufficiently on the entitled, destructive extractiveness in his continuing dependency. Underneath his more superficial willingness to relinquish his infantile demandingness was an angry, vindictive refusal to give up his claims on others as parents. Thus, at the end of the analysis, Mr. X dreamed of being in a department store and realizing that he had lost his MasterCard. He talked about having to leave behind the world of masturbation and homosexuality, what he called "the perfect world without any no's" and accept ordinary human frustration. As he spoke, he was appropriately sad and guilty, and I felt pleased. It would have been better had I continued insisting on his refusal fully to integrate and relinquish his malignant extractiveness.

Mr. X's repetitions within the termination phase of the analysis expressed his rage at ending and leaving, which he attempted to subvert, and expressed his ongoing wishes to perpetuate his dependency. In his repetitions, Mr. X could express anger but he sought to discharge or get rid of it rather than to integrate it. These repetitions, however, were not merely an artifact of the termination process. That is, this patient continued craving a dependent relationship and continued attempting to avoid full integration of his rage and destructiveness, which he feared.

Let us consider further Ms. D's (from chapter 4) shift into a sadomasochistic stalemate within the analysis. Having become aware of the intensity of her angry hunger and of the difficulties this caused her with others, she consciously attempted to change her behavior and to dissociate herself from her enraged, destructive, and hungry feelings and impulses. The critical shift was that her transference anger was now in the service of maintaining an angry, protective connection with the analyst, rather than for integration and working through of her anger and for further individuation. This defensive, repetitive enactment became the central issue to understand and to interpret. Ms. D needed to be shown consistently how much she wished to remain in a hateful, hopeless relationship with the analyst as bad mother, so as not to have to face what she dreaded within herself. Although she argued that she was (at least partly) newly expressing anger to the analyst in this mode of relating, she had to gain conviction that this defensive activity not only would not lead to change but sought to preclude it.

At times Ms. D could fantasize that she wanted to provoke the analyst into demonstrating concern for her, setting limits with her, making her behave herself, as an angry but caring father would do. The analyst should feel so frustrated and angry with her that he takes her across his knees, spanks her, and proves that he loves her. But she seemed unable to take such fantasies seriously or to connect them with her provocativeness with the analyst. Indeed, she was committed to viewing the analyst as a critical judge who, by disapproving of her badnesses, protected her from having to experience and own these. The analyst needed to acknowledge for himself and for the patient that she wished to draw him into a sadomasochistic bond and that she was succeeding. Then he needed to extract himself from this, to interpret the patient's unconscious wishes in preserving a sadomasochistic relationship with the analyst, while leaving it up to the patient what she did with these wishes. At the same time, he needed to interpret her denial that she was thereby defensively derailing a productive analysis. The analyst interpreted that Ms. D wished to be locked into an endless relationship, in which the analyst would pursue her forever and try to help her to change, while she would spurn and defeat his efforts. Such interpretation was partially successful. Ms. D was shown how in this sadomasochistic engagement, she could avoid her terror of being on her own and of having to feel responsible for what she dreaded inside herself, especially her destructiveness and her wanting to be loved and loved sexually. Because of her terror of her destructiveness, her quasi-delusional conviction that she would lose control of her anger and go berserk, she felt reassured to express and contain her hatred as justified as a reaction to the analyst and the analysis. The more she learned about her anger, the more terrified she felt that she could not control it. She clung to guilty and defensive identifications with other family members who had become violent. Then she would not have to hate them further. She could not believe, even intellectually, that she would eventually become capable of managing and containing her intense anger.

It was especially difficult for Ms. D to grasp how much she wanted to retain (especially in the transference to the analyst) the hateful mother–daughter relationship, on which she had been raised. At times, temporary breakthroughs would occur, in which Ms. D could take distance from this repetitive, defensive position. Soon again, however, she would close off and reenact the hateful mother–daughter transference with the analyst, with little awareness of her own intentions. Nevertheless, consistent interpretation of her willingness to run home to the safety of a mutually hateful mother–daughter relationship was helpful. The predominant motivation for her clinging to this mode of object relationship was her terror of her destructiveness, when she felt more separate and less contained and protected by the bad parent/analyst (see Novick and Novick, 1987, on the centrality of containment and punitive protection in fixed beating fantasies).

The analyst needed to become convinced that Ms. D was, indeed, seeking to destroy the treatment situation through her repetitions in the analysis, that this behavior was not merely defense and resistance. She was repeating a vindictive/spoiling way of relating that she had earlier enacted with her parents. In this repetition, she avoided acknowledgment of how enraged and destructive she felt. Then the analyst needed to insist firmly to Ms. D that the evidence was clear that she was destroying the treatment. He then needed to interpret her denial, her masochistic protests of helplessness, and her counterattack. The serious destructiveness underlying the sadomasochistic transference repetition had by now become painfully clear to the analyst. The earlier focus on her wishes endlessly to preserve a sadomasochistic mother–daughter relationship with the analyst had not sufficiently engaged her. Demonstrating that, despite all her conscious efforts at control of her anger, she was destroying her analysis alarmed her sufficiently so that she again become concerned about her rage. Now she could feel that, indeed, she did want to ruin anything good in the treatment, to make the analyst pay for her childhood neglect and deprivation. Ms. D could now feel how much she wanted to torture and destroy her parents/analyst for their disregard and exploitation of her. She could acknowledge that she had felt and behaved the same way with her parents. She again felt her violent rage; she could feel how much she wanted to smash her fist through the analyst's wall, to tear his office to pieces. At some point, however, Ms. D would become terrified and need to dissociate herself from her rage, as she feared violent action or disorganization into psychosis.

THE AIMS OF REPETITION

The concept of repetition for mastery is optimistic and progressive. At the same time, in clinical descriptions of repetition, the conservative, nonadaptive aspect is usually indicated by wishes to repeat infantile gratification and to remain protected. The ego's defensive activities can similarly be viewed from these dualistic perspectives of conservatism and progress (change, adaptation). Emphasis on mastery of painful affects and trauma leads to a view of the ego's defensive efforts as adaptive and forward-seeking. Since much of the clinical psychoanalytic literature on repetition has focused on trauma, it has emphasized such positive defensive mastery. An alternative perspective on defensive repetition emphasizes, instead, avoidance of change, protection against danger, clinging to what/who is safe. We think both of inertia and flux and of repetition and change.

Here we distinguish between repetition for mastery and integration (integrative repetition) and repetition to preserve the status quo (nonintegrative repetition). We need to differentiate between what seems to be repeated in a patient because it continues unchanged and what is repeated so as to protect against hidden dangers. Defensive repetition should refer to the latter. Defensive repetition would refer to that aspect of repetitive behavior whose aim is to protect against hidden danger. This aim would contrast with the aim of organizing and integrating within the ego what had previously been regarded as too dangerous to face. I prefer not to primarily contrast the relative influence of the id and the ego within defense. Instead, we can, more usefully, differentiate the ego's aims of organization and integration from aims of avoidance, riddance, or isolation. In the latter, which we usually regard as defense, dangerous content is avoided or kept apart affectively so that it does not count. For example, a patient, fearful of his own destructiveness, may need to repress, deny, project, undo, or isolate destructive affects and wishes. Simultaneously, he may need to repeat reassuring behaviors and aspects of relationships that defend against feared destruction of others. Also, he may need to isolate (keep separate) different aspects of himself: dangerously destructive/active, assertive; fearful, passive, submissive/inactive, or immobilized. Isolating the conflicted aspects of himself reassures that the more dangerous aspect is not a central part of oneself but only incidental or peripheral.

We can think of a hierarchy of defensive activities that range from immediate attempts to avoid dangerous affects and wishes to more complex efforts to keep apart, get rid of, or minimize dangerous aspects of oneself that have, to a degree, been tolerated transiently. Defensive efforts at isolating, compartmentalizing, minimizing, or hiding dangerous aspects of the self contrast with progressive ego aims of integration. Within an ongoing analysis, our attention shifts from immediate defensive efforts against feared affects and wishes to such more complex defensive attempts not to let what has been transiently faced really count. Thus we assess the progress of an analysis.

Unlike Klein (1976b; also see Appendix), I would regard the ego's attempts at assimilation, synthesis, and integration of what has been dissociated as one aim of defensive activity. But this issue is one of definition. I understand defense as involving both avoidant, nonintegrative aims and progressive, integrative aims. Regarding both of these ego aims as aspects of defense allows us to see more clearly that similar defensive maneuvers can sometimes lead to avoidance and stasis and can sometimes allow for change and growth. Thus, within a hierarchic model of ego activities, we must examine what is then done with a given defensive activity. In examining defensive repetition, this differentiation must be emphasized.

In my own earlier writing about sexualization (1981a), I did not differentiate among the aims of sexualization as defense. My own emphasis was especially on defense against hostile aggression (also painful affects and narcissistic needs). It was implicit, but not elaborated, that behavioral repetition was essential for sexualization to function effectively as a defense. I did propose that active repetition and re-creation serve to master childhood sexual overstimulation. I suggested, using Waelder's (1930) model, that sexual drive pressure and the ego's attempts to master this are used by the ego as a vehicle to express and master other conflicts. So, repetition was posited as a key factor for mastery (of infantile trauma, traumatic affects, overstimulation) and, by implication, for more general defense. I described sexualization's defensive function as involving temporary and illusory transformation of destructiveness into sexual excitement. I did not differentiate between such defensive repetition, which aims to deny destructiveness, and more successful attempts to integrate it. I should have stated that sexualization ordinarily serves not to master destructiveness but to avoid it. This distinction is not just a theoretical nicety! When sexualization is used extensively for defense, the clinical analyst needs to be alerted to the patient's terror of his destructiveness and his attempts to run away from it. It is all too easy to collude with the patient in believing that anger has somehow been transformed (gotten rid of) into sexual excitement. As in the vignette of Mr. X, the analyst needs to be fully aware that destructiveness is not being faced and integrated because of the patient's recourse to repetitive defensive (sexualized) enactments. Otherwise, the patient's persistent, defensive avoidance will be relatively successful.

Why is sexualization involved so much in repetition, as Bibring (1943) noted (see Appendix)? Largely, I think, because of how useful sexualization is in protecting against fears of destructiveness. Although sexualization is discussed separately in chapter 8, here let us note that sexualization especially creates and preserves the illusion that destructiveness is not harmful but the stuff of excitement. Badness in oneself and in the other is seemingly transformed into something desirable, arousing; hate is turned into desire. The excitement in such repetition is pursued because of its meanings, which usually involve some admixture of forbidden, incestuous, and grandiose specialness, and because of its defensive gains. Note clearly, however, that it is only an illusion that rage and hatred are transformed into libido during sexualization; no such change occurs.

SOME BACKGROUND ON REPETITION COMPULSION

Remember that the repetition compulsion was elaborated by Freud in conjunction with destructiveness or at least an earlier model (death instinct) of human destructiveness. Destructiveness must be modulated or regulated for life to proceed. Actually, in our theory building, fantasies of destructiveness (unrealistic, exaggerated, fantastic) and the associated anxiety and guilt become the dangers and hence the motivation for defense. We seek reassurance that we have not destroyed our needed objects or those parts of ourselves linked with these objects. Of course, destructiveness and needs of objects are not simple constructs but involve issues of narcissism, separation-individuation, painful affects, sexuality, and so on. What is repeated in repetition compulsion? No longer can we say that repetition is only a function of the id. If repetition compulsion is viewed as a compromise formation, then, of course, we would say that id, ego, superego, and reality all contribute. Is repetition compulsion beyond the pleasure principle? Perhaps the best way to deal with this question is in the terms of "Beyond the Pleasure Principle" (Freud, 1920), of life and death, change and status quo. That is, we can differentiate repetitions that allow for change (mastery, synthesis, integration) from repetitions that preclude change. For assessing the progress of an ongoing psychoanalysis, this distinction becomes crucial. It is important for us to be able to identify stable defensive repetitions, which aim permanently to avoid integration of dangerous psychic contents. Such repetitions contrast with defensive repetitions, which temporarily avoid facing and integrating what is dangerous, in order to prepare for this task later.

This discussion is not intended to mean that the death instinct is a biological force of "negative entropy." Nor should this be misunderstood as an espousal of those schools of psychoanalysis that overemphasize primitive destructiveness. Repetition compulsion should no longer be regarded as a mystical force distinct from the mind's general tendency to solve problems through repetition. Repetition compulsion should be understood within the context that repetitive thinking and acting are basic efforts to deal with mental contents. Certainly, from one perspective, such repetition can serve defensive purposes, while, from another perspective, adaptive and progressive aims can be observed. Psychoanalysts tend to regard defense and progressive adaptation as interconnected, on a continuum. This view is a unifying, holistic trend in contemporary psychoanalysis. Although this makes sense in theory, in clinical practice, I think it is preferable to contrast stable defensive repetitions, which aim to preclude change, from other defensive organizations, which can more easily be modified within a psychoanalysis. But psychoanalysts do not like to think of such differences in defensive organizations; they believe instead, that all defense is relatively difficult to modify. Psychoanalysts tend to believe that, to a degree, defenses are ultimately capable of being understood and analyzed. The position I outline here dissents from this view and focuses instead, on certain defensive organizations, that are much harder to modify than others.

DANGER AND DEFENSE.

Brenner (1982) clarified the targets for defense to include drive derivatives, aspects of superego functioning, and the painful affects aroused by them. In Brenner's view, defense is one perspective from which the ego can be viewed. Any ego function can serve defensive purposes; no ego function serves only for defense. With this view I fully concur. If the fantasied danger inherent in internal conflict is too great, then this danger must be reassured against, precluding the possibility that the conflict can be faced and integrated. I suggest that the degree of terror, experienced and imagined in relation to one's drive derivatives and superego judgments, determines what can be integrated and what must be (repetitively) avoided. This terror seems to involve especially intense destructive wishes toward objects, which one believes must be preserved. Or, perhaps somewhat more broadly, this refers to the need to preserve a relationship with an object, which is heavily contaminated by destructiveness on both sides, in self and other. If the hatred and destructiveness in self and other cannot be fully faced and integrated, repetitive behavioral enactments will aim to protect the patient from the terror of the imagined destructive encounter. The more frightened a patient is of hatred and destructiveness, the more he may feel unable to manage himself; the more he may then feel he needs someone else to regulate him. The more the relationship is infiltrated by rage and hatred, the more endangered the relationship is then felt to be. Hence, it becomes even more essential to reassure against one's destructiveness and against destruction of one's vitally needed object. Such is the function of these repetitive behavioral enactments in fantasy and in action on the outside world and on others. When I have presented some of the clinical material from which I have formulated this position, analysts have been eager to suggest that if patients feel sufficiently safe within the analytic situation, then they can tolerate facing more of what has been avoided. Although that suggestion is true to a degree, it too quickly moves away from focusing on what certain patients cannot tolerate in themselves and on their stable, repetitive avoidances of this.

THE AIMS OF DEFENSE AND OF DEFENSIVE REPETITIVE ENACTMENTS

We need to sort out further the aims of defensive activities. The immediate aim of all defense is, of course, protection from anxiety derived from internal conflict (safety). Stable and enduring compro-

mise formations bind anxiety by synthesizing and expressing conflicting wishes. This formulation need not mean that ongoing work is
not required to preserve such balancing between conflicting wishes.
The ordinary neurotic patient is relatively able to express and
synthesize conflict in fantasy, to handle it within his own mind.
When patients are unable to handle conflict within fantasy, they are
impelled to enact it repetitively so as to manage anxiety. Repetitive
enactments may, of course, occur in fantasy as well as in actual
behavior, which involves the external world. Fantasizing is certainly
a behavior, although one, we ordinarily assume, that does not affect
the outside world. Actually, that assumption is not accurate. Our
fantasies do involve and affect our representations of the outside
world, of others. Thus, they will affect how we relate to the outside
world. Repetition in fantasy may be regarded by the patient as an
action, as in undoing destruction or reconnecting to another person.
My differentiation has to be somewhat artificial between repetition in
fantasy and repetitive behavioral enactments, which directly affect
the outside world. Although it need not always be true, my impression is that, generally, repetitive behavioral enactments, which involve the outside world directly, tend to indicate that the patient
believes that the danger cannot be managed intrapsychically, within
fantasy alone.

Action and the (mis)use of other people aim to manage what the
patient is unable to manage for himself. Repetitive, magical undoing
and protective enmeshment with others, in fantasy repetition or in
actual behavior (usually these coexist), are pressured denials of
destruction and separateness. Here, too, we need to acknowledge
defensive possibilities of mastery, synthesis, integration, and change
inherent in such magical action and use of other people. But the
counterpart to the relatively stable compromise formations in fantasy
ordinarily possible for the neurotic is this repetitive enactment, which
is required to regulate one's inner world. This distinction between
relatively stable neurotic compromise formation in fantasy and repetitive action and use of others is not intended to mean that neurotic
patients do not, at times, need to regulate themselves in these latter
ways. When compromise formation in fantasy is insufficient to allay
anxiety, other, more powerful defensive modes are utilized. The
overriding aim, however, is then not mastery and integration of what
is threatening within oneself but avoidance and protection from this.

From this perspective, dependency, sexualization, sadomasochism, and perversion are action modes, intended to use real and
fantasied others in defensive, repetitive enactments. I am using these
terms not as diagnoses but as descriptions of pathological modes both

of defense and of object relations, which are especially difficult to analyze (i.e., change). The dangers include loss, separateness, helplessness, destruction, and narcissistic injury, the last, in part, through superego condemnation. Whatever one cannot tolerate and take responsibility for in oneself is disowned, gotten rid of, transformed, in magical, illusory ways, into something more acceptable. The pressure for repetition derives from the intensity of the dangers to be avoided. Conflict that cannot be adequately expressed and handled within fantasy leads to (endlessly) repetitive enactment so as to validate essential illusions. This idea is best known to us in perversion. It applies as well to these other forms of defensive repetitive enactment, which tend to resemble perverse object relations.

In my view, with such fragile parents, the child/patient may become terrified of his destructive ability (and defensive need) to overwhelm/intimidate the parents. This terror will exaggerate the patient's dread of his omnipotent destructiveness, and further bind him to the pathological relationship with the disturbed parent. Defensive, omnipotent illusions, attributed to self (sadistic omnipotent control) and to the object (in masochistic surrender to an aggrandized object), are further drawn on to reassure against such feared destructiveness. It is as if the patient keeps repeating his destructive attacks on the other so as to reassure himself that he has not really destroyed anything. The wish totally to annihilate and extract from the needed other is obscured in the endless repetition within which nothing/nobody changes. The patient disowns the destructiveness of his repetitions, in which he aims to endlessly torture and drain the other because of the latter's imagined failings. Repetition indeed, becomes a refusal to change, to lead one's own life separate and apart from the parents, who will forever be attacked, demanded of, and clung to as deficient.

Action tends to have a magical, defensive quality (action "makes it so"), that contributes an addictive quality to repetitive, defensive enactments. The magical quality of action tends to be derived from childhood experiences in which fantasies seem to have been actualized. Such experiences can include childhood seduction or abuse or the contrary, experiences in which the child has succeeded in intimidating vulnerable parents; in the latter case it is as if the child's destructive wishes have been actualized. These experiences contribute to the illusion that magically the child's wishes have been actualized. Repetitive "magical happenings" may then be used to deal with frustration and painful affects. These parents often provide a model for identification of the defensive use of (repetitive) action to deal with painful affects, which they believe they cannot tolerate.

Remember that trauma has always been associated with repetition compulsion. Here, too, with childhood trauma, action becomes overinvested because of what actually happened. That is, fantasies of danger and disaster have been actualized. Identification with the doer or aggressor and repetitive attempts to master trauma and traumatic affects also contribute to (repetitive) action tendencies. Illusions of magical protection through intense involvement, as with provocation, supplication, and submission, contribute to action tendencies, which repeat aspects of the child–parent relationship.

THE USE OF OTHERS FOR DEFENSE

The patient believes, usually erroneously, that on his own he is unable to manage what is inside him; a relationship with another is thus required. Although he may have conflict about such a relationship with another person, to some degree the other person is used to provide certain necessary illusions. Predominantly internal defensive operations may include repression, isolation of affect, undoing, reaction formation, denial. But note clearly that here, too, defensive operations, to a degree, affect the external world, including other people. Thus, when the Rat Man (Freud, 1909) replaces the stone in the road (undoing), action, rather than symbolic maneuvers alone, occurs in the context of an ambivalent, narcissistic relationship with his lady. Other defensive operations, which are usually, sometimes erroneously, regarded as more primitive, more readily show involvement of others in repetitive enactment as part of a complex defensive constellation (Balint, 1950; Ogden, 1979, 1983; Räkköläinen & Alanen, 1982; Modell, 1984; Dorpat, 1985; Sander, 1989). There are the unwise risk and temptation in such emphasis on the interpersonal of dismissing the intrapsychic or of dismissing traditional psychoanalysis. It is far better to integrate new areas of emphasis with what is already valuable, so as to enrich the whole psychoanalytic enterprise.

What I am after here is linking stable, defensive repetition with pathological modes of object relating. I want especially to emphasize modes of defense that involve another person, whether they operate intrapsychically only or interpersonally as well. For those conflicts for which a person cannot take responsibility, he will engage another (in fantasy, in an actual relationship, or in both) to protect against this danger. Interactive defensive modes, which involve another person in fantasy and/or in an actual relationship, are difficult to relinquish because of the imagined sense that the patient is unable to manage himself. Interactive defense modes also repeat aspects of a parent–

child relationship that has emphasized that neither one can handle what is inside of himself. As a result, it is more difficult to let go of such pathological modes of object relationship and of defense to integrate what is frightening within the patient himself. Thus, dependent relationships and magical action are both always involved in the kind of defensive, repetitive enactments here considered.

For example, projective identification is a defense that must involve both internal and external objects. Primitive idealization, devaluation, omnipotent control, and splitting also affect both internal and external objects. There is not just an externalization of internal defense but a need to involve other people in these complex defensive constellations. To interrupt such defensive repetition, the analyst must focus the patient's understanding on what it seeks to accomplish.

My view is that projective identification and transference repetition are linked in their defensive functions. I would regard these examples as attempts to protect against what cannot be tolerated within oneself by involving another person repetitively in one's own conflicts. I suggest that this view is a useful way to consider transference repetition, by understanding and interpreting of its functions. What is attributed to the analyst is to be understood as a method for managing some internal conflict that the patient feels he cannot handle within himself. With highly dependent patients it is essential to focus consistently on how the patient needs to make use of the analyst. Parent and child may each have used such defensive techniques, within the parent–child relationship, to disown and externalize what is unacceptable in oneself. Projective defenses and transference thereby become linked in their defensive, repetitive functions. What the patient feels guilty about, in recognizing the likeness between himself and the parent, is, of course, whatever reprehensible quality they share. The risk is of regarding such behavior primarily as turning passive into active or as identifying with the aggressor, without sufficient emphasis on the patient's own "badness." Focus on the defensive functions of the repetitive behavior, whether conceived of as projective identification or as transference repetition, is essential. The hatred and destructiveness, in both patient and parent, must now be acknowledged, as replayed with the analyst. Defensive oscillation between the roles of child and parent, conceived of as victim and aggressor, may aim to avoid the destructiveness in each position. In these defensive, behavioral repetitive enactments, affect is both induced in, and projected into, the other. What cannot be tolerated in oneself is attributed to, and put in, the other.

TOWARD SELF-RELIANCE AND TOLERANCE
FOR INTERNAL CONFLICT

When we explore repetitive behavioral enactments, a predominant emphasis on defense seems most useful. Thus, even pleasure, gratification, unsatisfied childhood needs, trauma, and fixation may not be the best perspectives from which to understand repetition. When the patient continues to repeat, we need to continue asking why this is and what advantages ensue from it. Dependency and transference repetitions in analysis can most usefully be explored in terms of how and why the object is being used by the patient. This approach then leads to questioning what the patient is afraid to take responsibility for in himself so as to be able to synthesize and integrate. One set of explanations for repetition compulsion consists of persistent, regressive, dependent attachment (see Sandler and Sandler, 1978; Shapiro, 1985; Wilson and Malatesta, 1989), which the patient fears relinquishing. Here, too, we need to question the defensive purposes in such attachments and avoidance of autonomy. The most helpful question seems to be: What is the patient afraid of, in being without an object on whom he is dependent?

Conscious awareness of the defensive functions served by such repetitive enactments is often insufficient for their relinquishment. Therefore, this perspective in the literature (e.g., Bibring, 1943; Loewald, 1971b; Klein, 1976b; Porder, 1987) seems overly optimistic. Patients may be well aware that they are stuck in repeating aspects of the child–parent relationship without successfully relinquishing this. Usually a partial denial of the repetition persists because of fears of relinquishing the dependent relationship and fully facing, in a responsible, integrative way, what is frightening within oneself. The patient may be able, at times, to face this in himself, only then to repress, deny, externalize, surrender to others, or sexualize.

From the perspective of compromise formation, repetitive behavioral enactments satisfy each psychic agency, albeit in a nonintegrative mode. Illusions of safety are sought in the face of dangers. Some aggression is discharged, without sufficient responsibility, however, to allow for its integration. Superego components of punishment and containment appear in the parent–child, dependent, sadomasochistic, or perverse relationship that is re-created. Responsible guilt, which could lead to change and integration, is avoided through punishment/torture; externalization of responsibility, for oneself and for the hatred, onto the other; sexualization of hostile aggression; defensive idealization of love and sexual arousal to deny destructiveness. The ego's aim in such defense and adaptation is to avoid synthesis and integration of the dangerous psychic contents by a variety of mechanisms that seek illusions of safety by attempts to reassure oneself that the badness is gone; is present in, and belongs to, the other; is not really bad but something good or exciting; does not count because of one's entitlement; or is justified as self-defense. Intellectually the patient may know much better than to believe these reassurances. It is easy to lose the ability to tolerate and take responsibility for one's own hatred when one plays these repetitive defensive games that embroil oneself with a re-created parent. Confusion easily occurs as to who is responsible, whose fault it is, and who started it, just as occurred once upon a time in the child–parent relationship.

Just as children tend to identify with and adopt parents' defensive styles, so, too, do they identify with parents' defensive aims. When parents have avoided responsibility for their badnesses by intense denial, projective defenses, and interactive defensive modes (dependency, sadomasochism, sexualization, perversion), the child will tend to identify with the parent's avoidance. Such projective and interactive defensive modes encourage the use of others for protection against one's dangerous psychic contents; this motivation becomes central in one's object relationships. Simultaneously, these projective and interactive defensive modes discourage responsibility and ownership of what is dangerous within. They also interfere with separateness and protect against it. The ordinary neurotic patient and his parents defend themselves, as we all do, but such defensive activities tend to be more circumscribed, encroach less on reality and object relations, and usually allow for more responsible guilt and autonomy than with repetitive behavioral enactments.

When we schematically examine a defense mechanism, it may be impossible to determine whether the aim is integration or avoidance, riddance, or disavowal. Even if the immediate goal is the latter, this still may allow for later facing and integrating. Think, for example, of Ogden's (1979) processive view of projective identification or of denial temporarily alleviating the pain of illness or death, so that it can be gradually assimilated. Dorpat (1987) elaborates this view that not all defensive activity is to be regarded as pathological, that is, not adaptive. Only in an overview of a patient's defensive processing within a psychoanalysis can we judge his overall defensive aims. Thus, we view the ego's defensive aims within a hierarchy of defensive activities.

Illusions or quasi-delusions that separateness is death and that no one is really able to tolerate facing what exists within contribute to the terror of self-examination and responsibility for oneself. These illusions all accentuate the need for defensive repetition so as to avoid, get rid of, or isolate what is dangerous within and to reassure that a defensively needed object and relationship persist. To the extent that a person fears and feels guilty about his destructiveness, he must avoid responsibly integrating this. Then he will need to cling to his objects, fear their loss and destruction, and undo such damage by immobilization, inactivity, surrender, and a general reversal of destructive affects into quasi-loving ones. Avoidant, nonintegrative defense and repetition contrast with the mature ego aim to organize and integrate within the ego's core, what had previously been regarded as too dangerous to assimilate and hence had been dissociated. Like Klein (1976b), I believe that these two ego aims are usually in conflict. For the patients focused upon in this book, the balance tilts much more toward persistent, nonintegrative defensive repetition. These two conflicting ego aims explain, I believe, the two contradictory aims of the repetition compulsion.

7

THE SENSE OF DEFECT

The sense of defect persists as a defensive avoidance of facing and integrating certain painful affects, especially rage. Every patient considered in this book relies on some negative, fantasy compromise formation, like the sense of defect, to protect and preserve himself. This is the price people pay for being unable to tolerate and integrate their "badnesses," so that they need to remain submissive to a destructive parental introject, which offers the illusion of protection. That is, we are here describing pathological dependency from the perspective of the awful feelings such a person has about himself. What is so awful is the willingness to maintain a degraded self-image to perpetuate pathological dependency.

This study of the sense of defect was originally prompted by my concurrently having in analysis two patients who had significant physical defects, and who regarded themselves as defective. I was surprised to realize how many of my other patients in psychoanalytic psychotherapy also had significant physical defects or regarded themselves as psychologically defective. These are not necessarily the same, nor is it the case that one is objectively real and the other is only fantasy. People vary enormously in how they process trauma and physical and emotional disability. It may be as surprising to see certain patients able to value and respect themselves despite considerable physical defect as it is to encounter patients with a sense of physical defect related to something that is objectively trivial, until, of course, it becomes clear within the analytic process how each has come to manage good and bad in the way he has done. An external observer's assumptions about the meanings of a given physical defect to a patient often prove erroneous. Such meanings must be clarified within an analysis, underneath the usual initial, intense, denial. The analysis must attend to the patient's processing or, more commonly, failure with such processing, of external reality (trauma, illness, physical defect, or disability), as well as to the patient's compromise formations in fantasy.

Besides the patients described later, the group of patients I have seen included one patient who had had a severe gastrointestinal illness as a child; two who had severe visual impairment, one with dyslexia; and three (one of whom also had a learning disability) who had had plastic surgical corrections for "realistically trivial" concerns, under great internal pressure to present an attractive face. To this group, I added a man I had previously analyzed who had been born with a genital defect, corrected surgically at age two.

How does a person with a physical defect come to view himself as defective? How does a person without an obvious physical defect come to view himself as defective? What does such a sense of defect refer to? Why does it persist? Why do some patients with a self-image as defective despair of ever being able to feel ordinary or adequate, even though realistically no one else would evaluate them as defective?

The sense of defect, physical or psychological, is regarded here as a fantasy, a compromise formation, involving conflict and attempts at conflict resolution among the psychic agencies. Psychoanalytic emphasis is directed to the motivations for the persistence of this sense of defect, rather than primarily to etiology (trauma) or genetic history. I (Coen, 1986), however, have been surprisingly misunderstood as discounting biological reality, as if it does not count (see Downey, 1987; Coen, 1987c). That view is certainly not my intention. What I am after is what is done with biological reality and why. Analytic data are presented to develop dynamic and genetic hypotheses to explain the persistent inability (and need not) to integrate the sense of defect.

The advantages, for the progress of an analysis, of viewing the sense of defect as a compromise formation are emphasized. This argument is buttressed by normative observations of children that suggest that self- and body images should be viewed not as actual, fixed structures but as compromise formations.

SOME CLINICAL SKETCHES

An analysand mentioned repeatedly that his elderly mother still questioned regularly whether he had had the nevus on his buttocks examined to make sure it had not turned malignant. Mr. B believed this nevus made his backside unattractive and that it was a cause for concern. As a six-year-old he had played with another boy who had a large, ugly nevus on his buttocks. They would take their pants off and chase each other. Mr. B had felt pleased and relieved that the other boy found his buttocks appealing.

One day the analyst asked the patient about the reality of the nevus. I was startled to learn that it had been just barely visible during childhood and had become virtually invisible. When Mr. B became the teacher's pet in first grade, his mother expressed her doubt to him that he could be so appealing to the teacher. Besides the many varied meanings of Mr. B's concerns about his buttocks, why could he not acknowledge his anger at his mother's destructive attacks on his self-esteem and body? Physical defectiveness, aside from his "small penis," did not play a central role in this man's pervasive feeling that he was deficient. Intense guilt and shame prevented him from facing his rage at his parents; he turned this against himself, so that he continually felt dissatisfied with himself. An injunction from both parents had to be strictly observed (reinforced by religious pressure) that he not upset his troubled mother and not see clearly and respond (with anger) to his mother's paranoid, depressive behavior. With the analyst's help, Mr. B was able transiently to acknowledge his anger. But he could not make this acknowledgment stick so that he could develop conviction that he had reason, indeed, to feel angry. Mr. B continued to feel too frightened of his destructiveness really to be able to confront it and work with it over time. Submission to others' negative, attacking views of him served to protect him from his rage.

Mr. E had a deeply etched sense of himself as physically defective, although this was split off and hidden by denial. He had been in treatment the better part of a year before the analyst accidentally discovered Mr. E's "defects" by inquiring casually about an unclear reference to his having worn glasses as a child. Since Mr. E wore contact lenses, the analyst had not been aware of his visual problem. It turned out that the patient was virtually blind without lenses. As a child, Mr. E had been warned by his first ophthalmologist that he would be totally blind by adolescence. Slowly, he revealed also that he had a small skin tag on the underside of his penis that would, at times, accumulate secretions; an extra, small lobe on one ear; and a nevus on his buttocks; small stature as a child and that he was left-handed—all of which he regarded, under his denial, minimizing, and secrecy, as defective. In a way, however, he did not fully know consciously that he viewed himself as defective, while, at the same time, of course, he really did know.

The following incident exemplifies his intense feelings of shame. In high school, while he led a tour for new students, one contact lens fell on the floor. He froze, terrified that the others would notice and regard him with contempt. He continued the tour for hours, despite his difficulty seeing and his fear that his mother would be angry with him for having lost the lens. He would not call attention to himself!

Fears of being ridiculed paralyzed Mr. E, so that he could not feel and express anger, wishes, ideas, opinions, and, to some extent, his free associations on the couch. If others became annoyed with him, they could humiliate him through criticism, especially through references to his "defects," as his mother had done. Mother would "show off" the strawberry nevus on his buttocks to company because of how "cute" it was; Mr. E would feel humiliated but helpless to stop her. This nevus also turned out to be less than an inch in diameter and to have faded since childhood. Mr. E believed his mother had simply been uncritical of his accomplishments, so that she would show off what he had done; in contrast, he regarded his having written a poem or song as just a beginning effort. His mother's boasting about him turned out to have been destructive, humiliating attacks, thinly covered with fatuous praise. In the analysis, to confront his anger at his mother's destructiveness seemed to invite further ridicule (or rejection) of himself as defective. Passive submission to others' narcissistic needs allowed him to feel tolerated; this, together with his view of himself as defective, protected him from his dangerous impulses, especially anger and sexual longings for mother, which led to further taunting.

Mrs. C had been a pretty girl, seemingly attractive enough for her narcissistic mother, until age five. Then she developed disabling neuromuscular symptoms and bodily and facial disfigurement. She was hospitalized in a distant city for an extensive workup; the diagnosis was uncertain, and her life was considered at risk. Surgery was performed to remove an endocrine tumor, although the family was not given a clear diagnosis. Her symptoms persisted, some for several years, while some disfiguring symptoms continued permanently. None of these residua were especially notable to me. Mrs. C was a physically attractive woman, although she could not feel her attractiveness. She could talk about her breasts being firm and prominent, and she could understand that she was shapely—she just could not feel attractive. Like Mr. E, Mrs. C had split off and denied her sense of herself as ugly, scarred, damaged, and stupid. Learning in school had been interfered with by her quasi-delusion that she was stupid as well as her difficulty with being alone to study. During the treatment, she discovered to her surprise and delight that she enjoyed reading fiction and history and that she had no difficulty with comprehension. She bought an expensive fur coat and watch as if they could make her feel attractive and intact (phallic, a man-woman, anything but herself as damaged). Mrs. C exercised regularly to counteract feeling that her body was ugly. She could not get away from her intense feelings of defectiveness. She continued to see herself as if she were still the young, disfigured girl. She would avoid sex if her abdomen was not flat, for example, if she had been constipated for a day or two, for then her large scar was more visible. She was very uncomfortable appearing nude or even with her hair wet. Much of her (narcissistic) fantasy life was aimed at repairing her feelings of defectiveness.

Multiple surgical procedures (including also intravenous infusions and tests, physical restraints during her hospitalization and surgery, and so on) had added to her terror of passivity and helplessness. She mistrusted doctors, felt that they had and would harm her, feared the analyst's interpretations as hurtful penetrations, and could not relax during intercourse with her husband or reflect on the couch on her associations or the analyst's interpretations. She had to be active, in motion, and could not hold still with her own feelings and perceptions of herself.

Denial, externalization, projection, and undoing were so intense and persistent that Mrs. C had marked difficulty dealing with what was wrong within herself. She had little compassion for what she had been through as a child. Repeatedly, she would report how touched others had felt listening to the medical and surgical traumas of her childhood. They had cried; she had not. Mrs. C felt touched and surprised each time someone was empathic and kind to her. She had great difficulty with such an attitude toward herself or toward her husband or son. She had identified with her mother's sadism and rejection of her feelings and needs. The same applied to her sense of defect, which was not to be discussed, as if it were too horrible to tolerate, as, indeed, her mother had felt about it. What was wrong with her was concrete, factual, not a set of very painful feelings about which she could first be comforted and then helped to integrate her terrible trauma.

When her son was expelled from school and assessed as having much more severe emotional difficulties (and a guarded prognosis) than first thought, Mrs. C simply could not work in analysis at her own difficulties. Her identification with her son as damaged (and her guilt) led to the imperative need to undo the son's disturbance. This, together with her sadistic provocation of the son, made the home situation increasingly destructive.

During this period Mrs. C's analytic hours became almost exclusively devoted to projective attacks on son and husband and urgent demands that the analyst and others do something. She was helped by sitting up and our shifting to a face-to-face psychotherapeutic focus on what the son required, so that he would not become more self-destructive. That is, I had to take her in hand and explain that since she did not want her son to kill himself, she could not allow herself to criticize him and that she needed to try, as best she could, to support his fragile self-esteem. Mrs. C had not been able to grasp, despite my interpreting her behavior and her denial of her own contribution, that her picking on her son and continual dissatisfaction with him (her own sadism, together with her identification with her sadistic mother) were leading him to feel suicidal. Now that she was sitting up, Mrs. C was delighted with being able to look at me and to see my concern and acceptance of her. She was pleased that I leaned forward, toward her, indicating, she thought, that I was trying hard to help her with the home crisis and that I was not repelled by her. It really surprised this woman, who was realistically quite attractive, that I could like her or feel attracted to her. She felt relieved that the pressure was temporarily off her needing to face her own sadism and destructiveness. Now, under my guidance, she had a program for helping her son, within which she could feel acceptable. It gradually became possible again, some of the time, to work with her on her feeling of being entitled to berate others by virtue of her being an exception. The latter also expressed her intense anger and bitterness, identification with the attacker (or doer), and terror of passivity. The crisis with the son had intensified a guilty judgment of herself as destructive, bad, and damaged. This had, at all costs, to be warded off by projection onto the son or husband or, at times, the analyst or the son's analyst. Intense, angry destructiveness led to abrupt shifts in her attitudes toward herself and others from idealization to devaluation.

Mrs. C's sense of unacceptability was razor-sharp. She felt her narcissistic mother had been repelled by her ugliness and had been critical of her defects and of her anger. She felt hopeless to satisfy mother's wish for a "sweet girl." In contrast to her attitude toward the patient, the mother seemed warmer and more accepting of the patient's brother. Mrs. C consciously wished to have a penis to be able to do the penetrating, to have a visible organ, to feel strong, powerful, intact—not a scarred, damaged woman, herself. Heterosexual and homosexual fantasies established her as dominant, exercising an attraction on others who reassured her of her desirability by their sexual responsiveness to her. Even in her fantasies, she resisted letting herself respond to being touched or aroused, so that she would not have to feel passive and helpless.

Sex was limited largely to narcissistic reassurance of her attractiveness, which was very important indeed. Mrs. C liked to dress up in black hose and garter belt, and standing, play phallic dominatrix to her husband. The only men with whom she had been orgastic in intercourse had been passive, safe men who she felt sure would not hurt her. She dreamed repeatedly of being robbed, invaded, hurt by people who were not concerned with her needs. Eventually she was able to become a better mother and felt grateful that, as she claimed, I had taught her mothering. Her sadistic attacks on her husband continued; we could not repeat here what we had done in her relationship with her son. Negative, hate-filled transference, and competitive phallic rivalry with me, including wishes to castrate me so as to grab my penis for herself, were all present but largely disowned. Mrs. C simply could not hold still with her destructiveness so as to take responsibility for it and attempt to integrate it. In effect, it became someone else's problem; someone else became the victim of her sadism, which she disclaimed. Her sense of entitlement, because of her childhood traumata, allowed her to attack others and to feel that they deserved such treatment.

NOTES ON THE LITERATURE

Attention to the importance of the mother–child relationship for integration of the child's physical defect began with Freud (1933). He pointed out that Emperor Wilhelm II's narcissistic vulnerability derived not primarily from his withered arm but from his mother's withdrawal because of his defect. This position has been advanced by Lussier (1960, 1980), Solnit and Stark (1961), Lax (1972), and Kohut (1972). Psychoanalytic authors have implicitly or explicitly emphasized the central importance of narcissistic pathology in patients with bodily defects: the persistence of narcissistic injury; problems with self-esteem regulation; compensatory self-aggrandizing and self-perfecting fantasies, with related, intensified hostile aggression; and fantasies of revenge, rebirth, and bisexual and castrative themes, which both express the sense of damage and attempt to redress it (Niederland, 1956, 1965, 1975; Lussier, 1960, 1980; Kohut, 1972; Bornstein, 1977; Yorke, 1980). Body deformity has been regarded as a chronic state of traumatization that becomes an organizing and concretizing experience (Greenacre, 1952, 1956, 1958a) for psychic development (Blos, 1960; Niederland, 1965; Castelnuovo-Tedesco, 1978, 1981). Additional trauma may include hospitalization, immobilization, separation from parents and home, medical tests and procedures, surgery, enforced passivity, helplessness, and loss of control (A. Freud, 1952; Jessner, Blom, and Waldfogel, 1952; Robertson, 1956; Plank and Horwood, 1961; Lipton, 1962). When the body defect occurs, it affects developmental processes and phase-specific conflicts (Moore, 1975; Dubovsky and Groban, 1975; Earle, 1979; Castelnuovo-Tedesco, 1981). Passive, submissive wishes (with or without masochistic or castrative elaboration) may exacerbate the long-term consequences of illness, hospitalization, surgery, and deformity (A. Freud, 1952; Blos, 1960; Kavka, 1962). Ego deformation may result, with impairment in learning, memory, thinking, and time and space perception (Blos, 1960). This ego deformation has been related to the defective body image and to maternal attitudes and prohibitions against acknowledgment of the defect.

All psychoanalytic authors have emphasized fantasy elaboration of body defects, which involves attempts at conflict resolution. Previous discussions of body image distortion in patients with physical defects, however, have tended to regard such distortion of the body image as concrete, fixed, and factual, rather than as a compromise formation. When psychoanalysts elaborate body image distortion from the perspective of childhood development and of the tasks of separation-individuation and the integration of self and object concepts, a fixed and static concept of the body image may emerge. Recall that fantasy and compromise formation involving the body image do not exclude reality, except partially in psychosis. In Waelder's (1930) model, the ego actively attempts (in its constructions, such as fantasy and compromise formation, more generally) to master and assimilate reality, the repetition compulsion, the id, and the superego into its own organization. To my knowledge, there is, surprisingly, no psychoanalytic literature devoted specifically to the psychological sense of defect in patients who are physically intact. Although this concept is well known, such patients have been considered to manifest signs either of castration anxiety or of a "defect" in psychological development. That is, there is a risk that "defect" is regarded too literally, outside of our usual perspective on compromise formation.

NORMATIVE OBSERVATION AND THE SENSE OF SELF

My argument that the sense of defect is most usefully viewed as a compromise formation is derived from the psychoanalytic situation.

Nevertheless, some brief consideration of the development of the sense of self will help provide perspective that, even in early childhood, the sense of self and a sense of defect should not be viewed as fixed, concrete structures. Central to this argument is Lichtenstein's (1961) view that the mother does not mirror back to the infant a preexisting, actual image of himself.

I agree with Lichtenstein (1961) that the term "mirroring," when used to describe the early development of the sense of self, overemphasizes the visual element of the experience. Lichtenstein proposed that, in a complex sensory responsiveness and interchange, the child is established, partly, as the sensory instrumentality of the mother, for the satisfaction of the mother's own unconscious needs. Lichtenstein's idea derives, in part, from Greenacre's (1958a) writing and Lorenz's (1935, 1937) etiological work on the "innate releaser mechanism." Emphasis is placed upon the early patterns of bodily relatedness between mother and infant, through which the mother's needs help give shape to the infant's first experience of himself.

We now believe that when a person looks in the mirror, he does not simply see what the mirror reveals. He sees himself as he needs to see himself because of his entire psychological makeup, reflecting varied conflicts and contributions from each psychic agency. Similarly, when the child sees himself in the mother's eyes, he does not see himself as he "really is." Rather, he experiences himself, within the mother–child relationship, in terms of the needs, wishes, and conflicts of both partners. Mahler and McDevitt (1982) emphasized that the early self-schema derives most from (1) the child's own inner feelings (or states), from proprioception first and gradually from sensory perception; and (2) the whole spectrum of caregiving by the mother. They noted the integration of hand, mouth, and vision into the body schema. Visual mirroring is an important, although only one, factor influential in shaping the self-concept. Greenacre (1958a) and Freedman (1972) had earlier agreed that it is not until the second half of the first year of life that vision becomes a principal sensory modality for early self-definition. Stern (1982) has described three ways mother and infant can be with each other: complementary interactions, state sharing, and need gratification. All of these contribute to the sense of self. Stern's three types of relatedness seem interconnected in life, so that mother and child have to mediate a whole set of conditions in order to share mutual engagement. Our perspective is amplified when we also include the earliest constitutional and experiential contributants to the basic core. Weil (1970, 1978) and Solnit (Panel, 1979) regard the infant's ability to engage the mother and the degree of resilience to neglect as genetically determined. Weil considers the problems posed for the mother–infant pair by infants with especially low or high stimulus barriers, sensitivity, or responsiveness. Each calls for a different kind of maternal responsiveness. I assume that for the mother and child to be mutually engaged, for the sort of responsive maternal mirroring that leads to the child's successful adaptation, successful negotiation of all these (and more) varied tasks is required.

I believe that the concept of mother as mirror or of the analyst's role as mirror (Winnicott, 1967; Schacht, 1981; P. Kernberg, 1984) derives from an aspect of child analytic work. A perspective is emphasized here in which the child analyst is to be extraordinarily careful not to be intrusive or unresponsive, in order to validate the central importance of the child as a unique person. Imitation, parallel or similar behavior, it is argued, is central to the task of helping children establish a self-concept. The parent or analyst is to help the child see what is actually already there within him, an image he needs to have reflected back. Where the mother has been depressed and unresponsive or has intruded her own needs into the mother–child relationship, it may well be essential for the child analyst or, later, the adult analyst to be extraordinarily respectful of not introducing anything other than what the patient brings to the treatment. Winnicott's (1967) emphasis on the mother's face as mirror should, I think, be taken metaphorically and from the clinical perspective of the child analyst's attempting to repair psychological damage. For child therapy with certain children, the creative, subjective, shaping role played by the child analyst may need to be markedly restrained. In theory building, this perspective may lead to an overemphasis on imitation, similarity, echoing, and literal mirroring as central to the development of the self-concept. In real life, I believe the mother needs to be not an imitative mirror but, rather, a loving, empathic shaper, a transforming creator of the child's experiences. So, too, in much more sublimated form, does the analyst need to work. Schafer (1983) has written movingly that neither imitation nor identification conveys what the psychoanalyst does in feeling empathically with his analysands. Like Lichtenstein, he stresses the creative, transformational aspect of empathic encounters.

P. Kernberg (1984) has recently studied the young child's developing use of the mirror in relation to the establishment of self-awareness and self-recognition. Such investigation is important for our understanding of the development of the child's sense of self. Her preliminary formulation is that the young "child's visual reaction to the mirror is that the image is predominantly mother." Let us note that when a child says her own mirror image is "mommy," we cannot be sure what this comment means. Nor is it yet clear to us what it means when a child searches for mommy in the mirror or behind the mirror. It seems more circumspect for now to assume only that the mother is somehow connected with the child's self-examination, that the mother's presence infiltrates the mirror so that when the child looks at herself in the mirror, she experiences the mother's presence as well as her absence. Winnicott (1967) wrote, "When the average girl studies her face in the mirror she is reassuring herself that the mother image is there and that the mother can see her and that the mother is en rapport with her." He writes about *"getting* the mirror to notice and approve" (p.114, italics added).

This discussion applies to adult analysis as well. The psychoanalytic situation can be metaphorically represented, as it is by many patients (in fantasy and dream), as a new looking in the mirror. The presence of the analyst infiltrates the mirror, and makes close examination safer and more bearable. Sometimes, when looking seems especially dangerous, the patient will need to feel the reassuring presence of the analyst more concretely. This is needed to assist differentiation of dangerous transference from reality (who the analyst really is) and management of frightening affects and wishes, just as the mother once did or should have done. Dreams of the analyst undisguised or of mirrors, as well as fantasy preoccupation with the analytic transference and the analyst, may, as one of their functions, help with such differentiation and modulation of dangerous transference and dangerous affects (Bradlow and Coen, 1975; Coen and Bradlow, 1985).

What kind of mirroring does the patient with a sense of defect seek from the analyst? Certainly there may be multiple, varied wishes. Several issues stand out in my clinical material; two are primarily defensive, and one is progressive and integrative. Defensive wishes in mirroring include that the analyst assure the patient magically of phallic intactness or collude with the patient that the sense of defect exonerates the patient from superego criticism about unacceptable wishes. On the other hand, what the patient needs from the analyst is an acceptance of the patient's feelings of defectiveness and help with tolerating and working with the multiple feelings and conflicts that preserve the sense of defect as a compromise formation. Here the analyst reflects back to the patient not the surface appearance of defect but what is, indeed, invisible to the patient's emotional perception.

THE PSYCHOLOGY OF THE SENSE OF DEFECT

An adult patient who regards himself as defective sees himself neither as he really is nor as his parents saw him. The sense of defect is more complex. A bodily defect is not always the nidus around which a sense of defectiveness is organized, but realistically trivial bodily defects may become organized into concrete representations of defectiveness. The sense of defect is experienced concretely, as fact, which is emotionally deeply etched (Blos, 1960, made this point in cases of cryptorchidism). At the same time, the sense of defect is usually vague, poorly defined, not easily verbalizable as to what is wrong. Although there is a profound awareness of something being wrong with oneself, this aspect of the self or body representation is usually split off, unintegrated, exhibitionistically repaired, and per-fected. There is an intense, pervasive hopelessness about ever being good enough, acceptable, or lovable. This, too, may be energetically defended against, unsuccessfully, by varied maneuvers—narcissistic, exhibitionistic, masochistic—to deny such frighteningly hopeless feel-ings of unacceptability. Such superego judgment is especially difficult to deal with because the patient knows neither the source of the criticism nor its content, which remain dissociated. What is wrong and why it is wrong must not be known. This psychological defi-ciency may become part of the sense of defect, in that the patient cannot do his own self-evaluation and support his own self-esteem. It is as if hating oneself were more tolerable than knowing the truth. If the truth is not known, magical attempts to reverse the self-hatred can be perpetuated with a kind of promise that one day a reversal may be possible, if only one tries hard enough, behaves well enough, becomes successful enough, and so on.Unable to look at himself and inside himself, the patient frantically scrambles for reassurance and assessments from others that, indeed, nothing is wrong inside or that he is, nevertheless, exonerated or, perhaps more accurately, is accepted especially because he has refrained from accurate self-examination, as his inner parental voices have dictated.

On the other hand, this contrast between the concreteness and vagueness of the sense of defect allows the patient to focus a substantial part of his internal conflict away from the core of himself, by splitting the conflict off onto the "defect." What is wrong is his defect, not the rest of himself. What is wrong is thus crystallized, localized in the "defect," so that magical repair, denial, and projection are allowed and the remainder of himself is spared as intact, good, and acceptable. The focus in concrete bodily terms of "defect" tends to obscure the complexity of intrapsychic conflict, and allows the patient some freedom from guilty responsibility for what is wrong within. It is not his fault; it has just happened to him; or nothing can be done about it anyway—all these can be defenses against superego criticism.

For our purposes, the confluence of bodily defect and psychological sense of defect involves this infantile promise that perhaps one will be accepted if accurate perception and evaluation are not attempted. At issue is not just the magnitude or time of occurrence of a physical defect but what dangers would ensue from attempts at integration of the defect. In this sense, similar conflicts attend a bodily, as well as a psychological, sense of defect. Paradoxically, the hopelessness that one can ever be loved and accepted keeps one inside the closed system of not questioning the basic premises and leads to intense character rigidity. A more secure person would have less terror about examining himself and his own psychological world. Once a person is convinced of his defectiveness, fears of permanent abandonment, rejection, ridicule, or criticism are too frightening to permit questioning the rules. Although some of these patients can feel furious at demands made on them by others, they tend to submit passively to the inexorable demands of their own conscience, as if that submission were the only hope for any acceptance.

For many patients with a sense of defect, accurate perception and evaluation of themselves and of others (parents) have been interfered with by parental injunction. If it is too frightening and forbidden to examine oneself, as one is, in relation to one's parents, one can never become one's own evaluator but will tend to remain dependent on the judgments of others and mistrust oneself. The most common genetic history in my patients with a sense of defect involved one parent with serious psychopathology, usually narcissistic, depressive, or paranoid, with the other parent encouraging the child's compliance with the collusion of not questioning what is wrong. The basic premise these patients share is that what is wrong is almost exclusively within themselves. The interaction between self and parents, real and fantasied, cannot be clearly known. The patient remains uncertain as to what is wrong, in whom it is located, and how it has come about. Thus the defect, physical or psychologically fantasied, becomes the nidus around which so much crystallizes. This is then offered up to the parents, especially the more disturbed parent, as an appeasement and seduction aimed at helping this parent feel better about himself by agreeing that the child is, indeed, the cause of what is wrong. Where the parent has projectively identified a bad or defective self-representation onto the child, such compliance by the child may be essential for the maintenance of the parent–child relationship.

Of course, these genetic hypotheses about the parent–child relationship have been derived from anamnesis within the analysis and analysis of transference. These hypotheses cannot command the same level of certainty as direct observation of the parent–child

relationship. Nevertheless, within the analytic situation, these hypotheses seemed not only formally correct but functionally effective
for intrapsychic change and the progress of the analysis. Additional
support comes from Blos's (1960) finding in three cases of cryptorchidism, a finding, based on child therapy and interviews with the
mothers at a clinic, of maternal prohibition that the child "recognize
his physical defect clearly or . . . think rationally about it" (p. 119).

Note clearly that I am describing patients both with physical
defects and with a psychological sense of defect. All the patients I
consider here with physical defects had a psychological sense of
defectiveness. But some patients with a psychological sense of
defectiveness did not actually have physical defects. Of course, given
the diversity of such patients, there will be differences in their
psychodynamics. Nevertheless, there are important similarities that I
want to stress. In all of these patients, the hostile interaction between
child and parents could not be acknowledged. Parental destructiveness had to be regarded as concern or caring or as deserved because
of the child's badness or defectiveness. They could not fully feel or
understand their own hatred but felt it either diffusely and indiscrim-
inately or predominantly as self-hatred. The patients with physical
defects were encouraged to ignore them, rather than to mourn and
integrate them. Their ability to examine their own and their parents'
responses to the defect was interfered with. The patients with a
psychological sense of defect felt prohibited from experiencing and
examining their own impulses and affects, as well as those of their
parents'. They felt they had to remain ignorant of what was inside
them and what was inside of the parents. Where a parent had been
paranoid, the child was terrified of disturbing the parent, felt under
pressure to comply with the paranoid parent's rules, and abandoned
his own developing standards. A child with a sense of defect who had
a narcissistic or depressed parent had felt especially vulnerable to the
parent's rejection, criticism, or withdrawal and was under greater
pressure than the ordinary child to comply with the parent's needs.

A parent's need for pathological enmeshment with a physically
damaged child will interfere with the parent's ability to help the child
to assess the defect, to mourn it, to rely on the parent to repair the
psychological sense of damage, and to move beyond this. An
insufficiently individuated parent lacking an integrated, confident
sense of self will tend to confuse self and other and experience a
child's physical defect narcissistically as a self-defect. The child is
resented and rejected as having failed to heal the damaged parent.
But the child is also welcomed as the container for the parent's own
bad and deficient feelings, as the parent now focuses his internal

sense of defect onto the child. Paradoxically, the rage, rejection, and projective identification further tie the dependent parent emotionally to the damaged child. So long as the parent needs to exaggerate the child's defect because of the parent's needs for attachment and avoidance of a sense of deficiency, the child will tend to become trapped and surrender further to his feelings of defect, as was the case with each patient with physical defects I have described here.

CHARACTER RIGIDITY AND THE SUPEREGO

Character rigidity in patients with sense of defect involves marked submission to superego prohibitions, especially in relation to intense hostile-aggressive wishes. The compromise formation of the sense of defect allows disguise and punishment of such aggressive strivings. These patients are very angry, and have much reason to be angry but simultaneously are very intolerant of their anger. The psychology of the exception in patients with sense of defect was more usefully viewed as a superego defense than as a superego defect (see chapter 9). Indeed, the demand for narcissistic supplies and the right to mistreat others largely served for defense against superego criticism. That is, the fantasy of oneself as an exception and as defective was used so as to feel more acceptable and worthwhile in the face of unacceptable hostile-aggressive wishes. Vengeful wishes aimed not only to undo past narcissistic trauma but especially to keep the patient in a safer, active, attacking posture, in contrast to feeling intensely vulnerable, passive, or helpless. Playing the role of fate, as an avenger in fantasy, protected against the terrors that fate and other people could inflict. Sadistic wishes to humiliate others as defective, allowed in the role of an exception, were most usefully viewed as defensive attempts to avoid direct experience of the patient's own passivity, humiliation, and rage.

Intolerance of passivity, activity as defense, and identification with the aggressor or doer (Segel, 1969) were interconnected with wishes to play the role of a sadistic avenger (fate). Passive longings and passive situations, such as reflecting on themselves and on the analyst's interpretations, were very difficult for many of these traumatized patients. This difficulty was most especially related to childhood passivity and helplessness in the face of trauma. None of these patients was able to be appropriately empathic and accepting of what was wrong within him. They would be very moved by the concerns shown them by others (including the analyst) but found it very difficult to identify with such an attitude. This felt foreign to them, unfamiliar, as, indeed, it had been. Empathic acceptance would threaten to undermine the rigid character structure, which required submission to the parental authority within the conscience. Such acceptance would lead to the danger of liberation of intense rage, causing the patient to feel unacceptable and frightened, both of his destructiveness getting out of hand and of being gotten rid of.

Two male patients with genital defects used their sense of defect as a bribe to their superego to be allowed exception from the oedipal laws. They had enjoyed especially seductive relationships with their mothers. The mothers had also apparently used the image of the son as genitally damaged and bisexual, so as to obscure the heterosexual seductiveness. Both of these mothers' seductiveness was tinged with taunting of the son as damaged, both exciting and humiliating him sadistically. Both patients felt great shame and rage at their intense sexual desires for the mother. Each man felt especially afraid of being aroused by a woman, only to be ridiculed by her as defective. One patient elaborated and enacted fantasies of being a "sadistic seducer," able to overcome and arouse others, so that no one could resist him (see chapters 8 and 9). Most centrally, he attempted to disprove that his genitals were defective and to master his own passive helplessness, arousal, rage, and the taunting humiliation by the destructive and overly seductive mother. Unconsciously, all these patients used the fantasy of defectiveness not only to hide unacceptable affects and impulses but to appeal to the superego that they had already been punished (castrated).

Wishes for transformation of gender and identity were marked in many of these patients. Gender change was linked to riddance of the humiliation of feeling defective and disadvantaged, willingness to give up the competitive struggles with others of the same gender, disguise of heterosexual incestuous wishes, and the magical wish for rebirth as a perfect specimen of the other sex. Phallic magic was sought by exhibiting oneself as flawless, intact, perfect, through dress, possessions, or accomplishments. Reparative attempts at exhibiting oneself as now intact and accomplished were closely related to the specific defect (Niederland, 1965). For example, Mr. E, nearly blind without lenses, became an accomplished photographer who wanted to dazzle others with his very large-format slides, which, nevertheless, were perfectly clear. Change of identity was similarly linked to narcissistic repair of the defective self-image and to becoming someone truly admirable, at least anyone else who had been spared one's own trauma. Note that such wishes for change of gender and of identity are not only linked to genital defects or a psychological sense of genital defect. The wish to be an intact person, even of the other sex, may transcend a sense of genital or gender defect or insufficiency. One wishes to start life over again and have the same opportunities and endowment as others.

CONCLUSION

From the perspective of adult psychoanalysis, it would be simplistic to view an analysand's sense of defect as deriving predominantly from the mother's inability to provide adequate mirroring responsiveness because of the latter's narcissistic injury, derived from the child's defect or defectiveness. Certain writers (Lax, 1972; Lussier, 1960, 1980) have tended to overemphasize this aspect. A balanced perspective certainly must include the reality of actual trauma, physical and emotional, deprivations, or developmental interference. What seems most useful, however, is to emphasize the dynamic motivations for the persistence of the sense of defect. Clinically, throughout this book, our focus is on defensive (and adaptive) factors that require preservation of psychopathology and "resist" change. From this perspective, the sense of defect, physical or psychological, is a fantasy, a compromise formation serving multiple functions. Since it is experienced almost in a concrete way, it may lead to confusion that it is not fantasy but reality. Real trauma such as congenital deformity, injury, illness, or surgery or real experiences of ridicule, taunting, or rejection may be important, deeply etched determinants in the fantasy of defect. As with all fantasies, however, the real experiences are used in various ways, for various purposes. What these are and why they are maintained become the psychoanalytic questions. Thus, the sense of defect does not refer to an actually existing defect, either in the body image or in the self-representation. It does not per se refer to physical or psychological disability, that is, to objective reality, say, as viewed by a psychoanalyst evaluating the patient. As a compromise formation, the sense of defect attempts to balance certain wishes against certain dangers.

When the analyst tends, reflexively, to regard his analysand's sense of defect as realistic, realistically derived, or appropriate, a countertransference collusion with the patient may be involved. That is, analyst and analysand, in agreeing about the sense of defect, make this factual rather than fantasy. The same may occur when the analyst overemphasizes the parents' contribution in terms of the latter's narcissistic injury to the patient's defect. Holding such attitudes may tend to preclude systematic analysis of the sense of defect in terms of what the patient has been unable to investigate and feel within himself and within his parents.

The reality of what is defective, physically or psychologically, need not determine one's sense of defectiveness. The sense of defectiveness is most usefully viewed as a fantasy, rather than as a structure, as Grossman (1982) has suggested more generally about the concept of self. We could describe a number of "defects" in ego and superego functioning in the class of patients who view themselves as defective. For example, think of interference with accurate perception and evaluation of oneself and others; excessive fear of, and submission to, a harsh, primitive, sometimes partially corrupt, superego;[1] pathological dependency; affective inhibition; at times, inhibition of memory, judgment, and thinking; intense anxiety of panic proportions; terror of bodily damage; passivity; claustrophobia (often related to childhood surgery, immobilization, and traumatic interferences with the body); speech disorders, and so on. Patients vary in their conscious or unconscious elaboration of such psychological "defects" (as evaluated by the psychoanalyst as outside observer) into a fantasy of the self as defective.

Most patients with pathological dependency but without physical defects do tend to regard themselves as defective, usually without understanding why they do so. In pathological dependency, the sense of self is usually regarded as inadequate, damaged, incomplete, unable to function alone; as bad, reprehensible, disgusting, shitty; as deserving of abandonment, rejection, and attack. To a degree, the bond with the other in pathological dependency requires taking the badness and deficiency in the other on oneself. One agrees to be "the bad one" for the other (parent) and to collude in denying that this surrender has been the price paid for acceptance. Self-hatred must contain and transform rage at the vitally needed other. There are enormous disappointment and anger, including at oneself, for the pathologically dependent patient's apparent inability to manage himself. The patient will need to learn that his conviction that "I can't manage without you" is a plea and seduction aimed to appease an angry, needy parent-imago who dreads and forbids separateness. Until then, such (exaggerated) emphasis on his emotional disability goes hand in hand with intense self-contempt and a sense of defectiveness. I cannot say that the sense of defect occurs only in patients with pathological dependency, although I can say that it is usually a prominent feature of them. Of course, milder, focal versions

---

[1] As with Ms. C, some elements of superego functioning may be corrupt (entitled, extractive, destructive toward others), while other aspects are overly harsh and restraining toward the patient. Inconsistency and lack of integration of superego functioning are common.

of defectiveness occur more commonly, expressing a variety of feelings of damage, castration, inadequacy, and insufficiency (cf. A. Freud, 1966), for example, the small penis syndrome. Typically, the man feels unconsciously that he has a child's penis and envies the large, powerful, magical paternal penis. Such men have usually not worked through their phallic envy and rivalry so that they could, in fantasy, tolerate accomplishing the robbing (castration) of the father and claiming the paternal phallus, power, and prerogatives for themselves.

For example, Ms. R revealed her feeling during analysis that her breasts were not large enough. This statement could have been accepted as factual (she seemed to have quite small breasts) or responded to analytically: "Not large enough for what?" This question opened the door to her feeling that she lacked what was necessary to heal her mother's serious depression so that mother could love her. If only she could have nurtured mother as mother's mother with large and full breasts or as mother's lover with a generous penis, then perhaps she could have gained mother's love. Her fantasy of having a penis was consciously elaborated and enacted during late latency and early adolescence by stuffing toilet paper into her panties so as to pretend she had a penis. Homosexual fantasies continued into adulthood of her seducing and healing another woman; she would be the man with the penis who could satisfy the other woman. Thus, she felt she lacked what she should have gotten from mother (and from father); she had too little good stuff inside her or on her. This young woman did have pathological dependency, which she was able to analyze successfully and relinquish. Ms. R resolved her sense of defect and homosexual conflicts, and she was able to have a satisfying relationship with a man.

The fantasy of the self as defective is, then, to be regarded as a compromise formation, involving conflict and attempts at conflict resolution between the psychic agencies. This perspective is not intended to minimize the role of actual trauma during childhood. What actually happened during childhood is, of course, important (A. Freud, 1956) and may even be irreversible if too much damage has been done to one's feelings of confidence and ability to deal with oneself and others. Nevertheless, a patient's sense of himself as defective is most usefully approached as dynamically motivated, to be understood psychoanalytically.

For example, Mr. E's terror of being ridiculed at times seemed to be so deeply etched that the analyst wondered if it could be changed. Remember him as having "defects" in vision, penis, earlobe, the skin of his buttocks, stature as a child, and handedness. He certainly was "actually" ridiculed about his physical defects by his mother and, at times, by his siblings and peers. He feared repetition of these traumatically paralyzing experiences, which had filled him with helplessness and abject humiliation. When he felt the need to assert himself with others, he would become terrified of being ridiculed as defective. This terror paralyzed many areas of his adult functioning. With the analyst, he felt constrained to "cater to" what he felt the analyst wanted. Although he knew otherwise, he regarded the analyst, as he did others, as self-centered and narcissistic and as demanding submission. But within his extreme passivity and indecisiveness, he enacted an angry refusal to satisfy others, a fantasy that he was exempt from really having to be considerate of others' needs, that he would secretly frustrate and dominate them. The problem for the analysis was his fear of feeling, more directly, his own angry destructiveness in relation to that of his parents (and analyst). In the fantasy of himself as damaged was the reassurance that he could not damage others, that he did not have it in him. As he began to approach competitive feelings toward other men and wanted to regard himself as an "ordinary guy," as well as an extraordinary guy, he felt terrified that others would ridicule his defects. This fantasy, too, contained a denial and appeal to the superego that his aggression, coming from such a weak and damaged man, need not be taken seriously as destructive. Gradually, from behind his fear of being ridiculed, emerged rage, wishes for revenge, sadistic wishes to humiliate others by exposing their defects and to dominate and control others, and especially the demand that he be regarded with respect and appreciation as a worthwhile person. Conviction and tolerance for his rage developed as we focused, more and more, on the negative transference, on his enraged and despairing view that he could never satisfy me, that I would always want to find something wrong with him. He could begin to hate me (and his mother) for this destructive disparagement and dismissal of him. He then wanted to seize the power of judgment for himself and to destroy me. Of course, he simultaneously felt better about himself, stronger, and more capable.

The limiting factor to analyzability and change in patients with a prominent sense of defect is often how deeply etched this has become. The degree of psychological scarring is not necessarily related to the reality of the physical defect. When the patient continues to view himself through childlike eyes, what has been wrong physically and psychologically may seem enormous, grotesque, and immutable. Such a patient may have become stuck, feeling helpless and hopeless about what has been wrong physically and emotionally in the parent–child relationship. Such feelings encourage the kind of pathological dependency discussed in this book. To change, the patient would have to be able to risk bearing his rage, in an ongoing, responsible way, at fate and at the parents, as focused now on the analyst. The patient would have to face his terror of retaliation (abandonment, humiliation, attack) from the analyst, perceived as intolerant of the patient's difficulties, feelings, and wishes.

Part III

THE NEED TO AVOID DESTRUCTIVENESS

8

SEXUALIZATION

"Nothing's villainous if it causes an erection."
Marquis de Sade, *The 120 Days of Sodom*, p. 532.

S exualization is a complex defensive operation very much implicated in defensive repetition as it occurs in pathological dependency, especially in sadomasochistic object relations and perversion.
When extensively used, it tends to become a key factor in patients'
difficulty with integrating what is wrong within them. The meaning
of sexualization emphasized here is the repetitive defensive attempt
to transform destructive feelings magically into excitement.

In the 1970s, the concept of sexualization was used extensively in
psychoanalytic writings about narcissistic personality disorder, especially by Kohut (1971, 1977), Goldberg (1975), and Stolorow (1975a,
b), to describe sexually expressed neediness. Sexualization could be
clarified (Coen, 1981) by focusing on the defensive functions of
sexual behavior and fantasy, in contrast to sexual arousal and
pleasure. The patients reported by these authors made extensive use
of sex for defensive purposes.

Sexualization has been used to refer to three different levels of
phenomena, usually without clear differentiation among them. First,
there is description of behavior, ordinarily nonsexual, which seems to
have been transformed into something apparently sexual. Analysts
decide, in such cases, that the behavior is excessively sexual and that
predominantly nonsexual purposes are being served. An example of
this behavior is erotization of the transference, an extreme (usually
highly pathological) form of erotic transference, where the patient's

123

behavior does not fit what analysts ordinarily expect of analyzable patients. Most commonly, such patients regard the analyst as an idealized and omnipotent figure, who is to be seduced to provide them with love and closeness, to bring them to life and heal their emptiness, lethargy, and disturbed sense of self. The approach to the analyst is childishly seductive, with emphasis on exciting the analyst so that he will respond lovingly and sexually to the patient. Second, using the energic model, analysts propose that excessive amounts of libidinal energy have become attached to a mental process. This mental process may then be used in a substitutive way to cope with the associated libidinal energy, or it may lead to inhibition of function. Think, for example, of so-called mental masturbation, in which repetitive thought involves disguised erotic gratification. Third, sexualization was regarded as a process whereby aspects of severe narcissistic pathology may be defensively elaborated in some perverse behavior. For example, the self psychologists proposed that perversion especially aimed to manage problems with self-esteem and self-cohesion. In doing so, however, they did not consider sufficiently what this process of sexualization was or how it functioned.

Two themes have since become clearer and now warrant emphasis: sexualization precludes integration of what is wrong, especially destructiveness, and is centrally involved in defensive repetition within pathological object relationships. Although sexualization is prominently involved in perversion and sadomasochistic object relations, it also plays an important role in other forms of pathological dependency. Crucial to pathological dependency is the attempt to transform angry, critical feelings into something wonderful and exciting. How sexualized such efforts become to transform magically what is wrong will vary in pathologically dependent patients. The psychodynamic mechanisms of such attempted magical transformation in pathologically dependent patients share similarities with sexualization. Such attempts to turn badness into goodness, in the other and in oneself, do, indeed, often become sexualized; the reason, most likely, is that sexual feelings seem so effectively to transform one's perceptions and feelings from bad to good.

Others have been here before. The Marquis de Sade, in *The 120 Days of Sodom*, explicitly recommends sexualization for dealing with pain: "One has got to learn how to make the best of horror; there is in horror matter to produce an erection. . . . This thing, however frightful you wish to imagine it, ceases to be horrible for you immediately it acquires the power to make you discharge. . . . Nothing's villainous if it causes an erection" (p. 532). Again, Sade recommends in *Justine*, "There was nothing one ought not do in order to deaden in oneself that perfidious sensibility" (p. 460). In *The 120 Days of Sodom* Sade's narrator seeks to eradicate sentimentality, concern, and affection by replacing them with sensuality. The Duc reports (*The 120 Days of Sodom*, pp. 293–294) that the keenest delight he has known was murdering his mother. When a young girl, whose mother has recently died, cries at hearing this speech, the Duc has himself masturbated by an older woman so that his sperm ejaculates at the entrance to the girl's vagina. Sexualized use of others especially helps the Sadian hero to protect against intense need, wishes to surrender to others, and feared total destruction of them.

TOWARD A HYPOTHESIS: A CASE WITH PREDOMINANT USE OF A SEXUAL MODE OF DEFENSE

Let us return to Mr. X, whom I described in chapter 6. He had recently begun to regard the termination of his analysis as inevitable and desirable, even though he still felt overly attached to the analyst. When the analyst acknowledged as appropriate his wish to work toward the end of his analysis, among his feelings were hurt, rejection, and anger that the analyst would really be willing to let go of him. He wanted to remain as my only child, promising that he could satisfy me better than anyone else, male or female, could do. As he had earlier, he now once again attempted to seduce the narcissistic, self-absorbed analyst–mother, so that he and I would remain together forever.

Recall how Mr. X enacted his telephone perversion, by calling a male model with whom he arranged a date. He would then masturbate with the fantasy of seducing this man homosexually. He associated this with masturbatory fantasies of seducing a male student into having mutual masturbation. In these fantasies, he focused on observing how he is arousing the other one, who is helpless to resist him. He associated this wish with his wife and especially with the analyst. Earlier in the analysis, his bisexuality had been more prominent. In his telephone calls to male models, he would talk to the other man about the size of the latter's penis, while he masturbated to orgasm. We were able to work with these telephone calls as an acting out of the transference; the analyst was to respond excitedly to him.

Mr. X's emphasis in these vignettes was on maintenance of

omnipotent control via seduction and sadism, to reassure himself that he was the "irresistible seducer." This grandiose self-representation served to counter his fears of change and uncertainty as he approached the end of analysis and defended especially against fears of separateness from his analyst and his wife.

Earlier in the analysis, Mr. X had been a witty and entertaining storyteller and comedian. He would continually try to bring the analyst to life, to elicit a response, preferably a smile, but even irritability or annoyance would do. Better to actively provoke the analyst than have to endure the helplessness and humiliation of the depressed, self-absorbed analyst-mother's uninvolvement with him. Mr. X could feel sure the analyst-mother was engaged with him only when there was intense affective interaction. This hungry man especially longed for bodily contact, for something tangible he could grab hold of and trust.

In the analysis, Mr. X wished for and feared that his transference longings would be fulfilled with me. He lacked the assurance most analysands have that this fantasy enactment of transference is to remain imaginary. When I interpreted, in as nonseductive a manner as I could, that his reaching his hands behind the couch in an apparently absent-minded way expressed his wishes to touch and be touched by me, he thought that I, too, craved such contact, that we were both hot for each other; he became excited, frightened, and confused. That is, his hunger and excitement led to temporary interference with his reality sense.

His profound feelings of isolation and neglect contrasted with the danger that his incestuous wishes for his mother would be enacted. Mother and child each seemed to have longed for exciting body contact with the other, without the safeguard of adequate limits. Mr. X's mother was a depressed, infantile, self-absorbed woman who had had a postpartum depression following his birth and remained depressed during his childhood. She developed a disfiguring disease, probably just before he was conceived, but she linked his birth with the onset of her disease. The mother's father died when she was a small child. She and her sibling spent the following year in an orphanage, her own mother having then been unable to care for them. A sister, who had served as a mother substitute, had died not long before Mr. X was conceived. His father had been seen by Mr. X through mother's eyes as weak and ineffectual, but also, in contradiction, as a "gangster," a potentially violent hoodlum. This latter image of the father represented a projection of the mother's hostile aggression as well as the wish for an exciting, dangerous man to enliven her.

Mother had been very seductive with Mr. X, often exposing herself to him. She would encourage him to come into the bathroom while she was bathing, to hand her the towel, and then to dry her, rub her back, or dye her hair. At times, they would lie in bed beside one another. The plausible reconstruction was made, from Mr. X's transference behavior, fantasies, and dreams, that the mother had arranged and encouraged his seeing her masturbating anally, with his having become sexually excited and overstimulated by this behavior. There seemed little question from the analytic material that Mr. X's inert, depressed mother had come alive, especially during sexually stimulating experiences with him. Intense bodily stimulation, as we have reconstructed, seemed to have been used by the mother to counter her feelings of lethargy, depression, and deadness. This emphasis is not intended to minimize the mother's own expression of her sexuality toward her son or even the fact that this was a pleasurable and significant way for mother and son to share closeness.

It turned out that Mr. X had been frightened of actualizing his incestuous wishes with mother, fearful she would "egg [him] on," without providing reassurance and control that this teasing was just seductive play. Nevertheless, both Mr. X and his mother had focused defensively on the specialness of their sexually seductive relationship. Later in the analysis, Mr. X mourned the loss of this "specialness": "No other son has been allowed the intimacy my mother and I have shared." Underneath this specialness were intense feelings of depression, deadness, unresponsiveness, loneliness, rage, and humiliation. There were frequent fantasy and dream images of stone, statues, deadness, inertness. This deadness represented Mr. X's image of the dead, depressed mother and his introjection of this in the pattern of masochistic object relations. It also represented the deadening of his own sadism and the sadism he had introjected from mother, as well as his identification with mother's dead father and sister in the effort to bring them to life for her.

Mr. X had attempted to elaborate and cling to moments of narcissistic splendor in which the revitalized mother, by smiling at him, had allowed him to share in her grandeur and omnipotence. Masturbation and sexual seductiveness with others were employed to evoke and affirm images of self and other in excited reciprocal response to each other. Mr. X invested his self-image with the illusion of an omnipotent, irresistible seducer to counter the image of himself as unable to affect the unresponsive mother and his associated feelings of helplessness, rage, and depression. Personalization of the penis was similarly used dramatically to enact the relation between narcissistic mother and son. The patient "picked on [his] pecker" as his mother picked on him and his father, and he alternately treated his penis with contempt and reassured himself that he could affect and excite someone, that is, his own penis. He pretended that his penis was another person. Although the focus here is on the defensive and reparative functions of Mr. X's sexuality, there is no question that heterosexual, incestuous longings, as well as homosexual strivings, were prominent. Full analysis of Mr. X's defensive uses of sexuality would have to include the defensive interconnections among his heterosexuality, homosexuality, and autoerotism and how each simultaneously expressed and screened the others.

During the termination work, as earlier in the analysis, Mr. X feared and tried to assimilate the dangerous maternal imago, experienced then as frightfully envious and devouring. He sought to protect himself from the cannibalistic maternal introject by reassuring himself of his own omnipotence, of the analyst's omnipotence as idealized powerful father, or of his own omnipotent ability seductively to transform the analyst at will. Here seductiveness functioned in the service of the transformation of self and object images to preserve the illusion of omnipotent and pleasurable control of the representational world and the preservation of the self. Sexualization assisted Mr. X's efforts to evade dangerous destructiveness in himself and in the other. Avoiding integration of destructiveness represented the limits of Mr. X's analyzability, interfered with the achievement of full separateness, and so contributed to the persistent and intense wish for, and danger of, attachment to another.

HOW TO USE THE TERM SEXUALIZATION

Sexual fantasy and behavior, like all fantasy and behavior, subserve multiple functions and can be examined from many sides. Waelder's (1930) model of psychic acts had eight perspectives, representing the intersection of eight vectors: the outer world, the repetition compulsion, the id, the superego, and the ego's attempts to master each of these by assimilation into its own organization. Clearly, in sexualization, sexual fantasy and behavior blatantly express sexual and aggressive drive derivatives. In clinical examples of sexualization, however, defense has greater urgency and significance in the patient's motivational hierarchy than does sexual drive gratification. This formulation does not negate the sexuality in sexualization. Nor is sexualization equivalent to sexuality.

In my view, sexualization should be used only to designate

phenomenologically that aspect of sexual behavior and fantasy whose goals and functions are not sexual arousal and pleasure but defense. Sexualization implies no specific, underlying metapsychological concept other than motivation for defense. Hence, failure of defense, if it is presumed to be responsible for the intense sexual content of a psychic act, should not be regarded as sexualization. Since defense is always one possible perspective on behavior/fantasy, sexualization is always one possible way of viewing sexuality. For the term sexualization to be useful clinically, however, it should refer to the extensively elaborated, defensive use of sexual behavior and fantasy. In Waelder's model, sexual drive pressure and the ego's attempts to master this are used by the ego as a vehicle to express and master other conflicts. How sexualized defense is accomplished and why in this sexual way remain to be explained. So sexualization refers to the ego's defensive use of sexuality without further assumptions about mechanisms and purposes. When sexualization is described clinically, an attempt should be made to designate specifically which mechanisms have been used for defense and to provide a genetic hypothesis, if possible, as to why a sexual mode has been chosen.

Sexualization as defined here occurs not only in patients with perverse sexual behavior. Recall that in its broad meaning, as the defensive perspective from which sexual behavior and fantasy are viewed, sexualization is an aspect of all sexual activity. In its narrower meaning, as the extensively elaborated defensive use of sexual behavior and fantasy, sexualization may be found occasionally in all patients. It may be used as a predominant and repeated defense constellation by narcissistic, borderline, and psychotic patients. Far less frequently, it may, at times, be used by patients with neurotic character integration. The exception to this generalization involves patients with neurotic character integration and with prominent pathological dependency, especially with, but not limited to, sadomasochistic object relations or perversion. Elements of sexualized defense play an important role in all patients with pathological dependency, regardless of the level of their psychic organization.

Is there nondefensive sexualization, the "libidinization of ego functions"? To preserve clarity and consistency, I prefer to restrict the use of the term sexualization to defense. Hartmann (1950) referred to the use of certain ego functions for the expression of drive derivatives; however, he understood that failure of neutralization was involved in instinctualization of ego functions. He (1955; see also Kris, 1956a, p. 262) also assumed that defensive ego functions operate with less neutralized energy than autonomous ones. To my mind, this view implies that libidinization of ego functions requires failure of the ego's integrative and synthetic ability for neutralization, together with defensive ego activity simultaneously subserved by the expression of the drive derivatives that have influenced the given ego function. Kris's (1956a, b, c) clinical descriptions of the libidinization of the ego functions of memory, fantasy, and integration emphasized their nonsexual defensive purposes. For example, Kris's well-known discussion of the Proustian libidinization of reminiscence connected this with defense against object loss. Despite my emphasis on the ego's defensive use of sexuality in sexualization, note that libidinization of ego functions may represent concomitantly direct expression of drive derivatives. Libidinization of perception ("sexualized looking"), as an example, certainly does involve both defensive and drive expression functions. My argument is that we understand this phenomenon best by inquiring how the ego is using the particular ego function, ordinarily autonomous, as well as the given drive derivatives, that is, the genetic, structural, and adaptive factors that are involved.

A GENETIC HYPOTHESIS ABOUT SEXUALIZATION

Here I shall retrace my steps and present a genetic model for the development of sexualization, that derives from perverse patients. Such perverse patients are pathologically dependent. The reader will see striking similarities between the genetic roots of patients with sexualization and the more general group of patients with pathological dependency. In each, there is collusion between at least one parent and the child to focus on idealized, wonderful, often exciting aspects of their relationship in order to obscure for both parent and child what is wrong between them and within them. In each, the child identifies with the parent's predominant defensive style, which involves avoidance of facing internal conflict. In each, magical efforts are made to transform hatred and destructiveness into love, caring, or excitement.

For certain patients, most commonly regarded as perverse, who use sexualization extensively, sexualization was significantly involved in the mother's defensive activities and in the mother–child relationship. That the mother protects herself from oedipal conflict by a seductive pregenital relationship with the child provides only part of the explanation. The typical mother of such patients is a depressed woman with substantial impairment of her ability to relate to the child as a unique person in his own right. Mother, child, and usually

father, too, collude in protecting the mother from fully acknowledging the extent of her psychopathology. There may be an actual
injunction from the mother, usually supported by the father, that the
child not perceive accurately the mother's disorder and that he not
show mother in any way what is wrong with her.

This hypothesis draws on Khan's (1979) model of perversion. What
is emphasized here, however, is that the sexual seductiveness between mother and child is more than just one aspect of the mother's
psychopathology. The mother's use of a sexualized mode of defense
and the child's identification with this are stressed. The collusion
between mother and child involves mutually shared pleasure in their
most intense and intimate way of relating to each other and defensive
emphasis on the sexual stimulation between them.

Mother and child both focus on the external surface of the body, its
appearance, its sensations, as well as on hypochondriacal anxieties
and sexual feelings, instead of on what is inside, what each really
feels. Seductive bodily stimulation particularly helps the mother to
come alive, and she seeks this from the child. Intense bodily
stimulation has the effect of countering the mother's feelings of
lethargy, depression, and deadness. The mother focuses on her
sexual feelings to obscure her psychopathology, and she focuses, for
herself and the child, on their special, seductive relationship to
obscure her deficiency as a mother. The child identifies with mother's
mode of defense to preserve the object tie with her. This identification
involves additionally obscuring from himself clear knowledge of
mother's pathology and of the deficiencies in the mother–child
relationship. Sexual seductiveness eventually becomes the child's
predominant mode for relating to others and for expressing his
intense object hunger. For purposes of explication, the gratifying
aspect of the seductiveness with mother, in part interpreted by the
child as representing vitally needed maternal nurturance, is high-
lighted here. "My mother adores me!" becomes heady and irresistible, indeed. It becomes very tempting to focus on this seeming
maternal adoration to deny one's rage at the unloving aspect of the
mother. This exciting specialness intensifies clinging to the mother
and interferes with integration of the contrasting images and feelings
associated with her.

Because of the unpredictable quality of the mother's empathic
responsiveness to the child and the child's ensuing feelings of
helplessness, overstimulation, rage, and depression, his role as
enjoying with her a special, seductive relationship, forbidden to other
children, is emphasized defensively. At another level, feelings of
entitlement because of deprivation are used to defend against oedipal

guilt. The child focuses on his self-image as an omnipotent, irresistible seducer to counter his rage at feeling exploited and manipulated by mother for her own needs without significant recognition of himself as a unique, differentiated person. This defensively elaborated self-image is preserved and enhanced through masturbation fantasies. The ability to manipulate others, especially by sexual seduction, is also used to validate this grandiose self-image. Seduction, in fantasy or act, also represents the active repetition for mastery and pleasure of passively experienced infantile trauma, including childhood seduction and maternal deprivation.

When threatened, especially by feelings of helplessness, to affect an external object, such patients attempt to reassure themselves that they are, indeed, capable of inducing response, sexual response, from anyone, including themselves. Masturbation with fantasies of being an omnipotent, irresistible seducer is extensively elaborated so as to serve a central defensive role, with multiple functions in relation to narcissism, object relations (internal and external), painful affects, aggression, and attack by harsh superego forerunners, as well as the specifically sexual dangers of sexual aggression and fusion, homosexuality, and incest.

Patients who use sexualization extensively will tend to reassure themselves that they can transform the analyst by seduction into an idealized, omnipotent paternal object. This illusion reassures the patient against the risk of being left alone with the dangerous maternal introject. The father imago and the analyst as an ordinary human being cannot be relied on to protect the patient adequately from the maternal introject. The patient will attempt to elicit concrete proof of the analyst's omnipotence, which he then hypercathects and clings to like an amulet to preserve himself from destruction during the rage-filled confrontation with the maternal introject. Behind the image of the analyst's omnipotence, however, is the illusion of the patient's own omnipotent ability seductively to transform the object into a needed image. The analyst is not, at such times, regarded as if he represents a transference fantasy. On the contrary, there is a partial denial of the reality of the analyst's identity so as to feel omnipotently able to transform him at will and to clutch concretely at the illusion of omnipotence in the patient and in the analyst. A fantasy is not strong enough stuff to rely on for these patients.

It is not my intention to reduce sexualization in this genetic hypothesis to a theory of infantile trauma and seduction. I have outlined one infantile prototype for the predominance within the child's inner world of a sexualized mode of defense. Sexualization in other patients may have a completely different genetic background and serve other defensive functions. My current view is that sexualization functions dynamically in neurotic patients very much as I described in perverse patients. Even the genetic background I elaborated occurs in patients with neurotic character integration who use sexualization extensively. With neurotic patients, however, the contrasts between the good and bad mother seem sharper. The mother may, at times, be depressed, unavailable, and, at times, overly seductive. But this view of the mother is oversimplified, especially with neurotic patients. There is also an aspect of the mother that is able to be caring, empathic, and helpful to the child's forward and separate development. But the maternal attitude seems to be inconsistent; it is hard for the mother to remain the good mother, seeming to need mothering herself to sustain herself and her mothering role. Without sufficient nurturance, she tends to become depressed and more overtly and diffusely angry and to withdraw from appropriate child care. She seems to be in conflict about separateness between herself and the child. The healthier part of the mother wishes this for the child, while the infantile part of her wishes for unending attachment between them, so that the child can tend to her needs.

Blum's (1973) formulation of erotization in the neurotic patient as involving the active repetition of childhood traumatic seduction is congruent with my hypothesis but different in emphasis. So is his fourfold set of purposes of erotization as defense against hostility, loss, narcissistic injury, and homosexuality. Sexualization as defense against specifically sexual dangers, such as homosexuality, should not be overlooked. Also to be remembered are heterosexual incest, sexual aggression, and sexual dissolution. Gedo (1979, p. 184) postulated varying goals of sexuality in relation to levels of psychic organization. In order of increasingly mature organization these goals are: restoration of organismic equilibrium, confirmation of the integrity of the self, confirmation of gender identity, enhancement of personal worth, and subserving the creation of personal relationships. These goals, which are regarded as crucial to the level of psychic organization, must be accomplished in any way possible. Although I agree with Gedo, my question remains how and why sex has become implicated.

I agree with Blum's emphasis on a parental model of seductive style and superego corruption, together with instinctual overstimulation. Blum suggested that the parental denial of complicity in the seductiveness between parent and child, which is paradigmatic of parental superego corruption, especially contributes to similar superego pathology in the child. As emphasized throughout the present book, parental behavior and attitudes establish a model within the superego in which one need not be responsible for how he abuses others. My view is that sexual (sensual) feelings have played an unusually significant role during early development because of the mother's seductive overstimulation of the child, together with her relative neglect of his emotional needs. The child then draws on the predominantly available mode of relating with mother to compensate for her relative unavailability and to stimulate her renewed interest in him (see Brody, 1960; Escalona, 1963). Precocious sexual stimulation may have been used to deal with early traumatization and neglect (Greenacre, 1960). Sexual feelings are then intensely available early in life for defensive use by the ego. As previously described, identification with the mother's predominant mode of defense combines with the patient's need for defense against his painful affects and dangerous perceptions of her. Sexual overstimulation is mastered by active repetition and re-creation. I believe strongly that an unusually large quantity of aggression, from early frustration, teasing overstimulation, and deprivation, at times alternating with inconsistent parenting involving good enough care as well as indulgence, can be successfully defended against (avoided) through sexualization. Depression, loneliness, helplessness, and anxiety can all be assuaged by sensual bodily stimulation. Problems of tension regulation (understimulation as well as overstimulation) can be monitored by sensual self-stimulation. Last, I would point to the role of illusion and needs for omnipotent control offered by sexualization in those patients who use it as a predominant mode of defense.

Recall Dr. S from chapter 5. Although Dr. S and his mother did not share intensely sexual experiences, both certainly did focus on their joint specialness. Dr. S became adept at stimulating his depressed mother by reminding her of the wonderful things she could do for him. He would rouse her to participate with him by his enhancing her self-esteem and seducing her, in effect, once again to become his special, beautiful mother. Through this deception, they each camouflaged mother's disability, her rejection of the patient, and his rage, hurt, and disappointment with her. Idealization of the bits of goodness between the couple covered over and erased all that was wrong. Our other patients with pathological dependency have also had a parent–child relationship similar to the one that has been described here for sexualization.

MECHANISMS BY WHICH SEXUALIZATION SUBSERVES DEFENSE

By considering mechanisms by which sexualization serves defensive purposes, we can get closer to the ways that erotized repetition functions more generally in patients with pathological dependency. Further psychoanalytic study is needed of the mechanisms by which sexualized defenses function. Let us briefly outline those mechanisms well known from the psychoanalytic literature, and let us confine this review to masturbation, so that we can make our approach to this problem a little easier. These mechanisms can be grouped under five categories: (1) the role of bodily stimulation and sexual pleasure to counter painful feelings and fantasies, to feel more vital and alive, to achieve self-definition and self-cohesion, and to provide the illusory presence of another person—this illusion extends to identification with the comforting mother to restore the symbiotic duality; (2) illusions of omnipotent control obtained by self-sufficiently producing pleasure through one's own sexual act; (3) the illusory actualization of fantasies during masturbation. Alteration of consciousness aids partial denial of painful, intrapsychic reality and the substitution for it of the positive world of illusion; (4) attempted defense against hostile aggression: seduction of the aggressor, reaction formation, and concrete representation of self and object representations to demonstrate their preservation; and (5) sexual attempts at self-differentiation from the maternal introject: hypercathecting the self-representation as phallic and masculine; illusory recovery of the paternal phallus or of the male love object as father.

Note clearly that we are not attempting a general discussion of adult masturbation as an example of sexuality, but we are examining how it is used in the service of defense. The goals of the five mechanisms outlined, although to some degree generally applicable to all patients, apply especially to those who are more disturbed; the reason is that most psychoanalytic writing about sexualization has dealt with such patients. Extensive and repeated use of sexualization, as indicated, is most common among narcissistic and borderline patients. It is, however, to be found in neurotics, especially pathologically dependent patients, and occasionally sexualization can be used by anyone. I assume that, during development, masturbation and masturbation fantasies have been idealized as the patient's private world (as they were for Mr. X), his secret garden of delight, to which he retreats, separate and apart from the insufficiently available and inappropriately responsive parent, to comfort and soothe himself. In his masturbatory world he reigns supreme, able to produce his own pleasure. At the same time, he can amplify and cling to images of himself lovingly and sexually accepted by the (relatively) unloving parent. Masturbation may enhance illusions of omnipotent ability for magical manipulation. The masturbator's magical manipulation of his own genitals transforms them from a limp, dormant state into an excited, alive, erect, gravity-defying one, all under his own control and direction. The image of the genitals coming to life may serve as reassurance that the dead, fragmented self or inert or dead maternal imago can be resurrected. For the more disturbed patient, such masturbatory experiences may serve to validate the illusion that the representational world can be omnipotently and pleasurably manipulated and controlled. For all patients, and this function is common to the five listed mechanisms, masturbation assists attempts to transform negatively toned, aggressively infiltrated images of self and objects into more positive, pleasurably regarded ones.

Let us expand the concept of the "illusory actualization of fantasies" during masturbation. Nydes's (1950) idea was that with alteration of consciousness during masturbation, accompanying changes in body feeling states with increasingly sensual and tactile pleasure, the masturbator's fantasies become almost real. Nydes emphasized that these bodily changes enhanced illusions of power. Eissler (1958) and Lichtenstein (1970) stressed confirmation of existence during orgasm as well as attempted validation of certain unconscious fantasies about the nature of sexual reality (e.g., the phallic woman). This view is akin to the idea (Deutsch, 1932, 1944; Greenacre, 1960, 1968; Khan, 1965b) that the pervert needs to provide concrete representation to preserve self and object images, especially because of the fear of destruction.

Imagine that masturbation fantasy is enacted on a kind of stage. Onto this mental screen are projected the images of self and object(s) that will play in the masturbatory drama. The role of illusion is enhanced during sexual arousal by the continued alteration in body image, sensations, and state of consciousness, contributing to the intensely vivid existence of a drama between the masturbator and his internal object(s). During sexualization, especially for the more disturbed patient, the masturbatory stage serves as a screen for projection of negative, aggressive aspects of self and object(s). While feeling and watching the intensely pleasurable sexual sensations he produces in himself, the patient attempts to transform the negative, aggressive images of self and object into positive, excited, sexually responsive ones. Negative aspects of the self can be regarded as not-self, and feared, powerful aspects of the object can be regarded as properties of the self. Since his object is now so passionately responsive to him, the patient feels reassured that he need not lose, fear, hate, or destroy his object or himself. Seductive transformation of the harsh parental superego presence is attempted in the screen of the masturbatory stage; an invigorated, more accepting superego presence is reintrojected, further validating the self as good, alive, and whole. A dangerously aggressive confrontation between self and other has been treated as a make-believe ceremony, a ritualized masturbatory game. The heightened sense of illusion aids denial of the enduring validity of each discrete (painful) image or affect. In this masturbatory world of illusion, bad becomes good, good becomes bad, self and other may be interchanged; nothing is or need be the way it seems. The scene is concluded with reintrojection, by vision and touch, of the transformed self and object images. Variations on the theme of the masturbatory transformation of images in sexualization include use of a mirror as well as impersonation. There is a need for concrete representation of internal fantasy images so as to render them more valid and credible. There is, then, a spectrum of need for, as well as ability to accomplish, the illusory actualization (and transformation) of fantasies during sexualization.

Condensation of oedipal strivings with primitive aggression has been reported as typical of the borderline patient (Kernberg, 1974). Sexual feelings may then be so interwoven with primitive aggression that they become frightening rather than exciting. The patients I have referred to so far use sexualization successfully enough for defense against aggression so as to experience fantasies of sexual aggression as pleasurable. Indeed, such fantasies reassure the patients against the fear of destruction of the object or of the self during fantasied sexual union. Sadomasochistically elaborated illusions of omnipotent domination and control help provide such reassurance. Other patients, instead, become terrified by fantasies of sexual aggression. I assume they are unable to preserve the exciting illusion of transformation of bad into good, so that their destructiveness returns in too raw a form. This second group of patients requires further defense against the dangers of sexual destruction. Autoerotism, fetishism, and homosexual object choice in behavior or fantasy may serve as regressive defenses against dangerously aggressive heterosexual wishes. This second group of patients includes some who must find a way to represent their fantasies concretely.

The explanation that splitting mechanisms allow the simultaneous expression of both primitive aggression and oedipal trends is correct but does not clarify sufficiently the complex layering of sexual and aggressive drive gratification and multiple defensive functions. Any sample of sexual fantasy or behavior may simultaneously represent heterosexual, homosexual, and autoerotic pleasure, as well as multiple defensive needs in relation to aggression and sexuality, object relations, and narcissism, all in complex interrelationship. A suitable psychoanalytic stance would be to regard such material as manifest content to be investigated for its latent meanings, in relation to drive and defense. For example, the borderline patient's fantasies of incest with the mother may represent all of the following simultaneously: oedipal sexual strivings; the wish for full differentiation out of maternal symbiosis versus the wish for fusion; validation of narcissistic needs for specialness, entitlement, and reparations; defense against the acknowledgment of dependent need by validation of the self-image as a tough, insensitive, lusty "mother-fucker"; substitution of sexual longings for greed and hunger; defense against homosexual wishes; defense against murder of the unloving mother or the despised part of the self (see Margolis, 1977, for some formulations about consummated mother–son incest).

Now let us connect these mechanisms in sexualization with pathologically dependent patients who are not perverse. Their use of sexualized defense, when this is focused upon in treatment, may make them seem perverse. We shall return to this distinction shortly. Recall Mrs. C from chapter 7, who as a child had had surgical removal of an endocrine tumor and who continued as an adult to feel ugly and defective. She enjoyed dressing up in black hose and garter belt and playing phallic dominatrix to her husband. Mrs. C's heterosexual and homosexual fantasies were of getting the other person to respond intensely to her while she remained aloof. She had conscious wishes to have a penis so that she would feel intact and powerful, able to penetrate the other, while she protected herself from passively giving in to needing the other person. Yet despite her terror of passivity, she was pathologically dependent. Mrs. C used sexualization to reverse feelings of helplessness, passivity, humiliation, ugliness, and defectiveness. Or remember Ms. R from chapter 7, who stuffed toilet paper in her panties so as to pretend she had a penis, especially with the meaning that she could enter and repair her depressed mother. Like Mrs. C, she had homosexual fantasies of seducing and arousing other women so that they would love and respond to her, as her mother had not. Or remember Dr. S from chapter 5, who wished to have women touch him so that he could pretend to be with his mother. In doing so during the analysis, he attempted to avoid his need, hurt, disappointment, and rage at the analyst's unavailability. Like Mr. X, he attempted to emphasize how special he was in being able to get whatever he wanted through his sexualized defense, rather than to face his powerful negative feelings. In these examples, sexualization in pathological dependency attempts narcissistic repair and the revival and transformation of a disappointing object relationship, so that rage, hatred, hurt, and disappointment need not be integrated.

Sexualization is effective in the temporary transformation of negatively toned, aggressively infiltrated images of self and objects into more positive, pleasurably regarded ones. It can become addictive and used repetitively for defense; then we regard it as erotized repetition. Through sexualization, some patients may elaborate aspects of a grandiose self-representation as an omnipotent, "irresistible seducer," which can then serve a central defensive role with multiple functions in relation to narcissism, object relations, painful affects, aggression, and superego conflict, as well as specifically sexual dangers. This grandiose self-representation is preserved and enhanced via masturbation and sexual seduction. The patient pretends that he can manipulate and control his inner world omnipotently and pleasurably. Nydes's (1950) concept of the "illusory actualization of fantasies" during masturbation has been elaborated into a mechanism whereby such sexualized transformations can occur within the representational world.

The more a patient feels pressured to eliminate what feels unbearable within himself, the more he may need to act in exciting ways, with the aim of transforming the bad into something that seems, for the moment, to be good. Since the illusory transformation does not last long, the patient feels driven to repeat the exciting, sexualized action again and again. Remember that such action can occur only within one's mind, on one's own body, or actually in relation to another person. Remember, too, that the power to get another person to respond, seemingly against his will, may be linked to varying degrees of sexual arousal. Exciting repetitive behavior includes getting the other person to react in sexual ways, in loving ways, or even in angry, rejecting ways. So long as the patient can demonstrate his omnipotent ability to induce response in the other, he can counter feelings of helplessness, neglect, and unimportance. Patient and partner play at reassuring the other that each cannot live without the other—heady reassurance, indeed! Since this reassurance is intended to cover all that is wrong within and between them, it must be endlessly repeated. Note the key role of sadism and the illusion of omnipotence in such behavior, what we would call sadistic, omnipotent control: "I can make you feel what I want you to feel, and you can't stop me!" Sadistic omnipotent control is the bridge to sadomasochistic object relations and more generally to all forms of pathological dependency, within which it plays a key role.

9

SUPEREGO ASPECTS OF ENTITLEMENT

Previous discussions of entitlement have emphasized the right to reparations and exemption from ordinary laws and morality because of past misfortune, as well as defense against varied danger situations involving negative feelings and negative self-images. My approach is congruent with certain writings about entitlement (Jacobson, 1959; Rothstein, 1977), although my emphasis is on defense against superego criticism.

Defectiveness, deprivation, and entitlement are to be regarded especially as attempts to placate the superego in the face of unacceptable destructive (and sexual) urges. That is, they should be regarded as justifying one's destructiveness: "It is because of what I've missed!" The "oral" clamor of deprivation and entitlement, together with dependency, submissiveness, and defensive uncertainty, screens hostile, aggressive wishes from every developmental level, preoedipal as well as oedipal. Typically, attitudes of entitlement are contradictory, unclear, and wavering. This contradiction results from conflict among differing ego ideal images and conflict among superego, ego, and id, about the sadistic extractiveness in these attitudes. Entitlement combines attempts to seduce the superego and to express sadistic, extractive drive derivatives. Entitlement involves a quality of perverse misuse of others in exploitative or extractive ways; sadism, to varying degrees, is a central feature.

The patients I describe are rigid character types. They differ from patients with more typical narcissistic personality disorders in having less of a firm conviction of their own specialness and entitlement to have what they want. Their entitlement always argues against opposite feelings. In this sense, we can think of negative entitlement, of not feeling entitled to the psychological essentials of life. Such patients cannot be sure they have the right to what they want, so long as they must compulsively (and defensively) undermine themselves and ask the opinions of their objects, internal and external. From negative positions (defective, unlovable, worthless), patients clamor about feeling cheated, deprived, and entitled, so as to justify their own rage and destructiveness. We will consider psychoanalytic tasks in the analysis of attitudes of entitlement.

The reader is referred to Rothstein's (1977) discussion of the literature on entitlement. This chapter should be considered complementary to Rothstein's, with specific focus on superego aspects of entitlement in certain rigid characters. Rothstein outlined a variety of defensive functions served by ego attitudes of entitlement in narcissistic patients, especially in relation to feelings of rage, helplessness, and separateness. He, too, considered a need for defense against accurate perception of the parents (mother) because of these affects as well as a deficiency in maternal relatedness. Separation-individuation has been incomplete, with defensive clinging to fused good self and object images.

Although Jacobson (1959) considered Richard III as having a superego defect, she discussed a "dangerous masochistic need for punishment" (p. 133), either hidden by feeling oneself to be an exception or as a defense against an underlying rebellion. This view seems similar to the view expressed in this chapter of contradictory attitudes toward entitlement as involved with superego conflict. Levin (1970) noted that excessive and restricted attitudes of entitlement may occur in combination. Murray (1964) implied that attitudes of entitlement protect against and justify destructive wishes. It should be noted that attitudes of entitlement and feeling oneself to be an exception refer to similar issues (Freud, 1914, 1916; Jacobson, 1959), although this similarity has not been made explicit. In clinical discussions, analysts tend to use the terms interchangeably, without, however, consciously acknowledging this use. From my perspective, what one is entitled to and what one is an exception to relate to similar attempts to influence the superego, so as to feel acceptable in the face of one's own hatred and destructiveness. What I emphasize with regard to pathological dependency, in contrast to earlier discussions of entitlement, is defense against superego criticism in the face of one's own dangerous impulses. The emphasis is shifted from past grievances, reparations, (defensive) orality, and dependency, to current dynamic conflict in which extenuating circumstances (exception, entitled, cheated, deprived, defective) are argued before the superego to justify hostile aggression (and sexuality).

VARIETIES OF ENTITLEMENT: SOME VIGNETTES

Dr. G complained that every ordinary misfortune of life that befell her was further proof that nothing ever worked out in her favor. Chronically angry, envious, demanding, insatiable, she continually felt cheated and mistreated. She got fewer patient referrals than her colleagues, and she, unlike them, was not appointed to important staff committees at her hospital. Dr. G found it very difficult to explore her own demandingness within her analysis. Her early life gave her good reason to feel what she did. She felt entitled to have whatever she wanted, while simultaneously feeling she would never have what she wanted.

In analysis Dr. G developed an intense maternal transference, within which she consistently and insistently demanded that her life be made easier by the analyst through various accommodations to her: mother–analyst and daughter could each exploit the other. Dr. G had great difficulty in differentiating transference from reality, maintaining her reality sense when her angry neediness interfered, acknowledging her entitled attitude, and connecting her self-criticisms with her "crimes." Partly, she struggled against feeling subservient to the analyst–mother, who set the rules and made the decisions (interpretations), by arguing and not agreeing. More specifically, Dr. G kept insisting that the frustrations and deprivations of her analysis were greater than those of anyone else she knew in analysis. There was marked resistance to acknowledgment of the transference repetition in this behavior especially of her own aggressive demandingness.

She was jarred when the analyst repeatedly emphasized the awfulness of being stuck within a destructive, mother–daughter, mutually exploitative relationship, which barred any possibility of freely offered concern, affection, or love. She protested that she only did the same as the analyst and others did to her. The analyst interpreted that her insistence that each did the same to the other protected her from guilt about her intentions toward the analyst. She was then able to feel that her destructiveness was inappropriate, that the analyst did not, indeed, deserve this.

In general, Dr. G found it difficult to accept responsibility for her destructiveness so that it counted and so that she would wish, more consistently, to change it. She had tried so hard to convince herself she was not bad; by the same token, if she was bad, then so was the analyst. If the analyst was bad, then Dr. G did not have to fear having loving and sexual feelings for him, which frightened her. Heterosexual loving and sexual feelings toward the analyst entailed destructive, competitive rivalry with mother and theft and appropriation of the paternal penis, together with other fantasies of aggressive sexual hunger. Infantile dependency defended against such dangerous womanly wishes. Dr. G needed to keep protecting herself by justifying her angry hunger as derived from current (and recurrent) deprivation and mistreatment.

Mr. H was a successful opera singer who sought analysis when his career temporarily flagged and he felt depressed. He felt angry and hurt that he was not better appreciated and offered the parts he wanted. He sensed that he turned others off by his depressed and complaining style, and feared this made him less desirable when he auditioned. Mr. H felt enraged about having to audition, demanding, instead, immediate and unconditional acceptance. He felt comfortable performing only when he had already been accepted for a role. During rehearsals, he felt angry and indignant at direction and criticism. Even once he felt secure in a role, he remained overly sensitive to, and demanding of, the audience's enthusiastic admiration of him. With friends, wife, and analyst, he was tyrannical; if he did not get his own way and was not the center of attention, which he greedily craved, he would withdraw into silence and sulk. He was indignant when the analyst arrived at the office only ten minutes before a session. He wanted more time to go to the bathroom, relax, and sit in the waiting room before a session.

Mr. H was a rigidly controlled man. At times, he could feel angry, but frequently, instead, he experienced somatic expressions of his angry feelings. Mr. H emphasized how special and indulged he had felt with his mother. Although this indulgence, indeed, seemed to have been one aspect of his experience with her, as it was reflected and investigated in the transference, he felt special only so long as he enhanced the mother–analyst's own self-esteem. Mother's indulgence turned out to have entailed a destructive infantilizing of him, which led him to feel undermined as a competent boy. Father had seemed distant, depressed, and envious of the mother's narcissistic relationship with Mr. H. Coexisting with his sense of himself as special and entitled was a sense of being unwanted, inept, and worthless. He gradually became aware of his rage at his mother's decidedly conditional acceptance of him and her exploitation. Like the other patients described here, Mr. H found it very difficult to stay with his angry perceptions and criticisms of his parents and analyst. It was especially difficult for him to accept his lonely, isolated, unloved feelings, which contradicted his feeling special. Indeed, he had felt so unwanted and afraid of abandonment that he had been under great pressure to constrict his experience of his world and remain submissive to his mother. His rage at feeling unloved and unwanted was split off and displaced. His worried, complaining, self-critical approach to others and to the analyst expressed his hunger for connectedness in identification with his mother's own style. He emphasized feelings of disability and deprivation as pleas for connectedness with parents and analyst. Here entitlement is used as a mode of relatedness.

Mrs. C (see chapter 7) is the woman who had a sudden transformation at age five; an endocrine tumor altered her appearance, threatened her life, and left her with some permanent, disfiguring symptoms. Recall, however, that as an adult she was objectively a very attractive woman, at least as far as her appearance went. To my mind, what marred her were not her scars, which were invisible to me, but her character ugliness. She continued to feel entitled to attack her son, husband, and others for their failings. She exempted herself from the responsibility of managing her own rage and destructiveness. If she felt angry, critical, and dissatisfied, as she felt most of the time, she believed she had the right to dump these feelings on the other person. Or she could easily justify why she should have what she wanted, whether a very expensive watch or fur coat to enhance herself or her husband's being just the way she thought he should be. Indeed, the self-justification for her angry, destructive, and greedy wishes tended to preclude analysis. Nobody was going to interfere with her now! At least much of the time, it was difficult to arrest her attention so that she felt troubled about her own internal conflicts. Her childhood trauma, sadistic mistreatment, and deprivation excused her demandingness, rage, and destructiveness. What was wrong was now the problem of others; they were to repair this because they owed it to her. When such entitled self-justification failed to defend Mrs. C against her sadistic superego, she felt intense self-loathing. Recall from chapter 7 that when her son felt suicidal, Mrs. C could neither contain her own self-hatred nor work with it in analysis. At this point we interrupted her analysis and sat her up. From this perspective, her entitled defense was needed to support her self-esteem against the harsh superego, especially the sadistic maternal introject.

Through her treatment, Mrs. C eventually learned to become

somewhat more empathic with her son's difficulties. She would emphasize that the analyst had taught her about empathy, which she had experienced little of in her early years. Intellectually, she could understand the analyst's interpretation that she displaced her feelings of defectiveness onto her husband and son and then attacked them for these failings. Or she could understand that she identified with fate as an attacking avenger, ever ready to get her husband and son for their imperfections. Nevertheless, she had great difficulty working in treatment with her vengeful destructiveness. She would repeatedly insist she was only responding to the aggression of her son or husband; nobody else would be able to tolerate their behavior.

Early in the treatment, Mrs. C had little awareness of what she had lived through (her illness and surgery; her relationship with her narcissistic and sadistic mother) and little compassion for herself. She felt that mother had forbidden such an attitude. Even later in treatment, she found it very difficult to maintain an attitude of compassion for herself and to connect her current rage and "bitchiness" with anger about her life. She continued to dissociate herself from her awful experiences, as if they had happened to someone else. The analyst could often help to calm her frequent destructive tirades against son and husband by relating her outrage to what she had felt and still felt about how she saw herself—as an ugly, scarred monster. She would suddenly soften, look quizzically at the analyst, and ask in a subdued, childlike voice, "It really was that bad, wasn't it?" One day she reported a variant of a repetitive dream: "I was in the bathroom with J [son]. I was on the toilet, having a bowel movement. A large piece of feces came out, and it and the water in the bowl overflowed. I tried to keep it in the bowl, but it went all over the place. I felt badly that it would get on J." The analyst said to her that she wished she could contain her "shit" and not take it out on her son but that her controls over her anger were poor; she felt moved and troubled about herself. Although she could acknowledge that she was an angry woman, she had to struggle consistently to ward off negative transference with the analyst. She said for the first time, "Sometimes I feel so angry in these sessions that I can't do anything productive but just give vent to it!" Typically, she quickly repressed this insight.

Terror of passivity (from her childhood traumata), wishes for control, and identification with the doer (fate) kept her in the role of an avenger. She repeatedly tried to do to others what had happened to her. Her sexual fantasies and behavior largely involved narcissistic support for her attractiveness and desirability, with the other, man or woman, responding to her caresses, while she kept herself aloof.

Within the treatment also, it was very difficult for her to maintain a (passive) reflective stance, and, unconsciously fearful of attack, she had to stay active by changing the subject, usually by picking on others. Mrs. C's entitlement, because of her childhood trauma, allowed her to disown responsibility for what her superego found so disgusting in her, her sadism and destructiveness. Her mother had responded with disgust to both her childhood loss of attractiveness and her anger. Mrs. C's terror of rejection by her superego because of these failings (ugliness) precluded her becoming responsible, in an ongoing way, for her own hatefulness, which she continually attributed to others.

Mr. E (see chapter 7) is the man with multiple physical defects (virtual blindness without lenses; a small skin tag on the underside of his penis; an extra, small lobe on one ear; a nevus on his buttocks; small stature as a child; left-handedness) who regarded himself (unconsciously) as defective. He had more difficulty acknowledging his feelings of deprivation than the other patients reported. He was afraid really to feel sorry for himself. After seeing the film *Careful, He Might Hear You*, his lover wanted him to hug her, because she had felt identified with the unhappiness of the child in the film. Mr. E was critical of the film and of his lover's behavior and was annoyed at such childishness. His lover, also in analysis, correctly interpreted to him that he was afraid of how much he wanted to be hugged.

Similarly, feelings of entitlement and angry, vengeful feelings were more hidden and dissociated from consciousness by Mr. E than by the other patients. On the surface was Mr. E's "negative entitlement," that is, the attitude that he was entitled to very little, that he was so terrified of rejection that he was content just to be kept around. Indeed, because of his terror of being discarded as defective, he masochistically restrained his desires and hostile aggression, so as to placate the hateful, rejecting other. Slowly through his analysis, we were able to liberate a more positive, insistent, even demanding entitlement that others regard him with respect, at least as an equal. Then later we could open up his sadistic, dominating, and vengeful feelings to be the boss and force others to feel humiliated and submissive.

Invariably, Mr. E needed to justify his anger, especially toward me in the transference, as realistically derived. His conscience would not tolerate his feeling angry unless he had a good excuse. The "excuse" was his childhood trauma: his defects and the deprivation and sadism with which he had been raised. It was not just that ultimately this trauma is what he felt angry about but that whenever he felt anger, he needed to justify it, indeed, to plead that he was entitled to feel angry. On the contrary, what he often sought to demonstrate was that he was now entitled to others' (analyst's) providing him what he had missed, so that he did not have to hate his mother for having hated him.

Although his behavior indicated the feeling, he did not feel how defective he regarded himself to be; his sense of defect had been largely split off and denied. Remember that I only discovered Mr. E's defects accidentally after a year of analysis. Mr. E's terror that others would ridicule or reject him as defective had paralyzed him emotionally. As a result, he had felt under great pressure to be compliant, not to think for himself, not to have his own wants and needs.

He was very afraid of the anger that lurked beneath his sense of himself as defective, anger in himself and anger in his parents toward him. He attempted to avoid anger in himself and in the other by passive submission to others' views and narcissistic needs of him. At a Thanksgiving weekend at a friend's house, toward the end of the meal, Mr. E assumed he was free to devour, without asking, what remained of two of his favorite foods. Later, his girlfriend pointed out to him that he should first have asked and that she knew their hosts had wanted more of these delicacies. Mr. E felt angry and criticized by her remark. He was not in touch with what seemed obvious to his girlfriend and then to the analyst: a hunger to be indulged and to have what he wanted. On the contrary, what he felt was fear that others would be critical of his having anything he wanted. It was only later in the analysis, as Mr. E would recall this incident, that he could tolerate feeling what he had enacted. Now he could feel how much he wanted to push everyone else out of the way, so as to grab the good stuff of which he felt so long deprived. Later, Mr. E could tolerate transiently feeling greed, rage, demandingness, sadism, hatred, and competitiveness, but these were very difficult for him to stay with and integrate.

Early in the analysis Mr. E was very compliant, terrified I would neither accept him nor keep him unless he kept me satisfied. He then seemed anything but demanding and entitled! Mr. E would feel pressured and self-critical if he could not confirm what I interpreted to him. The analyst must be correct, and Mr. E must be deficient. He was astounded when I told him that the analyst's interpretations could not always be valid or therapeutically useful and that Mr. E's responses and associations would help to determine if they were. Similarly, he felt very hesitant to follow his own leads and inclinations in free association.

Mr. E felt he had to justify his anger with the analyst; there had to be a good reason for him to feel angry. His conscience would not tolerate his being angry with me, unless he could demonstrate that I had failed somehow at being therapeutic. He feared that I would not tolerate his resentment unless he could persuade me that it was reasonable. He began to feel disappointed and angry that the analyst did not actually provide him with loving warmth and then was angry at the analyst as a transference version of the rejecting, distant parents. In the fantasy of being damaged was the reassurance that he could not damage others, that he did not have it in him. He then expressed wishes for revenge; sadistic wishes to humiliate others by exposing their defects and to dominate and control others; and especially the demand that he be regarded with respect and appreciation as a worthwhile person.

DISCUSSION

Each of these patients showed a striking contrast between feelings of defectiveness or worthlessness and a special, entitled attitude that he was allowed what others were not. A view of entitlement as involving demands for reparations for past mistreatment is certainly relevant here but may overly emphasize past grievances, with the risk of insufficient attention being paid to its current psychological purposes. Focus on the defensive functions of entitlement (Rothstein, 1977) helps to clarify its contemporary dynamic functions.

Each of these patients had been under great pressure to constrict his perceptions, evaluations, and feelings so as to preserve an insecure relationship with a hostile parental imago. Each patient had had a demanding, rejecting, narcissistic mother by whom he had felt unloved. Each had an intense fear of abandonment and a prominent sense of defectiveness, undesirability, or unlovability. As a result these patients felt great internal pressure to believe in a parental worldview in order to make their childhood tolerable and to lessen the dangers of abandonment and rejection. Because of the dangers of unacceptabilty and rejection, developing ideals and standards were overly skewed toward compliance with internal and external objects (Sandler, Holder and Meers, 1963). Identification with the hostile parental imago was most marked in Mrs. C but also present in each of the other patients. This identification did not indicate integration of the introject within the ego or superego as a metabolized identification (Rapaport, 1957). Rather, this identification was defensive, aimed especially at reducing feelings of guilt, helplessness, and anxiety (Sandler, 1960). Dread of the superego was intense in all patients, including Mrs. C ("the avenger"), and required them to avoid awareness of their own "badness." Character rigidity was manifest by fearfulness toward experiencing one's own feelings and wishes, great pressure to conform to internal parental standards, mistrust and undermining of themselves, and idealization of, and submission to, parental authority (Shapiro, 1981).

For the two patients with a physical sense of defect, accurate perception and evaluation of self and others (parents) had been interfered with by parental injunction. (see chapter 7). The sense of defect was offered up to a parent as an appeasement and seduction, aiming to help the parent feel better about himself by agreeing that the child was, indeed, the cause of what was wrong. This mechanism applied, to a degree, to the other two patients as well; they did not, however, experience such actual parental injunction against accurate use of the ego functions of perception and evaluation. These two patients also clung simultaneously to illusions of specialness in submission to mother and her views.

All patients manifested defensive confusion about what was wrong and in whom it was located. This confusion applied especially to feelings of defectiveness and to hostile aggression. Who the worthless, unlovable one was and who the bad one was were central organizing questions for these patients. What was most difficult was consistently to face their own hatred and destructiveness and the hatred and destructiveness in the parents. To a degree, it could be reconstructed that all these patients had felt rejected, unwanted, exploited, criticized, or ridiculed in childhood, as they now felt. Such awful expectations were their psychic reality and certainly seemed to have once been their actual experience with the parents. What should be emphasized, however, are the dynamic functions played by the hostile, rejecting parental introject within the patient's psyche. For a patient (child) who is so afraid of abandonment and unacceptability, it is comforting and reassuring to feel the presence of such a parental introject, even when the latter is critical or rejecting (Schafer, 1960). The introject becomes the repository for, as well as the guardian against, the patient's (child's) unacceptable strivings (aggressive and libidinal). These very angry patients are afraid of their anger and of abandonment and unacceptability.

Their intense anger can be largely explained by their past trauma and relationships with a cruel mother and a distant, neglectful father who abandoned the patient to the mother. Superego development was uneven and incomplete, with persistence of harsh, primitive, personified superego forerunners, which had not been fully tamed during oedipal phase conflict and resolution. These patients varied as to oedipal phase progression. The two patients with physical defects had phallic-narcissistic derivatives but had not fully entered into the passions of oedipal conflict. The other two patients had progressed further; preoedipal and oedipal conflict each served to screen the other. None of the patients could be regarded as having had a mature superego. They were unable autonomously to regulate their own self-esteem, impulses, and affects. A dependent relationship with another (internal and external) served these functions. Unable to rely on and to trust themselves and what was inside themselves (and to regulate this), these patients remained rigid, frightened of their own internal "monsters." They were also afraid of the loss of dependent protection and of their rage at such loss.

The repetitive enactment of placing others in the role of one's own judge has two layers. First, there is the repetition of feeling "bad" and angry in relation to a rejecting parent, now with the external assistance of another person who is to modulate and survive the fantasied destructive relationship. Second, there is the wish to escape one's own internal judgments about "badness" and one's "crimes" by relying on the opinions of others. Finding fault outside oneself is contributed to, in part, by relative developmental failure. Such faultfinding indicates a relative inability to assess reality (and oneself) accurately. It also has the dynamic meaning that others have failed the patient, that something further is required from outside for the patient to progress further. Such external faultfinding contributes to the sense of entitlement and of being an exception in its emphasis on what must be obtained from others.

Each mother (and Dr. G's father) had altered the sense of reality to serve internal needs, confused the patient as to what was real, and encouraged identification with the model that reality is not to be reasonably and clearly defined. This parental behavior provided the background for a superego that need not accurately assess reality in the service of adaptation (Nunberg, 1932; Rapaport, 1957; Furer, 1972) but sanctions demands that the external world accommodate itself to the patient's pressing needs. Denial and mistrust of perceptions and feelings were prominent in each patient.

Conviction that one is unacceptable and threatened with abandonment and rejection leads to intense character rigidity: extreme efforts are made toward compliance with parental dictates and restriction of one's own needs, affects, perceptions, and ideas. Each patient felt himself to be unlovable and unacceptable as he was. To be tolerated by others required special efforts of accommodation to others' needs. To feel tolerated required complicated defensive efforts against intense superego criticism. Thus, these patients both hungered for narcissistic supplies to feel lovable and made strenuous efforts to persuade their own conscience that they were not bad, deficient, or disgusting. Feelings of entitlement played a prominent role in defense against such harshly critical superego judgments. Entitlement established a position of specialness, of being better than and more deserving than others, a position that defended against terrible feelings and perceptions of self and of others. Feelings of deprivation, mistreatment, and entitlement are exploited by the patient to justify his own unacceptable impulses from every developmental level, especially destructiveness from preoedipal conflict as well as from phallic-oedipal conflict. "It is because of what I've missed" and "I've been cheated" become rallying cries to justify destructiveness and to avoid responsibility for it. The patient is continually arguing, as if before a judge, that there have been extenuating circumstances. Simply to feel angry, without explanation or justification, is frightening, as if the patient will then be condemned as irreparably bad, defective, or disgusting. All patients could transiently acknowledge their own exploitative, demanding, and destructive attitudes toward others. Relinquishing the entitlement to infantile need satisfaction (Murray, 1964) and struggling with his own destructiveness as a psychoanalytic issue, rather than justifying it, were the foci for each analysis.

To feel entitled and to have and to do as one pleases derive from past trauma, deprivation, or abuse; from identification with parental attitudes of exploitation or extractiveness (Rothstein, 1977); from teasing overstimulation when coupled with neglect or alternating indulgence and deprivation; and from the parental model that the superego need not assess reality accurately. Included in these latter three factors is the parental example of (perverse) misuse of object relations for need satisfaction without sufficient regard for the needs of the other (especially the child). Entitlement involves this quality of (perverse) misuse of others in exploitative or extractive ways; sadism, to varying degrees, is a central feature. The spectrum of attitudes of entitlement extends to more severe superego pathology, intense sadism and destructiveness, highly exploitative and parasitic object relations, and pathological narcissism (O.F. Kernberg, 1984). It is beyond the scope of this chapter to discuss fully all such forms of malignant entitlement. We should note, however, the tendency of some of these patients simultaneously to attempt to seduce the superego and to express sadistic, extractive drive derivatives: "I am allowed to do what is forbidden!" It is precisely this attitude, that one is allowed what is forbidden to others, that enables attitudes of entitlement to aid the expression of multiple forbidden wishes, such as we see in other forms of malignant entitlement. We should note, too, that what is most forbidden to the patient and what he yet expresses in the entitled state may not at all be what he connects consciously or preconsciously with the sources of, and rationale for, his entitlement. For example, Mr. X exploited feelings of entitlement, derived from deprivation, his genital defect, and the inconsistently seductive relationship with his mother, to justify his wishes to seduce and castrate the analyst. Because of all he had already suffered, he was now free to do as he pleased! Of course, he needed to keep arguing and justifying this position to his conscience, which sought to repay him in kind for his exploitative and destructive wishes. It is especially impressive how patients with pathological dependency cloak their phallic-oedipal desires with orally entitled justifications.

Although it may appear on the surface as if malignant entitlement serves primarily for drive expression rather than also for superego defense, this view is not correct. Defense is necessary against criticism about sadism and extractiveness from a poorly integrated superego with harshly aggressive, personified, superego fore-runners.[1] In addition to the defensive techniques already discussed, patients with malignant entitlement tend to make the other, rather than themselves, feel guilty and expiatory through their sadistic demandingness and their use of projective identification. Parasitism and exploitation of others are justified, consciously and uncon-sciously, by intense rage at aggressively distorted parental figures for their neglect, mistreatment, or abuse. Sadomasochistic bonding in such (parasitic, exploitative) object relations, external and internal, attenuates the felt dangers of destruction and separation.

In pathological dependency, patients' feelings of entitlement are contradictory, unclear, and wavering. The clamor that they are entitled always argues against opposite feelings, that they have no such right, that they are confused about what should be their fair share. On the one hand, ego and superego seem to sanction these entitled demands. On the other hand, there is awareness of the sadistic extractiveness of such attitudes, so that the patient must disown them. Simultaneously, these patients maintain and repudiate entitled attitudes and keep themselves defensively confused as to what they believe. Ego ideal images of being good, considerate, and respectful conflict with images that one should have what one needs (and has missed). The rigid character types described here seem to differ from more typical narcissistic personality disorders in that these patients have less conviction of their own specialness and entitle-

---

[1] See Glover (1964) and chapters 13 and Appendix in this volume about a similar need for defense against sadism in perversion.

ment. These patients have not felt sufficiently and consistently indulged by a narcissistic parent to be able to maintain a grandiose, entitled view of themselves. To be sure, some narcissistic defensive overvaluation of themselves, as well as ambivalent entitlement, is present. Dependency wishes, however, together with self-under-mining as defense against, and punishment for, unacceptable impulses, keep these patients uncertain about their own value, so that they give the final say over to others (external or internal).

HOW TO ANALYZE ATTITUDES OF ENTITLEMENT

In treatment, feelings of deprivation and entitlement are, in part, transformed into supplications, demonstrating the patient's submission and inability to manage alone. The dangers of autonomous functioning include thinking for oneself, differentiating oneself from the parental imagoes by accurate perception and evaluation of reality, and tolerating one's own hatred, destructiveness, competitiveness, and the limitations of what has been possible with the parent(s). What is at issue is not merely that the patient has been deprived or feels entitled to reparations because of this deprivation. That contention is the manifest content through which patients maintain their submission to a parental figure and justify their unacceptable wishes. The deprivation may have been real, and the patient may feel hungry and cheated and crave what he has missed. These id derivatives may be very intense and may seem to fix the patient on a craving for "dumplings" (Freud, 1915). Freud meant that certain patients insist on actually obtaining transference love from the analyst; they are unable to settle for analyzing this as a set of wishes that cannot be fulfilled. Freud wrote:

> [There is] one class of women with whom this attempt to preserve the erotic transference for the purpose of analytic work without satisfying it will not succeed. These are women of elemental passionateness who tolerate no surrogates. They are children of nature who refuse to accept the psychical in place of the material, who, in the poet's words, are accessible only to "the logic of soup with dumplings for arguments." With such people one has the choice between returning their love or else bringing down upon oneself the full enmity of a woman scorned. In neither case can we safeguard the interests of the treatment. One has to withdraw, unsuccessful; and all we can

do is to turn the problem over in one's mind of how it is that a capacity for neurosis is joined with such an intractable need for love [pp. 166–167].

Viewed within a conflict model, however, this intractable need for love is best understood and interpreted as an attempt to placate and seduce the superego in the face of dangerously unacceptable impulses. Without the illusion of specialness and magical protection afforded by submission to parental authority, there is terror of all that has been wrong and all that is wrong. Patients who have felt so unacceptable, defective, or worthless have been too frightened not to see themselves as the parent did, to move outside the closed circle. Paradoxically, this shift would allow them to view themselves more realistically (not through the imagined eyes of an aggressively distorted parental imago).

Each patient tried to deflect focus away from himself onto others as bad, defective, or disgusting. Someone else, not the patient, was the bad one, the disgusting one, the one who deserved to be ridiculed or picked on. The patient then deserved to be loved, and a competitor (sibling, parent) deserved contempt. Picking at others was used to persuade the superego that the latter was wrong about the patient, who was, indeed, better than a rival (Lax, 1975).

Having the right to pick on others added to the claim of exception from ordinary morality. Beyond guilt reduction, this exceptional status helped to protect the patient from vulnerability to feeling passive and helpless in relation to others and to fate. Each patient became a powerful avenger in meting out punishment vengefully to others. To be "fate," as Mrs. C was, the picker or attacker, created the illusion of safety from the terribly frightening vicissitudes of fate (illness, deformity, surgery, and so on) or parental moods. It was as if Mrs. C kept insisting: "I myself am fate, the agent of my destiny and that of those around me. I no longer need fear what can be done to me." What Mrs. C expressed so loudly was also found in unverbalized forms in other entitled patients who pretended to possess the power of the universe, which was being enacted through them. Although we are here stressing that impersonation of fate defends especially against dreaded feelings of helplessness and passivity, such omnipotent claims were also used to avoid responsibility for the patient's sadism and extractiveness. It is as if the patient is merely serving as the agent of a higher, natural law, as, indeed, Mrs. C felt. Mrs. C and Dr. G would each insist that she was only asking others to adhere to reasonable standards of right and wrong. Each woman thereby attempted to obscure and justify her sadism and demandingness. Identification with the aggressor or doer (Segel, 1969) and turning passive into active were involved. Each patient had good reasons to fear helplessness, passivity, and neediness and good reasons to be mistrustful of others. The patient's continued identification with the sadism and extractiveness of the parent avoids acknowledgment and integration of the patient's rage and disappointment.

When the analyst attempts to interpret the patient's feelings of deprivation and entitlement, the patient may feel accused of being excessively and unrealistically demanding. In contrast to responsible guilty concern or even terror of punishment derived from primitive superego forerunners, "entitled" patients are all too able to ignore their conscience or to misuse the claim that they are being criticized by the analyst to justify further the entitled stance. Or the patient may simply continue to clamor for more, while demonstrating how he is continually shortchanged. Such defensive avoidance and inattention need to be demonstrated to the patient for the entitlement to become seriously engaged. Even if the patient can accept that these feelings of deprivation refer to the past, he still feels stuck with them in the present. Interpretive focus on the patient's willingness to submit to another's (parent's) view, with the multiple protective illusions this submission offers, may be more helpful. So long as the patient must compulsively undermine himself because of his fears about his destructive wishes, he will turn to another (parent figure) for the latter's opinions. Entitlement, at its deepest level, is a question of what the patient is, indeed, entitled to. Interpretive focus on the patient's doubtfulness about the legitimacy of any of his claims, from the most exploitative to the most basic and unassuming, may help to avoid countertransference reactions of frustration, helplessness, and anger when tyrannized by such patients. Of course, frustration, helplessness, and anger are what the patient himself feels in his dependent submission to the authority of others. Interpretation of both the genetic roots for this dependent submission and its current dynamic basis is necessary.

10

PSYCHOSOMATIC AVOIDANCE OF CONFLICT*

The pressure to avoid internal conflict in pathologically dependent patients may often lead to the transient development, sometimes to the persistence, of a psychosomatic symptom complex. When dangerous conflict and dangerous feelings cannot be tolerated, the body may be drawn upon as a regressive means to get away from what feels overwhelmingly threatening. In this respect, we can liken the defensive use of psychosomatic symptoms to action tendencies in pathologically dependent patients. When the patient's defensive organization is unable to manage conflict intrapsychically, more drastic defensive modes are drawn upon, which may involve driven repetitive action or the exploitation of bodily symptoms. To varying degrees, pathologically dependent patients generally turn to some form of behavioral enactment with others so as to avoid internal conflict.

I stress avoidance, rather than integration, of internal conflict via the psychosomatic symptom. What I describe here applies to various common psychosomatic entities such as irritable bowel syndrome, chronic headaches, peptic ulcer, or psychogenic dermatitis. I focus on low back pain syndrome as a paradigm of psychosomatic attempts by patients with pathological dependency to avoid facing and integrating conflict. I do so because I have had considerable experience with low back pain syndrome; a large number of my patients were referred initially because of it by John Sarno, M.D., who runs an

---

* An earlier version of this chapter was originally written in collaboration with John Sarno, M.D. (Coen and Sarno, 1989).

156

extensive educational-psychological treatment program for patients with back pain at the Rusk Institute for Rehabilitation Medicine in New York City. Most of these patients are rigid character types, the most treatable of which are those with pathological dependency. That is, the more severely narcissistic and paranoid of these rigid characters have accomplished little in therapy from which they have usually fled quickly. This chapter emphasizes understanding and treatment of psychosomatic symptom complexes in patients with pathological dependency. I stress avoidance of conflict in psychosomatic disease in preference to such vague and difficult to demonstrate concepts as somatization, hypochondriasis, or conversion as causative factors.

For most of the patients I describe, such psychosomatic avoidance of conflict is relatively transient, and it alternates with other stable defensive modes. Through the paradigm of back pain syndrome, I want to indicate how to manage such psychosomatic episodes psychoanalytically, so as to gain access to the underlying conflicts. The analyst's ease and confidence in working with such psychosomatic crises correlate highly with the patient's relinquishment of the psychosomatic symptom and the shift toward analysis of conflict. The psychosomatic symptom has often been a good entry route into psychoanalytic psychotherapy or psychoanalysis, once the patient becomes convinced how much he works at not feeling and not facing what is wrong within himself. Once the focus shifts to the patient's general, intense defensive activities within what is usually a rigid character structure, the back pain recedes in importance and usually disappears, except for very brief recurrences. These may reappear when the patient is again unable to tolerate and manage what he is feeling. For most patients, once access to what is wrong is regained, the psychosomatic symptom rapidly disappears.

Various affects and various conflicts may be discerned in patients with such psychosomatic symptom complexes. Given the ubiquity of the back pain syndrome, this fact is not surprising. Nevertheless, what is most typical of all patients I have seen with psychosomatic syndromes is difficulty tolerating destructiveness and dependency. This chapter focuses on psychosomatic crisis in patients with underlying pathological dependency. The patient feels the need for containment and punishment, on the one hand, and caring and enhancement of self-esteem, on the other. Underlying fantasy complexes typically involve some version of "the crippled child." I mean not that this fantasy is enacted as conversion but that once the psychosomatic symptom complex appears, meanings are attributed to it and uses made of it, as the patient needs. "The crippled child" motif expresses both rage at the psychological damage/disability in oneself, to which others/parent(s) have contributed, and the claim that deficient care and nurturance must be made good. From the position of "crippled child," kept down in pain/bed, the patient feels safer with his own hatred and destructiveness, than if he were to rise up with it. The imagined punishment and mutilation reflect guilt about, and the need for protection against, rage and destructiveness in the presence of intense need for the object.

I want to indicate the ease of helping patients out of low back pain syndrome and of engaging certain of these patients in psychoanalytic psychotherapy or psychoanalysis, by explaining the defensive function of the back pain and the patient's excessive attention to guardedness and protection. I saw the patients described here in consultation or in psychoanalytic psychotherapy or psychoanalysis because they did not respond sufficiently to Sarno's educational-psychological program. Those who were able to engage in an intensive therapy were able sufficiently to open their dependent wishes toward me to allow a treatment process to proceed. Some could not do so. These patients vary in their willingness to be influenced, protected, and rescued. Thus, suggestion that permanent structural damage will not occur varies in its role here. That patients can give in to wishes for rescue and protection seems to help them to recover from back pain syndrome and to become engaged in a productive therapy. Such temporary surrender within a psychotherapy or psychoanalysis allows the patient the magical illusion of protection from his back pain and from his feared internal conflicts. This illusion seems to permit recovery from the psychosomatic crisis. The problem then becomes the wish for dependent (magical) protection from what threatens the patient from within. Once this can become engaged, the psychosomatic symptom can be relinquished and a therapeutic process can proceed. We also consider how to deal with the occurrence of episodes of psychosomatic symptoms within an ongoing treatment.

Sarno's (1981, 1984a, b) opinion is that the majority of neck, shoulder, and back pain patients, including those whose symptoms are attributed to most structural abnormalities (e.g., osteoarthritis and herniated disc), suffer from the tension myositis syndrome (T.M.S.). This is a psychophysiologic disorder characterized by postural muscle tenderness in a very consistent pattern, varying degrees of neuropathy, and, in some patients, tendonalgia. That T.M.S. is psychosomatic is suggested by the concurrence of other common psychosomatic processes in the histories of 88% of patients with T.M.S. (Sarno, 1981) and the relative ease with which the process can be permanently and rapidly resolved through an educational-psychological program of treatment in the majority of cases (Sarno, 1984a, b). Most patients who have back pain syndrome and are seen by physicians have a psychogenic etiology. What the patient claims has been caused by trauma (exercise, lifting, strain) usually turns out not to be so. The moment of "trauma," to which he prefers to attribute its etiology, is when the patient became aware of his back pain. The commonsense view that muscle strain perpetuates back pain syndrome is incorrect, even in people who do heavy lifting (Sargent, 1946; Walters, 1961; Sternbach et al., 1973; Sarno, 1974, 1976, 1977, 1984a; Gentry et al., 1975). The largest number of patients with back pain syndrome will have T.M.S., complicated in some by what has been called conversion pain (named psychogenic regional pain by Walters, 1961). In our experience, the only structural lesions of consequence to be ruled out are tumors, benign or neoplastic, and intrinsic bone disease. Bony or disc abnormalities of the spine are rarely responsible for pain. Sarno (1981) has postulated the etiology of T.M.S. to be an anxiety-induced myoneuralgia, mediated through the autonomic nervous system and leading to regional ischemia and muscle pain, due to alterations in lactic acid metabolism and episodic tetanus. Ischemia of nerve roots or peripheral nerves is an additional source of pain and may produce other sensory and occasionally, motor changes. Tendonalgia also appears to be part of the syndrome.

Theoretically, therefore, the majority of back pain syndromes should be diagnosed by the primary physician, who is seldom the one to make the diagnosis. If the pain does not resolve spontaneously, patients are referred to an orthopedist, neurologist, or neurosurgeon or seek out healers on their own. The result is that a structural diagnosis is maintained that leads in many cases to a chronic, often worsening pain syndrome. Thus medicine contributes to the perpetuation of the disorder it is attempting to cure. There are cases in which structural somatic pathology can be demonstrated to be the cause of back pain. Careful physical examination, together with appropriate clinical studies, must decide this diagnosis; however, the first rule of medicine, to do no harm, is violated by traditional, conservative treatment of back pain syndrome. Of approximately 4,000 patients with neck, shoulder, and back pain seen by Sarno over 15 years, over 95% were diagnosed as having T.M.S. Awareness that most cases of back pain syndrome do not have a primarily structural etiology leads to dramatically effective psychological treatment.

Tension in this syndrome refers both to anxiety and to a state of defensive hypervigilance and guardedness in preparation for danger (Schur, 1955). Emotional intolerance for some affect and some conflict increases the patient's state of tension and guardedness (anxiety and defensive state), with involvement of the musculoskeletal system. Conflict is avoided rather than stably resolved by compromise formation. A secondary absorption in the somatic symptoms further avoids (and is infiltrated by) the underlying conflicts. Levels of T.M.S., from mild to most severe, can be differentiated based upon variations in degrees of anxiety and hypervigilance. Mild versions of T.M.S. are common and may occur in anyone. The T.M.S. patients who have consulted Sarno have tended to be conscientious, responsible, driven; the more anxious have been compulsive and perfectionistic. Only 5–10% have required psychiatric referral because they did not improve sufficiently in Sarno's program. They represent a distinct subgroup, characterized by character rigidity. They are more anxious, more cautious, more rigid and perfectionistic, more guarded and hypervigilant. These are their chronic character attitudes, in back pain or not.

It is usually sufficient for Sarno, as the physiatrist, to provide empathic explanation of the role of anxiety and defensive states in causing back pain, together with reassurance that this is a reversible, self-limited process, for patients to recover. He presents a series of lectures to his patients with back pain syndrome. Sarno especially emphasizes that since there is not true somatic pathology, there will not be permanent tissue damage. The whole process is reversible if the patient can accept the psychosomatic diagnosis and his own role in the syndrome and tolerate the feelings he has been avoiding. Recovery does not require insight into deeply unconscious conflicts. Awareness of the psychosomatic process and confidence that it is easily reversible seem to be curative for most patients, within two to six weeks.

Patients with "psychogenic regional pain" are harder to treat, and they more often require hospitalization. Hospitalized patients in Sarno's program have intensive, daily, individual or group psychotherapy as well as physical therapies.

The psychoanalyst is referred only the more difficult patients who do not recover within Sarno's program (5–10% of Sarno's total group). My experience with a large number of such patients is that they recover from their back pain easily, whatever their psychiatric diagnosis and however their psychotherapy or psychoanalysis proceeds. Some tend to have brief recurrences of back pain during psychotherapy but easily recover from it. It has been impressive how easy it has been for so many people to shed their back pain, even when it had become chronic and disabling. I have seen very few patients of the group of chronic, intractable back pain invalids or those with "psychogenic regional pain." Most of the seemingly chronic, intractable back pain invalids I have seen made full recoveries. That it seems so easy for most people to recover from back pain syndrome without resolution of intrapsychic conflict makes it seem unlikely that back pain syndrome is a stable compromise formation. I prefer to view it as an attempt at avoidance of conflict.

Patients who develop back pain syndrome become frightened of what is wrong and of what will happen to them, even before they consult a physician. This fear tends to be reinforced by most physicians, even if conservative treatment (bed rest, muscle relaxants, tranquilizers, and so on) is prescribed. That is, patient and physician worry about permanent neuromuscular damage, the future possibility of surgery, or at least the prospect of increasingly more frequent and longer recurrences. The patient's worries about what will happen to him increase his anxiety and hypervigilance, with consequent aggravation of low back pain and nerve symptoms. Warnings from physicians about the necessity for strict bed rest (to relieve imagined nerve root compression) make these careful, tight people even more attentive to the dangers of causing themselves further damage.

In T.M.S. there is not nerve root compression; this fact can be established by CAT scan. Patients who continue to fear and believe that they have structural impingement on nerve roots are referred by Sarno to a competent neurologist or neurosurgeon to clarify this issue for the patient. The pathophysiology of T.M.S. has not been fully established, but it is postulated that regional ischemia leads to pain in muscles and, at times, in nerve roots or peripheral nerves. For patients to recover from T.M.S., they must believe that they do not suffer from structural pathology of the back. The more rigid the patient with back pain syndrome, the more that fear of damage (destructiveness) is a central issue. A parallel situation would be if it was believed that unless a tension headache was relieved promptly, a brain tumor or essential hypertension would result.

Typically, for relief of the back pain syndrome, the diagnosis must be established by the primary physician or physiatrist. The cases reported here were referred following diagnosis by the physiatrist. When back pain syndrome develops suddenly during an ongoing psychoanalysis or psychotherapy, it is also helpful for the physiatrist to make the psychosomatic diagnosis. This not only hastens resolution of the somatic symptoms but facilitates analysis of the underlying conflicts.

SOME CLINICAL VIGNETTES

Mrs. J, in her 60s had spent seven years as an invalid with back pain. She had obtained little permanent help from the many treatment centers she had attended in the northeast. Because of her symptoms, she and her husband left the idyllic spot in the Caribbean where they had retired. She traveled supine in the back of a large Cadillac, with her husband as the chauffeur. A distinguished psychoanalyst whom Mrs. J consulted doubted that she could be helped because of her dissociation from her early trauma. Mrs. J's mother developed tuberculosis when Mrs. J was one-year-old, and mother died when the patient was 2 1/2. It seems likely, from what her family told her and from her treatment behavior, that mother's ability to care for her was severely limited once mother became ill. After mother's death, Mrs. J was raised by various, not very caring relatives, until early adolescence. Then her father remarried, and she lived with him. Father kept his remarriage secret from Mrs. J for a year, presumably so that he would not have to keep her with him. Within her treatment, she recovered many memories of her disappointment with her father and of the marked emotional deprivation she felt.

What was most remarkable (she was the first patient with severe back pain I had treated) was the complete remission of somatic symptoms within six weeks. One day she removed her heavy girdle and forgot it in the waiting room bathroom. She spontaneously spoke about Lourdes and a miracle cure from the analyst. As her back pain receded in importance, she actively and consciously attempted to actualize with the analyst the loving care of which she felt so much deprived. The analyst was to be mother, father, husband, and lover. Indeed, Mrs. J had been very demanding with her husband, but her invalidism had justified this demandingness. She seemed to have been waiting for someone to heal her, to adopt her, and to love her. Her hungry demandingness and rage were extreme, especially in the analytic transference. Mrs. J had identified with her sick mother, wanted to cling to her, and wished that someone would come really to care for her. Mrs. J's perception of herself as frail and ill made her feel more lovable, a little less like the abandoned "little match girl." It was also used to demand care and to defend against guilt about rage and demandingness.

It was very difficult for Mrs. J to tolerate and integrate her intense, hungry rage and demandingness. She would try to stifle it, to behave herself, to pretend this was no longer present. Her rage felt overwhelming to her. So did her wishes that the analyst love and fulfill her. These had to be diluted and justified, over and over again. Otherwise, she insatiably, irresistibly craved sexualized or sexual merger with the analyst. She had to deny how extractive she was by pretending that she was being loving. But she wanted to lead her life through and with me! She consciously attempted to live her life in imitation of me, to maintain the illusion that we were one person or, at least, always together. Her home, country home, vacation, and work were all largely determined by doing what she either knew or imagined I did. Her wish to fuse with me was extreme; she had marked difficulty with boundaries and separateness. In the face of separation, her terror of abandonment and of being alone combined with her difficulty in preserving her psychological equilibrium and an internal image of a good, caring analyst/parent. Intense rage and fear threatened to overwhelm her during separations. Whether she had an actual defect in maintaining object constancy was not clear. Her tremendous hunger for loving parenting and the rage and terror at its interruption suggested that angry affects destroyed the image of the good analyst/parent.

When she felt endangered by interpretation of her wishes to empty me out, possess, devour, and become me or by the threat of losing or destroying me because of her rage, she would regress severely, spending weekends in bed, listening nonstop to country music, tuning out what was wrong. She would appeal to me not to say such terrible things about her, which she could not stand and which were not true. She would react to such interpretations sadomasochistically, insisting that I was merely angry and torturing her. Instead, we were to continue to pretend that our treatment relationship was really mutually loving. If I loved her, I could not think or say such things about her. Mrs. J obviously was a fragile, disturbed woman, with enormous feelings of deprivation. Back pain was a defense against the affective chaos within her. It was also the hint of an expression of her view of herself as a frail, damaged child who required care and who was too weak to be destructive.

Nevertheless, Mrs. J totally relinquished her invalidism, sought additional graduate education, and was able to function as a highly skilled professional. Within the limits of her severe psychopathology, her improvement was remarkable. She became able to sustain contentment and pride in herself and, to a degree, to enjoy being on her own. She is not an example of the successful analysis of a case of pathological dependency; however, through the treatment relationship and through some character modification, Mrs. J functioned at a much higher level. She continued to require a dependent relationship to sustain this improvement.

Mr. K, a successful businessman, presented with three years of low back pain, together with anxiety, approaching panic, and depression. Surgery had been recommended for a structural orthopedic problem, although there was question whether this had anything to do with the patient's back pain. Mr. K was terrified he would not be able to maintain his business, in an industry that had suddenly had a number of bankruptcies. Back pain appeared when Mr. K felt especially tense, worried, and fearful about what would become of him. He would compulsively worry himself, becoming tighter and more agitated, as if this behavior would ward off danger. At such times he was most out of touch with conflicted feelings and experienced only anxiety and helplessness. He would intensely crave dependent reassurance and protection, and his defensiveness and guardedness would be especially marked. Later in the treatment, back pain did not occur, and he tolerated conflicted wishes and feelings much more easily, with less need to ward off hatred and competitiveness. Within a dependent, idealizing transference (as he had had with previous physicians), he soon felt better.

Mr. K would come into the analyst's office, sigh repeatedly, and with tie off, shoes unlaced, and shirt partially unbuttoned, emphasize how much stress he was under and how much he needed to "relax." He could acknowledge how much he wanted the analyst to feel sorry for him, to be sympathetic and caring. Mr. K was a compulsive "do-gooder" in his attempts to win others over. He did not expect that such positive acceptance would be spontaneously available to him. On the contrary, he expected neglect, indifference, or contempt. Suffering (including his back pain) was used to induce the other to show caring, a pattern developed with his mother; dependent, masochistic submission functioned similarly. These patterns were also used as punishment and expiation and in the attempt to contain his destructiveness. Mr. K was a very controlled, rigid man who allowed himself little freedom in his feelings, wishes, and fantasies. He was the way he thought he should be. It was very difficult to allow himself time off to "hang out," as in watching television or in being with his children in unplanned situations.

When he had brief recurrences of back pain or other bodily illnesses, he would become more passive, constricted, and submissive. Hostile, aggressive feelings, especially angry, demanding, or competitive attitudes, disappeared from view, with Mr. K's becoming more worried about himself and craving reassurance. When this shift was interpreted to him, he could usually allow himself to rise back up again and to feel angry, challenging, and demanding. Fears of abandonment and loss of love were intense and were exacerbated by his imperfections, including worries about bodily defectiveness. He could open up his intense anger, feelings of deprivation, envy, and competitiveness, but he found it difficult to take responsibility for such feelings in an ongoing way. He would need to justify such feelings, blame others for them, or soon disown them, so that they did not really count. On the other hand, Mr. K was now well aware how deprived and angry he chronically felt and of how difficult this feeling was to tolerate in himself.

Terror of loss and rage at felt deprivation, in contrast to the intense special regard and admiration he craved, kept Mr. K very much in turmoil. When he first presented with back pain, he felt overwhelmed, unable to manage, almost ready to surrender, wanting very much to be rescued. This desire to be rescued was the transference role he sought with the analyst. Back pain screened great shame about his childlike neediness and closed in his intense rage and envy. So long as he could feel esteemed and admired, he could manage. When he felt deprived of such narcissistic supplies, which he demanded and sought on a grandiose scale, he felt depressed, enraged, sadistic, attacking, and again unable to manage all of these feelings. Back pain was one indication of Mr. K's more general difficulty with facing and integrating his destructive affects.

PSYCHODYNAMIC ETIOLOGY: MECHANISMS

Let us now, using the paradigm of low back pain syndrome, focus on how the psychosomatic symptom complex serves to avoid intrapsychic conflict in patients with pathological dependency. Keep in mind that patients with other common psychosomatic syndromes share similar psychodynamic mechanisms. Think, for example, of irritable bowel syndrome, chronic headaches, peptic ulcer, or psychogenic dermatitis. When patients develop the psychosomatic syndrome, they seem relatively unable to tolerate experiencing some affect related to some conflict. The specific affect or conflict may vary from patient to patient. The fact of emotional intolerance for some affect and some conflict increases the patient's state of tension and guardedness (anxiety and defensive state), with the production of the psychosomatic syndrome. Psychological equilibrium in patients with psychosomatic syndromes is unstable. Generally, their conflicts do not appear to be resolved stably within a compromise formation but are avoided. A primary inability or failure to deal with the predominant conflicts leads to the somatic symptoms. Then a secondary absorption in the somatic symptoms further avoids (although it certainly is infiltrated by) the underlying intrapsychic conflicts. The psychosomatic syndrome does not seem to occur when certain, specific affects or specific conflicts are blocked from conscious experience. The etiologic mechanism does not seem primarily to involve conversion or discharge of affects via somatic channels. An intense, generalized need for defense, so as to avoid some threatening conflicts and affects, involves the body. The psychosomatic symptoms seem to be triggered by the high general level of anxiety. The anxiety seems to derive from the threatened inability to manage these dangerous conflicts and affects, that is, from an impending failure of defense. Hypervigilance is intensified, anxiety escalates, but the focus shifts to the body and concerns about the fate of the bodily symptoms.

Because of the intensity of the patient's fear of being judged unacceptable, by others as well as by himself, he must restrict awareness of anything negative within himself. Rigid character defenses are required against experiencing affects and wishes that would lead to judgments of unacceptability. Thus, the patient is intolerant of his own strong affects and clear perceptions of himself and of others. For example, awareness and expression of intense angry criticism make the patient anxious, penitent, and placating. Fears of being gotten rid of or of being unloved are heightened by awareness of "badness." The patient becomes more anxious, protects himself from awareness of such angry/destructive feelings, and seeks proof of acceptance through self-torture and demonstration of his "goodness."

Anxiety, from the conflict/affects and from the sense of failure of the defensive organization, seems to trigger the symptoms, in back pain and in other psychosomatic syndromes. Most commonly, the patient is unable to manage his intense rage and dependent longings, which feel frightening. A longing to surrender, to be cared for, and to be protected from what is threatening, within and without, intensifies. This regressive desire adds both to the patient's anxiety and to the wish to be ill. It is more accurate, however, to say that this wish, latent or activated in the patient, becomes exaggerated once the psychosomatic syndrome occurs. This wish contributes significantly to the persistence of the psychosomatic symptom and the patient's preoccupation with it. The threatened defensive organization seems to require additional assistance. This is provided by the shift in the patient's focus to the body and the legitimization, through illness, of the appeal to others for help. Self-punishment and greater self-containment occur in the psychosomatic crisis, relieving some of the pressure to manage rage and destructiveness. But note that such psychodynamic explanation is different from demonstrating etiology.

Rather than conceive of anxiety and anger as expressed somatically, we can more prudently posit a heightened state of danger, with a general intense need for defense against negative affects; anxiety and defense both implicate different body systems. This concept avoids a model of hypothetical "affect equivalents" being discharged within the body. The latter may be a relic of earlier psychoanalytic times, when there was concrete overemphasis on the economic point of view.

Once the psychosomatic symptom occurs, pathologically dependent patients feel freer to make use of it for expression of dependent longings (to be cared for as ill); defense against affects and wishes that cannot be tolerated and integrated (by preoccupation with the somatic symptoms, emphasis on passivity, and helplessness); punishment through pain and suffering; and unacknowledged angry and sadistic attacks on caretakers (internal and external objects) through one's suffering. The wish to be "a crippled child" can express these varied determinants, as they did in many of my patients.

Because of their difficulty in tolerating and integrating their negative qualities, these rigid characters are relatively unable to rely on themselves to provide ongoing self-assessment, self-guidance, and self-direction. This inability enhances their emotional dependence on others for reassurance about their own value. They tend to doubt that they are good and worthwhile. They live in a constant state of vigilant self-scrutiny to make themselves acceptable to others and to themselves. When such people become worried about not doing well or not being good (enough), they become more tense, vigilant, and careful about themselves and about everyone else. In this state, the psychosomatic syndrome is more likely to occur and to persist. For rigid, dependent patients to relinquish their psychosomatic symptom complex, they must develop compassion for themselves that they have felt so afraid of being unacceptable and that they have been unable to own the negative side of themselves.

These patients tend to have affective inhibition as part of a general character rigidity. They show overtly neurotic symptoms and character, unlike, say, McDougall's (1980) psychosomatic patients. They are troubled about themselves, and they have little difficulty feeling anxious (excessively). They tend to form dependent, idealizing, often sadomasochistic transferences rather than to remain detached and indifferent. Our patients do not have a deficit in the ability to experience and express affect (whether a biological "alexithymia" [Sifneos, 1974] or a psychological "affective stifling" [McDougall, 1980], which occurs so early and so extensively that these people virtually cannot experience emotion).

Can we then say that our patients are more disposed toward somatization than is the average patient? The rapidity with which the patients I have seen recovered from their psychosomatic syndrome without the substitution of another psychosomatic symptom argues against a basic need for somatization. The occurrence of other psychosomatic symptoms in these patients is also usually transient. What stands out most from our clinical material are the contribution of tension and chronic character defenses to the psychosomatic syndrome and, then, the uses made of the pain for dependency, for defense by narcissistic preoccupation with the pain, for punishment, and for expression of anger and sadism against caretakers (internal and external). When anxiety is intensified because of threatened failure of the defensive organization and psychosomatic symptoms are precipitated, these are then exploited so as to bolster defense in the ways described. Especially the wish to be cared for and rescued, now legitimized by the somatic illness, supports the failing defensive organization and allows expression of part of the underlying conflict. For some patients (including Mrs. J and Mr. K), failure of the defensive organization can lead to intense depression, infantile regression, disorganization, immobilization, or threatened psychosis.

Each patient previously described did, indeed, believe that illness was a vehicle for obtaining caring. Mrs. J's initial presentation could be described as a severe, general emotional breakdown, in which she presented herself as a sick, crippled child who desperately required care, bodily and emotional. Wishes to be a "crippled child" were expressed by many patients. It seems to us more prudent to conceive of the uses patients make of their somatic symptoms, once these occur. This approach avoids positing an innate tendency toward somatization as etiologically active; we have insufficient evidence for somatization, whether based on inability to process affects or on wishful or defensive identification as ill. That there is a wish to be a "crippled child" does not mean that this has caused the back pain!

Are these patients hypochondriacal? They certainly can be. They show increased preoccupation and concern with their bodies and excessive fears about the consequences of their somatic symptoms (Barsky and Klerman, 1983). Various fears and conflicts appear in such hypochondriacal concerns (Richards, 1981; Broden and Myers, 1981). Typical are fears of loss and punishment, especially in relation to hostile aggression. What Sperling (1968) has called "the psychosomatic relationship" may become activated in the face of fears about the psychosomatic symptom. That is, patients may regress to earlier or concealed modes of relationship in which dependent and sadomasochistic patterns are prominent. Dependency wishes are legitimized so that manipulation and exploitation of others are concealed. These patients seek to make others responsible for them and for what is inside of them. This motivation is powerful in hypochondriasis, as in dependency and sadomasochism. It is the link between psychosomatic avoidance of conflict and the other defensive modes described in this book. It is so much a part of the wish to be ill, physically or emotionally. To the degree that a person fears what is inside of himself and cannot tolerate this, he will need to be ill, to make someone else responsible for him. The somatic symptoms and failure to improve can be used against others (external and internal) sado-masochistically, demonstrating others' failure and neglect. We especially noted hypochondriacal exploitation of physical symptoms for avoidance of internal conflict, dependency, and defense against varied forms of hostile aggression; hypochondriasis includes warding off superego criticism for such feelings by placating and submission in the sick role.

Thus, our view is that there is potential for hypochondriacal elaboration in these patients with regressive dependent and sadoma-sochistic modes of relationship. This view avoids having to conceive of the somatic symptoms as themselves expressing such wishes (Wisdom, 1959; Atkins, 1968; Sperling, 1968). This dependent, sado-masochistic potential is, however, a basic part of pathological dependency.

Defensive, narcissistic elaboration of the somatic symptoms is an important factor in secondary avoidance of the predominant underlying conflicts. That is, the somatic symptoms and the patient's preoccupation with them absorb his emotional interest to a degree and may become "the focus of narcissistic regression" (Schur, 1955). Schur is correct that a regressive focus may relieve unbearable conflicts. The patient's attention shifts to the body and its claims, away from conflicts with others (external and internal). This shift serves to tune out what the patient cannot tolerate feeling in himself. The somatic symptoms and his worry about them are used to enhance self-esteem and entitlement (through suffering) and to appeal to the superego that aggression and demandingness are justified. Dependency and deprivation similarly can be used to justify and obscure one's badness. The patient expresses feeling overwhelmed, unable to manage, wanting someone else to lift the burdens of life. Use of such metaphor should not imply conversion of such wishes into somatic expression. What feels overwhelming are the intolerable pressures of internal conflict, also represented externally as the pressures of life, and it is these from which the patient wants to be rescued. The internal conflict must be avoided in these multiple ways. For most of our patients, unlike those of Schur (1955) or Sperling (1968), somatic symptoms do not seem to protect against psychotic disorganization; however, the threatened failure of the defensive organization may, indeed, endanger some of these patients with regressive disorganization, depression, masochistic surrender, or more overt psychotic collapse, as with Mrs. J and Mr. K.

This chapter emphasizes that the meanings and uses of a psychosomatic symptom need to be differentiated from its etiology. Defensive gains of the somatic illness have been regarded as evidence of conversion of affective conflict into physical disease (Ziegler, Imboden, and Meyer, 1960; Raskin, Talbott, and Meyerson, 1966; Kornfeld, 1985). Too much speculation enters into deciding whether conversional physical symptoms have been used for psychological defense in the past or whether they are now being used (successfully) to solve a conflict. Even in true conversion reactions, we expect a symptom not to resolve conflict (as these authors do), but to serve as a compromise formation involving conflict. Our impression agrees with these actual case reports that conflict is not resolved but avoided in "conversion" pain. Escape from conflict has been confused with defense against, and somatic expression of, conflict and affect. Symbolic meanings and intrapsychic uses of pain are not the same as the cause of that pain. Each of these three studies provides useful criteria for gauging the probability that physical symptoms are largely psychologically derived. This finding does not demonstrate a process of conversion. When, indeed, there is good evidence (specific fantasies) that intrapsychic conflict is enacted in a pain syndrome, this evidence should be described. This perspective preserves Fenichel's (1945, p. 230) definition of conversion as the translation of "specific fantasies into a body language."

FROM PSYCHOSOMATIC SYMPTOM TO THE ANALYSIS OF PATHOLOGICAL DEPENDENCY

The reader should not be surprised by our therapeutic optimism. This is solidly based on extensive clinical experience. We emphasize the relative ease of helping patients out of their psychosomatic symptom complex. What must the psychoanalyst do to help the psychosomatic patient? He must maintain confidence, expressed or not, that the psychosomatic syndrome is psychologically derived and is self-limited. The patient must be shown his intolerance and fear of his own wishes and feelings. The more severe the case, the more imperative it is that the patient's hypervigilance and character rigidity be interpreted immediately. He must be shown his extraordinary watchfulness over his bodily functioning, behavior, feelings, and wishes. He must be shown how strongly he believes that anything negative in him makes him unacceptable. He must be told that his psychosomatic syndrome will not disappear until he is able to stop scrutinizing his physical symptoms and believing that he is worthwhile only if he is all good. Some preliminary genetic construction needs to be given about why the patient had to become so perfectionistic. At the very least, for the sake of his somatic recovery, the patient must question the rigidity of his internal standards. He will need to relax his adherence to these standards. Empathic explanation and beginning psychotherapeutic work on why the patient has had to be so afraid of not being good enough to be wanted will help to lessen his intense self-scrutiny, hypervigilance, guardedness, and panic, and this intervention is usually sufficient for the psychosomatic symptom to disappear.

Similarly, the patient's defenses against, and fears of, relying on the analyst need to be modified so that the patient can turn his needs for magical protection to the analyst. This shift takes the pressure off the patient's fears of bodily damage from his psychosomatic syndrome as well as his terror of his internal conflicts. The analyst temporarily becomes the protector from both dangers. Then the patient has to be shown how he runs away from what is wrong within himself toward wanting someone else to protect him. This theme becomes a central focus of the treatment, just as it does in analyzing other varieties of pathological dependency. That is, the psychosomatic patient arrives in conflict about his dependency (and his destructiveness). He cannot bear simply to wish for the other to care for and protect him. He needs a good excuse (illness) to justify such wishes. This conflict over his needs for others must be engaged immediately so that the patient can relinquish his psychosomatic symptom and the treatment can proceed. The emphasis shifts from the psychosomatic symptom to the patient's conflicts over his needs of, and uses of, others (analyst). It is characteristic of such psychosomatic patients that they are both highly dependent and intensely intolerant of dependency. Those who, indeed, cannot bear their needs for others will flee treatment. Those who are able to tolerate their neediness will begin to become responsible for it and understand its functions. Thus, the therapeutic goal with these patients is to shift the patient's focus from his psychosomatic symptom to his pathological dependency. If the dependency can be engaged within the analytic situation, the psychosomatic syndrome can be relinquished, and the patient can proceed with his analysis.

The capacity to tolerate one's affective life seems, in effect, to preclude psychosomatic syndromes. The better able patients are to tolerate what they feel, including their anxiety, vigilance, mistrust, rage and destructiveness, and depressive feelings, the less troubled they will be by psychosomatic symptoms (Rosenberg, 1949). Intolerance of affect and of internal conflict, such that ordinary defense proves insufficient, is the setting for the psychosomatic illness and its prolongation. Psychosomatic illness, viewed this way, is another means for attempting to avoid what the pathologically dependent patient fears he cannot tolerate facing in himself.

Part IV

THE PATHOLOGICAL
NEED FOR THE OTHER

11

SOME PROBLEMS FOR THE ANALYST IN ANALYZING PATHOLOGICAL DEPENDENCY

In this chapter, I describe some of the analyst's difficulties in the systematic analysis of pathological dependency. I especially emphasize the analyst's collusion with the patient in preserving the defensive addiction to signs of acceptance, both inside and outside of the analysis. Analysts may rationalize such collusion by deciding that the patient is too needy to do otherwise, that his deprivation requires such current provision, or that this collusion is necessary for building new ego function and structure. Indeed, I have described (see chapter 3) that the patient's dependency must become fully engaged within the analysis and that the patient's devouring hunger, neediness, destructiveness, loss, sadness, inability to be alone, and everything else needs to be drawn into the analysis and, as much as possible, onto the person of the analyst. To do so, the analyst must be comfortable with his own regressive, dependent hunger, his own primitive desires in all their cannibalistic, murderous, acquisitive, and destructive forms. Otherwise, he will not be able to facilitate the patient's access to such desires in the progressive deepening and unfolding of a regressive analytic process. To the degree that the analyst shares the pathologically dependent patient's defensive style of avoidance of the dark side by emphasis on love and caring, systematic analysis will be interrupted in favor of some form of pseudo-loving sharing between the analytic couple. Insofar as the analyst is frightened of his own cannibalistic hunger, wishes for merger, and escape from autonomy, he will retard the full emergence of these regressive desires in his patient as expressed toward the analyst. I describe the analyst's techniques of justifying such self-protection through the misuse of clinical theory in the analytic setting.

SOME CLINICAL VIGNETTES

Professor M, a distinguished scholar, took great pride in his literary accomplishments. During his first analysis, he felt better about himself, became more secure about his talents, and seemed to be somewhat more at peace with himself. When his move to another university and city ended the analysis, however, he became depressed, self-tormenting, and doubtful about himself and his abilities. In his second analysis, he quickly tried to establish similar dependent ties with the analyst. He reported, and his transference behavior and fantasies with the second analyst indicated, that he derived considerable comfort and support from the analytic relationship. He sought to use this relationship to attenuate his anxieties and insecurities. The first analyst (analyst X) had emphasized strongly that Professor M's childhood deprivation and neglect were predominant factors in his hunger for attention and caring. As reported by Professor M, an analytic situation had been established in which he was shown the power of his dependent longings as primarily derived from real events (neglect, deprivation); ultimately he would have to renounce these wishes. Analyst X, an experienced and well-regarded person, seemed to have interpreted other defensive functions in Professor M's attachment to the analyst and other parental figures. What the second analysis indicated most, however, was that Professor M had become stuck in a satisfying, dependent relationship with analyst X, which apparently had not been systematically analyzed.

Professor M fantasized and suspected that analyst X had regarded him as a protegé and had enjoyed his creative abilities and literary productions. During the first analysis, the patient had, in fact, written about areas that overlapped with those of the analyst. He guessed that certain childhood experiences and conflicts were similar in himself and in analyst X. According to his report, analyst X seemed most irritable with him (a most unusual occurrence) when the patient suggested early in the analysis that analyst X and he shared certain similarities of deprivation and neglect. For his evidence, he referred to certain of the analyst's emphases.

Analyst Y was able to maintain a more consistent analytic perspective on Professor M's dependency and questioned rather than gratified it. Alerted by what the patient reported and indicated by his material, analyst Y emphasized the patient's willingness to settle for dependent attachments, including analysis, rather than under-standing the defensive functions these attachments served, especially in relation to hostile aggression. The patient's guess seemed plausible to analyst Y, that analyst X had, at times, tended to confuse himself with the patient and to enjoy a mutually shared dependent relation-ship. Analyst X, a distinguished classical analyst, was not attempting to apply a self-psychological acceptance of the patient. As far as analyst Y and Professor M could reconstruct, analyst X and Professor M had tended to settle for the patient's actual dependent attachment to the analyst, which presumably also gratified certain of analyst X's needs. The problem for this reanalysis was to take apart the patient's willingness to "be in analysis" so as to make the analysis productive rather than a stalemate in which the patient lived out certain childhood dependent patterns he had had with both parents. Various "seductive" interventions by analyst X had added a quality of reality to Professor M's needs of the analyst. This interaction had encour-aged extra-analytic goals and emphasized the patient's disability, rather than consistent psychoanalytic understanding of these. In the second analysis, it became possible to open up the patient's terror of loss of control of his anger so that he could bear it. Professor M was able to integrate his anger and relinquish his considerable dependent pressures.

Ms. T, an unmarried artist in her 40s, was in psychoanalytic psychotherapy with analyst Z, a younger analyst, who sought consultation. Ms. T had been orphaned as a small child. After a brief period in an orphanage, she was raised by various relatives. She did not recall feeling wanted. The threat of abandonment involved fears of being sent back to the orphanage. This fear added to her childhood terror of the intensity of her needs and her angers. The rapid development of an intense, erotized transference surprised both patient and analyst. Well aware of the intensity of Ms. T's childhood trauma and neglect, the analyst tended, at times, to be overly warm and supportive, responding to the patient's emotional pressures on him. This behavior tended to actualize the relationship between them and increased Ms. T's feeling that the analyst was the parent she had never had and so desperately wanted. The analyst had alternated between being overly satisfying and attempting to interest Ms. T in understanding her attachment to him. He was unsure of the cause of Ms. T's paranoid, depressive responses to his interpretations of the uses she was making of the treatment. Did her responses derive from her own pressures, from the fluctuations that had actually occurred in this treatment between gratification and understanding, or from the interpretations per se? If the last, he was worried as to whether

Ms. T could tolerate interruption of the modus vivendi established in the treatment.

Consultation clarified that analyst Z's inexperience and theoretical view that more direct involvement and activity were required in the psychotherapy of a patient with such massive deprivation were only part of the problem. When analyst Z was able to clarify, through consultation, where his own neurotic needs and fears had impinged on Ms. T's psychotherapy, she became somewhat less demanding, tolerated frustration in the treatment situation more easily, and became interested in a more sustained way in understanding the dilemma of her attachment to the analyst. Analyst Z satisfied himself that the patient did not "really" need signs of his concern about her. On the other hand, sustained psychoanalytic understanding of the transference was hampered by the reality of what had transpired in the treatment; thus it was more difficult for Ms. T to relinquish the illusion that analyst Z could provide her with the love she had missed. But beyond this was her terror of fully facing her angry destructiveness, which had to be hidden under a cover of positive feelings. It was frightening and humiliating for Ms. T to attempt to face her hostile aggression within the erotized "love" she wanted from the analyst. The degree to which she wanted to intrude, take, use, devour was alarming, indeed, in its force, its primitiveness, and its seeming acceptability to her conscience. Hunger, attachment, and rage all came together in her insistent demand for dumplings (Freud, 1915) and were ultimately the limitation of the treatment.

Some of Mr. X's (see also Coen and Bradlow, 1982; and chapters 6 and 8, this volume) twin transference illustrates aspects of the analysis of pathological dependency. Mr. X would often enter my office with a superior, slightly contemptuous air, his head thrown back, his nose in the air. This entrance had a studied quality, as if he were working hard at convincing both himself and the analyst of his invulnerability. It would quickly become apparent that he was trying to ward off his longings, hurt, and anger, usually in relation to a frustrated transference wish, as his demeanor, speech, and affects would quickly change. He was exquisitely sensitive to any sign of my having a life of my own, whereupon he would feel disappointed, rejected, insignificant, and outraged. Mr. X's impersonation of the analyst was striking in its intensity and vividness; it often conveyed the conviction that he was the analyst, not a fantasied imitation of him. For example, Mr. X would leaf through my mail in the hallway, ask a woman patient for a date, and gesture and speak on the couch, at times, as if he were the analyst. He would become excited, arrogant, and pontifical as he made or restated interpretations. I would feel startled, as if he had actually appropriated something of mine. When I would interpret to him that he was behaving on the couch as if he were literally the analyst, Mr. X would become startled, just as I had felt earlier. He would feel jolted, confused, momentarily unaware that he had just been playacting. During such imperson-ation and for a brief period of time following the analyst's interpre-tation of it, he could not integrate the idea that his wish to imper-sonate the analyst did not and could not transform him magically into the analyst.

Mr. X would prepare himself for possible changes in the analytic routine by attempting to create the illusion that he actively brought about what he had to endure passively. It would often happen that as we approached a holiday or vacation interruption, he had prepared plans to leave just before he expected I would. He would save this information and disclose it immediately after being informed of my plans. This behavior would give the impression that he had thought of leaving first, that he could do whatever the analyst could do. His need to have the upper hand in the treatment process was manifest similarly by attempts to keep me uncertain about his behavior and his collaboration in the treatment. Mr. X taunted me with the idea that he was untrustworthy, that even the fantasy and behavior that he reported in the hours were unreliable.

Like the other patients described here, he strongly wanted direct gratification of his wishes. He would transiently experience his wishes for contact with me as mutually shared. He told me, "You are what I've always wanted to be!" He seemed to believe that I was an embodiment of his images, that I could not be different from what he imagined.

In the third week of the analysis, just before our first holiday interruption, he dreamed:

I'm lying on a psychoanalytic couch which is made from the bottom of egg crates. It molded to the shape of my body. I was talking to a psychologist I know. She was at the head of the couch [later he moves her to the base of the couch]. She touched my knee sensuously. I pulled my knee away. The couch was very long. She caressed the bottom of my leg.

He later reluctantly added that a penis, like a broomstick, extended from her body. He associated to feelings of loneliness and depression in relation to the separation. He hesitantly referred to the analyst's making sexual advances to him. He worried: "You know all my secrets; you've made up your mind about me. What if after five years,

I turn out to be what you first thought?" He followed with the claim, "I can be what I want to be." This dream was the first one in analysis; it revealed clearly the initial transference paradigms. The initial understanding of the dream, as an example of Feldman's (1945) typical dreams in analysis, was the wish to transform the analysis into a seductive gratification. Additionally, in retrospect, certain themes become clear: images of molding and fitting together; reversal from head to base; body contact and seductiveness in the service of maternal closeness; the importance of the phallic mother fantasy. There are already glimpses of the intense fear and wish that he has been, is, and will be only an idea in the analyst-mother's mind and of the need to defend against this danger. Fantasies of fitting together into complementary roles between patient and analyst to make one unit in a very fragile relationship were soon to emerge.

Following the holiday, he reported this dream: "I was performing fellatio on one of my students. As I was doing it, he seemed to grow larger and larger, not just his penis but his entire body. As he got bigger, I felt myself shrinking." He talked about a father-son relationship or one between brothers, where one grows larger while the other shrinks, with both tied together as a unit. Another dream reported in the hour featured depressed homosexual overtones and referred to the wish to change names, his own into the idealized analyst's, and the beginning of his fantasy play of condensing our names into one, into various combinations of each first name with a contraction of the two last names. Each person would be so addicted to the other, by an unbreakable bond, that separation would be impossible. In the third month of the analysis, he reported fantasies that he and I were twins, not two different people. Whatever was present in one was also in the other. Most prominent, then, were fears of his intense need for the analyst's help and fear of his destructiveness toward, and envy of, the analyst.

He repeatedly fantasied making "you into me." After six months of analysis, he reported several fantasies: the analyst does not leave the office; he has a twin who goes out to shop while the other stays inside; he does not have an existence apart from the patient but exists only in his presence. Before the first summer vacation, prominent oral, visual, and anal incorporative longings appeared; he dreamed of getting safely and deeply inside the body of another. He wished to be the only child living within the analyst-mother's womb and replacing or destroying the other imagoes within the analyst's mind or womb. There was a despairing tone to his wishes for surrender, for giving up his own wishes for life and growth simply to exist within the mother. A more optimistic wish was actively to replace the mother's needed objects, to fulfill a complementary role for her, so that she would then be sufficiently revived to mother him. He felt depressed and feared the regressive danger of becoming only a microscopic speck within the mind (womb) of the other.

DISCUSSION

Fantasies that the analyst was his twin served to protect Mr. X from needing another person fully separate from himself. By impersonating the other as twin, he became the other; he could with safety then be himself and, as it were, himself as the other. He feared giving in to the analytic process because of fears of loss of control over his intense hunger, greed, envy, and rage and his fearful expectations of frustration, disappointment, and hurt, as well as fears of masochistic surrender to the analyst as mother. The omnipotent illusion that he could impersonate the analyst served to protect him from such dangerous need and frustration. Because of his fearfulness of helpless inequality and surrender to the analyst, he sought to validate an illusion of twinlike equality. Denial of difference between self and other primarily defended against separateness and fears of destruction of, or surrender to, the object. Mr. X needed most to protect himself from his intense neediness of an object regarded as unavailable, exploitative, and neglectful of his own separate needs and traumatically seductive, while he still maintained an object tie.

In his twin fantasies, Mr. X partially substituted himself for the object so as to screen the danger of his intense need for the maternal object. This fantasy is a narcissistic defense against full acknowledgment of object need by representing the sought-after object as combining aspects of self and other. Intense object need persists with the comforting illusion of some influence or control over the object by partial, magical grafting of the self-image onto the object image. For Mr. X, the phallic mother imago represented a twinlike object invested with the important, differentiating aspect of the self. The fantasy served the aim of further differentiation from the archaic mother. Mr. X's prominent use of the phallic mother imago seemed to represent the partial substitution of himself for the dangerous object, with the aim of power over, or at least the wish for, equality with the object. Sexual and sexualized wishes to penetrate and remain within the mother's body led to fear of loss of separate identity. Twin fantasies, doubling, and visual validation of his phallic identity also reassured against fears of castration and loss of separate identity in getting inside the fascinating but dangerous archaic mother.

Mr. X was able to change considerably. His wishes to surrender, as in the twin transference fantasies, shifted from incorporative hunger to more overtly destructive wishes to rob, take, devour, and destroy. He could relinquish the twin fantasies to face in himself, to a degree, what he had needed to attribute to the powerful other. He continued, however, to use another for protection and as the container of his envy and destructiveness. His twin fantasies and his more general willingness to mix up self and other were narcissistic defenses against his fears of destroying a separate but vitally needed other. Put another way, narcissistic object relationships attenuated the danger of losing or destroying an object regarded as differentiated from, and not under, the influence of the patient. Incomplete separation-individuation is here used defensively. To the degree that he could not fully integrate his destructiveness, he continued to feel incomplete, as if a substantial part of himself were missing, as in a late dream (and associations) in analysis of picturing himself as only half a man, split down the middle. He continued to crave someone else to complete (protect) him. Through his seductiveness and prominent use of sexualization, he avoided the task of integrating his considerable rage.

Symbiotic illusions of magical protection are seductive, convincing, and difficult to relinquish. In pathological dependency, patients cling to another for such protection and feel unduly frightened of relinquishing it. Tasks in the interpretation and resolution of such unrealistic, magical, symbiotic illusions have been considered in chapters 2 and 4. Interactive defensive modes encourage children/patients to rely on someone else for their psychological management. A climate is established that to be alone psychologically is tantamount to death, that no one can manage this aloneness. Instead of the child/patient's increasingly being helped to tolerate and integrate his intense affects and wishes, so as to become an autonomous person, he becomes more frightened of his world, inside and outside. Self-doubting and self-undermining originally served to obscure angry criticism of parents and then continue to erode the patient's confidence in his feelings and judgments, so that he must look to others for answers. But the symbiotic illusion of reassurance, that everything will be all right so long as the couple is together, becomes too appealing to set aside, so as to feel one's dark side. This illusion becomes the (usually unconscious) emotional setup in the analysis. The patient, then, is primarily motivated by the desire "to be in analysis," even if he seems to work diligently at problems. The motivation will usually be clearest at times of separation, when the patient feels panicky. Or it can be seen when the patient seems content with himself and the analysis, primarily because of the illusion of the analyst's magical protection, without feeling motivated to work out further what is wrong within himself. This may be the case, even when the patient takes a complaining stance toward the analyst. Complaining may still cover the illusion of protection, through remaining in treatment. It is easy for the analyst to become impatient, critical, and angry with the patient about the latter's lack of motivation for change. Lack of motivation for change is precisely the problem. The patient with pathological dependency is terrified to let go of the illusion of magical protection. He is afraid to face, in a consistent way, his rage and destructiveness, which have been denied and reversed for so long, by turning the other from an object of hatred into a powerful savior.

Once these illusions can be successfully challenged in the analytic transference, then the underlying rage and destructiveness, now toward the analyst, must be consistently faced so as to be integrated. There is always the risk that analyst and patient will find it too difficult to bear their mutual hatred and destructiveness in the transference/countertransference interplay. This hatred is, indeed, the hardest part of analysis (Bird, 1972; Stein, 1981), the part that is most easily, at least partially, avoided. With the patients under consideration, it is all too easy for analyst and patient to collude in providing support and acceptance, unrealistically expecting too little of the patient. Not every patient can tolerate such analytic goals, and the analyst does not need to be unduly depriving and "tough." What is necessary is to balance the patient's needs for acceptance and support, in all their varied forms, against the need to work through such pathological dependency to the underlying rage and destructiveness.

Similarly, the patient's addiction to obtaining signs of love, from others and within himself, needs to be repeatedly interpreted as reassurance against unbearable hatred in himself and in the other. It is such a relief when the patient feels calm, at ease, good, and loved, in contrast to the "dis-ease" of feeling his own destructive anger and that of his object. Such patients will continually run from bearing some of their hatred to the (false) reassurance that all is well, that they are loved and lovable, and disown their terrifying rage.

The greater the patient's neediness, anxiety, demands, and sensitivity, the more difficult it may be for certain analysts to persevere with the analytic task. To relieve the analyst's distress caused by the patient and the reactivation of the analyst's own early conflicts that have been inadequately analyzed, extra-analytic interventions may be used. To the degree that the analyst must rationalize these interventions and is unable to understand his own distress and conflicts, the patient may consciously or unconsciously believe (sometimes correctly) that the analyst actually wants to join in a mutually gratifying, dependent relationship. This wish can be hidden from the analyst's own introspection under cover of a "friendly" analysis or by attributing the neediness entirely to the patient. That the patient unconsciously recognizes the analyst's gratification in their relationship further fixes the goal of actualization of dependent longings (as with patients Professor M and Ms. T). It is not by the analyst's words alone that such patients move away from their demands for dumplings (Freud, 1915) to participate in genuine, collaborative, psychoanalytic exploration of their neurosis. Such patients do considerable testing of the analyst to determine what he is willing to do for them and really wants of them—psychoanalytic goals or otherwise.

THE USE AND MISUSE OF THEORY

When stressed by difficult patients and by their own unintegrated neurosis, analysts may defensively use clinical theory so as to protect themselves. Analysts may easily misinterpret the extent of the new real-object relationship with the analyst, which Loewald (1960, 1970, 1971a, 1975, 1979), Gitelson (1962), and Greenson (1971, 1972) recommend. Loewald (1979) emphasizes that the transference relationship is akin to drama, not to be actualized, and that the analyst is there as a new object for instinctual investment, while consistently renouncing instinctual gratification (for self and patient) in favor of understanding and growth. While regarding the psychoanalytic situation as an interaction between two unequally positioned (especially in terms of level of organization) participants, Loewald does not advocate "interpersonalized mutualization of the transference" (Valenstein, 1979). When Greenson (1971) writes that the resolution of the transference neurosis occurs by its replacement by a real relationship and that resolution does not occur "by interpretation alone," the ambiguity may lend itself to defensive misuse by other psychoanalysts. Brenner's (1979) criticism of Greenson, although extreme, to my mind, has the virtue of preserving the analyst's task of understanding or, at least, attempting to understand and interpret, instead of leaving the analyst free to waver between offering and withholding warmth and concern. That is, Brenner advocates consistent interpretation of conflict rather than the provision of warmth or concern.

Similarly, when Gitelson (1962) wrote that concern and care by the analyst are what tends to cure, he is describing only the first phase of analysis and is not recommending the provision of anything extra, outside of standard technique. The diatrophic attitude, according to Gitelson, is implicit within standard technique. This attitude refers to the mother's concern for her child's care. It does not require active intervention, support, or corrective emotional experience. Gitelson claims, paradoxically, that the analyst's diatrophic attitude leads not to increased infantile neediness but rather to "the partial relinquishment of the anaclitic attitude" (p. 325), together with cooperation, identification, and collaboration. Friedman's (1969) warnings about the dangers of not interpreting transference longings in a first phase of analysis are relevant to analysts' uses of Gitelson (1962), Kohut (1971, 1977), and Modell (1976). To the degree that illusions are accepted, that is, not confronted and interpreted, the more they tend to be regarded as reality rather than fantasy. With patients Professor M and Ms. T, the illusion of a special dependent relationship with the analyst had, to varying degrees, been actualized, making this more difficult to interrupt and interpret. There was no evidence that any of these patients had actually required a long period in which such attachment to the analyst was not interpreted. On the contrary, in each example, once the analyst could clarify his own needs and goals with the analysand and proceed to analyze the dependent attachment to the analyst, significant change occurred within the analytic situation and within the patient. The limitations of analyzability then became more clearly those of the patient himself.

It should be clear that the patient's pathological dependency must be fully engaged within the transference to analyze it. To do so, the analyst must help the patient work through his fears, mistrust, and defensive avoidance of fully relying on the analyst, so as to allow regressive transference wishes to be felt. Of course, patients with pathological dependency vary as to how much they must protect themselves against this emerging within the treatment. The technical problem is how to encourage such regressive transference developments, while keeping the patient concerned with understanding his dependent attachment to the analyst and ultimately working his way out of it.

With needy, sensitive, anxiety-ridden patients with pathological dependency, as with anyone, the analyst must make the analytic situation tolerable so that an analytic process can unfold. The needier the patient, the greater may be the risk of behaviors that are common at times to analysts: warmly encouraging him, speaking more to alleviate the patient's anxiety and loneliness, occasionally joking, sharing a common interest, reassuring him, advising, telling anecdotes, and so on. The issue is not whether this is standard technique;

witness Gedo's (1979) anecdote about Loewenstein—while whistling may not be an appropriate interpretive vehicle for the analyst, telling a Jewish joke is. The analyst's efforts to engage the patient emotionally and to provide some comfort, "support," and a warm ambience may tend to actualize the patient's illusion that the dependent relationship with the analyst is real. The more the analyst actually gratifies the patient's wishes for dependent support, the more this gratification leads to a dependent enmeshment that is "beyond transference" because the patient has been encouraged by the analyst to seek the provision of functions, the patient feels unable to supply (as with patients Professor M and Ms. T). It may be very difficult for the analyst to avoid such interventions with more infantile patients who have ego deficits in managing themselves and their world. They may feel especially grateful to the analyst for "teaching" them what they have not yet managed to learn about regulating themselves and relating to others. The temptation may become very intense to put oneself in the analyst's hands, as if he were the Messiah. When contact with the analyst is so calming and reassuring, relieving the patient's terror of being alone, it can become so seductive to settle for this mode of relationship. It is far better, instead, that patient and analyst try to work through the patient's conflicts as far as possible rather than to assume that the patient will require lifelong support.

These concerns are especially relevant with patients who tend to confuse and deny the distinctions between transference and reality, between what is inside and what is outside. Bak's (1956) concept of defensive "overflowing" between self and object as a defense against destructiveness is relevant here. Denial of the outside world, based on a kind of magical omnipotence, is a significant part of such defense. Confused identification and projection mix up who is who, similar to what we have seen with Mr. X's twin transference. Such identification and projection lead to a defensive, narcissistic object relationship, one designed especially to protect against the danger of destruction and loss of the object. Defensive confusion occurs not only in psychotic patients; Professor M, Ms. T, and Mr. X (and even Freud in relation to Fliess) showed some of this defensive confusion between self and other, especially when threatened by their fears of killing the other (analyst). If self and other are defensively confused, the danger of losing or destroying the other is abated. The other's power is taken over, while one's own (destructive) power is given over. Sharp differentiation of self from other is undone, so that self and other, in at least partial merger, are regarded as magically omnipotent, invulnerable. Incomplete separation-individuation is here defensively exploited. It is essential that the analyst be clear and repeatedly clarify for such patients the latter's defensive tendency to confuse transference wishes toward the analyst with the actuality of the psychoanalytic situation. To a degree, such patients seek to transform the analytic situation into the illusion of their full control over the omnipotent analyst (world). The dependent transference, within which they feel good/loved/special, evokes this grandiose, invulnerable paradise. The patient, in effect, says, "When you accept me, then everything is fine; nothing can go wrong; I am protected and safe." The regressive, defensive purposes served by such illusions of being loved/loving must be explored both in the analytic transference and in the patient's childhood if the patient is to move beyond this position.

At some point, every analysand must relinquish dependency in the transference in order to grow. Patients, of course, vary in their needs to experience and maintain aspects of dependent transference. The risk for all patients and especially for those under focus here is of unconsciously clinging to illusions of magical omnipotence in partial, dependent merger with the analyst. The patients here considered tend to ignore the analyst's consistent interpretation of their wish for grandiose, omnipotent merger with the analyst because they would then feel threatened by separateness. Or they then feel intense hurt, rejection, rage, and a paranoid sense of betrayal. The patient feels that if the analyst loved (cared about) him, he would accept what the patient wants so very much and not give him such a hard time about it. It may be very difficult, indeed, for such a patient to believe in the analyst's sublimated concern in wanting to see the patient grow further. To be loved now (and to share in a grandiose, omnipotent merger) is an urgent demand. To be admired later for how one gives this up is too mature (tame) a substitute!

In contrast to Gitelson (1962), I am concerned with how the dependent transference may interfere with the patient's growth and further individuation and encourage feelings of inability to provide for himself, with a real, rather than wishful, turn to the analyst. The actualization of the patient's intense wishes for the provision of functions he feels unable to render (by an object on whom he is dependent) may interfere with their analytic resolution and actually attach the patient to the analyst. The standard, wishful transference setup, which emphasizes so starkly the contrast between transference wishes and the reality of the psychoanalyst qua psychoanalyst, may be attenuated and replaced by a real dependent relationship. We know from follow-up studies and reanalyses that it is not uncommon with patients who seem to complete analysis successfully that the apparent changes are in (large) part due to the actual presence of the analyst and the patient's emotional attachment (Oremland, Blacker, and Norman, 1975; Shapiro, 1976; Kohut, 1979; Levine, 1979; Szalita, 1982). Later, without the analyst's presence, such gains may soon fade.

Concepts such as the diatrophic attitude, holding environment, real relationship, and empathy—all useful concepts—may be used clinically to rationalize the analyst's interventions so as to lessen his own distress. When the analyst speaks more, this speaking may be because the patient requires it or because activity lessens the analyst's anxiety and reduces the pressure to do something for the complaining patient. The concept of the analyst as a new object is especially apt for exploitation by the analyst to handle any difficulties with preserving an analytic stance with respect to pathological dependency. It may be used to justify the provision of actual supplies for the patient because of the analyst's own emotional difficulties in the psychoanalytic setup with certain very needy patients. The problem is not the analyst's theory but the need to hide from himself his true intentions with analysands under the guise of theory. Strachey's (1934) emphasis is relevant as to the sharp distinction between fantasy and reality in order for transference interpretations to be mutative. There is a danger that the analyst will become the good object the patient seeks, even if only at times, rather than helping the patient to work through transference wishes. In Strachey's terms, the analyst here becomes not a good but a bad object. Certain functions, such as tension and anxiety reduction, may occur automatically in the presence of the analyst without the latter's doing anything specifically. How the patient uses the analyst for this purpose, together with the wishes and fantasies about the analyst that come together here, becomes subject to analytic scrutiny. For the analyzable patient, the analyst does not ordinarily seek to fill in missing functions and structures but to join the patient in understanding himself. To do otherwise is to usurp the patient's own role. Such intrusion into the patient's life and mind may arrest further individuation during psychoanalysis, with the neurotic potential for sadomasochistic dependent submission to the authority of the analyst. To regard the patient, even temporarily, as the incapable child he fantasizes himself to be precludes the understanding and integration of the defensive functions of this regressive fantasy within the totality of the patient as a competent adult. Even with seemingly infantile, demanding, dependent border-line patients in psychotherapy, far better results are obtained by confronting the aggression, impossible demands, entitlement, and masochism than exclusively "empathizing" with the patient's felt deprivation and disability (Kernberg, 1975).

The analyst may feel pressured to speak, gratify dependent wishes, or alleviate the patient's distress in order to disavow such intense aggression in the patient, as well as in himself. The patient's pressure on the analyst to "do something" may be specifically related to making destructiveness in oneself disappear, while "blaming" the analyst for the patient's being stuck with his hatred. Or pressure on the analyst to "do something" may derive from envy and destructive spoiling by the patient of what the analyst does give. The danger here is the analyst's use of the concept of holding environment, diatrophic attitude, new object relationship, and so on to sanction activity intended to avoid destructive feelings and wishes in the analysand and in the analyst. Of course, the clinical issue is to assess, sensitively and tactfully, what the patient can tolerate and to respond to the patient's genuine need rather than the analyst's defensive need. In large measure, the patient can go only so far as the analyst can. If the analyst is able to integrate his own destructiveness, without avoiding this by pathological, interactive dependent modes (here with the patient), the possibility is open for the patient to do the same. But if the analyst cannot manage the patient's destructiveness, he will need to collude with his analysand in protecting both of them from the full force of each one's feeling rage and hatred within the transference-countertransference interaction. It is so much less painful and so much more gratifying for patient and analyst to focus on good, loving feelings between them, rather than to persist with the analytic task of fully experiencing destructive anger. The temptation may, indeed, be great for the analyst to leave the patient alone with his addiction to feeling loved. It is so much more difficult continually to show the patient his hunger to be loved and then to interpret how this protects him from feeling his continual underlying rage. The analyst himself has to have been able to relinquish such defensive undoing of destructiveness by compulsive/addictive reassurance of loving. The analyst must be comfortable with his own aggression in repeatedly frustrating the patient's illusions and turning the patient back on his hatred and his hatred of the analyst. At the very least, the patient will hate the analyst for the latter's relentless pursuit (even when it is carried out with tact and sensitivity) of the patient's dependent avoidance of integrating his destructiveness and for the analyst's thereby repeatedly spoiling the patient's illusions and defensive infantile gratifications. Beyond this reason for his hatred, the patient will have to become comfortable with his rage and destructive aggression from every developmental stage, as repeated with the analyst, to let go of his pathological need for another.

12

THE EXCITEMENT OF SADOMASOCHISM

Consideration of sadomasochistic object relations is important in this book because it is frequently, although not invariably, found as a clinical phenomenon in patients with pathological dependency. The conceptual issues involved in understanding and analyzing sadomasochistic object relations overlap with the dilemmas of pathological dependency. Finally, part of the therapeutic impasse in pathological dependency often involves sadomasochistic enactment. Even if the treatment relationship in pathological dependency does not become frankly sadomasochistic, its analytic management is very similar. It should not be surprising that relationships within which the partners' roles are so unequal will be similar.

The psychoanalytic literature, by and large, regards the etiologic differences between masochistic character disorder and masochistic perversion as unknown. The interrelations between masochistic character disorder and masochistic sexual excitement are complex. It is not sufficiently appreciated that sadomasochistic enactments, both sexual and not explicitly sexual, are exciting, often intensely so. We will focus on this excitement, sexual and nonsexual, in sadomasochistic object relationships. This focus will help us to explore patients' difficulty with relinquishing sadomasochistic relationships.

Stoller (1976a) proposed that sexual and nonsexual excitement involves rapid oscillation among fantasied danger, repetition of prior trauma, and fantasied triumph and revenge. He especially emphasized sexual excitement as defense against anxiety. Shapiro (1981) suggested that what is exciting for the sexual sadomasochist is playing at giving in to fantasies of dominance and submission. This dynamic, however, in no way distinguishes the moral masochist from the masochistic pervert. This formulation leaves us wondering why all moral masochists are not perverts inasmuch as they all share conflicts about dominance and submission.

It will be helpful to bear in mind Freud's (1905) early proposal that sadism and masochism are erotic expressions of aggression. That is, a focus on the erotic in sadomasochism will keep us close to the excitement. Sadomasochistic object relations are a way of loving (and hating) others and oneself and are especially concerned with intense ways of engaging another so as to mitigate dangers of separateness, loss, loneliness, hurt, destruction, and guilt. Aggression and sexuality are adapted to this end of intense connectedness with another person. Multiple defensive and adaptive functions are subserved. Sadomasochistic object relations can be viewed schematically as a complex defensive system against destruction and loss, within which relationships are continually pushed to the brink, with the reassurance that the relationship (at least some imaginary parent–child relationship) will never end. To the degree that separateness is too frightening to be tolerated, the patient will fear and be unable to relinquish such sadomasochistic bonding. Despite the threats, fights, provocations, and excitement, sadomasochistic object relations tend to be stable, enduring, and highly resistant to change.

Here is a brief sample from Sacher-Masoch's (1870) *Venus in Furs* to illustrate the need to manage both separateness and destructiveness in sadomasochism:

> *Severin*: "I want your power over me to become law; then my life will rest in your hands and I shall have no protection against you. Ah, what delight to depend entirely on your whims, to be constantly at your beck and call! And then—what bliss!—when the goddess shows clemency, the slave will have permission to kiss the lips on which his life and death depend" [p. 163].
>
> *Wanda to Severin*: "You are no longer my lover, and therefore, I am relieved of all duties and obligations towards you; you must regard my favors as pure benevolence. You can no longer lay claim to any rights, and there are no limits to my power over you. Consider that you are little better now than a dog or an object; you are my thing, the toy that I can break if it gives me a moment of pleasure. You are nothing, I am everything; do you understand?" [p. 164].
>
> *The contract between them*: "Mrs. von Dunajew may not only chastise her slave for the slightest negligence or misdemeanor as and when she wishes but she will also have the right to maltreat

him according to her humor or even simply to amuse herself; she is also entitled to kill him if she so wishes; in short, he becomes her absolute property" [fragment, p. 184].

Usually, layers of anxiety, defense, and guilt cover the excitement of sadomasochism. In my experience, patients with sadomasochistic character disorder have sadomasochistically distorted sexuality (not, however, structured perversions). Like the excitement more generally, this distortion is not readily apparent; it is uncovered only by analysis.

Certain similarities in defense and adaptation should be noted between sadomasochistic object relations and sadomasochistic perversion. The content of the excitement and the dynamic uses made of it are similar in both. Sadomasochistic excitement involves entering into what is ordinarily dangerous and forbidden: incestuous, exploitative, inappropriate, hurtful, infantile, regressive. Excited, intense feelings and experiences substitute for genuine love and caring and defend against negative feelings in oneself and in the other. When one feels unloved and unloving, illusions of intense, excited involvement with another are substituted. The couple has difficulty being separate and feeling valuable, so that they must be with each other and at each other. This dilemma is then idealized as if it were wonderful love. "You can't stand to be without me; you can't resist me; I'm the most important person in the world to you!"—such grandiose, exciting, seeming adoration fills in the gap of one's feeling unloved. When the promise of such adoration is frustrated, then rage, hurt, and rejection are evoked. These feelings threaten disruption of the bond and lead to more provocation and attack so as to reconnect, even more intensely, with the partner. Such patients become addicted to the exciting illusion of special (grandiose) adoration. This becomes the background for erotized repetition. Genetic and dynamic links, especially in relation to defense against hostile aggression, are described among sexual seductiveness, sexualization, and sadomasochism. Similarities are noted in the object relations (perverse misuse of others) of certain patients with sadomasochistic character disorder and sadomasochistic perverts. Patients with masochistic character disorder are relatively able to express conflict in fantasy, to handle it within their own mind. Masochistic perverts differ in being impelled to enact unconscious fantasies into concrete reality so as to render them valid and credible. They cannot accomplish this process intrapsychically; their ability to symbolize and to resolve conflict in fantasy is impaired.

EROTIZED REPETITION

Contemporary psychoanalysts have tended to overly desexualize masochism. (See Maleson, 1984, and Grossman, 1986, for discussions of this). These writings have helped to differentiate moral masochism from masochistic perversion and to trace Freud's views of sadism and masochism as component instincts. Further, a multiple-function approach to masochism must certainly emphasize the variety of nonsexual meanings encompassed in clinical descriptions. Nevertheless, this tack has tended to minimize the motivational pressure, the driven excitement, in sadomasochism. Defensively sexualized repetition (see chapter 6) remains a useful perspective from which to view clinical samples of sadomasochism. Sexualization of hostile aggression is an important contributor to sadomasochism. Sexualization as defense is usually considered in relation to painful affects, hostile aggression, and narcissistic needs. To be sure, not all samples of sadomasochistic behavior can be demonstrated to involve defensively sexualized repetition. But I am impressed with the confluence of moral masochism with defensively sexualized repetition. Similar genetic and dynamic issues tend to occur where sexualization is used as a predominant form of defense and in sadomasochistic character pathology. Separateness, loss, helplessness, and destruction are central dangers to be defended against by sexualization and by moral masochism. Sexualization and sadomasochism are both especially useful ways to manage intensely frightening destructiveness.

It is exciting to feel able to induce intense affective responses in another person, to overcome the other's barriers, to feel in control and dominant, able to make the other feel bad, guilty, weak, inferior, defective. It is exciting to hold another person in the palm of one's hand, to push another to the point of losing control, attacking, and leaving, and then to be reassured that this loss will not occur. Others can be simultaneously gotten rid of and held onto. When one is terrified of separateness and destructiveness, it is very reassuring, indeed, to feel able to combine getting rid of and holding on. It is not my intention here to attempt a comprehensive review of the literature on masochism. What I am after, instead, is focusing on why masochistic object relations are held onto so tenaciously. Parkin's (1980) view of masochistic enthrallment is relevant as the attempt to share in and borrow the mother's power and fury. I prefer, however, to emphasize the masochist's willingness to surrender to the hostile (critical) parental view of him in order to feel the illusion of magical protection, caring, and specialness under the domination of the powerful (destructive) parent. Surrender protects both child and parent from the dangers of the hatred and destructiveness in both of them and makes possible some relationship between them. The child (patient) accepts his role as the worthless, defective, shitty one in submission to the hostile, rejecting parent as the good, idealized one. This becomes a kind of "seduction of the aggressor" (Loewenstein, 1957). It is seductive, indeed, to offer the other the grandiose prospect of doing whatever he pleases with you. The child (patient) can then extract some caring from the parent, protect the parent from his guilt at hating/rejecting the child, and enhance his own worthiness through his suffering. He plays at the illusion that since he is the bad one, when he finally becomes good, the parent will love him. To face the fact of the parent's inability or deficiency in loving and the parent's hatred and destructiveness is too barren a prospect for the child. To face one's own rage and destructiveness is too frightening. The masochist seeks mastery and control and associated narcissistic enhancement through the provocation and exaggeration of suffering. The willingness to continue to view oneself through the hateful and distorted eyes of a rejecting parent, because of all of these defensive and compensatory gains, can be strong, indeed. The wish to surrender, to hate oneself, to feel depressed, shitty, worthless, incapable, crippled is in these terms, an appeal to a parent for love, caring, and protection, especially from the rage and destructiveness in the patient and in the parent.

Underneath the layer of game playing in sadomasochistic object relations is a more serious destructiveness—destroying another's integrity, self-respect, autonomy, and free choice. This point is where it becomes frightening to face the parent's destructiveness in wanting to cripple oneself as well as one's own destructive hatred of the parent. If one feels terrified of separateness and of one's destructiveness and continues to crave parental loving, it becomes impossible to integrate one's hatred and destructiveness and to let go of the pathological relationship with the destructive parent. Sadomasochism's combined destroying/getting rid of and holding onto avoids this more mature integration. Instead of facing what has been wrong, the patient becomes excited in repeating what a parent (mother) did with one. Indeed, the excited, erotized repetition serves to ward off the horrors of destructiveness, mother's and one's own. Erotization tames destructiveness; one can pretend that it is a kind of loving relatedness, an exciting game sought by both participants. Playing this game is very different from acknowledging that one person hates, envies, and begrudges another his own life and his own separateness and autonomy and wants to destroy them. Dangers of fusion through passive masochistic surrender are defended against by the illusion of sadistic omnipotent control, the ability to render another helpless. That is, the masochist is hardly just a passive victim. Under that pose are his hungry destructiveness, his wish to control, dominate, rob, and despoil the other. Submission to a stronger object serves to protect the masochist from fears of his own destructive wishes and affects.

THE GENETIC BACKGROUND OF EROTIZED SADOMASOCHISM

One common genetic background for both sexualization (when extensively used) and sadomasochism is a relationship with a relatively unavailable, depressed mother who is sometimes inappropriately and overly seductive but much of the time is unresponsive and unempathic. Extractiveness in the service of mother's pressing needs combines with her sexualized defense against her own destructiveness and rejection of the child. These motivations are commonly expressed in a sadomasochistic relationship between mother and child. Terrors of loss and destruction are countered by the illusion that mother and child will remain tightly bound together forever. Such mothers resent the burdens of child care. They wish to be the one who is cared for. They envy the child his new chance in life, his autonomy, capacities, strength, youth, attractiveness, phallus (i.e., whatever they feel they lack). Out of envy and hatred, the mother unconsciously wishes to destroy these attributes of the child. She cripples the child and bonds the child forever to her, with a reversal of roles. Idealization of pretended loving (reaction formation) and seductive overstimulation emphasize that the mother–child relationship is good and loving rather than exploitative and destructive. The child identifies with mother's predominant defensive positions and relates to her in a complementary way. This encourages both sexualization and sadomasochism as defensive and adaptive phenomena to contain and soothe intolerable affects.

Sadomasochistic provocation of a child can lead to overstimulation of sexuality and aggression, overwhelming the child with affects of arousal, rage, hurt, and humiliation. Being the object of such intense attention from a parent, in sexually seductive or sadomasochistic ways, stirs feelings of specialness and exception. These alternate with feelings of neglect and loneliness, guilt at one's transgressions (sexual or sadomasochistic), overstimulation, rage, and helplessness at one's exploitation and neglect. Defensive identification and erotic or sadomasochistic repetition aim to master the overwhelming affects, as well as to repeat the idealized pleasures. Being the child of sadomasochistic parents can be a chronic strain trauma. That is, the child is frequently and chronically flooded with anger and sexual arousal, without adequate parental protection for modulating these affects. As with Q, whom I shall describe shortly, there may be a lack of clear boundaries between family members. Autonomy is not to be respected, but to be destroyed in the service of intense neediness. Family members are not to be separate and different, each responsible for tolerating and resolving his own difficulties. The destruction of autonomy encourages and perpetuates interactive defensive modes, pathological forms of object relating, and defensive analization. Mixing and merging of self and other, of good and bad confuses boundaries, identity, and psychic contents. One blames the other and tries to make the other responsible and guilty for what is wrong within oneself. This mode of relating must interfere with separateness and increasing tolerance and responsibility for one's own affects and wishes. The more uncomfortable a person feels with his own psychic contents, the more he must turn to another for protection. Once this tendency has become automatic, change, even within a psychoanalysis, can become very difficult indeed. Bear in mind that masochism need not have this particular genetic background; there need not have been sadomasochistic parents. What is emphasized here are the consequences of having had sadomasochistic parents.

Here is a brief example, reported to me by the horrified father, my patient. Q, a toddler, was watching her parents in another intense, sadomasochistic fight. Mother was screaming obscenities at father and trying to claw at him; she seemed to be out of control. Father, angry and helpless, grabbed his wife's hands and yelled at her to stop fighting in front of Q, who became excited, overstimulated, overwhelmed. She, too, began to scream, "Shut up, you fuckin' bitch!" and grabbed at her mother. Father was appalled, thinking that Q looked just like his wife—she was becoming a toddler sadomasochist!

Q had been overindulged, the parents making conscious attempts to keep her from feeling frustrated. Q had been allowed unlimited access to the parental bed and to the mother's body; the mother had overidentified and confused herself with the frustrated child. Q had not been provided with reasonable limits to her need satisfaction and reasonable experiences of frustration. These would have been necessary for her to develop tolerance and patience while learning to soothe and comfort herself. She was encouraged to identify with both parents' urgent demandingness and wish that there be no frustration or (reasonable) separateness. Parents and child repeatedly re-created an exciting and entitled primal scene from which none of them was to be excluded. Q, too, could go after whatever bodily gratifications she desired. In these fighting scenes, this young child had to deal with her parents' being out of control, enraged, and destructive. There was a temporary loss of a protective parent to help modulate her affects.

PSYCHODYNAMICS OF EROTIZED SADOMASOCHISM

The child attempts to get and maintain some mothering in an otherwise very difficult situation. Rage, hurt, humiliation, exploitation, neglect, and betrayal require powerful regressive defenses. Both sexualization and sadomasochism are especially useful for the illusion that destructiveness is caring. Excited, intense feelings and experiences are idealized and defensively focused on. Here are important dynamic similarities among sadomasochistic character, sexualization, and perversion. The excitement, from mixing together intense hostile aggression and sexuality, allows such patients, like perverts, temporarily to master rage and other negative affects. During imaginary, as well as enacted, seductive and provocative encounters, there occurs a temporary defensive transformation of negatively toned, aggressively infiltrated images of self and other(s) into positive, pleasurably regarded ones. Sexual arousal, masturbation, and enactment of seductive fantasy all help temporarily to disown negative aspects of the self and to appropriate dangerous aspects of the object. Sexual responsiveness, in fantasy or in actual enactments, reassures against fears of loss or destruction of the object or oneself.

An extreme example of a sexualized defense occurred in Ms. W, a psychotically delusional patient whose analyst spoke to her about hospitalization because the patient and the treatment relationship had become unmanageable. For the entire session, she smiled, stared seductively into the analyst's eyes and insisted she would never leave him and he could never leave her. Words did not count, nor did they have anything to do with what was real—an intense, exciting, passionate bond that could never be broken. The more she feared loss or destruction of the relationship with the analyst, the more Ms. W needed to tempt, seduce, and provoke the analyst into excited interaction with her. She had long overtly and implicitly offered to be the analyst's most adoring one, so that she and he would share the grandiose splendor of being god and goddess of the world. This union was now to be consummated. Ms. W would never be apart from him, a merger that she attempted to enact! She covered over her destructive wishes to devour and drain the analyst with seductiveness, adoration, and loving words; however, her hungry destructiveness (and primitive guilt about it) and terror of separation broke through the "loving" cover to spoil it. Ms. W refused to leave the analyst's office, followed him home, phoned him repeatedly during the night, and tried to enter his home. She dealt with her guilt about her hostile aggression by insisting that the analyst was now the cause of the problem. If only he would leave his family, live with her, and love her, everything would now be fine!

In less extreme form, in neurotic sadomasochism, the illusion of loving conceals destructiveness and the wish to misuse the other. We could also discuss "aggressivization" of object relations in sadomasochism; abundantly available aggressive drive derivatives infiltrate libidinal object relations in the service of intense attachment, relatedness, and domination.

In the sexual seductiveness of sadomasochistic object relations, the object cannot be left alone, outside of one's own orbit. The pair can neither be comfortably together nor be apart. Hatred drives the couple apart; fear of separateness and loneliness forces them together. Control, domination, submission, and arousal of intense affects by omnipotent manipulation keep the couple engaged. Denial and projective identification aim to put into the other what cannot be tolerated within oneself. The other is made the "bad one," who must then seek absolution and loving forgiveness from oneself. Badness is then repeatedly made not to count. It is magically turned into goodness. Fixed, clear moral standards have little force. What matters is to be accepted by the other, however this acceptance is accomplished. During phases of sexualized reunion, each partner feels accepted, forgiven, and no longer bad. The badness in each has been magically repudiated. Both partners are now good; it is others who are bad.

CLINICAL VIGNETTES

Ms. O complained of feeling depressed and hopeless that she would ever have a satisfactory love relationship. She had again broken up with Xa, although this relationship was, she thought, the best she had yet had. Xa had told her repeatedly that he would not tolerate her provocative fighting. They had just resumed their relationship after another "ending." On Christmas Day, Ms. O gave Xa a number of gifts. The previous day she had complained on the phone that Xa had not gotten her any gifts. He arrived with a lovely bouquet of flowers.

As Xa unwrapped the gifts Ms. O had gotten him, she became more and more incensed that he had not gotten her anything besides the flowers. She tried to ignore her feelings but, instead, found herself boiling up, wanting to go at Xa. Finally, she could not resist. She attacked Xa for his lack of generosity and worked herself and him into a frenzy. He tried to calm her down and briefly got her interested in sex, but there was no stopping Ms. O. Xa left, again announcing that the relationship was over. The patient called his home repeatedly, then took a long cab ride to his home. She left him a note and multiple messages on his answering machine and apologized, saying that she wanted to see him again. This provocation was a repetitive pattern. When she felt ignored, neglected, or abandoned, Ms. O would attack the other person; she would try to provoke him into fighting with her and make him feel guilty and responsible for her. She was now well aware how exciting provocative fighting was and how difficult it was for her to resist the temptation to engage others in such scuffles.

With the analyst also, especially before separations, she would be provocative, attacking, guilt provoking, trying to worry him and make him responsible for what would happen to her in his absence. She sought to elicit some intense reaction from the analyst that would reassure her that she, in effect, would be emotionally inside him during the separation. If the analyst felt worried about her, guilty or angry with her, she could imagine that she was with him during the separation. The patient would repeatedly become more demanding and difficult with the analyst up to the point where he was expected to lose control, get angry, and threaten to get rid of her. When she feared this result might happen, she would quickly change and behave herself to undo the danger of being gotten rid of. In this enactment of a beating wish, she also wanted the analyst to restrain and contain her hatred and destructiveness. The analyst was to spank her and thus show her that he both loved her and was strong enough to protect both of them from her intense destructiveness. She could not at all take for granted the analyst's concern and ability to help her to contain her destructiveness.

The reader will need some background to appreciate why Mr. P felt so anxious and uncomfortable on an initial date with V, an attractive, capable woman. Mr. P was a very rigid, consciously paranoid and schizoid, single corporate executive who was afraid of his own feelings, of intimate contact with others, and of others' controlling and dominating him. With me, Mr. P was controlled and guarded, fearful of really becoming emotionally involved, of any spontaneity. He was referred to me with low back pain syndrome. His hesitation to resume his life fully, while some leg pain persisted, conveyed the feeling that, if he actively made a move on his own behalf, he would be punished. That expectation is, indeed, what he had felt as a child with his tyrannical, sadistic, alcoholic mother as well as in relation to a serious gastrointestinal disease. Mother was prone to rage attacks and torturing of the family, especially of the father, who was repeatedly humiliated (as not being a man) in front of the children. Mr. P's passive father seemed to surrender at home to mother's sadistic attacks, and he seemed uninvolved with the patient. Mother would competitively exhibit her intelligence to Mr. P, so that he felt stupid and worthless by comparison. His childhood gastrointestinal disease, not diagnosed until he was six, also contributed to his intense self-restraint and sense of defectiveness. Unpredictable vomiting, diarrhea, failure to gain weight, hospitalization, and violent reaction to foods were all part of his early years. Life became easier for him once this disease was diagnosed; he could then have more control over his body by avoiding certain foods.

Mr. P had good reason to be guarded and mistrustful, to expect nothing good from other people. His best feelings as a child involved helping mother to admire herself, usually at his own expense. Intense feelings of disappointment, neglect, deprivation, hunger, rage, and sadism were warded off by Mr. P's sadomasochistic, paranoid system, in which all emotion was carefully regulated. He maintained object ties through his negatively experienced contact with "tormentors" at work. Mr. P was very frightened of closeness with others; he had not had any satisfying intimate relationships. Especially when he seemed to want to feel closer to others, he would experience them as wanting to force him into "being friendly," behavior that he would resent and resist fiercely. His need not to give in to others or to himself was striking.

It was touching to observe this very schizoid man begin to cry for himself about his deprivation and abuse and begin to want something more for himself. He began to feel the right, less colored by shame, to want the analyst to be there for him, really to help him. So much of the time he had tried to go through the motions of just talking for the sake of talking and wanted nothing from the analyst. He began to allow himself to feel angry at the analyst's absences, to want caring and intimacy with the analyst. I was moved when he was able to complain that I seemed less involved in a particular session, that he wanted to feel my concern. He was surprised to discover that he could turn to me for help during a particularly difficult period; not only would I not turn him away, but I welcomed his allowing himself to need me. He sobbed as he allowed himself to thank me; he contrasted my emotional availability with his childhood neglect and rebuff. Increasingly, he began to tolerate and integrate his considerable rage from underneath his masochistic submissiveness, self-hatred, and self-restraint.

Now let us return to his date with V. That V had been "all over him" physically that night had especially made him anxious. He thought there was an inconsistency between her apparent strength and her so quickly coming on to him. Mr. P's anxiety was related, in part, to his own wishes to have sexual control over V. He was very uncomfortable with his wishes that V would become so aroused sexually that he could do anything he wanted with her. She would go helplessly out of her mind with desire, so that Mr. P could, in effect, lead her around by her genitals. He relished V's feeling humiliated and debased as she abjectly desired that he satisfy her. He would be cool, indifferent, powerful, strong. Then Mr. P would not have to fear that V could humiliate or hurt him.

To the wish sexually to dominate V, Mr. P associated an adolescent memory he had recently recalled. When he was 16, mother had had one of her usual drunken fights with the entire family and had especially taunted father for not being a man, for being a fairy. Removing her blouse and bra, mother had stood, bare-breasted, in front of their home and defied father and patient to stop her, inviting sexual attack from "anyone man enough to handle her." Mr. P recalled, and now could allow himself to feel with hatred, lust, and tears, how much he wanted to go at his mother. He wanted to teach her a lesson, to make her behave herself; she should act like a normal mother, who would not humiliate and attack his father and himself. He also wanted to possess this wild sexual animal that was his mother. Mr. P could now connect his masturbatory fantasies of strangling women by squeezing their necks with his hands with wanting to shut his mother up. By attacking his mother, he would stop her from saying all those horrible things. He wanted to destroy mother (women) while also enjoying her body as he pleased. In this necrophilic fantasy, the woman was safe only if totally dominated (dead). The intensity of his sexual sadism frightened him. He quickly resumed his defensive posture and felt anxious, insecure, vulnerable; his aggression was again projected onto others.

If Mr. P did not control and dominate the woman, he feared becoming trapped forever. It was difficult for him to tolerate his own wishes for passive masochistic surrender. He was eventually able to describe wishes to get fully inside the body of the woman, where he would feel safe from her critical attacks, neglect, or abandonment. If he became part of the woman, she would not attack herself, so she would not hurt him. The only way he felt he had connected with his mother was by entering into her world. He had seductively offered to give himself up for her greater glory: "My mother couldn't resist that I would give up everything for her. That was too seductive!" It remained very hard for him to believe that anyone would want him otherwise, for himself.

Eventually, Mr. P came to acknowledge that underneath the image of the dangerous mother was his view of how fragile and vulnerable she seemed. He had been so afraid of his mother's emotional collapse in the face of his criticism or anger that he had felt constrained to be protective with her. Much of his terror of his sadism and destructiveness was connected with this exaggerated danger of his power. When he became freer to criticize me angrily, he would quickly feel the need partially to undo attack and would acknowledge how I was helping him. He was able to feel his fearfulness that I could not withstand his angry attacks.

ON THE WAY TO PERVERSE ENACTMENT

In both sexual seductiveness and sadomasochistic object relations, intensity of arousal and connectedness substitutes for genuine love and caring. The more that negative feelings in oneself and in the other must be denied, the more need there is for repetitive arousal of the other and of oneself. Erotized repetition seeks to recapture and cling to aspects of infantile love because one does not feel securely loved and safe. Simultaneously, erotized repetition attempts to master hostility, fears of loss, narcissistic injury, and even specifically sexual conflicts, such as about homosexuality (Blum, 1973).

Both sexual seductiveness and sadomasochism between parent and child lead to attempts to idealize the intensely exciting encounters. What becomes special and emphasized for the parent–child couple is their intense, exciting bond. They do what others dare not. Each will give himself totally to the other, will do whatever the other wants. That this enmeshment is mutual using and extracting, not love and respect for a separate other, is denied and covered over by passion. The psychology of the exception not only is used as protection against guilt about such transgression and misuse but also is elaborated more generally to protect against hatred and destructiveness (see chapter 9). Superego corruption is fostered between parent and child by denial of complicity in such seductive and sadomasochistic transgressions (Blum, 1973). Specialness, entitlement, and the ability to seduce and arouse others are all used to defend against superego criticism for one's destructiveness. Such patients have, by and large, not completed the task of superego integration; they remain with harsh, personified, poorly integrated superego forerunners. During childhood, the ordinary rules and expectations did not apply. At times, a parent could do as he wanted, regardless of the consequences for the child. Reality was not reasonably assessed and clarified for the child by the parent. Reality could be what such a needy parent deemed it to be. Such children had to struggle between times of great indulgence and attention, with sexual and sadomasochistic arousal, and times of feeling ignored, neglected, and abandoned by the parent, who could not remain appropriately emotionally involved with the child. Of course, such children will seek to reengage the parent in whatever ways work (sexual seductiveness or sadomasochistic provocation). They will have little reason to assess themselves according to ordinary reality. They will seek to share in the parent's narcissistic specialness as expressed in special indulgence, stimulation, excitement, and even special shared guilt. Here they can again feel grandiose rather than worthless. Erotized or sadomasochistic repetition seeks to recapture such specialness.

One aspect of what is exciting is the sense of what is ordinarily forbidden, what should not be, which is transgressed: incestuous, exploitative, inappropriate, hurtful, infantile, regressive. The excitement itself and excited repetition serve to ward off guilt at awareness of what one should not do. Immersion in the excitement and idealization of the forbidden and wrongful behavior are focused upon to distract from more realistic, guilty self-assessment. Sade prescribes sexualized excitement clearly: any horrible feeling can be avoided if only one gets sufficiently excited. Sadomasochistic excitement, like sexual seductiveness, involves similarly entering into dangerous and forbidden territory. It always has the meaning of special adoration, which feels magnetic, irresistible. The masochistic patient gives in to regressive wishes to escape from autonomy by becoming embroiled with another in hostile aggressive and erotic contact. This interaction stirs up and mixes up who is who, in an exciting and consuming surrender. Remember that this merger need not be psychotic. At neurotic levels, such defensive analization of object relations (reversibly) plays at merging and mixing. This protects against separateness, destruction, responsibility (and guilt) for what is within oneself and whatever is dangerous about the other (by pretending that it is one's own, a kind of introjective denial in fantasy). The knowledge that this behavior is wrong, destructive to oneself and to the other, and infantile and regressive adds to the excitement (and guilt). The patient disclaims responsibility for his behavior. He plays the sadomasochistic game with the analyst, who is to try to stop him—or become so frustrated, angry, hopeless, and defeated that he is unable to help the patient. But in his angry frustration, the analyst is never to let the patient go, thereby proving his love and reassuring that separation will never occur. What is dissociated here is the patient's difficulty with autonomy and self-regulation and acknowledgment of the serious destructiveness embedded within such sadomasochistic game playing. The excitement of the game denies the seriousness of the intended destructiveness.

Sexual seductiveness and sadomasochism tend to come together in nonperverse masochistic patients once defenses against such awareness have been interpreted. It becomes exciting for such patients to make another person vulnerable or to become vulnerable oneself to being controlled, dominated, exploited, and humiliated through sexual arousal. With interpretation of defense, nonperverse masochistic patients, to a degree, tend toward playing at perverse sexual misuse of others. This does not become structured perversion but perverse sexual desires, which are partly enacted and partly contained in pleasurable fantasy. That is, the patient does not become a sadomasochistic pervert, although his desires to torture and be tortured may become sexually exciting. In analyzing masochistic, pathologically dependent patients who are not perverts, the analyst should expect such perverse trends to emerge often. That the patient regards perverse sexual misuse of others as "play" conceals his more destructive intent. To arouse and control another through his own intense sexual arousal makes the patient feel powerful, an irresistible seducer, and it gives him the illusion that he is loved. Negative qualities in the object and in oneself are warded off by emphasis on one's own magical ability to bring the other to life sexually. For the moment it is as if nothing else matters. The need to seduce others, too, may repeat childhood patterns of seductiveness in a sadomasochistic relationship with a parent. Exploitation, misuse, and humiliation of the vulnerable one, with associated rage, hurt, and betrayal, are defended against by excited sexualized repetition. Even though there is a reversal from passive to active in the initiation of such scenes, the patient inwardly clings to the regressive and destructive parent–child relationship. Excited repetition puts off until another day the need to relinquish the parent–child relationship and to take responsibility for one's own affects and wishes.

Sadomasochism, in this sense, is a complex regressive defense against varied dangers of autonomy. It is a kind of running home to what is safe and familiar. One person is to beat and punish another repetitively to contain and atone for what is "bad" within himself. The patient runs away from what frightens him within himself and runs toward his craving for protection against such dangers. To the degree that autonomy (and responsibility for one's own wishes and affects) is frightening, regressive defensive solutions will be sought.

We have not discussed sexuality other than as an excited, sado-masochistic capturing or surrender to another; however, we are still not in the area of perversion. Patients may, indeed, feel driven to arouse, seduce, and conquer in the service of sadomasochistic exploi-tation, bondage, and domination. Unless this behavior is obligatory for adult sexual functioning, unless there is no other way, this is not structured perversion. The need to enact seductive fantasy with another, who is made to fit one's own fantasies, does move toward perversion.

SADOMASOCHISTIC PERVERSION

The sadomasochistic pervert, in contrast to the neurotic, tends to have a sexual fantasy life that is rigid and impoverished. He has only one way to become sexually aroused. Unlike the neurotic, the pervert is relatively unable to resolve conflict solely within fantasy. Hence, the patient's obligatory fantasy must be repetitively enacted so as to validate his needed illusions. I find it useful to make a schematic division of perverts into higher and lower level types and to think of higher and lower level functions within these types (see chapter 13). The higher level sadomasochistic pervert uses perverse behavior primarily to permit sexual functioning and orgasm as a defense against castration anxiety and oedipal guilt. He attempts by his act to validate his unconscious fantasy (of the phallic woman: signifying that castration does not occur) in order to defend against intense castration anxiety, so as to be able to function sexually. The lower level sadomasochistic pervert uses sexualization in the service of narcissism, closeness, need satisfaction, defense, repair, adaptation, and the preservation of psychic equilibrium and structure. Of course, the lower level pervert is also enabled to function sexually through his perversion, although that function is not his primary goal. Rather, he needs to use sex to accomplish other, more pressing tasks.

The object relations of the higher level sadomasochistic pervert can resemble those of neurotics, except for the focal sector of the concretely perverse defense against castration anxiety and oedipal guilt. The object relations of the lower level pervert are grossly impaired. Typically, there is incomplete self-object differentiation, with extensive use of projective identification. The external object is used primarily to satisfy the lower level pervert's needs, with little acknowledgment of the other as a separate person entitled to the satisfaction of his own needs.

Sadomasochistic perversion involves some humiliation or suffering, usually not intense physical pain. For example, the man may be insulted or humiliated by the woman, tied or blindfolded, urinated on, or symbolically dominated. At the highest level, the humiliation or suffering represents a punishment, symbolic of castration but precluding castration, for incestuous wishes and actual sexual functioning. By participating with him, the woman reassures him against castration and is a willing accomplice to his incestuous wishes. By participating with him and administering a token "punishment" under the patient's absolute control and staging of the performance, she undoes the danger that she will actually castrate him. Seduction of the castrator, a variant of Loewenstein's (1957) term, seduction of the aggressor, is an apt way to describe this attempt to change the woman's image from aggressive and threatening into accepting and participating. The woman usually is dressed in "phallic" clothing to counter castration anxiety further. Dangerous qualities in another and in oneself can be changed, easily and magically, by change of clothing, gesture, or appearance. This sexual magic is theater (see chapter 13).

The patient's control and staging of the performance must be respected by his actress. If the woman steps out of her assigned role, the game is spoiled; for example, if she hits too hard, enjoys her role too much, or functions too autonomously.

The masochistic pervert, more than the neurotic masochist, exploits and clings to erotization and action. For the pervert, action has a magical defensive quality (action "makes it so"), involving repetitive reenactment of childhood seductive experiences. The magical quality of action for the pervert may be partly determined by the fact of childhood seduction or seductionlike experiences. Childhood seduction contributes to the illusion that, magically, the child's wishes have been actualized. "Magical happenings" may then be used to deal with frustration and painful affects. Sexual magic is not only used to achieve sexual arousal; the magic of action becomes an important defensive illusion, which is sought to eliminate whatever cannot be tolerated. The exciting sexual event (for example, "She lets me do anything I want with her") disavows absence, hurt, and rage with someone, like the analyst, who cannot be so fully controlled. Other nonperverse patients also tend to go into action so as to avoid painful feelings ("action tendencies"). Here the emphasis is on the exploitation of excitement and specialness in the service of varied defensive needs. Confusion between reality and fantasy protects against negative affects and frightening perceptions associated with childhood sexual overstimulation (Shengold, 1963, 1967, 1971, 1974; Blum, 1973). Denial and/or destruction of reality assumes a prominent role in defense. Masturbation and seduction of others become vehicles for demonstrating one's magical powers to affect oneself and others. Illusions of magical ability protect against felt helplessness and inadequacy. Even in nonperverse sadomasochistic object relations, action tends to be regarded as magical. Especially where there has been childhood parent–child sadomasochistic overstimulation, does this mode of relationship bear similarities to perversion: the magic of action and the specialness of what has transpired between parent and child become central to the psychopathology. This concept of the magic of action complements the view that repetition of seductive gratifications is both desired and attempts to master and repair the associated traumatic affects of overstimulation, rage, and helplessness. Further genetic and dynamic consideration of perversion is presented in chapter 13.

THE PERVERSITY OF OBJECT RELATIONS IN SADOMASOCHISM

Note the similarity in the object relations of lower level perverts with patients overtly involved in sadomasochistic object relations. The other person is, to a degree, to be used for the patient's imperative needs. A partial denial of his separate identity allows for his illusory transformation into a needed fantasy object. Dehumanization, degradation to the status of part-object, projective identification, omnipotent manipulation, and exploitation occur in both. The other person is to be controlled within one's own subjective world and denied his separateness and autonomy. Of course, masochism is seen at every level of psychic integration and object relations. Patients for whom sadomasochistic excitement becomes irresistible tend to resemble perverts in what they need from their partners, in the illusory games they play, and in their relatively perverse misuse of others. Sexual, sadomasochistic, and perverse excitement is similar in the promise of what will occur with one's partner. The patient is beckoned by something forbidden, something that should not happen, something dangerous, appealing, leading backward. He returns to the exciting, special games of yesterday. Once again he is embroiled in a dangerous, destructive relationship with an enticing, exploitative parent. If he can keep repeating the excitement that beckons him, then he need not face the horrors to which he has made himself a party. Excited, endless repetition avoids the truth of abuse, neglect, misuse, and exploitation—destructiveness in the parent and destructiveness and complicity in oneself.

Repetitive exploitation is, indeed, perverse misuse of others. The child/patient felt used by the parent, who tended to destroy the child's (and the parent's own) perception of objective reality and the validity of the child's separate needs in favor of the parent's own neediness. Hence, the patient now feels entitled to enact a reversal of misusing others. We cannot, however, claim that every such patient was actually exploited by a parent. Feelings of hatred and deprivation, without sufficient ability to contain and balance these feelings against some sense of feeling loved and cared for, can similarly evoke a pathological relationship involving misuse. The patient feels entitled to extract what he desires from the other, who exists predominantly to gratify him. The patient's rage, demandingness, and destructiveness in such misuse of others tend to be dissociated and justified. In embroiling himself in repetitive excitement with the other, he makes the other responsible for him and uses the other to manage what the patient feels he himself cannot. This mode of relating is a form of pathological dependency in which one invites, entices, insists that the other must take care of him. The other is to provide the illusion of caring and love, of which the patient feels so deprived. The other is to reassure the patient against his terrors of separation, loss, destruction, castration, and guilt, by his responsiveness, continual availability, and punishment or forgiveness. The other becomes the repository for whatever the patient cannot tolerate in himself: aspects of id, ego attitudes, and superego judgments. The relationship with the other is to take the place of, and deny/undo, whatever is wrong within the patient, which no longer counts. This becomes extractive, destructive misuse of another person for one's own needs; the separateness and needs of the other are then denied and ignored. The excited illusion that the couple is involved in the most special kind of loving hides the ruthless exploitation and destructiveness. To the degree that the patient can extract the illusion of being loved, he can temper and disown his rage and destructiveness. The addiction to feeling loved is needed to calm one's destructive anger.

13

PERVERSION

HOW DO PERVERSE ENACTMENTS IN
PATHOLOGICAL DEPENDENCY DIFFER FROM
OBLIGATORY PERVERSION?

Perversions are regarded here as a form of pathological dependency in which another person is sexually engaged so as to
provide essential defensive reassurance against certain basic dangers
that cannot be managed alone. The pervert requires another person
for his psychic functioning, not just for his sexual pleasure. We have
already considered perverse object relations in which there is exploitation of the other, which, to varying degrees, is sexualized. This
book regards the hallmark of pathological dependency as the "perverse" misuse of others. We have defined perverse object relations as
involving exploitation, extractiveness, and destructiveness with the
partner, whose own separate needs and identity are obliterated in the
service of the patient's own urgent defensive requirements. Such
"perverse" object relations need not be sexualized, although defense
analysis tends to reveal and to liberate more frankly sexualized
perverse trends (see chapter 12). There is a spectrum in pathological
dependency of sexualization of object relations, as well as of defensive functioning. The more sexualization there is in pathological
dependency, the more sexually perverse becomes the exploitation of
others. So we need to clarify further perverse object relations within
pathological dependency by examining perversion as well as to
discuss perversion as a form of pathological dependency.

We need to make clear that there are now two different approaches to perversion. The traditional (rigorous) definition, to which I have adhered, following Bak (1974), regards perversion as an adult psychopathological formation, consolidated through adolescent development, which is obligatory for adult sexual functioning (see Coen, 1985a). The looser attitude has been to consider bits of perverse behavior that serve important defensive requirements, whether or not they are obligatory for the patient's sexual functioning, to be the equivalent of perversion (e.g., see Novick, 1990). Although I would not call the latter perversion, the similarities are worth stressing, especially in the study of pathological dependency. Recall the "perverse" behavior we have already noted in the pathologically dependent patients we have described: telephone perversion in Mr. X, whose mirror perversion we will soon consider; Ms. C, the phallic dominatrix; Ms. R, who stuffed toilet tissue in her panties to pretend she had a healing and penetrating penis; Dr. S, who wished to have women touch him so that he could pretend to be with his mother; the perverse sadomasochistic excitement of Ms. O, Mr. P, Ms. D, Mrs. J, Ms. W (the psychotically delusional love addict), and toddler Q. We will meet Professor U briefly to learn about his sexual addiction to pornographic movies and massage parlors. Consideration of obligatory perversion will help to illuminate these bits of perversion. The reader is referred to the Appendix for some comment on current psychoanalytic approaches to homosexuality as well as a critique of the literature on perversion and gender development.

ON THE WAY TO PERVERSION: CLINICAL SAMPLES OF PERVERSE ENACTMENTS IN PATHOLOGICALLY DEPENDENT PATIENTS

Let us return to Mr. X, whose telephone perversion we considered in chapter 8 in the context of rage and clinging to the analyst during termination of the analysis. He was the man who wished for and feared actualization of his transference longings with the analyst. He imagined the analyst would be like his inconsistently seductive and available mother, who did not preserve clear safeguards against incest. Mother sometimes sat with her legs spread, her nightgown moving up, so that he could observe her genitals clearly. She had developed a disfiguring disease that led her to feel deformed and ugly. Mr. X had prominent memories, dated mostly to age five or six, of mother, warm and perspiring, walking about the apartment in a filmy nightgown, her fat buttocks sticking to the transparent fabric. When he objected that she should not expose herself to him, she would taunt him and say that he was ashamed of her appearance, that she was not attractive enough for him, or that he was still her "tot," that he and his penis were still little. His "little penis" was a particularly sensitive issue. He had been born with a genital defect, which was surgically corrected when he was two. The procedure left him with a tiny skin tag on the underside of his penis. Mr. X had a profound sense of himself as castratable.

In the middle of his analysis he revealed that he had frequently masturbated in front of a mirror during middle and late adolescence when he was left alone at home. Masturbation before the mirror after the patient reached adulthood was relatively infrequent; occasionally, it involved the use of another man's underpants taken from things discarded in an incinerator room. Dreams and associations led to his revealing his masturbation before the mirror. He explained about his masturbation:

It's like how a doctor examines you. I check it to make sure it's all there. Sometimes I look in the mirror or TV screen. It reassures me I have a penis and that I'm not tugging at something that's not mine. I'm creating a person watching me do it. He's making sure I have a complete kit. It's like my telephone calls [to homosexual men who have advertised]. I have an orgasm, then I want to hang up. Maybe it's to have somebody with me while I masturbate and tricking them. Like mother asking what you are doing in the bathroom, but knowing perfectly well the answer. After ejaculating, I don't want to speak to that person anymore. I'm saying, "Hey, I'm a man. I have a penis and I can use it very well."

The following session Mr. X reported a dream:

I see my mother in her nightgown, the outline of her buttocks. She's pulling the nightgown away from her skin as if she's lifting it and exposing herself. I feel I must not see this or at least pretend not to have seen it. My excitement, shame and guilt mount as I fantasize my mother taunting me to fuck her. At the same time I feel sad about my crazy mother.

Three sessions later he described another dream:

"I am having an analytic session in which I tell a dream about a cat coming up to my chest and purring. It changes from a docile kitten into a tigress ready to tear out my eyes, and then back into a kitten. I am aware something is going on behind my back. I find you sitting there without pants, wearing a pink shirt and tie with the buttons open, covering your erection with a notepad. Your body is dark, orangey, semen dripping down the shaft of your penis. I say, "What are you doing? You're masturbating while I'm telling you this?" You have a glare in your eyes, demonic, with two huge pockmarks on your face oozing blood like you'd been stuck with a cigarette. You are staring at me. I'm in disbelief.

He wondered what kind of analyst would masturbate while listening to his patient, like his mother with himself. Was he crazy, or was his analyst/mother crazy? Mr. X described his mother's becoming defensive when he would protest about her exposing herself. Then he said, "I can't look at myself in the mirror and say to her . . ." He noticed the slip and commented, "I see myself in the mirror as my mother."

A few sessions later he reported that the previous night he had taken a pair of jockey shorts from the incinerator room, put them on, cut them up, and masturbated.

He said: It was like mutilating my own body. Some man had worn them. Like Samson's hair, some of his masculinity, power, would penetrate my skin, increase my testosterone. I'd absorb his masculinity and destroy it. I'd cut the guy to shreds with the scissor, castrate him, soil his pants with my semen, show him that my penis works!

Mr. X then confessed with considerable shame and guilt that, as an adolescent, he would put on his father's underpants, open his father's closet, which had a mirror inside the door, and sit on his father's chair facing the mirror. He would expose his penis before the mirror and watch it become erect as he masturbated to ejaculation. "I would think I was that other man in wearing father's underpants—that I'm father, since I'm wearing a garment of his which gets so close to his penis. His penis goes into mother's vagina, so it's like fucking mother one person removed."

The following day he related a dream:

I have a vision of my father walking into the bathroom naked. I can see the end of his penis. I get a side view of his leg, the indentation of his buttocks; part of his penis is masked by his step. [He interjected:] It was so difficult yesterday. I'm disgusted by what I did, it's perverted. . . . I could see myself masturbating in my father's underwear by the mirror. I can't go on. . . . It's painful to talk about these fantasies. I awoke over and over last night. [Then he continued with the dream:] I'm sitting in father's chair seeing father's body. Father is like a somnambulist. He knew if I turned around I'd see him naked. My impression was that he didn't care that I saw him naked.

Soon after he dreamed:

I'm in the men's room of a railroad station. It's all white tile, two sinks, mirrors, a row of urinals. I'm nude. I decide to urinate into a urinal, to piss at a distance. I'm stretching to get a trajectory, target practice. I shoot for one of the urinals. I'm not successful, I'm really pushing myself. As I'm shooting, a guy walks in, dressed, maybe it's you, in a business suit like a commuter. I pounce on him, grab him by the shoulders, I throttle him. I pin him down to the floor. I rip off his clothes. I fellate him. I'm biting off his balls. I can feel my teeth at the shaft of his penis, like I'm a buzzard. I'm out to eat him up. I'm burrowing my head, gnawing at him. It's cannibalism, I'm ripping him open, getting as much flesh into my mouth as I can.

He associated:

If I can't lick 'em, eat 'em! I want so badly to be a man, a kingshooter, to put those urinals down, to show how far and how much I can ejaculate. But there's no audience, nobody's watching me. Each urinal's like a monument, a cemetery. I'm telling the world I'm a man, the biggest shot you've ever seen, but nobody's there. Then this guy breaks my act. An ordinary man finds this crazy guy jerking off in the men's room of Grand Central Station. He comes in on the show, an impersonation of a transvestite, like posing for a statue. I'm playing to a house with no people in it. I'm angered by your interrupting the show. I become extra powerful like a beast gone mad. Then I eat you. I'm sucking you into me. I'm out to incorporate you. I can't get enough of you.

When this material emerged in Mr. X's analysis, he was struggling with heightened feelings of aloneness, as well as a fear of actual incest, in relation to the analyst as mother and father. He sought to

incorporate the analyst-father's potency so as to consolidate his own
sense of himself as a man. He wished to excite the analyst-mother
into sexual response/incest with him but feared its actual consumma-
tion. Two men together, himself and the analyst-father, as enacted in
the mirror masturbation, could better withstand the sexual and
regressive (surrender and merger) dangers of entering mother. Mirror
play in adolescence seemed like an important attempt at mastering
traumatic experiences of childhood overstimulation with accompanying feelings of excitement, rage, and helplessness. Sexualized
looking in the mirror was used in Mr. X's defensive attempts to
transform multiple frightening images into exciting ones: his own
sense of genital defect; mother's deformed appearance; mother as
overstimulating; mother as dead, depressed, unavailable; father as
passive and unappreciative of the patient as a man. Mirror masturbation during the analysis served to reassure Mr. X that he could
safely expose and contain, with the analyst's protection, his incestuous desires in the transference toward the analyst as both father
and mother. We shall want to return, after describing Professor U, to
consideration of the need for perverse enactment in pathological
dependency.

When he felt bereft of emotional support, Professor U, an accomplished author and lecturer, would turn to pornographic movie
houses and sexual massage parlors, to which he had a sexual
addiction. Since he did not require this behavior or even fantasies
about these experiences in order to have intercourse with the woman
with whom he lived, we did not regard this behavior as an obligatory
perversion. But this behavior is the kind of perverse enactment, like
Mr. X's perverse play using telephone and mirror, that is more
common in pathological dependency than is obligatory perversion.
Professor U's pathological dependency and separation anxiety led to
his pressure to replace the absent or unavailable analyst with a sexual
masseuse. He would watch films at the pornographic movie theater
in an enclosed cubicle. By putting coins in a slot, a window would
open through which a woman would offer her breasts or vulva for
him to suck or rub. With a sexual masseuse, he would have a warm
bath, a regular massage until he was relaxed; then it would get
sexual. Professor U describes:

> Suddenly they're kissing your genitals, you're kissing their
> vaginas and breasts. All of a sudden you're carried away. I
> don't know if they are, they pretend to be. I gradually get
> excited during the massage. You know there'll be sex. So maybe
> if someone's seducing you, it makes you feel loved and

wanted. . . . I'd also enjoy giving the woman cunnilingus and getting her excited. But now there's the health risk in kissing a woman's vagina. I'd get so carried away, I couldn't stop without kissing her vagina. I certainly don't care about the woman per se. I'm just getting something instead of giving something. It's almost like you get lost in her when you're giving cunnilingus. She's opened herself up to you, so I'm getting a feeling of real connection and intimacy, even though it's phony.

The masseuse had to be attractive, kind, seeming to be patient, concerned, and responsive with him. If she were too obviously a prostitute or brusque or impatient, he would leave. She had to be a good actress, to play a role with him, which conveyed the illusion that he was special, as he had felt some of the time with his mother. When the illusion was punctured, as when the masseuse went on to the next customer, Professor U became depressed and resentful. The masseuse herself had little importance; she was easily replaceable, so that he did not have to fear her loss. Even if he had lost his mother, there could be an endless stream of masseuses, and he could dispose of the masseuses as he had felt mother had done with him. If Professor U had an ordinary massage, he would feel more relaxed, but he would not feel cared for, as he would when the masseuse would masturbate him. It was better when he would suck the masseuse's breasts or vulva or play with her anus or have her stick her finger in his anus. The greater the liberties allowed, the more excited he would feel and the more he would later use memories of these experiences for masturbation: as with either one of them penetrating the other's anus by finger or tongue or the masseuse's rubbing his penis and allowing him to ejaculate between her breasts or through her hair. Once he got sexually aroused, he could pretend that the masseuse wanted to respond to him and so was caring for him.

To analyze Professor U's sexual addiction, we needed to interpret his going into action so as to avoid his feelings and longings, here especially in relation to missing the analyst and feeling angry, hurt, and disappointed when he was left on his own. The more he was able to tolerate his intense desires to be with, and take from, the analyst, the less urgent was the pressure of his sexual addiction. Heterosexual and homosexual longings for the analyst as both mother and father were expressed and defended against through Professor U's perverse enactments during the analysis. He especially craved continuation of feeling special in relation to mother, in contrast to her depressed withdrawal. With the analyst-father he sought support and admiration for his accomplishments, and he sought to rob the analyst of his magic phallus so as to acquire the analyst's power and authority.

Mr. X, unlike Professor U, had experienced the typical childhood sexual overstimulation that is drawn upon for the framework of perverse enactments. Professor U's mother had been inconsistently seductive, but not in a really sexual way. Mother, an accomplished writer, would at times peruse and marvel at his youthful literary attempts and encourage him to share a kind of narcissistic specialness with her, within which he could imagine that one day he would become as creative as she was. At such times when he could hold her attention, mother would seem to admire him as another one of her remarkable creations. On the other hand, Professor U craved the touching he felt he had missed with both parents; he now wanted this from a woman who would pretend to let him do as he wanted with her. I cannot explain satisfactorily why Professor U developed a sexual addiction instead of some other psychopathological entity.

Patients with pathological dependency tend to identify with the action tendencies of their parents, so that they avoid feelings and needs by action. When these patients are unable to manage internal conflict within their own psyche, they turn to others to spare them. One mode of engaging the other is sexual. The more defense and object relations are sexualized in pathological dependency, the greater is the likelihood of perverse enactment. Repetitive seeking of excitement is used to cover over all that is wrong in oneself, in the other, and in the relationship. Both Mr. X and Professor U were addicted to repetitive attempts to stir up feelings of sexual excitement and specialness to defend against negative feelings and negative assessments of self and other. In this regard, they did function like perverts. But notice that we are here describing the keystone of pathological dependency, the idealized and excited misuse of another to defend against what is most threatening within. Hence, in this sense, all patients with pathological dependency tend to be perverse in their misuse of others. What varies is how sexualized this becomes and how much sadomasochism and perverse enactment are developed within the context of pathological dependency. Now, let us consider obligatory perversion directly.

OBLIGATORY PERVERSION

Perversions are stable defensive organizations, like pathological dependency more generally, that are highly resistant to change because of their central role in defense against destructiveness and preservation of object need. Psychoanalysts now emphasize that perversions can be understood and treated, in contrast to older, more pessimistic views. Although there are perversions (fetishism and transvestism performed alone) that do not require the presence of another person for their enactment, intrapsychically the need for the other persists. Perverts usually emphasize their freedom from dependency, their ease of exchanging objects as they idealize their excitement and pleasure, rather than their need of the other. This emphasis on the interchangeability of objects is aimed at protecting against the danger of intense need of the other, which exists in most perverts, despite their vigorous and rage-filled protests to the contrary. For example, at the end of the Marquis de Sade's *The 120 Days of Sodom*, not everyone has been murdered. Certain vitally needed people, such as the three cooks, must be preserved! Even Sade's most notorious libertines must know when to stop! The danger for Sade's perverse characters is depletion, loss, abandonment, total destruction of needed objects, so that one is truly alone. The dependent pervert, feeling enraged and impotent, in Sade's description, denies and attempts to reverse his helplessness and bondage by attempts to seduce, exploit, dominate, denigrate, mutilate, or murder the object. To the degree that one feels unable to manage alone, the vitally needed (internal) object cannot really be gotten rid of, no matter how loudly one talks about murder. Such fantasies of escape from bondage by murdering the needed object, at some point, must be undone. External objects can easily, endlessly be replaced.

Contemporary psychoanalytic writers have attempted to help other analysts to overcome their transference bias against perverts so as to be able to understand and analyze some of them. This shift is akin to revisions in our biases toward narcissistic and borderline psychopathology. Perversion can now be viewed as a solution to intrapsychic conflict, which, to varying degrees, is analyzable. Three factors have tended to diminish psychoanalytic appreciation of the central role of conflict resolution in perversion. As we all know, Freud's (1905) original point regarding perversion as the negative of neurosis has been misused and has contributed to the idea that perversion represents the direct discharge of drive components without modification and conflict within the psychic agencies. The hungry demandingness and the seeming insatiability of certain perverts and patients with erotized transference contribute to the view that perversion is nonconflictual, unmodifiable, and unanalyzable. Finally, the view that perversion represents repetitive reliving of infantile trauma, even if this reliving is for active mastery of the original trauma with its associated affects, adds to the perspective that perversion is not primarily involved with the resolution of intrapsychic conflict. The relation between infantile trauma and conflict resolution in perversion will need to be clarified.

PERVERSE ENACTMENTS: THEIR NATURE AND MULTIPLE FUNCTIONS

A tension between conservative and progressive trends runs through all of the literature on perversion. That is, the pervert, more than the rest of us, struggles between preserving himself—repetition, rigidity, overcontrol, ritualization, inhibition, or impairment in his imaginative capacities—and radical, illusory reconstructions of meaning validated through his actions. The pervert, in these terms, is an ultraconservative revolutionary! The pervert oscillates between viewing his activities as literal, concrete, real and viewing them as make-believe, only a game, play-acting. The object relations of the pervert are not just repetitive, driven, defensive activities aimed at guaranteeing the survival of his psyche, identity, and self-esteem. It would be overly schematic to believe this simplification; real people are not constituted this way. There are possibilities for warmth, intimacy, and love (given as well as received) in the pervert's love affairs. At the same time as we acknowledge that the pervert, like the rest of us, wants to love and be loved, he is limited by his intense need for control over himself and his external objects, his fear of passive surrender to his needs and his objects, and his defensive need (and perhaps, for some, developmental inability) not to accord the other autonomous status [without regarding him as a part object to be used and onto whom he can project aspects of himself and his internal objects.]

Psychoanalysts agree that perverts have some constriction in their use of sexual fantasy and that they tend to enact in perverse behavior vital defensive illusions that they cannot sustain intrapsychically. Analysts differ about whether perverse sexual fantasy defines perversion or whether it is simply an aspect of ordinary neurosis. That is, some analysts consider rich (perverse) sexual fantasy as characteristic of neurotics rather than of perverts. Most analysts believe that the repetitive need to enact certain highly specific perverse fantasies defines perversion. The pervert's driven, defensive need to turn to sexual action when he seems unable to manage conflict intrapsychically has been stressed by contemporary psychoanalysts. I think it is crucial to maintain the distinction between neurotic sexual fantasy and perverse sexual enactment. Perversion simply is not the same as neurosis, despite the similarities. Our task in this book, however, is to examine this borderline of perversion within pathological dependency and to highlight the similarities and the differences with obligatory perversion. Our attention has especially been drawn to perverse enactments in pathological dependency, which we have contrasted with neurotic attempts to resolve conflict within fantasy alone. Our focus has become why and how certain pathologically dependent patients have developed a sexualized turning to another so as to manage internal conflict.

We need to understand the motivational hierarchy in the pervert's need for action. It was far simpler, at an earlier time, to think predominantly of castration anxiety as the force to be surmounted for the pervert to function sexually. The motivation was then simple and clear.

I find it useful to make a schematic division of perverts into higher and lower level types and to think of higher and lower level functions within these types. Such thinking is implicit in most contemporary writing on perversion. Socarides (1978) divides homosexuals into oedipal and preoedipal types. It should be kept in mind that this division is heuristic and that actual patients may not fit neatly into such models. The higher level patient uses perverse behavior primarily to permit sexual functioning and orgasm, by defense against castration anxiety and oedipal guilt. Here Bak's (1968) idea applies that the ubiquitous, unconscious fantasy in perversion is the "phallic woman." The pervert attempts by his act to validate this unconscious fantasy to defend against intense castration anxiety so as to be able to function sexually. Note that thus far we have referred to the purpose of the perverse behavior as a sexual one, to permit sexual functioning. At the lower level, the primary goal is no longer to accomplish adequate sexual functioning but to use sex for other, more pressing requirements. As for the higher level pervert, however, the perversion does allow sexual pleasure to occur. We are then referring to sexualization (see chapter 8), that is, the extensively elaborated, defensive use of sexual behavior and fantasy, in which defense has greater urgency and significance in the patient's motivational hierarchy than does sexual drive gratification. Most perverts represent "more disturbed" patients, largely narcissistic and borderline types. They differ from other patients with lower level character integration in the predominant reliance on sex for need satisfaction and closeness, defense, repair, adaptation, and the preservation of equilibrium and psychic structure. Remember that pathological dependency includes patients from varied degrees of psychic organization. In this sense, it is not a diagnosis of patients' structural organization.

Although pathological dependency can be assessed in diagnostic interviews, its prime importance is in the assessment of progress or lack of progress within ongoing analytic treatment. Even for higher level perverse functioning, we still need to ask why oedipal guilt and castration anxiety are defended against through perverse sexual behavior rather than in ordinary ways.

ETIOLOGY AND PSYCHODYNAMICS

When we inquire into the etiology of perversion, we do well to distinguish between the form of the perversion and its predominant functions. All authors seek to connect the form of the perversion with infantile, usually traumatic determinants, and that connection may not be difficult to make. Whether this tells us what the perversion seeks to accomplish is another matter, however. Indeed, it may even be correct that the outline of the perversion seeks to turn childhood trauma from passive into active for the purpose of mastery and revenge. It is certainly to be expected that patients will create their perversions, just like their neuroses, from what is available and pressing during development. Even when we can demonstrate infantile trauma and seduction, we need to understand the intrapsychic consequences, constructions, and uses that have been made of such experiences. Too often we stop prematurely at making linkages of elements in the perverse behavior with childhood determinants rather than continuing to inquire into a hierarchy of functions of the perverse behavior. What is the importance of reenacting childhood seduction? Why is this done? I would speculate that the magical quality of action may be partly determined by the fact that childhood seduction or seductionlike experiences contribute the illusion that magically the child's wishes, which he knew were supposed to remain at the level of fantasy, have been actualized: it really happened! A background of seduction may establish a precedent for "magical happenings," which may be drawn on to deal with frustration and painful affects. Confusion between reality and fantasy usually results as to what has and can really happen. Such confusion serves defensive requirements against the negative affects and dangerous perceptions associated with childhood sexual overstimulation (Shengold, 1963, 1967, 1971, 1974; Blum, 1973).

Denial or destruction of reality and its replacement by illusion become a predominant technique of defense. Alternatively, a dual reality is maintained in which partial denial obscures painful reality and covers it with perverse illusion. Masturbation and seduction of others then become vehicles for demonstrating one's magical powers to affect oneself and others. This idea complements the concept that repetition of the seductive gratifications is desired, together with the need to master and repair the associated traumatic affects of overstimulation, rage, and helplessness. The illusion of magical ability defends against felt helplessness and inadequacy, as usually occurs with childhood seduction experiences.

Khan (1979) is the author who has been most specific about etiology and the sexual component in perversion. Most, though not all, authors agree about maternal seductiveness in the childhood of the future pervert. Khan emphasized the mother's depression and her "organized defense" against it, obsessional defenses with denial, so that neither mother nor child is generally consciously aware of mother's depression. Mother and child collude to protect mother from awareness of her pathology. The mother is sexually seductive with the child. The child "libidinizes" the body, including the genitals, in response to deficiency in maternal care. That the mother was simultaneously experienced as intrusive contributes to the child's regarding his own private bodily and fantasy experiences as sacrosanct. Masturbatory reveries are involved with preserving and idealizing the good aspects of the mother–child interaction apart from his rage at her. Khan postulated that a part of the self is kept separate from the mother, does not surrender to her or to her moods, and is validated by the masturbatory reveries.

SEX IN PERVERSION: DEFENSE

Khan's (1979) formulation gives us a hypothesis about why sexual fantasy and experience are especially turned to for defense. Remember that perversion was originally thought of in terms of facilitating sexual functioning. If a person was impaired in his gender or sexual identity and functioning, the perverse sexual ritual, it was thought, offered a way to repair temporarily this disability so as to allow sexual performance. This explanation is still good, especially for higher level perverse functioning. The pervert tries to do the best he can with sexual pleasure and performance and chooses from among the varieties of sex the one way in which he is capable of functioning sexually. For understanding why sexuality is predominantly used for defense (the lower level aspect of perversion), our formulation needs to be more explicit about the choice of sexuality. What needs to be added is a clearer understanding of how sex functioned in the mother–child relationship and of the mechanisms by which sex is adapted to serve defensive aims. Here we are subjecting the "frame-work" in perversion, as Arlow (Ostow, 1974) called it, to analysis. Sexualization will be emphasized as the predominant defensive operation in perversion.

My own model for the development of sexualized defense as a predominant defensive operation involves three principal factors: the intense availability of sensual feelings early in life, far in excess of what is ordinarily experienced; the prominence of sexualized defense in the mother–child relationship; and the usefulness of sexualized defense for mastering large quantities of hostile aggression. One genetic model for the abundance of early sensual feelings, which I elaborated in chapter 8, is the mother's seductive overstimulation of the child when it is associated with her relative neglect of his emotional needs. Sexual drive pressure and the ego's attempts to master this are then available for further use by the ego to express and master other conflicts. To compensate for mother's relative emotional unavailability, with the hope of reviving her flagging interest in him, the child turns to the predominantly available mode of relating with mother (Brody, 1960; Escalona, 1963). In such a setting, the child himself, at a very early age, may already have turned to sexual stimulation to cope with felt trauma and neglect (Greenacre, 1960). When the mother's own predominant mode of defense has been sexual, identification with this combines with the child's needs for defense. Efforts to master sexual overstimulation by active repetition and re-creation engender a model in which multiple other defensive functions can be simultaneously served. The preponderant drive derivatives, affects, early defensive patterns, and identifications are drawn upon for vital defensive and adaptive needs. Not only sexuality but also an unusually large quantity of aggression must be confronted. This results from early frustration, deprivation, and teasing overstimulation.

When sexualized defense has been significantly involved in the mother's psychic organization and in the mother–child relationship, this defense serves to obscure her psychopathology and maternal deficiency. In chapter 8, I described the typical mother under consideration as a depressed woman with substantial impairment of her ability to relate to the child as a unique person in his own right. Mother and child collude in their mutually shared pleasure in, and defensive focus on, the seductive bodily closeness, in contrast to other forms of relating. The depressed mother comes to life with seductive bodily stimulation, which she seeks from her child. Sexual seductiveness eventually becomes the child's predominant mode for relating to others and for expressing his intense object hunger.

Masturbation and masturbation fantasy are the arena in which sexualized defense becomes elaborated in the future pervert's childhood. In his masturbatory world, the future pervert attempts to comfort and soothe himself, separate and apart from the insufficiently available and inappropriately responsive mother. He idealizes his masturbatory pleasures and his self-sufficiency and omnipotence in creating them on his own. Magical doing is contributed to by masturbation; illusions of omnipotent ability for magical manipulation are enhanced by the masturbator's magical manipulation of his own genitals.

Defense is required against feelings of helplessness, overstimulation, rage, and depression, in relation to the unpredictable quality of the mother's empathic responsiveness to the child and his feeling exploited and manipulated by mother for her own needs without significant recognition of himself as a unique, differentiated person. The pathological object relationship is idealized and clung to, emphasizing how special, irresistible, and inseparable each is from the other. The mother's inability or deficiency with loving her child is patched over with sexualized excitement and the illusion of adoration. This excited, adored feeling is endlessly, repetitively sought. When the mother is unable to provide even this for her child, his rage is intensified; he then fears losing and destroying their relationship. This fear and rage lead to more clinging and more need for defense by idealization and sexualization.

Not everyone is able to tolerate, use, and be aroused by intense hostile aggression in his sexuality. For most, this will turn off their pleasure. Yet we are suggesting that the pervert is able temporarily to master his rage, as well as other negative affects, through sexualized defense. How is this mastery accomplished? My own model emphasizes defensive transformation of negatively toned, aggressively infiltrated images of self and objects into positive, pleasurably regarded ones during masturbatory fantasy enactments within one's own mind. Masturbation fantasy is played out on a kind of mental stage, on which the images of self and object(s) to be enacted are projected. As the masturbator feels and watches his own sexual sensations and increasing arousal, the role of illusion is enhanced by the continual changes in body image, sensations, and state of consciousness. The fantasied relationship between self and others becomes more vivid, more real (Nydes, 1950). Negative aspects of the self can be disowned, and dangerous aspects of the object can be appropriated as the masturbator experiences and observes his drama. The object's passionate responsiveness assuages the patient's fear of loss or destruction of his object or himself. Superego components are brought into this game for the same purpose of temporary, illusory transformation. The scene's finale consists of reintrojection, by vision and touch, of the transformed self and object images. A make-believe ceremony, a ritualized masturbatory game, has disguised and eased a dangerously aggressive confrontation between self and other. This masturbatory game is the preparatory training for perverse seductive behavior. We are establishing a gradient of sexualized fantasy: played out within one's own mind, with the aid of external inanimate objects, or with the aid of other people.

FROM NEUROTIC MASTURBATORY FANTASY TO PERVERSE ACTION

Most authors agree that the dividing line between neurosis and perversion is that the neurotic is relatively able to express conflict in fantasy, to handle it within the province of his own mind, and usually to distinguish (sometimes requiring the help of another person) the identity and reality of others from his transient transference uses of them. Note that within this definition the pathologically dependent patient seems more perverse than neurotic. This finding has led us to define a borderland of neurotic pathological dependency and perversion. The pervert, unlike the ordinary neurotic, is impelled to enact into concrete reality his unconscious fantasies so as to render them valid and credible. His own mind is insufficient for accomplishing this. Other people are then assigned parts in the drama the pervert stages so that he can authenticate himself, his fantasies, and his defensive transformations. Of course, for the pervert to play out his dramatic scenes requires that others submit to his direction and control. Dominating and controlling others are also his intention, so that he need not fear their influence over him or his need of them. The nonperverse, pathologically dependent patient, although he may vary in the level of his psychic organization, tends to be more capable than he believes, and than the pervert actually is, of resolving conflict intrapsychically. For heuristic purposes, we can say that the pervert has no choice but to enact his perverse dramas, while the typical, pathologically dependent patient does not know that he has a choice about how he manages his conflicts.

Khan (1979) regarded perversion as "auto-erotism à deux . . . an engineered re-enactment of masturbatory practices between two persons as a compensation for that insufficiency of maternal care which is the pre-requisite of infantile auto-erotism and narcissism" (p. 24). Khan does not literally mean that masturbation and perversion are synonymous. Perversion should not be reduced to masturbation. Nevertheless, the similarities are worth stressing; we can think loosely of perverse practices as enactments of masturbatory dramas. In perversion, is there always another live person present? When does masturbation, also the enactment of fantasy, become perversion? When another substitutive object, clothing, mirror, or fetish is added? (Bradlow and Coen, 1984). For the many reasons already presented, it would be incorrect to argue that the transvestite and fetishist are basically heterosexually oriented and related and that this perverse behavior serves only to ready them for intercourse.

Greenacre (1968) raised the question of why the pervert needs a concrete image or experience. Deutsch (1932, 1944) and Khan (1965b) emphasized that the pervert needs to provide concrete representation to preserve self and object images, especially because of the fear of destruction. Eissler (1958) and Lichtenstein (1970) stressed confirmation of existence during orgasm as well as attempted validation of certain unconscious fantasies about the nature of sexual reality. Greenacre (1968) noted that some men can handle their castration anxiety during intercourse by fantasizing about, or focusing upon, the woman's breasts as phallic substitutes; others actually require a fetish. Greenacre's answer to her own question about "concreteness" is primarily the intensity of the infantile trauma, which has not been mastered, so that there is a persistent need for visual, tactile, and olfactory denial and introjection. Other answers include severe, internal psychic deficiency, with the need for magical incorporation; defense against sadism and aggression, the concreteness demonstrating that nothing has been destroyed; definition of body boundaries by use of a phallic integrating agent. The pervert's need for concrete images and experiences is part, but not all, of his action tendencies.

Instead of the omnipotent self-sufficiency that the masturbator may arrogate to himself, in perverse behavior, omnipotence and control are demonstrated in relation to a partner or substitutive object. A partner or substitutive object is used to actualize one's needed fantasies and tends to make these fantasies more real, less illusory. But these games are also illusory because no matter how much the pervert transforms his object into identity with his unconscious images, he is not psychotic; the differentiation between the other and his assigned role is maintained. The deadly seriousness with which the psychotic must insist that his object is identical with his own delusion of him and attempt to transform him differs radically from the illusory, playful, reversible games/dramas of the pervert. I would regard this latter as an example of defensive analization of object relationships. Magical (anal) mixing of self and other, good and bad, shit and love seeks to blur the boundaries between self and other, as well as between love and hate, especially as protection against loss and destruction. But such defensive, reversible, temporary mixing and merging are not psychosis, even if, at times, they resemble a kind of playing at craziness!

Remember the distinction of the higher level pervert, who defends against oedipal guilt and castration anxiety so as to permit sexual functioning. His relation to his partner will be very different from that of the lower level pervert, for whom sexualized defense is urgently needed to preserve himself. Other than in this focal sector, the object relations of the higher level pervert will resemble those of neurotics. Domination, control, and omnipotent illusions are needed only for defense against castration anxiety and oedipal guilt. What the lower level pervert has to accomplish with his partner is vastly different; his object relations are grossly impaired. Typically there is incomplete self–object differentiation, with extensive use of projective identification. The external object is used primarily to satisfy the pervert's own needs, with little acknowledgment of the other as a separate person entitled to the satisfaction of his own needs. Omnipotent control of the external object aims to prevent frustration or the provocation of guilt, when sadistically attacked. The danger of emotional surrender, usually with passive masochistic wishes, to affects and to another human being tends to keep the pervert from needing and responding directly. Khan (1965b) describes well how the pervert seeks to maintain control, to induce surrender in the partner, and then to identify vicariously with him. The greater the danger of sadistic destruction or passive surrender, the more distance may be required from live human beings: an aspect of voyeurism/exhibitionism, fetishism, autoerotism, and celibacy. Instead of genuine human connectedness through the sexual experience, excitement and intensity are focused upon. Separateness and closeness with a needed object must be carefully balanced against each other.

What comes across as most perverse is the relation to the partner when this is stripped of ordinary human tenderness, warmth, and concern for the other's individuality and differences. Extractive misuse of others in seductive/sexual ways, together with a partial denial or destruction of reality, is a central aspect of perversion. Freud's task in the "Three Essays" (1905) was to demonstrate the central role of sexual impulses in human behavior and specifically in neurosis. Sexual expression may vary, but as variants of the normal. For our purposes, however, the pervert's relationship with his object, its humanness or lack of it, is our best guide to perversity.

Within the psychoanalytic situation, our baseline problem may be the pervert's urgent demand for gratification and for loving and affirmation, from the analyst as from everyone else. Unless we can interest him in understanding the purposes this demand serves, there will be no analytic process. If the pervert feels sufficiently entitled to demand gratification as reparation for childhood deprivation and is anxiously driven toward continual defensive repetition without the freedom to examine and understand this, then we are, indeed, at a loss. A psychoanalytic perspective on the multiple functions served by perverse behavior—adaptive, reparative, defensive, gratifying, all complex and to be understood within a conflict model—is our best guide.

14

PATHOLOGICAL JEALOUSY

This discussion of pathological jealousy emphasizes the central role of defense against destruction and intense need of another and links it with our consideration of severe dependency. Indeed, I consider my patient, Mr. Y, whom I describe in this chapter, to be pathologically dependent. I would emphasize his dread of his dependent longings and the continual need to escape from them. Some of the same mechanisms apply, as well, to ordinary jealousy. I also describe intense but ordinary jealousy in a patient with pathological dependency. Ms. Z, like Mr. Y, also was far more fearful, guarded, and mistrustful in needing others than the typical patient described in this book.

Most patients with pathological jealousy who have been described in the psychoanalytic literature have been too disturbed to tolerate a standard psychoanalysis. Patients can be helped, however, by modified psychoanalytic treatment to relinquish their pathological jealousy if analyst and patient can understand the functions it has served.

Pathological jealousy, in contrast to ordinary jealousy, seems to be distinctly uncommon, indicative of severe psychopathology. Pao (1969) noted correctly that previous authors on pathological jealousy reported either psychotic patients, brief treatments, or transient symptomatology. As a result, their formulations have needed further evaluation. I emphasize the adaptive and defensive functions of behavioral enactment of sexual and angry feelings in pathological jealousy. Jealous behaviors are likened to perverse masturbatory enactments, which are required when conflict cannot be handled intrapsychically. Pathological jealousy is described as a substitute for, as well as a defense against, the fantasied dangers of full, loving intimacy with another single person, man or woman. The object choice in pathological jealousy is regarded not as a single person but as involving also a fantasied protector. The object choice is basically narcissistic, homosexual so as to protect against the dangers both of passive needs of another person different from oneself, as well as of aggressive destruction of the object.

NOTES ON THE LITERATURE

The clinical data presented by psychoanalytic authors on pathological jealousy have tended to be too brief and sketchy to permit reassessment by others. Pao's (1969) report is the only exception. Earlier authors tended, in the spirit of the times, to schematize their discussions and material into oedipal, oral sadistic, or homosexual conflict. Most authors have emphasized the severity of disturbance in pathological jealousy and connections with paranoia, serious narcissistic pathology, detachment, intense sadism, and object hunger. Intense early needs of objects, primarily for self-esteem regulation and drive control, conflict with the dangers of closeness, destructiveness, and need for control over the object (Riviere, 1932; Fenichel, 1935; Schmideberg, 1953; Pao, 1969). These are issues for pathologically dependent patients, including those who are terrified of giving into their intense dependent wishes. Other than Pao, these authors have exclusively emphasized oral sadism rather than presenting a more balanced view of aggressive conflict as derived from each psychosexual stage. As with perversion, underlying psychodynamics have been offered for pathological jealousy without sufficient attention to how this symptom complex functions for defense and gratification of the conflicts involved. This criticism is especially true for the functions of sexual arousal in pathological jealousy. Previous authors have tended not to focus on the functions and role of the behavior, affects, and wishes of pathological jealousy in the current life of the patient.

Most authors implied that the narcissistic and object-related disturbances in pathological jealousy derive from preoedipal conflict. A minority (Jones, 1929; Barag, 1949; Seidenberg, 1952; Spielman, 1971) argued, instead, that triangular oedipal conflict and guilt are central; however, they did not present convincing clinical material to demonstrate this point. Most authors emphasized the narcissistic dependency in jealousy. In my terms, a narcissistic dependency links the pathological versions of jealousy and dependency in terms of the driven need for support from others for one's self-esteem. Authors have disagreed as to whether the narcissistic dependency serves primarily as regressive defense against oedipal guilts and anxieties or as a basic mechanism for self-esteem regulation, involving oral fixation and defense against oral sadism. Pao (1969) was clearest about narcissistic pathology and emphasized "concern over narcissistic unrelatedness" as his patient's central issue. This narcissistic unrelatedness was not sufficiently explicated, however, as a determinant of the pathological jealousy. Pao tended overly to focus his patient's narcissistic pathology around orality and attachment during the second year of life. Unlike earlier authors, Pao implied interweaving of preoedipal and oedipal conflict, although he also tended to make a sharp dichotomy between them. I prefer to emphasize that the jealous triadic scene in pathological jealousy serves simultaneously to defend against, as well as to express, both dyadic and triadic conflicts.

The role of sexuality in pathological jealousy has been contested. There has been too much debate over the content of the sexuality, whether it is primarily preoedipal homosexual or oedipal heterosexual. The emphasis on sexuality as defense has been primarily against oral sadism; sexualization of other conflicts has not been explicitly presented. The dangers of passive homosexual wishes were stressed by Freud (1911, 1922), Brunswick (1929), Lagache (1950), and Pao (1969) and by applied psychoanalytic studies of Othello's jealousy (Wangh, 1952; Feldman, 1952; Smith, 1959). Heterosexual incestuous dangers were, of course, emphasized by those authors who posited triangular oedipal conflict as central. Riviere (1932) argued, instead, that the sexual component in pathological jealousy was only defensive, not an actual gratification; that is, oral sadistic conflict is defensively "genitalized." Seeman's (1979) psychiatric study noted actual sexual arousal: five women patients with more extreme pathological jealousy used homosexual fantasies about the rival for masturbation or during foreplay with the husband. Seeman pointed out that pathological jealousy helped to repair damaged self-esteem by justifying anger and by fostering efforts to become more like the fantasied rival (see Joffe, 1969, on envy). This view is congruent with my emphasis on the adaptive functions of this symptom complex.

Freud, as we know, divided jealousy into normal, projected (impulses of infidelity are projected onto someone else), and delusional. Freud related delusional jealousy to defense against homosexual longings and considered it synonymous with paranoia. In his discussion of paranoia, Freud, (1911) introduced the idea of homosexual object choice (which he would later call narcissistic object choice) as a normal developmental stage between autoerotism and object love. Thus, narcissistic object choice has long been emphasized in pathological jealousy (it was part of Freud's understanding of homosexuality).

Jones's (1929) contribution on jealousy played a pivotal role for later theorists. Jones described the phenomenology of narcissistic dependency in jealousy; however, he regarded this exclusively as regressive defense against oedipal guilts and anxieties. Jones noted intense, passive wishes to be loved and reassured and to possess the love object, who is regarded ambivalently; a fear of "being loved too greatly . . . of having his personality possessed by the love object" (pp. 336–337); incapacity to love, related to impaired self-esteem and fear of the relationship with the love object. Fenichel (1935) added that not only are such people incapable of fully loving others, but they also change their love objects "continuously and readily" (p. 349) and can become jealous even of people about whom they had been relatively indifferent previously. Fenichel disagreed with Jones's exclusive focus on the content, that is, guilt, to be reassured against by narcissistic dependency in jealousy. Fenichel, instead, stressed fixation on a primitive mechanism of self-esteem regulation in jealousy, a mechanism involving oral determinants, as well as oral fixation. External narcissistic supplies (being loved) are required from others to maintain self-esteem. I think this view is too extreme. Self-esteem regulation in pathological jealousy is related not only to deprivation, hunger, and oral sadism but to anxieties and guilt derived from each developmental level. Although the preoedipal psychopathology may appear predominant, this need not exclude defensive requirements against guilt from phallic oedipal conflict. Deprivation, hunger, and mistreatment may certainly be exploited for defense against varied aggressive and sexual guilts.

The role of unconscious homosexuality in paranoia, not specifically in pathological jealousy, has been debated by Frosch (1981) and Blum (1981). Frosch emphasized the organizing role of unconscious homosexuality in paranoia; passive anal wishes become humiliating and dangerous through actual experiences of humiliation inflicted by an important person of the same sex at certain key developmental phases, especially before sexual identity has been fully established. Such experiences tend to actualize wishes and guilts. Blum noted that the paranoid's homosexuality defends against destructiveness and serves to maintain an object tie. Blum stressed a more general, severe preoedipal disturbance in paranoia, with uncompleted separation-individuation, narcissistic arrest, and impaired object relations and reality testing. Ego integration, identity, and sexual identity are unstable, with serious narcissistic, aggressive, and sadomasochistic conflicts. I think these positions are compatible and complementary in explaining the functions of unconscious homosexuality in paranoia.

CLINICAL VIGNETTE

Mr. Y

Mr. Y was a bright, well-regarded, highly capable, and responsible man. He prided himself on his morality, ideals, and values. His pathological jealousy stood in sharp contrast to his reasonableness. He suspected his wife was having affairs with other men. He would search her diary, letters, notes, and papers discarded in the wastebasket. That she left these open to his investigations fueled his suspicions. Mr. Y performed a nightly examination of his wife's panties to determine the quantity of secretion and number of hairs. He decided that on those days when his wife had been at home, her panties contained little secretion and hair. When she had been out of the house, more was to be found in the panties. Sometimes the hair color in the panties was lighter than his wife's; sometimes there were fecal streaks or dried stains from secretions. These findings suggested to him that she had had sex with a man other than himself. In his sleuthing, Mr. Y discounted the vigor of her day's activities. Early in the analysis, he thought seriously of hiring a detective to follow his wife, tapping the phone, and having the panty secretions examined for semen at a laboratory. The fixity and intensity of these ideas were alarming to the analyst.

Indeed, there was no evidence (to the analyst) to justify Mr. Y's suspicions. He received little love, warmth, support, or even involved sex from his wife, although he, at first, would not acknowledge this fact. He struggled against his fantasies of involvement with other women. Rather than being adulterous, Mrs. Y seemed too restricted, controlled, angry, depressed, and paranoid to seek such pleasure. Her envy and phallic, masculine competitiveness with Mr. Y were intense. During intercourse, she would insert her finger firmly and painfully into Mr. Y's anus or bite his penis during fellatio.

Mr. Y was reserved, guarded, and afraid of the analyst's influence. He presented himself as likable, a good fellow, in contrast to being angry, aggressive, and mistrustful, feelings that he hid under his cover of normality. Thus, his "panty checks" contrasted with his predominant behavior on and off the couch—most of the time. During several sessions, for a few moments, Mr. Y could sound paranoid. Thus, when the analyst attempted to focus attention on understanding the meaning of Mr. Y's panty checks and diary searches, by emphasizing that there was not a shred of evidence that Mrs. Y was involved with any living mortal man, Mr. Y became livid: "Not a shred of evidence, you say! There is a shred of evidence! What's in her panties!" In another session, when the analyst suggested, perhaps once too often, that we needed to understand Mr. Y's need to be admired, he stormed: "I really like being with the leaders in the field . . . but you make that like dirt! You make me an inferior being . . . someone whose main theme in life is being with important people." In this second example, however, as at other times when he felt hurt and criticized by the analyst, he could recognize that the analyst had told him something painful and that it was less painful just to feel criticized. He would wonder from time to time whether he "shouldn't automatically reject what you say so as to demonstrate I'm not passive by not agreeing too quickly." Even when he agreed with the analyst's points, he would often need to change the subject so as to regain control.

He protested that the analyst had influenced his dreaming so that he was now dreaming what the analyst had interpreted, not what he himself was in conflict about. This idea applied, especially but not exclusively, to dreams with overtly homosexual content. The analyst interpreted, from abundant and alarming evidence, that Mr. Y feared that the analyst wanted to, and was, taking control of his mind. Mr. Y said that, of course, he believed no such thing. Yet despite his denial and attempts at riddance of what troubled him most, he was very afraid of a closeness with the analyst that would interfere with his own separate functioning. A collaborative dialogue with the analyst was most difficult for him in that he was mistrustful of holding still (passivity) and reflecting on what the analyst said to him. Typically, Mr. Y resolved to stop his jealous examination of his wife's panties and notes by an act of willpower and insisted that he had mastered this conflict. Still, during this period of treatment, during separations from the analyst or from the wife, the patient would resume this behavior. In retrospect, it seems that the disappearance of Mr. Y's pathological jealousy also coincided with his increasing attachment to the analyst (in an intense homosexual brother/father transference).

Even as he was getting married, Mr. Y had felt jealous and worried that his wife might be involved with other men, including a former

lover and his own brother, Bob. Mr. Y similarly felt pained and
jealous when women at work with whom he flirted showed trivial
responses to other men.

Mr. Y anticipated annoyance, irritability, and being barely tolerated by the analyst. Warm concern and genuine interest were not
what he expected. His many dreams of bleakness, barrenness,
loneliness, and coldness could not be explained just in terms of
current reality but reflected, he came to acknowledge reluctantly and
bitterly, pervasive, lifelong feelings. In this deprivation, he was able
to turn to his brother, Bob, for mutual comforting. Typically with
Mr. Y, this closeness was outside his awareness until the analyst
asked whether his relationship with his brother might have had some
of the warmth and tenderness reflected in his dreams and transference attitudes toward the analyst.

He did not want to think of the analyst as a human being about
whom he had intensely personal feelings and curiosity. The more
aware Mr. Y became of his dissatisfaction with his wife, the more he
craved and hated closeness with the analyst. Homosexual fantasies
and overtly homosexual dreams expressed, in part, such wishes for
physical closeness, admiration, attention, and masculine fortification.

On the couch, at times, Mr. Y would feel warmly sensual, with a
partial erection. Usually he would acknowledge that he felt "affirma-
tive" but would protest that these feelings had nothing to do with
longings for closeness with the analyst, if this interpretation was
suggested to him. Homosexual longings and homosexual transference intensified. He dreamed of the analyst as apparently homosexual in a "proper, stiff" English country setting. The analyst barely
acknowledged Mr. Y's presence in the dream and seemed to be
annoyed, not talking to him. He tried to get the analyst's attention. In
that session, when he thought the analyst had referred to him
affectionately, he became worried: "You might reach out and touch
me, when your voice sounded affectionate." A month later he
dreamed: "I'm in my childhood home, perhaps getting ready to go to
church. I was sitting down on the toilet and Bob came in. I threw a
washcloth at him, but kiddingly. 'Let me have my privacy!' He
laughed, and I guess he didn't come in." With embarrassment, he
reported fantasies of wanting the analyst to admire his long, soft
stools. He associated that his anxiety in the locker room mixed with
fascination at looking at men's genitals, especially uncircumcised
penises. When the analyst interpreted Mr. Y's wish that the analyst
serve like his brother in an intimate, warm, admiring relation with
him, Mr. Y could feel such wishes. Mr. Y wanted, however, to enjoy
such a close relationship with the analyst without acknowledging it in

consciousness. There was marked resistance to awareness of the transference. There were many examples of Mr. Y's longing for a close connection with the analyst and seeming to enjoy it, until it was interpreted to him. Usually his pleasure would diminish, he would deny the interpretation, he would protest that since he could not have a real relationship with the analyst, such wishes were pointless, and he would attempt to move further away from the analyst. Wishes for a close bond (union) with the analyst seemed so intense that Mr. Y could not allow them into consciousness, except fleetingly.

Two sessions later, he reported a dream:

I was playing with D's [wife's] vagina or whatever, and she was wet. The lips were parted. I was going back and forth, stimulating her. I was there with somebody else, maybe two other men who were also doing something with D, perhaps playing with her, stimulating her. As I went down D's wet vulva with my finger, there was another finger of somebody else in the vagina. That hurt me. I had the feeling of excitement, revulsion, sadness, anger. My next thought was oh, we shouldn't be, we should be delicate, he shouldn't hurt her by jamming his finger in hard. Then I felt sad for D. Among my feelings was anger, I guess.

He associated to not wanting D to be hurt, to feeling sad that D had two people poking at her. Although he referred to himself and the analyst poking around in/at his wife, this association did not have much conviction for him. At the end of this hour, in association to encountering another man in his wife's body, he acknowledged the emotional importance to him of the most distinguished fantasy lover he had assigned to his wife. It pleased him if this man found his wife appealing, in that he then became more attractive to the man. He was able to talk about his admiration for his father-in-law and his delight with the latter's gifts to him. He wanted to feel admired and accepted by fathers and important, successful men.

Soon after, he reported another "hateful" dream:

The guy next door whose name I can't pronounce [which is Jewish like the analyst's name] is naked. I'm lying on my back, and he's on all fours above me. His penis looks like mine. [He obsessively described a feeling in the dream similar to smoking a cigarette, that he'd become addicted, if he took just one.] I touch and stroke his penis. He touches mine in the same way. At one point I want him to lie down on me and copulate, but I

realize I haven't got any hole to go in. I don't think of the rear
end. I think I get an erection, and I think he may. Then I want
to put his erection in my mouth and I do.

Touching and sucking the man's penis were interesting. He
protested first, however, that he was being seduced into the situation; the man was ugly, and the dream was hateful. By the end of the
hour he reported his embarrassment at enjoying, at close quarters
with another man, a lively repartee that he experienced as frighteningly intimate. As he was getting out of the shower, he wondered
whether the analyst fantasized about "this terrific body I've got." The
analyst interpreted that the Jewish guy in the dream was the analyst
and that Mr. Y now wished for such intensely exciting physical
contact with the analyst. Mr. Y was more tolerant of his homosexual
wishes and a little more accepting of such cravings toward the
analyst. He was now well aware of his pleasurable interest in things
Jewish, of his wanting to share this connection with the analyst. In
the session before the summer vacation separation, Mr. Y was able to
understand, on his own, that involved in his fear that his brother and
wife were having an affair were "how much I wanted Bob to love me
and how much of a betrayal of that love it would be if he were to love
D." His loving feelings for the analyst as brother were clear, although
frightening.

As Mr. Y became more aware of the intensity of his hunger for
patient and warm acceptance—for someone concerned with Mr. Y's
needs rather than with his own—his anger surfaced. His angry,
destructive, and sadistic wishes toward his parents, however, were
displaced and enacted with multiple authorities, whom he would
repeatedly challenge and criticize as arbitrary, unreasonable, and
contemptuous of the needs and feelings of other people. Mr. Y was
relieved to find that his homosexual wishes also involved intensely
aggressive and competitive struggles with other men for power,
prestige, and the right to enjoy women sexually. Submissiveness,
dependency, and character rigidity defended against feared unacceptability and rejection for his intensely aggressive-destructive impulses. He would feel very guilty at directing such wishes toward his
parents, and he would quickly lose the evidence he had just elaborated for his criticisms of them. Nevertheless, he complained (and
erased the complaint) that his father had abandoned him to a
hypercritical, paranoid, depressed mother, with whom he was under
orders to behave himself and not upset her fragile equilibrium. He
remained on duty with his disturbed wife, just as he had with his
mother, ever ready to feel guilty in response to her attacks on him.

Mr. Y's fearfulness of needing either men or women made him tend to escape from both. In multiple situations with women who were capable of warm caring toward him, he had run away, frightened of their needs and of his own and fearing rejection or entrapment and passive surrender. For example, as he imagined what it would be like to feel involved with a warmer, more responsive woman, he dreamed of being caught in a web woven by a poisonous spider. He minimized his concerns that the woman was insatiable sexually, although he readily acknowledged his fearfulness (from multiple dreams) of mother and wife as poisonous, poisoning the air with their destructive criticisms and depressing negativism. The analyst pointed out that, in imagining closeness with a caring woman, Mr. Y feared his own insatiable wishes and his anger. As he began to feel himself to be more sexually potent, intensely competitive struggles with father-bosses (analyst) reemerged; Mr. Y now felt safer struggling with such wishes. With men, Mr. Y's fears of passive homosexual surrender were now complemented by angry, destructive, and competitive wishes that he could feel, made him preserve an emotional distance. Fears of closeness and of destructiveness in the other and in himself were now clear with both men and women. As a result, he feared he could not love.

Ms. Z

Ms. Z's intense jealousy emerged when she began to live with a man. She had regarded herself as undesirable, feeling insufficiently appealing and attractive. As a child, she had felt very much neglected and rejected by both parents. Initially, her unloved feelings were turned back on herself, as if she had been the cause of each parent's difficulty with being generously caring toward her. With me, she remained aloof and distant, often speaking with little feeling, as if she was going through the motions of complaining about continually feeling shortchanged. Indeed, Ms. Z had considerable difficulty tolerating interpretation of her defenses against fully relying on and needing the analyst. She would feel criticized and argue that she just did not feel much toward me. At times, however, her dreams and treatment behavior revealed her intense hunger for the analyst's nurturance. For example, in one dream a hungry, lonely kitten in a corner of the waiting room needs to be picked up, hugged, and fed. In response to interpretation of her distance with me, Ms. Z would insist that I regarded her as a patient only in a perfunctory way, that I certainly could not have feelings about her, other than perhaps boredom, impatience, irritability, or dissatisfaction. One day when she stressed that my attitude to her was as mechanical and impersonal as her own toward her clients, I told her—with more vigor than usual—that if that were so, I would be so bored with my work that I could not do it. I explained that for me to feel engaged with her, or with any patient, I had to feel strongly toward her. If I could not feel much about her, if she, indeed, did not matter to me, I could not be of help to her. Of course, I had to manage and understand such feelings in order to advance her treatment. This time (we had been here before) she was surprised and taken with what I told her. She cried and felt much more conviction as she connected the image of my perfunctory attitude with both parents' lack of involvement with her. She had tried so hard to believe that everyone would be the same with her. This time, she could begin to integrate how sad and angry she felt about her childhood deprivation.

Ms. Z had some reason to mistrust R's (boyfriend) commitment to her. There was evidence that R had difficulty allowing himself to feel fully loving with her without defensively needing to disregard her needs. But she was pained by the intensity of her jealousy when they were apart. She could not bear that he might enjoy being with anyone else. This concern applied especially to fears that he would have sex with another woman. Ms. Z could now feel how hungry she felt for someone to love and enjoy her. She wanted R to fill her up. Her previous overeating and overspending were now directed toward R. She felt insatiable, continually desiring sex, gifts, and attention from him. When they were apart, she felt intensely jealous, tortured by ideas that R might be with another woman. When there was, indeed, some evidence that he might have had drinks with a former girlfriend, Ms. Z would feel enraged and betrayed.

Ms. Z's jealousy linked with feelings of betrayal and rejection in relation to both mother and father. She could feel her disappointment and jealousy in relation to the birth of each of her younger siblings and her fantasies of what they got from the mother. She felt she had never really had much of a relationship with either parent. Mother and father may have each given something to the other from which she was excluded, but mother did not seem to do well with father. On the other hand, Ms. Z felt intensely jealous of father's second wife, with whom he at least seemed to be loving and devoted. When father left home as the parents separated, Ms. Z felt hopeless ever to gain father's love.

Unlike Mr. Y, Ms. Z's jealousy did not lead to uncovering intense homosexual desire, nor did it seem to be primarily a defense against intimacy and destruction. Her jealousy seemed to repeat and express, in an especially clear and intense way, sibling and oedipal rivalry, with condensation of preoedipal and oedipal longings to be loved exclusively. Deprivation, neglect, rage, and hunger were expressed in her jealous preoccupation that someone else might be getting some of what she desired so greedily. Despite Ms. Z's fearfulness and mistrust in allowing herself fully to feel need of the other person, we could not establish that her jealousy served to screen this danger. Nor did her jealousy seem necessary for the masochistic self-enhancement she so often provided herself. Her jealousy focused her chronic complaints about both parents onto her lover, as she complained that she was being unfairly neglected in favor of the selfish needs of the other or of others he (or she) preferred. Through her jealousy she seemed somewhat better able to tolerate and integrate her chronic rage, by justifying that she was, indeed, being treated with insufficient concern and consideration. Since facing and integrating her anger had been very difficult for Ms. Z, her jealousy helped to facilitate this therapeutic task and so was adaptive.

As Ms. Z's dreams became increasingly more violent, she first insisted that she could not feel such anger during waking life. The analyst consistently interpreted her fear of pulling together her anger and dissatisfaction, now with R and in the transference with the analyst and previously with her parents. Anger and sadness broke through her chronic blandness as she sobbed and screamed that she deserved better with each of us. I was, indeed, impressed that this very tightly controlled woman finally allowed herself such freedom within the treatment situation. She now seemed to feel more entitled to good care, to have the right to insist on it, and to feel angry when the other would not provide it. Terror of being alone forever kept her from leaving R so as to find someone better able to love her. It was, indeed, progress for Ms. Z to tolerate feeling her chronic anger without having to close this off and hide behind her chronic insistence that she simply could not feel the anger that I believed was inside of her. She could now much more easily connect her jealousy with her chronic angry feelings of deprivation. Before, she would insist that she just could not connect herself with the very lonely and unhappy child she described; the child felt like someone else. As a result, both Ms. Z and I felt less troubled about her jealousy. It became the door through which she could open up and feel her chronic bitterness.

DISCUSSION

Mr. Y's pathological jealousy, like any compromise formation, served multiple functions. Actual behavior, involving aggressive and sexual drive derivatives, featured prominently in Mr. Y's pathological jealousy: panty checks, diary inspections, and reading of the wife's notes. This behavior was repetitive and under his own control, behavior in which he again and again found "evidence" against his wife, subjected himself to her contempt and rejection of him, and became sexually aroused. Mr. Y's panty checks and fantasies about them served, to a degree, as his sexual behavior during the period under review. They were painful but sexually stimulating, leading him not only to fantasize about his wife's sexual activity with other men but to allow and encourage his own sexual fantasies about other women and (preconsciously and unconsciously) about other men. More generally, excitement and connectedness, with the couple and with each member individually, were important motivations. Early in the treatment, during separations from the analyst or from the wife, the patient would resume this behavior. My impression is that the intense homosexual brother/father transference contributed to the dissolution of the pathological jealousy symptom complex. That is, the pathological jealousy functioned, in part, for sexual and emotional connectedness to others. The analyst now became the needed other.

All defensive activity involves action on one's own affects, wishes, internalized objects, and, to varying degrees, on the external environment and external objects. This patient's need for behavioral enactment resembled perverse masturbatory enactments. Behavioral enactment may become necessary when conflict cannot be handled intrapsychically, so as to prevent regression or disorganization. The following dangers are emphasized in this repetitive behavioral enactment: intimacy in an exclusive relationship with either a man or a woman; aggressive destruction and guilt; and inability to regulate self-esteem. Behavioral enactment, like masturbation itself, through the associated excitement, tends to make fantasy more intensely realistic and enhances feeling connected to the (unavailable, dangerous) fantasy objects.

The need for concrete evidence in Mr. Y's pathological jealousy related primarily to defense against aggressive, destructive dangers. Because of his denial of his wife's destructiveness, Mr. Y would lose the evidence of it, just as he had with his mother's. The analyst as father witnessed the evidence of the mother-wife's hostility and helped Mr. Y to bear his own anger in response to it. Extenuating circumstances (evidence) were required to overcome the paternal injunction against upsetting the disturbed mother (wife). The evidence reassured Mr. Y that he had justification for his angry feelings. The need for concrete evidence testified to Mr. Y's defensive distrust of his own feelings, perceptions, and thoughts and of their destructiveness. External reassurance through enactments protected the patient's self-esteem from persecutory attacks by the superego. He needed continual demonstration of the validity of his angry criticisms, together with denial of his own destructiveness through the persistent survival of these inanimate objects with their "evidence." Mr. Y's intense guilt about his sexual and romantic fantasies about other women and wishes to leave his wife and children was attenuated by "proof" that his wife was guilty of the same sins and that vindicated his own desires. To the usual idea that projection of impulses toward infidelity is involved in pathological jealousy must be added the need for defense against guilt, the contention of being forced into infidelity, of having no choice because of the wife's similar behavior. Riviere (1932) made the need for defense against guilt explicit in such projection of impulses. The extensive behavioral enactment here described takes the jealous fantasy another step toward actualization of the other's crime as a superego defense. A rigid character like Mr. Y is under great pressure to submit to internal parental standards (such as the paternal injunction against upsetting the disturbed mother-wife), so as to preclude feeling unacceptable, rejected, or abandoned. Hence, he needs to justify his crimes, as if he were before a judge. Projective identification describes Mr. Y's simultaneous repudiation of his own sexual wishes, together with the excitement at their fantasied fulfillment attributed to the wife. That is, Mr. Y oscillated between being voyeur and exhibitionistic participant and experienced the sexual excitement of both roles.

Behavioral enactment of fantasy in Mr. Y's pathological jealousy also condensed aspects of masochism and pathological narcissism, which had been sexualized. In his sleuthing, he rubbed his own nose in his fantasies and experiences of the wife-mother's rejection of him. Mastery of such traumatic feelings was sought by active repetition under his own control. Demonstrating with concrete proof that he had been betrayed, humiliated, and rejected had greater value than just the unsubstantiated feeling. The connections between masochism and paranoia (Freud, 1919; Bak, 1946; Blum, 1980, 1981) are clear here. The dramatic enactment ("caught in the act") in his panty checks and diary searches made more real and credible these awful feelings. He called upon God to witness his mistreatment for self-aggrandizement and the right to be loved. Experiencing and demonstrating how he had been mistreated, wounded, rejected, and unloved were used to demonstrate and enhance his value as worthwhile and lovable. Ms. Z seemed better able to use her jealousy to face and integrate her chronic rage by validation of her neglect and betrayal.

Mr. Y had greater difficulty with integrating his anger. Sexual feelings for Mr. Y served as both defense and gratification; they attenuated painful feelings, which helped to defend against, and relieve guilt about, homosexual, heterosexual, and sadistic-destructive wishes. Hence, in contrast to Riviere's (1932) view that the sexuality of pathological jealousy is only defensive, my position is that the sexual arousal is a central determinant. It not only is defensive but also condenses heterosexual, homosexual, and autoerotic conflicts and may actually serve as the patient's sexual behavior.

Lonely, betrayed, rejected, excluded, criticized, Mr. Y repeated in his pathological jealousy basic affective determinants of his childhood relations with both parents. He was attached to such painful affects as constituting the nature of his ties to objects (Valenstein, 1973; Blum, 1981). He emphasized, however, the suffering he had to endure at the hands of his rejecting objects for narcissistic and masochistic enhancement. Despite his mistrust, that is, he knew that he could have more than he did in his relations with objects. It was just this discrepancy that served self-aggrandizement, love-worthiness, and guilt reduction. From this perspective, Mr. Y's pathological jealousy was a masochistically elaborated fantasy of exclusion from the primal scene. So was his acceptance of living in a loveless and sexually ungratifying marriage while longing for something better from other women. Mr. Y was frightened and mistrustful of loving and needed, instead, distance, control, domination, and objective reasons to be wary of his partner. Although Ms. Z was also frightened and mistrustful, she could abandon herself to wanting to be loved by her lover, although not by the analyst. Both patients were terrified of their intense regressive, dependent wishes. Each was a pathologically dependent person who, nevertheless, had to control and maintain distance in relationships. The choice of a partner (wife) who was similar to himself protected Mr. Y from greater intimacy, demonstrated that the other, not he, was frightened of loving, and was used in his masochistic demonstration that he was not being loved.

From this perspective, the primal scene triadic construction of Mr. Y's pathological jealousy protected against dangerous intimacy with one person. The woman was the object, the arena around which his homosexual wishes were deployed. The pressure and dread of actualization of his homosexual wishes required a continual connection to a woman. The apparent triangle of himself, a woman, and another man protected him from the danger of his desire for the man, by the woman's presence. But not only does the woman protect against homosexuality; the man protects against intimacy in a one-to-one relationship. Father and brother must protect the patient against being left alone with the disturbed mother-wife. Homosexual dangers involve the intensity of wishes for passive surrender (union), leading to castration and loss of separateness, as well as of aggressive destruction of the object and, in retaliation, destruction of the self by the object. Heterosexual dangers involve intense mistrust, expectations of rejection and unacceptability, and fears of entrapment and passive surrender (insatiability) and of aggressive destruction of and by the object. Simultaneously, this intense dyadic conflict screens a dangerously aggressive triadic oedipal struggle. Oscillation between participants and roles in the primal scene—male/female, exhibitionist/voyeur, adult/child, active/passive, sadist/masochist—protects against holding still in any one position of relatedness to another person, something Mr. Y found exquisitely difficult.

The object of desire in pathological jealousy is not a single person. Rather, the patient's imagined dangers in passive needs of the love object are protected against by the fantasied presence of another person who is appealed to as a protector from such dangerous intimacy. Freud's (1911) concept of homosexual object choice as a normal developmental stage on the way to object love, with homosexual object choice identical with narcissistic object choice, is relevant here. Relations with an object regarded as similar and equal to oneself (homosexual, narcissistic) are safer than intense needs of an unequal, different object (heterosexual, adult love). From this perspective, the object choice in pathological jealousy is homosexual and narcissistic, even with regard to the heterosexual component. The heterosexual object is regarded as phallic and masculine in her own right and is further pulled into the homosexual, narcissistic orbit by her fantasied connection with another man. Control, equality, and sameness in one's object relations defend against a variety of fantasied dangers in freely needing and loving another. Frosch's (1981) view, although suggestive, could not be confirmed here, namely, that there had been actual humiliation experienced for the expression of passive longings and leading to paranoid defense against homosexual strivings.

Thus, in cases of pathological jealousy, inability to love, which has been noted by earlier authors (Freud, 1911, 1922; Jones, 1929, Fenichel, 1935; Schmideberg, 1953; Pao, 1969), is here given central attention. The various explanations for narcissistic deficiency in pathological jealousy offered by previous authors should be considered complementary. Defense against dangers derived from all psychosexual levels, especially in relation to hostile aggression, as synthesized and integrated within the ego throughout development, requires continual reassurance from internal and external objects.

Joffe's (1969) view that envy should not be understood in terms of a specific psychosexual developmental level applies as well to understanding pathological jealousy. The narcissistic deficiency is a complex issue not reducible only to defensive regression from oedipal conflicts or to presumed developmental arrest or fixation; the conflict is understood as involving both oedipal and preoedipal derivatives. I have suggested an organizing focus for understanding this intense fearfulness of allowing oneself to love another single person. The jealous triadic construction serves, in the multiple ways outlined, to deal with this danger and need.

In contrast, Ms. Z's ordinary jealousy did not seem to serve as a defensive screen against loving intimacy. Although she, too, was terrified of commitment, she could allow herself somewhat more abandon within a love relationship. Neither patient could relax and enjoy dependency. Briefly, each patient could feel how much he or she wanted to be loved and cared for. But at some point each one would become frightened of just living with such dependent cravings and would close them off. For analysis of pathological dependency, the patient first has to be able to feel the intensity of the need for the other and then, later, to become troubled about the misuse of the other to defend against his own internal conflicts. Until the patient can hold still with his own intense dependent longings, the pathological dependency cannot be taken apart. Patients who are too terrified to allow themselves to rely on another person in a committed way over time cannot analyze their pathological dependency but will, instead, seek to avoid and deny it.

Ms. Z's isolation of affect, undoing, reversal, and repression contrasted with Mr. Y's persistent destruction of meaning within the treatment situation. Ms. Z's jealousy allowed her to sustain and vindicate her chronic rage, so that she could begin to integrate it. Mr. Y could appease his conscience through his jealousy that his anger was justified. But he would have to rid himself quickly of any angry conviction of mistreatment and make it meaningless. Both patients relied on masochistically elaborated pathological dependency to protect against separateness and destructiveness. Unlike Mr. Y, Ms. Z could tolerate moving further outside of this dependency, while observing her needs and fears with the other person.

Part V

CONCLUSION

TOWARD A PASSIONATE ANALYSIS
Technique in the Analysis of Pathological Dependency

S uccessful analysis of pathological dependency requires that the analyst be able to encourage and tolerate full opening up of the patient's rage and destructiveness, together with exploration of the multiple protective illusions attributed to dependency. To facilitate a passionate analytic process, the analyst must process and understand his own intense feelings of hate and love for his analysands. Managing and containing intensely passionate feelings of hatred or love are difficult for all of us, analysts and patients. At a recent panel, "Hate in the Analytic Setting" at the American Psychoanalytic Association (Panel, 1991), despite the focus of the topic, in each presentation there seemed to be relief for both patient and analyst once rage and hatred had become understandable and the patient was behaving more reasonably, less angrily. It should not be surprising that even our most capable analysts seem eager not to be burdened by hatred.

We need fuller consideration of how analysts struggle with their loving (and hating) feelings toward their patients and their various defenses against these, so they can best facilitate a passionate analytic process. Analysts need to welcome and draw upon their loving feelings, sexual desires, and wishes for connection with patients so as to learn more about the patient and to advance the work. The same applies to hating and destructive feelings. A distinguished analyst told an analytic audience on another occasion that he uses his fantasies of having an affair with his female patients to wonder how and why the affair would not work. From these fantasies he is usually able to learn something new about his patient. To be creative as a psychoanalyst requires access to, and tolerance for, intense feelings

247

and desires in and between patient and analyst, plus the ability to process and use these in the service of the patient's growth toward maturity rather than for the analyst's own needs.

Analysts' need for defense against rage and destructiveness interferes with analytic work. The analyst needs to feel secure that he can face, contain, and process intense need, desire, and hatred in himself, without action or avoidance. Of course, if he can be responsible for such intense feelings toward his patients, he can investigate these reactions to advance their analyses by separating his own needs and conflicts from his patients'. If the analyst cannot hate his patient who hates him, at least some of the time, the patient's hatred cannot be analyzed. I am skeptical of analysts who insist that they feel little hatred for patients who chronically hate them. Of course, analysts may respond with varied feelings, not only, or not necessarily, anger, to a patient's brief expressions of anger. But chronic hatred is much more difficult for analysts to bear. In the presence of chronic hatred, devaluation, contempt, and rejection of the analyst's attempts to interpret, it may become difficult for the analyst to persist with the analytic task. Of course, analysts vary in what they need to receive from their patients, in how angry, hurt, and rejected they feel when patients frustrate such needs, and in their tolerance for hatred and destructiveness in the patient and in themselves.

To successfully analyze patients with pathological dependency, the analyst has to bring their rage and hatred out in the open into the transference and enable the patient to keep them there, so the patient can take responsibility for and integrate these feelings. To do so, the analyst must tolerate his own rage and his patient's rage. We are quite far along when we have arrived at a point where the patient is expressing and owning his chronic hatred. On the contrary, what is much more typical of pathologically dependent patients, as we have seen throughout this book, is that they flee from taking responsibility for their anger and destructiveness toward helpless, idealized reliance on the now-transformed hated object. Initially, the analyst will have to struggle with his own frustration, annoyance, and disappointment that the pathologically dependent patient avoids analysis of conflict. Such anger in the analyst should be a signal of what is wrong within the treatment process. There is, of course, the risk that the analyst's efforts to engage the patient about his avoidance of facing what is wrong will become contaminated by the analyst's own anger or sadomasochism. That is, faced with a pathologically dependent patient who consciously and unconsciously wants merely to be in analysis so as to preserve the analyst as protective and containing parent, the analyst may feel inclined to exhort, bully, threaten, or get rid of the patient as insufficiently motivated for analysis.

The analyst will need to address both the patient's chronic character defenses that avoid processing feelings and wishes and the patient's dependent attachment to the analyst. This combination of rigid character defense and dependent relatedness may easily lead the analyst to feel dissatisfied with the patient, and then the patient may feel dissatisfied with himself and regard himself as an analytic failure. That is, to a degree, analyst and patient may actually accept that the patient is and will be an analytic failure. The analysis needs to address the patient's willingness to repeat with the analyst the patient's earlier acceptance of a role of disability, incompetence, or subservience in relation to a parent. Here, too, the analyst needs to use such sadomasochistic reactions in himself to understand further what the patient wants with him.

For example, recall from chapter 6 my efforts to analyze Ms. D's intensified sadomasochism with me. For us to work our way out of this impasse, I needed first to acknowledge that I had become stuck in a sadomasochistic engagement with Ms. D. But even more important, I needed to acknowledge that Ms. D was seeking to destroy the treatment and that she was succeeding. Until then I had used partial denial to obscure my own collusion in what was wrong and to avoid acknowledging fully how vindictively destructive Ms. D was being with me and with our joint work. Then I would not have to hate her so intensely; instead, I could shift to defensive attitudes of concern, helplessness, or self-criticism. There was also for each of us the danger of loss of the other if we each acknowledged hatred and wishes to get rid of the other. Once I could hold still with hating Ms. D for how destructive she was actually being with me and with her treatment and show her this, no matter how loudly she protested and fought, to a degree, she was able to move forward.

As with Ms. D, to analyze pathological dependency, analyst and patient both need to tolerate and face the patient's rage and hatred, which need to be kept out in the open between patient and analyst. Thus the various ways in which the patient avoids feeling and expressing his anger need to be consistently addressed so that the patient becomes able to feel and take responsibility for his anger. Once this anger is more consistently available, then we need to understand it psychoanalytically. That is, the patient must be helped to feel who and what he is angry at. Then, he needs to learn what defensive uses he makes of his anger. These are different. Pathologically dependent patients are chronically angry people; they need to experience these angry feelings and work with them in treatment. But they also need to discover how they exploit their resentment, nourish it, and use it to bolster various claims and protections. For example, anger can be used to create distance from others, to deny need and dependency, to spoil the good things others offer, to support entitled claims for reparations, to hold on to others in hostile ways, and so on.

I would differentiate the aims in hating to include getting rid of, as well as holding on to, an object. One danger of hatred for the patient is destruction of a needed person. To understand why the patient is so afraid of destroying his needed object, we need to clarify the patient's fantasies of why and how he expects his hatred will destroy the other. What may be most important here is the fantasied sense of danger in feeling one's feelings, of how this will endanger oneself or the other. The danger of destruction of the other will be exaggerated by the patient's vital need for the other, because the patient feels unable to manage alone. Hatred can move in the other direction, toward getting rid of the other and managing oneself separately, if, indeed, separateness can be tolerated. When one needs the other too much and cannot stand the need, one can endlessly want to dominate, humiliate, destroy, or kill the other. But if the need for the other is paramount, the other cannot really be destroyed or relinquished; the display of contempt, devaluation, and so on becomes so much posturing, denying one's own need and helplessness.

To analyze chronic hatred, the analyst needs to emphasize not only the patient's fear of destructiveness, but also the adaptive and stabilizing functions of chronic hatred, once it has clearly appeared within the treatment situation. Thus, chronic hatred and sadism may protect against psychotic disorganization as well as despair, immobilization, and giving up. The analyst must also pay attention to how the patient tries to manage his hatred. Sadomasochistic excitement, for example, is one way to manage chronic intense rage by attempts to tame it, sexualize it, and contain it within an object relationship. Yet, despite the excitement, only in illusion is the rage no longer present in sadomasochism. Sadomasochism moves the patient away from the immediate destructiveness of intense rage toward the containment of chronic hatred and chronically hateful relationships (in this respect, an ego-adaptive and defensive transformation of rage).

In my experience, chronic hatred may be a way of life for certain neurotic patients, not only for borderlines. This view is a major premise of this book. Patients with pathological dependency, while terrified of their destructiveness, are locked into chronically hateful relationships. Although the hatred may be denied, undone, or turned into its opposite, with the partner and the relationship idealized, it nevertheless persists. To be sure, at the start of an analysis, it may not be at all obvious that the pathologically dependent patient hates the very ones he seems to need. By now it should be clear that considerable and consistent interpretation of defense is required to reveal and liberate the rage of the pathologically dependent patient.

Hatred and intense dependent need are multiply interconnected in pathological dependency. The needy patient hates the one he needs so much and hates his own neediness. The affective force of hatred further binds the patient to his object. Fears of destruction of the object lead to greater need for attachment to the object to preserve the object; to reassure oneself the object survives; to contain one's destructiveness; to reassure oneself against superego judgments by reclaiming the object's acceptance, and so forth. Terror of one's own dangerous internal forces perpetuates the dependent bond by seeking to put one's badness into the other and to make the other one responsible for this and for oneself more generally. Inability to assume responsibility for oneself and for one's dangerous forces perpetuates the dependent solution.

Optimal technique for managing and analyzing hatred requires ongoing attention to the details of the patient's reasons for hatred and dissatisfaction with the analyst. Only insofar as the analyst is in possession of the details of why a patient hates him in the present can he interpret systematically the patient's defensive retreat from fully feeling his hatred. The risk, as in the panel presentations I have referred to, is the analyst's temptation to shift too soon from the force of the patient's hatred to relative emphasis on its other functions so as to relieve the tension between the analytic couple. When a patient is convinced that the analyst regards him with contempt and disinterest, even if the analyst systematically pursues investigation of this contention as it relates to the present and the past, the patient may yet hold to this conviction tenaciously. But analysis of intense transference hatred needs to begin with careful attention to why and how the patient feels the analyst deserves his hatred. Only later can the links with hatred of the parents be made; to do otherwise is to pull the patient away from the immediacy of hating the present object (analyst). Once the hatred has been engaged and worked with in the transference, the varied adaptive and defensive functions of the hatred can be explored. We should note that attention to the usefulness of hating facilitates the patient's understanding and willingness to explore what may lie beyond the hatred. Tolerating hatred and allowing it to flower in the transference should allow the analyst to go beyond the interpretation of destructiveness in his analysis. Hatred has multiple functions and intentions that go beyond destruction. Hatred certainly can be a form of relatedness. Hatred can screen and express loving wishes, serve to maintain distance and to preserve boundaries, reverse feelings of helplessness, worthlessness, and humiliation, and protect against disorganization and despair.

A sense of how hate may subserve other ends can be gleaned from the following declaration in the psychotherapy of an unusually hate-filled woman, Ms. F:

> I don't mind your hating me. What I mind is your indifference. This whole treatment and your supposed concern for me are not real. I pay you for it and you do your job. When I can feel you hate me, I have something I can believe in. The rest of the time, I'm tempted into an addiction to this treatment and to you which can't go anywhere, because it's fake. If you're not indifferent to me, then you can't stand being with me. I'm just a lump in the chair, a gross blob, a nothing. There is no way you could want to be with me.

When Ms. F allowed herself to feel need, concern, and caring between herself and me, she would relax and enjoy this closeness temporarily. Then she invariably would catch herself, close off, pull back into her chronic silence, disavow the connection, attempt to destroy my helpful effectiveness, fill up with hate; rejection, and pessimism, and miss a couple of sessions. She would disavow her sadism in seeking to hook me into a helping bond with her, only to cut me down and off and leave me to feel angry, teased, frustrated, and ineffective.

Early in the treatment, she would move to the brink of tempting both of us to end the treatment (and once she actually ended it and later returned) before she would again allow some connection to open between us. Slowly, she came to tolerate some closeness and need with me, without fully attempting to destroy them, even as she would pull back into prolonged silence and attempted disconnection. She had an uncanny knack for sensing just that point where I would feel I could not stand her destruction of the treatment anymore, at which time she would allow some renewed contact between us. I cite Ms. F to illustrate hatred as an adaptive bond, in which both the attempted expression and containment of intense rage and destructiveness served as a cover for need and love and as a means of reversing feelings of helplessness, vulnerability, shame, and humiliation into a sense of power and control. I want to draw further on this example to consider issues in the technique of analyzing hatred. In the malignant form of transference hatred, she continued to insist that my selfish indifference to her was real. Gabbard (Panel, 1991) described malignant transference hatred, in which the "as if" quality of the hatred disappears, with the patient's insisting that his feelings are veridical. Of course, malignant transference hatred will disrupt the therapeutic alliance and the treatment. Ms. F's hatred of me was a transference repetition (to both parents as indifferent and self-absorbed), which she was afraid to acknowledge more consistently, especially because it threatened her with the loss of hating me, which served to organize her and protect her from surrender to despair and crippling depression. It also threatened her defensive shield against needing me and wanting me to love her exclusively. This wish terrified her because of its all-consuming intensity (with merger wishes and fears) and her dread of hurt, humiliation, and ultimate rejection by me. Without the protection of hatred between us, loving feelings stimulated anxiety, intense mistrust, and mounting pressure to disconnect from me and her own feelings. What would happen next between us if she did not interrupt the loving feelings? She could not reconcile her contradictory views of me as loving/caring and as fake/hypocritical. Certainly, I would soon disappoint her and show her my true colors, so she had better not relax and enjoy the closeness with me. Ms. F needed to be connected to me through intense feelings, sometimes hating, sometimes loving, continually shifting. I want to emphasize my struggles to contain my patient's hatred and my own. Because of the disavowal of her destructiveness and her insistence on my failures with her, I, at times, would lose my tolerance of her accusations and of her. Then I would feel like insisting forcefully that she was the "bad one," not I. Since she could not reclaim this "badness" for a parent or herself, I had to tolerate being "the bad one" much of the time. I also had to carry the loving feelings for both of us, since most of the time she also could not claim these. I preferred her hatred and active rejection, through which she remained connected and invigorated, to her surrender to hopeless despair. That is, I both resented and enjoyed being chronically hated. The more I could accept and enjoy her hatred, which paralleled her addictive neediness and moments of affectionate and tender caring, the better I could help Ms. F to tolerate that she was bound to me by both hatred and caring. I needed to demonstrate repeatedly that despite her terror of relatedness to me and to others, it was better than her chronic disconnection and despair. I had to help her to reclaim her intense human feelings and needs from contempt, humiliation, and rejection (her own and the internalized parental imagoes), so that she could value and prefer the pain and pleasure of human relatedness to her chronic detachment and conviction that she was nonhuman.

SADOMASOCHISTIC STRUGGLES AND ANALYTIC PROCESS

I believe that patients with pathological dependency need to open up, face, and integrate a considerable amount of rage and destructiveness to achieve permanent change. Without sufficient "blood and guts" coming into the analytic setting, through the patient's experiencing violence and passion in an ongoing, sustained way in the analytic transference, pathological dependency cannot be resolved. If it is correct that many analysts are uncomfortable with rage and destructiveness in the other and oneself, how can they facilitate the patient's opening this up fully? Analysts may be tempted into participating in a sadomasochistic relationship with the patient so as to defend against and contain more nakedly destructive impulses in both partners, especially by alternating roles as to who dominates and stops the other. For example, the impasse Ms. D and I reached involved just such joint sadomasochistic avoidance of the rage and destructiveness in each of us. When I could remain clear that I hated her for seeking to destroy her analysis, then we could progress. But I had colluded with her in enacting a pattern of relatedness that refused to acknowledge in an ongoing way how destructively she was feeling and acting. That is, I would not stay with my assessment of how destructive she was being with me and with her treatment. After awhile I would seek a different answer for what was wrong between us. With Ms. F, I kept wanting her to acknowledge and to work therapeutically with her destructiveness. Not only was that expectation unrealistic with Ms. F, but I came to realize that I also wanted her to relieve me of the burden of hating her for making me the "bad one." I needed to relinquish, more fully than I had, the wish to transform Ms. F into a typical patient who would be able to address what was wrong more consistently. I had to keep catching myself, often with her help, at a partial denial of the severity of Ms. F's difficulties as a patient. I needed to remain more accepting of who Ms. F was and of her hating me and my hating her and not to fear that we would each act on our wishes to get rid of the other. When I remained convinced that we would remain together, hating each other for some time, I felt less angry and anxious with her. I was then under less pressure to attempt to interrupt this pattern by frequent interpretation, which, unfortunately at times, had become my mode of attack. Not surprisingly, I also then became freer to feel, underneath the rage, loving feelings between us. Now I was not turning to love so as to avoid hate. Ms. F had taught me that mutual hatred had to be the foundation of our relationship. She showed me in her silent and not so silent ways that caring could come from the acceptance of one's hatred without recrimination by the other.

A sadomasochistic relationship protects against both separateness and destructiveness and precludes the analysis of either. To get beyond it requires that the analyst grasp for himself and interpret for both patient and analyst what they have *both* been getting from the sadomasochistic enactment. Then its protective functions can be emphasized, so that the patient now has the choice to relinquish his satisfaction with preserving a (defensive) sadomasochistic relationship and to face what lies behind it. In this sense may sadomasochistic relationships preclude analysis. It is the same argument I have been advancing throughout this book. When patients are content with certain chronic, stable defensive organizations, of which pathological dependency and its variants, including sadomasochism, are my central example, there is insufficient motivation to propel an analysis forward. To develop the motivation to face his own internal conflicts and to want to change, the patient must become sufficiently troubled about his chronic avoidance, through settling for a pathological object relationship, of what is wrong.

For example, a patient was reported (Panel, 1991) who freely disclosed that she felt proud of her ability to provoke her analyst and that this reduced her feelings of helplessness. Her very skilled analyst revealed that, at times, he had difficulty focusing on the patient's accusations against him rather than "soothing" her or interpreting defense against desire between them. He seemed to be reluctant to confront and engage the patient's provocativeness with him. Instead, to a degree, patient and analyst lived out an interaction in which each rejected the other. The patient was critical, taunting, and devaluing of him. She contended that the analyst was trying to avoid his real rejecting feelings toward her. She chronically insisted that the analyst was dissatisfied with her; she charged that he was incompetent, selfish, unresponsive, not understanding, and disinterested in her and that he disliked her intensely. At the very least, the analyst did not seem to welcome hearing the details of how and why the patient felt he disliked her. He described his helplessness, frustration, dissatisfaction, and resentment of her. The patient seemed to attempt to address the sadomasochistic enactment within the treatment when she taunted the analyst with being a "masochist." A crisis occurred in the analysis when the patient caught the analyst looking at the mail in his lap at the start of one session. Unfortunately, he could not then (or before) acknowledge, for himself as well as for her, that, indeed, he felt angry and rejecting with her and then explain how she had contributed to these feelings. Obviously, in retrospect it would have been better to acknowledge earlier that, because of her feelings of helplessness, rejection, and inferiority, she sought to provoke the analyst and to have an effect on him and that she was capable of doing so and was, in fact, succeeding. Once that interaction was acknowledged between them, it would have been easier to address why the patient needed to do this. It seemed to me that the analyst's acknowledgment to the patient, at long last, that *each of them* was engaged in fighting was essential for the patient not to feel just like a helpless inferior. As in my struggles to regain my interpretive stance with Ms. D and Ms. F, such a statement by the analyst tells us that he now has the potential to disengage himself from the enacted sado-masochism by confronting his hatred of the patient's destructiveness with him. Such owning up to the patient by the analyst seemed to allow this analysis to proceed again. The analyst courageously acknowledged that he had tended to avoid analytic focus on the patient's rage and destructiveness because they made him anxious. We can surmise that beyond his fears of destructiveness in the patient and in himself, he feared losing her if he faced how much each one wanted to destroy, to get rid of the other.

Patients need to become able to tolerate, face consistently, and then integrate, contain, and manage their rage and destructiveness. Chronically angry people will not get rid of their anger at the end of their analyses. Hopefully, they will have a much better, more complex perspective on their anger, be able to accept and live with it without excessive self-hatred or constraint, and even come to value, enjoy, and use it constructively. Our question as psychoanalysts is how to facilitate a psychoanalytic process in which the patient can feel and work with as much passion (hate and desire) as he and the analyst can stand. The analysis of pathological dependency requires facing, feeling, and integrating intense violence and passion. This analytic task requires consistent attention to our patients' and our own needs to retreat from and avoid intense loving and intense hating in the other and in ourselves.

It should be clear by now that analysts' needs to rely on dependent and sadomasochistic defenses against separateness and rage will intersect with similar needs in the patient and will especially impede successful analysis of pathological dependency. The analyst's fear of destructiveness in the patient and in himself intersects with the analyst's fear of losing the patient because of the mutual wishes to destroy or get rid of the other. The analyst will then tend to move away from confronting the hatred between them toward efforts to bind the couple together through concern and caring, whether or not he actually expresses such wishes for connection and acceptance to the patient. My experience with Ms. F, that, indeed, hatred can be a stable bond, seems less familiar and less comfortable to most analysts.

Indeed, it is difficult to help dependent patients relinquish their chronic way of living, in which responsibility for oneself and one's feelings are disowned and invested in another. The analyst will need to demonstrate to the patient repeatedly the latter's willingness to live this dependent mode out indefinitely with the analyst, to refuse change, and to want to preserve the illusions of protection contained in their bond. The patient will need to be helped to develop firm conviction of how he has derailed his life, sold himself short, disavowed full acknowledgment of his abilities and passions, in order to preserve the pathological bond with the other. The patient will need to feel very sad and angry with himself, with his parent(s), and with the analyst about his selling out on himself, so that he can develop sufficient motivation to struggle against this. To arrive at this point requires that the analyst insist repeatedly on the patient's clinging to support rather than systematically facing what is wrong within. The analyst will both help and hurt his needy, sensitive, dependent patients by emphasizing their chronic avoidance of what is wrong so that they do not have to change. The patient may then feel rejected and unaccepted by the analyst so that the analyst needs to interpret that the patient seeks to feel accepted by the analyst rather than to change. Or patient and analyst can replay the childhood scene where the child/patient could not satisfy a parent. On the other hand, the patient may feel gratified that the analyst does really care enough about him to make an issue consistently of the patient's not changing. Here, too, this analytic approach may initially aid the patient's motivation to participate in the analysis. Ultimately, however, the patient will need to struggle with such wishes to be loved by the analyst in contrast to his own desires for change. The analyst needs to remain acutely aware of the effects of his therapeutic activity on his dependent analysand, so that the latter can be helped to work with this. Needy, dependent patients will feel connected and engaged by the analyst's activity, which they crave, in contrast to silence and lack of contact. The fact that the patient feels gratified by the analyst's interpretive efforts is not a valid reason for the analyst to refrain from engaging the patient about their therapeutic stalemate. Rather, the patient's hunger for contact and intolerance for being left on his own need to be engaged and explored in their multiple meanings throughout the analysis.

Such patients need to learn that they can, indeed, bear their pain, that not only do they not need to run from this but they will gain confidence in their strength through the ability to face what is most dangerous in themselves. Such an analytic attitude emphasizes the patient's strength and potential for autonomous functioning, beyond what he has allowed himself to imagine. The analyst needs to stress that change is terrifying for the patient and to show him how he keeps closing the door to full affective responsibility and autonomy. The focus here is on analyzable patients. Of course, not all patients can tolerate and manage such persistent analysis of their dependency as a regressive defense and face consistent exploration of their own internal conflicts. This differentiation is crucial. With all patients, however, it is better to focus on the multiple ways in which they hide and restrain their abilities and encourage them to discover what they can actually manage (and not manage) for themselves.

I certainly would encourage that analyst and patient attempt to discover together how far the patient can proceed with facing what is wrong within himself, without trying to guess this in advance. The patient's past history and initial presentation may not lead to an accurate assessment of the patient's analytic aptitude. Analyst or patient may err repeatedly in attempting to gauge what the patient is capable of facing and resolving. Analysis is always exploration of possibilities and meanings. Thus, my initial negative appraisal of Dr. S's (chapter 5) analytic capacity was based on past history and his intensely regressive dependent hunger. Within a trial of analysis, he was able to make constructive use of the analytic process. Interpretation of his regressive move toward remaining in bed and not working shifted this to the level of wish, which he sought to explore, understand, and modify. This shift reassured me both that analysis would not lead to a disorganizing regression and that Dr. S would profit from analytic exploration.

On the other hand, many pathologically dependent patients look better to themselves and to the analyst initially than they do later in the analysis. This point is a major premise of this book. Many of these patients function at a high level outside of the analysis, where their dependency is both obscured and gratified. Although the analyst can assess pathological dependency in the initial consultations, he will not be able to determine beforehand how much it will impede an analytic process. Several factors contribute to making patients with pathological dependency look sicker once analysis is under way. Their defensive style is devoted generally, rather than in selected areas, to not wanting to know and to feel what is wrong. Hence, they want to be analytic patients to feel protected and contained by the analyst but do not want to explore themselves analytically. Inhibition, avoidance, and confusion about feelings have become a way of life for them. To feel attached to the other person, they have learned in childhood to exaggerate attitudes of helplessness and disability and to submit to the other's authority without acknowledgment of their resentment. They are thus paralyzed as active agents of collaborative exploration with the analyst. Patients with ordinary dependency will soon feel freed and buoyed by the analyst's attitude of welcoming the patient's ability to join him as a collaborative explorer of the patient's inhibitions, symptoms, and pain. Pathologically dependent patients, instead, are threatened by such invitation to autonomous functioning and will tend to regress further to even more helpless, disabled surrender to the analyst as the good, capable one. The analyst's interpretation of the patient's defensive helplessness within the analysis may lead the patient to protest further that he does not understand what the analyst wants or that he just can not do any better. It is essential for the analyst to grasp that these patients must present such exaggerated versions of their worst sides in order to feel accepted.

Of course, not every pathologically dependent patient can be analyzed or even treated psychotherapeutically. Remember that pathological dependency is not a diagnosis that necessarily determines the level of the patient's psychic organization. All we know initially from it is that the patient relies on another to handle his own conflicts. We cannot know for certain at the start of treatment what the patient will be able to take over for himself. We assume that the patient has felt the need to exploit his lack of full autonomy and independence for varied defensive purposes. The trial of treatment consolidates our assessment of pathological dependency through the patient's treatment behavior. In this sense, pathological dependency is an excellent way to describe such patients' response to analysis. The definition of "not analyzable" given by the Kris Study Group (Joseph, 1967) is useful here. It refers to one who will, in the course of an analysis, for whatever dynamic reason, fail to progress beyond a certain point and tend to become stalemated, with a result that is inadequately resolved or otherwise unsatisfactory. All patients with pathological dependency at some point in their analysis will thus seem to be not analyzable. Only some of them will succeed in moving beyond this point so as to establish their own autonomy and independence.

The patient may initially seek to change in order to please the analyst. The analyst may choose to accept this motivation without interpretation at the beginning of the analysis as the patient opens up his hunger for the analyst's acceptance and love. Recall that in chapter 11 I warned that without early interpretation of the patient's dependent uses of the analyst, the pathologically dependent patient may come to feel that his attachment is actual, in a quasi-delusional way, rather than illusory, wish-filled transference. For a patient, say Dr. S (of chapter 5), who seems to be newly opening up his dependent hunger for the analyst as his defenses against this are interpreted, I would not be concerned with simply allowing the dependency to flourish. Indeed, I would even want, as I did with Dr. S, to draw the dependent hunger into the analytic transference. I would watch closely, however, for signs that the patient does not want just to settle for dependent wishes toward the analyst but seeks to actualize them into a quasi-delusional love relationship. With patients like Mrs. J. (chapter 10) or Ms. W, the psychotically delusional woman of chapter 12, early interpretation of the wish to transform the treatment into a love affair will probably not help much to head off this wish. With healthier patients, such as Professor M (of chapter 11), as soon as the analyst perceives that the patient wants to settle for a dependent relationship with the analyst, he needs to make an analytic issue of the motivation. The problem is not only one of early interpretation. More important is the analyst's willingness, usually out of his own awareness, to join the patient in a mutually shared dependent relationship that is interpreted only in token fashion, so as to preserve it for both partners. The analyst who is comfortable with his own dependent wishes can even enjoy the patient's early dependent turn to the analyst, until or unless it interferes with the patient's forward progress. The problem here is the analyst who needs to disown his dependency or who cannot relax and enjoy it and so enjoy the patient's dependent wishes.

In this sense I referred to the two patients in chapter 14 as being afraid to relax and give in to enjoying their dependent wishes. In some respects, dependency feels good to patients with pathological dependency. They have come to enjoy relying on someone else, who by caring for them reassures them that everything will be fine. Further, they have exploited such good feelings in being dependent so as to camouflage all that is wrong in their dependent enmeshments. Certain rigid characters (Mr. Y and Ms. Z of chapter 14; Ms. F of this chapter) dread the loss of control in passively allowing themselves to desire the other and fear they will be overwhelmed with destructive hungry desire, with dangers of merger, cannibalism, or murder of the other.

Eventually the patient needs to be confronted with his willingness to accept a relationship based on the need to satisfy the other. As the patient can grasp that he has needed to please the other because of his own insecurity and that such a relationship is a profound deviation from ordinary mutual human caring, he will become sad and angry and attack his own limited expectations of what is possible with others. This shift may become especially moving when the analyst demonstrates how awful it has been that the patient has needed to feel so afraid and restrained with the analyst. If this interpretation can open enough of the patient's fury in a sustained way, then forward movement becomes possible. The patient will need to be shown, over and over again, how ready he is to close off his rage, to pretend that he has resolved it, by flight to positive feelings. The patient will need to test, again and again, through the analyst's interpretive invitation, that the analyst will neither retaliate nor abandon him because of his rage and desires. On the contrary, the patient needs to be shown repeatedly how awful it is that he is willing to accept that, having been angry at the analyst today, he must be good tomorrow. In all of these ways, the dependent patient is made painfully aware of the awfulness of what he has needed to tolerate until now.

The analyst cannot pull the dependent patient forward. That would merely perpetuate the pathological dependency. The patient must be shown the choices involved in continuing this way of life, in contrast to tolerating his terror and exploring separateness and his own internal demons. Ultimately the patient must choose for himself how he will lead his life; the analyst cannot make this choice for him. The analyst, however, would be totally failing his dependent patient if he were not fully to engage the patient about the consequences and limitations of his dependent choice and to explore the patient's terrors in relinquishing this protected position. This change will not happen spontaneously, as with the ordinary patient. I am not advocating a modification of standard analytic technique. But analyst and patient need to be prepared that the patient is content to live out his transference and resistance rather than struggle to resolve them. That is, to a large degree, the pathologically dependent patient wants to remain dependently attached to the analyst, who will be responsible for managing him; not only does this wish not trouble him but he vigorously avoids any other possibilities. The dilemma is how to make this motivation an analytic issue without the analyst's impatiently, angrily, or sadomasochistically trying to force the patient to want to be on his own.

In effect, the pathologically dependent patient responds to the analyst's interpretation of the analytic stalemate with anxiety about the analyst's dissatisfaction with him, fearing the analyst will terminate the treatment. An ordinary analysand would respond to such interpretive concern in the analyst with his own concern about whether he can, indeed, address what is wrong. The analyst's concern would alarm the patient about himself rather than primarily about the bond with the analyst. The pathologically dependent patient, in effect, holds his breath and hopes the analyst will forget about the problem or change his mind and now be happy with the patient. Or he deceives himself that he has now resolved what is wrong and is now again "a good analysand." Somewhat like Mrs. J (of chapter 10), Mr. I (also see chapter 5) would respond by feeling hurt and criticized when I would attempt to show him how he was stuck in the treatment. He would either counterattack, retreat, or argue haughtily that I was mistaken, that he was getting "value" out of the treatment. Seemingly for years, he could not hear the content of my interventions about his difficulties with being an analytic patient. As with his family, Mr. I simply wanted everything to be fine between us. To a large degree, he was primarily moved by his grasp of my tone in interpretation rather than what I wanted to convey to him. He eventually cried when I told him that he was content to remain in analysis with me forever without changing and that my agreeing to this not only did not demonstrate concern for him but repeated how he felt his mother had infantilized and misused him. Similarly, after he had recovered from his hurt and rejection, Mr. I had cried earlier in the analysis when I had not accepted his Christmas gift. I had told him then that he had already spent enough of his life feeling that he had to buy people to like and help him. This man is an extreme example of a rigid, pathologically dependent character with intense narcissistic needs. But even with his feeling moved by these and many other analytic interventions, very quickly, sometimes as soon as the following session, the underlying difficulties would be set aside as if they had already been resolved. It was easy for me to move Mr. I to tears; he just could not or would not stay with what had made him sad. What was most helpful was my continually showing him how he was giving up on his own potential to manage himself. This interpretation would lead him to feel sad and cared about by me and at least lead to a little bit of concern about himself. Unfortunately, interpretation of his wish to keep me actively involved and responsible for him did not lead Mr. I to take over more of the responsibility for his analysis. My role continued to be to find ways to demonstrate his giving up on himself, not only without injuring his self-esteem but with helping him to feel sad and angry about how much of his development he had sacrificed with his mother and now was willing to continue to do so with me. I am reminded of Pao's (1969) report that for a long period early in the analysis of a pathologically jealous patient, he was confined to interpreting only that the patient was jealous again.

The analyst's intention with the pathologically dependent patient is to help the patient to become concerned in his own right about himself and where he has become stuck. To accomplish this goal, as with Mr. I, will require that the analyst consistently, but without hostility, interpret the patient's defensive avoidance and refusal to take responsibility for what is wrong in himself while denying that he continues to do so. The analyst will need to keep showing the patient his wish primarily to stay with the analyst rather than to change and will need to find a way of helping the patient to feel the awfulness of this selling out on himself.

With all dependent patients, not only those for whom dependency is grossly pathological, there comes a time when the analyst will choose to interpret the patient's insistence that he must receive passively what he wants. How long a given patient needs to imagine filling himself up by passively being given to by others, including the analyst, will, of course, vary with the extent of childhood deprivation, neglect, and trauma and terrors of rage, aggression, and separateness, as these have become integrated within the patient's compromise formations. Some patients may continue to argue that they want others to love them freely, that to demand this love of others, even in fantasy, would spoil everything. Or they may protest that you cannot pull love out of a loveless parent. Or they may continue to insist that they are not yet ready to relinquish the wish to be cared for by a parent. Of course, such patients need to struggle with such chronic attachment to being cared for by others. Indeed, that is what we mean by pathological dependency. But at some point the patient will need to let go of such regressive wishes, in order to consolidate and integrate his more active, aggressive, violent, and passionate desires. When patients protest that they cannot get caring through aggressive demand, usually they are stuck at demonstrating sadomasochistically how they are chronically being deprived. It is then helpful to interpret to the patient that his goal is not to be loved but to continue his lifelong, insufficiently acknowledged fight with his parents that they do not love him sufficiently. The patient needs to grasp how much chronic hatred and rage are embedded in such sadomasochistic fighting, which has been presented as "just wanting to be loved." The patient needs to shift from the position where he feels he merely needs to obtain what he has missed in order to move forward toward acknowledging his chronic war with the world. This shift includes dealing with his vengeful refusal to accept responsibility for himself and his conflicts, to accept the limitations of his childhood, and to manage himself now as best he can.

Angry patients who continue to feel deprived may persist with claiming in entitled ways that others must provide them with what they have missed. Such patients need to struggle with relinquishing the quasi-delusional claim that their hunger must now really be satisfied. This struggle is, indeed, difficult for certain patients who cling to an entitled insistence that others must remain responsible for them, that they have been too damaged to do so themselves. They may, indeed, seek to demonstrate repeatedly that they cannot manage for themselves and insist that the analyst must provide this help for them. For example, certain patients will insist that they cannot continue to feel angry, aggressive feelings on their own, that the analyst must consistently and empathically help them to do so. To a degree, this claim is accurate, but such patients easily exploit it in their chronic war with the analyst/parent. For example, Mr. E, the man with multiple physical defects (chapters 7 and 9), feared staying with feeling angry on his own without my protection. But he sadomasochistically protested that I had to be indefinitely responsible for helping him to feel enough compassion for himself so that he could remain outraged at his parents and at me. He would insist that he was angry that I really was not helping him enough to be able to continue feeling angry. Eventually I was able to help him to feel with conviction how much he now wanted to torture me as an inadequate analyst/parent, in a way that he had felt too insecure and frightened to do with his parents.

Interpretation needs to focus on the patient's willingness to give up on discovering and claiming his own abilities in order to perpetuate a hate-filled relationship with an analyst/parent who is accused of being insufficiently helpful and caring. The emphasis shifts from the patient's passive neediness and disability to his rage and hatred. Such patients have emphasized their sense of disability and deficiency in order to engage a parent, from whom they have sought to extract supplies. They have attempted to hide the power of their destructive wishes by insisting on their helplessness and passivity.

The analyst may feel helpless and discouraged by the patient's chronic protests that he cannot remain responsible for his own angry feelings or that he cannot remain connected with the analyst unless the latter preserves this connection by empathic interpretation of the patient's need. The risk here is that the analyst may feel like giving up and agree with the patient that he is too disabled to progress further. Or the analyst may retreat from his disappointment and resentment at how little the patient changes, if, indeed, the analyst needs this change from his patient, toward being unduly supportive of his patient as actually emotionally disabled. Of course, patients may need the analyst, especially early in the treatment, to be accepting, empathic, and involved and help the patient to bear his pain and his needs. The analyst needs to sort out how much of the patient's slow progress in the analysis expresses a vengeful war with the analyst in which the patient refuses to accept responsibility for himself and his conflicts. Vindictiveness is built into pathological dependency and must be analyzed for the patient to change. Here the analyst's frustration, disappointment, and resentment are useful clues to the patient's insufficiently acknowledged aggression. Such awareness and interpretation by the analyst help to transform pathological dependency into an endless, unsatisfying relationship based on rage and hatred. On the other hand, the analyst's frustration with the patient's slow rate of change may express the analyst's own neurotic needs of a patient who has marked difficulty with processing feelings and with changing.

Separately, the analyst needs to show the patient the multiple, magical, protective illusions that have encouraged the patient to cling to the other as a god. If, indeed, the analyst is the deficient one, as the patient maintains, then it is not the patient who is the bad one. When the patient insists that the analyst is unhelpful and inadequate, there is already movement away from more exclusive focus on self-hatred and defect, toward the patient's bearing his chronic anger. The analyst needs to foster the patient's chronic, explicit, and implicit criticism without turning the criticism back on the patient. The analyst may be made to feel guilty and deficient by the patient, or he may feel annoyed at the patient's repetitive, unvarying protests. If the analyst can grasp the patient's terror of acknowledging his destructive attacks on the analyst and the analysis, there is a way out of the stalemate. The analyst needs, then, to show the patient consistently how much he hates the analyst as parent and how he must deny and undo this in order to cling to the other. If the patient can come to bear his intense rage and relinquish his conviction that he cannot be on his own (with his rage), then he can begin to consider seriously his wishes to get rid of the analyst. The analyst will need to help the patient understand his guilt in wanting to be rid of the analyst (as deficient parent) and to have his own separate life. But once the patient can begin to tolerate and integrate his rage at the analyst and to value and enjoy his wishes for separateness, the stranglehold of pathological dependency has been partly broken.

As part of the therapeutic endeavor, the analyst intends to open up the patient's angry, aggressive, hungry, and envious desires to take from others, so that passivity is not the only option. The dependent patient will find ways to resist this shift. Nonetheless, as the patient begins to tolerate more of his aggressive/destructive wishes to rob others, he will feel stronger and more capable. This aggression will involve both preoedipal and oedipal desires. Especially as the patient works through envious and competitive desires to appropriate the good attributes of each parent and can fully tolerate his violence in devouring, emptying, castrating, and appropriating from the other, the patient will now feel that he possesses enough to sustain himself. If the pathologically dependent patient can integrate these angry, destructive feelings and wishes in himself, he can relinquish his envy and reliance on the other, who has seemed better than he. Often, however, patients will be tempted to stop after feeling only some of their destructive rage toward the parent/analyst, as if they have completed the work. Or patients will quickly again surrender to the other all they have taken and retreat back to dependency and envy of the other. Surrender and retreat represent an undoing of their destructive robbery, so as to contain the dangerous angry feelings. To keep the violence open so that it can be integrated requires that the analyst repeatedly interpret these defensive retreats. Through all of this work, the patient must increasingly come to value what he can do for himself and for others rather than what he can receive from them. In doing so, the patient needs to relinquish the infantile insistence on being cared for, so that he can feel generously able to nurture and provide for others. Hopefully, the patient will now feel much more pride, strength, and satisfaction in assuming the role of powerful and giving parent, so that the role of child is seen as a disappointing, regressive retreat.

Once the work begins to resemble ordinary analysis of neurotic character disorder, much of the battle has been won. For example, eventually Dr. S (chapter 5) began to feel much more capable, aggressive, powerful, and creative as we liberated his angry, destructive desires to compete with and rob the father-analyst. For the first couple of years of his analysis he had felt nothing of the sort. He was convinced that he needed to obtain ongoing nurturance from the analyst and from his mentors in order to function. During this period he wanted me as both father- and mother-analyst to admire him as a bright boy; he believed that the power and strength were in his mentors and in me. He was surprised when he first discovered that he did not want only to rely on the more senior professors in his medical school department but that he wanted to rob them of their offices, bookcases, and abilities. Dr. S was even more shocked when he found himself envying and wanting to rob the analyst of his brain and penis. He would quickly lose his newfound strength and creative ability and then long for the analyst to reinvigorate him. Dr. S both persisted with dependent longings to be passively cared for and defensively disowned his destructive rivalry and robbery with the father-analyst. But having discovered his own creative powers, he found passive dependency much less attractive. It was now clear to both analyst and patient that Dr. S felt much more motivated to pursue analysis on his own of his defensive retreats and his ongoing fears of his anger and destructive powers. Dr. S became a much more active and capable collaborator in the analysis, even in the analysis of his persistent dependent attachment to the analyst. He now wanted to be the analyst rather than the analyst's favorite child. He would still need to struggle to relinquish his powerful desire to support his self-esteem by exhibiting himself for others' admiration. That is, he had to acknowledge and let go of his wishes to analyze himself successfully so that the analyst would admire him. Of course, that task was difficult.

The patient must become able to struggle against the regressive temptation to retreat into dependent reliance on another, so as to avoid his own terror of rage and destructiveness. The patient needs to become convinced that he can manage such rage and destructiveness on his own, without another's containment, support, protection, or punishment. Even more, the patient needs to enjoy his anger, to draw on it constructively, to become less afraid of losing control of himself. Then his dark side need no longer be isolated and avoided but can be looked to for strength and power. Envy and competition become pathways to obtain what one feels he is missing from the other. By tolerating such wishes to rob, appropriate, mutilate, destroy, devour, and murder the other, the patient claims what he needs for himself from the other. If he can tolerate and integrate such rage and destructiveness, he can then consolidate what he has appropriated from the other, together with the power of his hostile aggression. If he can bear such destructive feelings in an ongoing way, without retreat to dependent surrender to others or punishment by them, he can then come to value himself as a strong, capable, autonomous person who can manage himself alone.

Notice that I do not differentiate men from women as I outline the tasks of relinquishing pathological dependency so as to move toward autonomous management. Although there certainly are differences in the developmental pathways and the contents of the conflicts of boys and girls, the similarities especially stand out. This book is not the place for discussion of the more general similarities between boys and girls in body envy of both parents, castration conflict (mutilation anxiety), and the tasks required to resolve oedipal conflict. Both male and female dependent patients need to face and integrate their childlike envy, rage, and competitiveness toward the creativity and strength of the parents, the mother's breasts and womb, the father's phallus, their brains and good insides. That is, the analytic tasks are similar with male and female dependent patients. Like Dr. S, each has to acknowledge that he or she is too capable to persist as a passive and helpless child. To do so, male and female patients alike need to face and integrate their varied angry, envious, destructive, competitive, and murderous intentions toward others.

For example, Ms. N combined outstanding success and ability in business with profound insecurity and dependency. This highly accomplished businesswoman had disowned full acknowledgment of her ability and success because these meant that she did, indeed, want to defeat and destroy others. She tried to convince herself and others that she had just been lucky or that she had charmed and seduced others to get where she was. As she relinquished her helplessness, defensive confusion, and willingness to be passively supported, she was able to feel how much she wanted to be the best, the favorite, at work and now in the analysis with me. Like Dr. S, she was initially startled by her aggressive fervor to get what she wanted, especially in the transference with me. Surprisingly, this high-powered executive now finally became comfortable with insisting that her employees must accomplish their work satisfactorily or they would be reassigned or fired. Sexual desire for me as the father-analyst was easier than envy, robbery, and rivalry with me as the mother-analyst. The more she could tolerate her angry and destructive desires, the stronger and more powerful she felt, so that she felt much less inclined than previously to turn to others for advice and support. Increasingly, she valued her own opinions rather than insisting that she was not smart enough or well educated enough to know for herself what was best. Large public presentations had made her very anxious; she feared others' criticism and envy. Now she could feel that she wanted to overwhelm her audience, to seize the number one spot for herself, to exhibit herself with all her success and ability. Onstage Ms. N could now enjoy men desiring her and her body and delight in outdoing the women in her audience; their envy now felt good rather than frightening.

I want to stress that pathological dependency involves, perhaps more prominently than other character disorders, intense regressive retreat from the dangers of intense feelings and intense desires (aggressive and sexual). Once the dependent patient comes out from behind the conviction that he can be sustained only by passive reliance on, and nurturance from, another, he needs to struggle with the intensity of his wishes to take what he wants from others so as to feel complete and intact. Powerful angry, aggressive, and sexual feelings have previously led to his running away from facing and integrating his active side, toward defensive emphasis on helplessness and passivity. To the degree that he has felt he could not be separate and alone and that he could not manage his passions on his own, he has needed to rely on another. Now he needs to tolerate and integrate his rage and hatred at the other on whom he has relied and his destructiveness and desire in appropriating the other's fantasied goodness, strength, and power. He needs to relinquish the illusion that the other can, indeed, protect him from the dangers of life, the dangers of his own passionate feelings and wishes and the ordinary external dangers of life. Then he can go his own way.

We should have no difficulty with a mixed psychoanalytic model that integrates conflict over drive and wish with object relations and hierarchical developmental organization. Similarly, we should take for granted that preoedipal and oedipal conflicts will become interrelated and, to a degree, condensed with one another. Further, we assume that each level of conflict may be used simultaneously to protect against full awareness of the other. For example, Dr. S and Ms. N were both much more comfortable emphasizing their preoedipal conflicts than acknowledging their destructive wishes for success and autonomy at the oedipal level. Certain other patients emphasize their phallic narcissistic needs, obscuring their more general (preoedipal) hunger for dependent support from others. Behind the surface of Dr. S's oedipal conflicts were persistent, primitive exhibitionistic needs. That is, the surface of the patient's current conflict within the treatment is regarded as the manifest content of the analysis, to be analyzed in its own right as well as for what lies behind it.

In the analysis of pathological dependency, the analyst needs to identify where the patient is stuck and help him to become troubled about his inertia, to face the reasons for his failure to move forward, and then to face and integrate the dangerous feelings and wishes that could heretofore be tolerated only transiently. By opening up the patient's ability to tolerate intense affect (hating, destroying, desiring, loving), both preoedipal and oedipal rage and destructiveness will emerge. But they will remain available only if the analyst keeps a consistent focus on the patient's defensive willingness to settle for protection, containment, and punishment from another.

In a successful treatment, first, the pathologically dependent patient will shift from helplessness and passivity to rage and active wishes to grab and take what he wants from others, as with Dr. S and Ms. N. Next, he will need to become convinced that he does not need to keep the other around. Otherwise, he will oscillate between anger and activity and passive retreat and surrender to the other. Thus, over a prolonged time Dr. S allowed himself to feel angry, aggressive, and capable and then would seem to lose this feeling. Once again, he would try to worry me that he could not manage in my absence, that he was even getting worse. He would feel depleted and depressed, desperate for my infusion of energy. We saw how afraid he felt that any sign of his ability to manage on his own would lead me to terminate the analysis. Dr. S also feared that he would destroy me in his desires to take the good things he envied in me. Then he would be alone and lonely without an analyst-parent to admire and sustain him. Hence, he would undo and deny the evidence of his destructiveness; he was once again only passive, weak, and helpless. Dr. S would go through cycles of fantasied robbing of me and then guilty surrender to me of all he had taken. In doing so, he contained his rage and destructiveness so that he did not have to feel fully how much he wanted to castrate and murder me. He continued to hold on to me.

Finally, the pathologically dependent patient can desire and enjoy wanting to get rid of the other, destroy him, and, once and for all, take what he has envied in the other. This shift is possible when the dependent patient no longer feels that he cannot manage on his own. Destructiveness and wishes to murder others are not so dangerous when the patient is no longer terrified to be alone. The pathologically dependent patient will still keep retreating toward idealization of the other and away from his rage-filled wishes to destroy the other. But here the analytic work becomes more like ordinary character analysis, once the dependent patient can tolerate separateness and autonomy.

APPENDIX
A Guide to the Literature on Repetition, Sexualization, and Perversion: Central Issues in Pathological Dependency

I have argued in this book that the concepts of repetition and erotized repetition, sexualization, perversion and perverse object relations play key roles in pathological dependency. Here, very, very briefly I want to indicate some of the interconnections among these issues. This appendix provides a literature review for the reader who wants additional background information on these strands of pathological dependency.

While pathological dependency as a specific phenomenon has not been previously discussed in the literature, clearly each of the three tributary streams—repetition, sexualization, perversion—has received extensive treatment in the literature. In this appendix I attempt to review these discussions and seek especially to tease out those lineaments of theory that I consider especially useful in confronting the phenomenology of pathological dependency. In doing so, I am, in part, retracing some of my own steps as I researched the literature in pursuit of the present topic. Then, too, I am attempting to provide an overview of where psychoanalytic theory currently stands with regard to the issues of repetition, sexualization, and perversion. Accordingly, the following discussions are meant to stand separately, each more or less on its own, as individual units.

SOME HISTORICAL BACKGROUND ON THE
DUAL NATURE OF REPETITION: STASIS
VERSUS CHANGE.

In *Beyond the Pleasure Principle* Freud (1920) elaborated a contrast
between "change," "development," and "progress" and what he
termed the "precise contrary—an expression of the *conservative* nature
of living substance" (p. 36). Freud located this opposition within the
instincts themselves. The theme of struggle between change and
conservative repetition that precludes change runs throughout
Freud's work and is a major theme of this book. The concept of
repetition for mastery is optimistic and progressive. Turning passive
into active to achieve mastery and to modulate painful affects (say, as
in the "Fort/Da" game, Freud, 1920) is usually regarded by analysts as
adaptive. At the same time, in clinical descriptions of repetition, the
conservative nonadaptive aspect is usually indicated by wishes to
repeat infantile gratification and to remain protected. The ego's
defensive activities can similarly be viewed from these dualistic
perspectives of conservatism and progress (change, adaptation).
Emphasis on mastery of painful affects and trauma leads to a view of
the ego's defensive efforts as adaptive and forward seeking. Because
much of the clinical psychoanalytic literature on repetition has
focused on *trauma*, it has tended to emphasize such positive defensive
mastery. There exists an alternative perspective on defensive repetition, however, that instead emphasizes avoidance of change, protection against danger, clinging to what or who is safe. Like Freud, we
think both of inertia and flux, of repetition and change.

Loewald (1971b) differentiated between passive and active repetition, between reproduction and re-creation. He drew on Bibring
(1943), who had earlier distinguished between a repetitive or repro-
ductive tendency in repetition and a restitutive aim to reestablish the
pretraumatic situation. Bibring's attempt to explain repetition compulsion in relation to *trauma*, led him to invoke trauma (in my opinion
without sufficient evidence) in some of his clinical material (pp.
494–496). Loewald (1971b) discussed the possibilities, within a psychoanalysis, of actively taking responsibility for one's own unconscious, so as to shape or re-create what previously had been passively
experienced. Loewald viewed repetition of unconscious phenomena
as due primarily to repression, so "that [it] is not exposed to the
influence of the organizing activity of the ego which would lead to
what we have identified as recreative repetition" (p.61). Loewald's
tends to be an optimistic view that emphasizes the possibilities
attendant on insight rather than emphasizing continued needs for

defensive repetition. He does not, however, lose sight of that aspect of the repetition compulsion which involves "the resistance to having to give up something that is precious, whether painful or blissful, in its intensity and uniqueness" (1971b, p. 95).

Waelder (1930) proposed that the ego actively attempts to master the repetition compulsion (as well as the outer world, id, and superego) by assimilation of it into its own organization. Kubie (1939) viewed repetition for mastery of traumatic experiences as within the pleasure principle. He argued that repetitive patterns may merely indicate the persistence and inflexibility of unsatisfied cravings. Bibring (1943) disagreed, citing Hartmann's authority, that such pleasurable instinctual repetition should be included within the repetition compulsion.

More recently, Segel (1969) described "identification with the doer" as a repetitive defensive effort to master or bind anxiety derived from infantile trauma (primal scene, threat of abandonment). In my work with pathologically dependent patients I (see chapter 7) have often observed "identification with the doer" in patients who had been traumatized by severe childhood illness, deformity, or surgery. Such patients do not merely seek to avoid passivity, helplessness, and narcissistic trauma by playing the role of the sadistic avenger; they also need to defend against superego criticism by emphasizing repeatedly that they are exceptions who are entitled to judge the badness of others, onto whom they project their own self-criticism (see also chapter 9). The more unacceptable such patients feel, the more they need to make themselves acceptable to others and to themselves by disowning or justifying their own badness. For certain rigid characters, this need will preclude integration of their own destructiveness; instead defensive repetitions will recur that aim to disown or justify what cannot be tolerated within the self. In Waelder's (1930) model, repetition for mastery of infantile trauma ("identification with the doer") is simultaneously adapted by the ego for superego defense.

Insofar as all defense involves an aspect of defensive repetition, we can view defensive repetition as one aspect of all behavior. I point this out because of the importance of defensive repetitive behavior in pathological dependency, which is used to avoid facing and integrating conflict. Fenichel (1941) differentiated between the impulse (id) and defense (ego) aspects in any sample of behavior. Our perspective toward the behavior determines which side we see. In this sense, all patients manifest defensive repetition. Valenstein (1971) followed Gill's (1963) idea that a hierarchy of defenses could be elaborated. Defenses that are lower in this hierarchy are regarded as passive in the sense that there is greater regulation by the id

(Rapaport, 1953). Defenses higher within this hierarchy are more active in the sense that there is greater regulation by the ego.

Klein (1976b) divided the ego's defensive activities into two groups: repression and dissociation as strategies of regressive retreat, avoidance, and stasis, on one hand, and "active reversal" as a growth promoting strategy, leading to reconstruction, innovation, and integration on the other hand. He, however, regarded only the former as defense. He distinguished the ego's integrative activities from defense proper. Klein proposed that the repetition compulsion derives both from this latter principle of "reversal of voice" and from "the activity of repressed ideas" (p. 264). Although for Klein defense was nonintegrative, avoidant, tending to fix the patient at an impasse, he stressed the interaction between defense and integration. Drawing on Waelder (1930), Rapaport (1953), and Loewald (1952, 1971b), Klein emphasized the ego's capacity for actively assimilating and integrating within its core what had previously been dissociated. Like Loewald (1971b), Klein was optimistic about the ego's capacity for active mastery, integration, and growth. In Dorpat's (1987) emphasis on denial as the prototypical defense, he has similarly contrasted the disclaiming of responsibility, denial (defense), and isolation with responsibility for avowed action, integration, and constructive adaptation. I am highlighting literature that contrasts defensive repetition as avoiding conflict resolution and change with the opposite possibility: that it opens the door to mastery and integration.

EROTIZED REPETITION AND SEXUALIZATION

That clinical examples of repetition compulsion in our literature usually involve defensively erotized repetition is not sufficiently appreciated. Bibring (1943), however, noted,

Perhaps the most frequent way of taking the compulsive repetition into the personality is through sexualization when, for instance, the repetition compulsion becomes linked with masochistic drives. By such libidinization the compulsive repetition is placed at the service of the pleasure principle of the id [pp. 507–508].

As an example, Bibring describes a case of "erotic transference" in which the woman patient "struggled with impulses to stretch back her arm to pull the analyst to her, or to jump up and embrace him" (p. 495). Bibring makes clear, however, that this is an aggressive erotization, not merely erotic transference, aimed at avoiding dependence on a man or on the "sovereignty of men" (p. 495) in the patient's terms. Through this aggressive erotization, the patient sought to capture the analyst's penis. Bibring reduces this phenomenon by hypothesizing that the patient must have felt traumatized on first seeing a penis, a formulation consonant with the then prevalent idea that repetition must be linked to trauma. But what Bibring has described is a repetitive attempt to turn helplessness, passivity, and dependency into triumph and domination. Abraham (1920) had previously described women who must repetitively "castrate" men. But Abraham was a skilled interpreter of narcissistic vulnerability, even as he reduced this to women's "penislessness." He described women's defensive, repetitive attempts to defend against dependent needs for men through erotization. Although this is not Abraham's actual language in this paper, like his earlier (Abraham, 1919) paper on narcissistic defenses against analysis, he implies that erotized repetition serves as an aggressive, narcissistic defense against object need.

Savitt's (1969) case of erotization emphasizes repetition compulsion, that is especially linked to loss, trauma, hunger, and rage. Blum (1973) linked erotization with regressive repetition. He viewed erotization as the turning of childhood traumatic seduction into active repetition for mastery and the continued pleasure of infantile love. His patient was analyzable, and Blum emphasized mastery and change as possible in the cases he reviewed. What is not clear in previous discussions of erotization, including my own (Coen, 1981) is whether it serves to master danger or primarily to avoid it.

In the 1970s, the concept of sexualization suddenly became popular in psychoanalytic writings about narcissistic personality disorder. Kohut (1971) reported the clinical finding of perverse sexual behavior in some patients with narcissistic personality disorder. He correlated such perverse sexual behavior with intense underlying narcissistic need. Sexualized wishes are often the mode of expression of incorporative longings to fill in missing narcissistic structure. At times of narcissistic injury, as with a breach in the empathic relationship with the analyst, the attempt to preserve narcissistic structures is often frantic, desperate, and sexualized. By sexualization, Kohut meant intense, driven sexual behavior designed to maintain the existence of psychic structure. The patient seeks to affirm, by the intensity with which he can feel, see, or touch his own excited body, that his psyche is intact.

In his earlier writings Kohut (1971) used the energic model to relate sexualization to impairment of the ability to neutralize narcissistic libido. This energic explanation made his use of the concept of sexualization unclear and contributed to the illusion that a discrete process had been designated and described. That is, the psychoanalyst was to think that somehow narcissistic energy had been transformed into sexual energy. What was important was the connection of serious narcissistic pathology with driven sexual behavior. Later, Kohut (1977) described sexualization, without the energic hypothesis, as perverse sexual behavior observable in certain patients with narcissistic personality disorder. He suggested that certain patients with narcissistic personality disorder had attempted as children to cope with lethargy, depression, and loneliness because of an unempathic or absent selfobject by "solitary sexual activities of a sexual, near sexual, or sexualized nature" (p. 272). Kohut related the use of a sexual mode to the need for intense feeling stimulation to reassure the self that it is alive and whole, for defense against depressive affect, and as a mode for the expression of incorporative wishes to fill in missing narcissistic structure. In other words, we emphasize the patient's sexualized attempts to obtain from others what he or she feels so deprived of—contact, soothing, caring, admiration, loving— as if adult sex were primarily what the patient needs!

Goldberg (1975) followed Kohut's use of the energic hypothesis in attempting to explain sexualization in perversion. According to Goldberg, it represents (1) "the more raw and primitive expression of the drive" because of deficient neutralization; and (2) the ego's defense against painful affects (p. 337).

Similarly close to Kohut's intent is Stolorow's (1975b) speculation that "the degree of primitive sexualization (as with primitive aggressivization) of narcissistic reparative efforts is a measure of the degree of narcissistic vulnerability and the acuteness of the threat of narcissistic decompensation" (p. 477).

Kohut's and Goldberg's use of the concept of sexualization reflects Hartmann's (1952) definition of sexualization as the situation in which "libidinal energy serving the functions of the ego comes too close to the state of instinctual energy" (p. 170). The ego functions involved are then said to have been invested with a "sexual meaning" (Hartmann, 1955, p. 217). Inhibition or disturbance of function may result. Hartmann's view was that sexualization occurs especially during regression, when the ego is unable to neutralize instinctual energies sufficiently to preserve the intactness of ego functions. This model of sexualization emphasizes the *failure* of the ego's integrative and synthetic ability for neutralization rather than an active process of transformation of drive, affect, or behavior.

For Freud, as for Hartmann, sexualization referred to the energic hypothesis and the excessive investment of libido in a given function. For example, Freud (1909) stated that in obsessional neurosis,

> the thought-process itself becomes sexualized, for the sexual pleasure which is normally attached to the content of thought becomes shifted on to the act of thinking itself, and the satisfaction derived from reaching the conclusion of a line of thought is experienced as a *sexual* satisfaction" (p. 245).

Regression, symbolization, displacement, and, for psychotics such as Schreber (Freud, 1911), the inability to master large quantities of instinctual energy were the mechanisms Freud designated explicitly as sexualization. Freud did not designate as sexualization its other implicit meanings or the nonsexual functions of sexual behavior. Freud's perspective contrasts with the emphasis contemporary psychoanalysts have placed on patients' attempts to manage intense nonsexual neediness through sexual activity. And we are now much more interested in how patients accomplish this.

Glover (1933, 1964) contributed to the tacit assumption that sexualization is a distinct and clearly understood process in psychoanalysis. First, he was influential in positing "libidinization" as the central mechanism in perversion. Second, using an energic model of the dual drive theory, he described libidinization as a process whereby libidinal energy neutralized unconscious sadism. This hypothesis was unfortunately thought to preclude further clarification of the functions of a sexual mode of defense in coping with hostile aggression.

Glover's reference to libidinization of anxiety in perversion was picked up by Gillespie (1952, 1956), Khan (1962, 1964, 1965a, b, 1969), and Goldberg (1975) without further clarification of the process involved. More generally, sexualization of affect has been referred to without specifying what it is. The one psychoanalytic paper on "eroticization of anxiety" (Laforgue, 1930) does not refer to sexualization but describes the situation where anxiety stands symbolically for libido. Descriptions of the use of sexuality as a defense against painful affects were provided by Eidelberg (1945), Bak (1953, 1956), Greenacre (1953, 1960, 1968, 1969), Khan (1962, 1964, 1965a, b, 1969), and Kohut (1971, 1977).

Defense against hostile aggression through sexualization is an explicit or implicit premise of most writing on the subject. Pathologically dependent patients seek the illusion that their destructiveness has been magically transformed into something exciting, something that is no longer dangerous to the other or to oneself. The literature, however, does not provide sufficient clarification of the mechanisms involved in the attempted management of hostile aggression through sexualization. The metapsychological metaphor of the taming of aggression by libido has been resurrected in this literature. This metaphor is most applicable to the theory of differentiation and integration of psychic structure within the dual drive theory. In the literature it has instead been translated concretely into clinical usage, as if it were explanatory of a sexualized defense against aggression, which it is not. Defense against aggression in sexuality was discussed by Freud (1922), Deutsch (1932, 1944), Bak (1953, 1956), Loewenstein (1957), Greenacre (1960, 1968) and Khan (especially, 1965b).

Let us now consider the genetic background for the development of sexualization as a predominant mode of defense. How and why does it develop during childhood? I especially want to elucidate those bits of parent-child interaction, patterns of stimulating relationship, and modes of interpersonal protection between the couple that are elaborated into the defensive style of sexualization. Much of this elaboration of sexualization will parallel the more general development of pathological dependency, in which patterns of relationship and of defense derive in substantial part from the child's early experiences with the parent(s). Of course, we need to consider the child's own contributions to the exploitation of sexualized modes of defense as well as the modifications of the pathological object relationship and defensive style that will be introduced during later development.

Sexualization in defensive constellations has been treated separately from a different standpoint, namely, the shaping role of childhood overstimulation in the etiology of the perversions. The part excessive sexual seductiveness in childhood plays in the etiology of perversion was noted by Litin, Giffin, and Johnson (1956), M. Sperling (1959), Khan (1965b, 1969), Stoller (1968, 1975), McDougall (1972), and Chasseguet-Smirgel (1974). Ferber and Gray (1966) suggested the same for patients with beating fantasies. The hypothesis is that the mother encourages the child in a seductive pregenital relationship with her, which is gratifying to the mother yet simultaneously protects her from her own oedipal conflicts. In the spirit of the times, this hypothesis made too sharp a dichotomy between oedipal and preoedipal wishes. The child's illusion of his adequacy as mother's lover may be encouraged, discouraging him from growing up, from identifying with father in his adult masculine role, and from further differentiation from the mother.

The goal for the pervert, according to Khan (1965b, who elaborated Winnicott, 1956) is "refinding and recreating concretely the original unity with the omnipotent nourishing breast-mother" (p. 70). The pattern of perverse sexual behavior with another person repeats aspects of an early pathological relationship with the parent(s). Khan stressed that, as a child, the pervert experienced the mother as intrusive, while she simultaneously maintained an "organized defense" against depression. The concept of an "organized defense" against depression comes from Winnicott (1948), and as Khan uses it, it refers to obsessional defenses with denial used by the mother so that she generally is not consciously aware of feeling depressed; neither is the child consciously aware of mother's disturbance. The child colludes with the mother to protect her from awareness of her pathology. The mother is sexually seductive with the child. The child "libidinizes" the body, including the genitals, in response to a deficiency in maternal care.

Greenacre (1960, 1968) and Kernberg (1974) suggested that libidinal development can be adapted to serve primitive oral and narcissistic needs. Sexual behaviors are prematurely developed to serve nonsexual needs and to obscure the patient's hungry, primitive qualities. This premise is implicit in all other writings on sexualization. Splitting mechanisms, Kernberg has suggested, allow such seemingly oedipal wishes into consciousness.

The literature on erotized transference has also contributed several relevant ideas about the functions of sexual seductiveness. Rappaport (1956, 1959) reported erotized transference as occurring only in borderline or psychotic patients whose reality testing and critical judgment were impaired. Seductiveness and sexual demandingness are used, in the service of hunger and greed, to stir up the analyst so as to maintain intense contact with him. Such patients also thereby exercise their power to elicit the analyst's response and to control him.

Blum (1973) disagreed with Rappaport that erotized transference occurs only in borderline or psychotic patients, although he acknowledged that it occurs only rarely in neurotic patients. Blum emphasized the patient's seductive style of defense and related it to a childhood history of parental seductiveness and denial of complicity, which provided a model of seductive style and superego corruption. The childhood sexual seduction during the oedipal phase provided instinctual overstimulation without adequate protection. Erotization, according to Blum, defends predominantly against hostility, homosexuality, loss, and narcissistic injury. It represents the turning of childhood traumatic seduction into active repetition for mastery and the continued pleasure of infantile love.

A crucial question here for the understanding of sexualization is how patients with structured perversion differ from those with severe character disorders but less sexualized psychopathology. This question has been insufficiently addressed. Even in descriptions of the psychodynamics in perversion the choice of sexual mode of defense has tended to be ignored. At the same time, analysts have differentiated lower and higher levels of perversion (see chapter 13), and emphasized the defensive and adaptive nonsexual needs of the lower level pervert.

Why a sexual mode of defense is chosen by patients of any type has not been sufficiently attended to in the psychoanalytic literature. Choice of defensive mode generally tends to be regarded as unknowable. The formulations that oedipal and preoedipal trends may be condensed or that sexual behaviors may be prematurely developed and adapted to serve earlier needs may foreclose consideration of choice of a sexual mode of defense. These formulations may presume too concretely that certain sexual behavior in the adult represents, in the form or mode of its expression, oedipal sexual strivings that are being diverted for narcissistic needs. The sexual mode of expression of these needs may not then itself be subjected to psychoanalytic scrutiny.

That sexual feelings are intense and pleasurable has been posited as a reason for their use as a defense. This explanation does not sufficiently differentiate their use from the use of other intense feelings, such as pain, or other pleasurable feelings, such as joy or satiation. Masochism, with its predominant emphasis on painful affect, has been investigated far more comprehensively than has been pleasurable sexual experience. Stoller (1976a) noted that the phenomenon of sexual excitement has received scant psychoanalytic commentary. More generally, sexual pleasure may tend to be regarded unquestionably as an entity in itself, a basic directing force of mental life (Klein, 1976a, took a similar tack). Although it is understood that other functions may be subsumed under sexuality, this overvaluation of sexuality may obscure recognition of its defensive uses. On the other hand, the pleasurable, driven aspects of sexual feelings, fantasy, and behavior should not be minimized. To my knowledge, no psychoanalytic author has regarded sexualization as merely an expression of sexual drive pressure. Sexualization has been understood as a defense or as a failure of defense. To clarify the defensive uses of sexuality, meanings and mechanisms need to be specified.

The mechanisms by which sexual feelings, fantasy, and behavior function in the service of defense require further psychoanalytic clarification (see Coen, 1981). Psychoanalytic authors have centered their discussion of defensive aspects of sexuality on defense against painful affects, hostile aggression, and narcissistic needs without much attention to how this is accomplished. Stolorow (1979), focusing on the functions of sexual experience for the pervert, attempted to specify functions for sexuality in relation to the development of the representational world. In my opinion his attempt did not go far enough. Following Kohut (1971, 1977), Stolorow limited his consideration of the functions of sexuality for the pervert to preservation of the cohesiveness of the self-representation; he omitted his earlier idea (Stolorow, 1975a, b) that the sexual sadomasochist also attempts to enhance his self-esteem and to counter painful affects. Stolorow's discussion of sexuality and development did not focus on the role of sensuous experience, but merely related each traditional psychosexual stage to certain ongoing tasks in the process of separation-individuation. Stoller (1976a) tended to reduce the "excitement" in sexuality primarily to the issues of active mastery of childhood trauma and problems with hostility.

Surprisingly, the role of sensuality during early development remains unclear. Its relation to the tasks of separation-individuation needs to be elaborated further. This lacuna contributes to the difficulty of understanding the defensive functions of adult sexuality. Jacobson (1964) and later Abelin (1971, 1975) proposed a developmental model in which sexual feelings for the parent of the opposite sex, perceived as separate from the self, together with rivalry toward the same sex parent, help to define one's social and sexual role. This sexual thrust is thought to promote differentiation out of the advanced subphases of separation-individuation. The idea that "I want her sexually just like he (the father rival) wants her" is distinctly different from "I want to imitate her so as to be a part of her." Parens and colleagues (1976) hypothesis that a biological heterosexual drive is the primary organizing influence for entrance into the Oedipus complex also supports the idea that heterosexual feelings enhance differentiation from the mother. Sexual drive pressure and masturbation would aid developmentally in the integration and consolidation of self and object representations and the move toward desiring an object perceived as separate from the self. Phallic exhibitionism (Edgcumbe and Burgner, 1975), viewed within this model, refers to the wish for admiration of the genitals, the whole body, and the self in a fixed gender role to consolidate the self representation and to enhance and firm up its value as existing separately from the maternal object.

PERVERSION

In the course of this book I describe perversions as one form of pathological dependency, as stable defensive organizations that are highly resistant to change because of their central role in defense against destructiveness and preservation of object need. The other person is misused sexually to serve a variety of pressing defensive needs, not all of which are sexual. Here I want to review some of the background literature on perversion. Since perversion has not been viewed as a variety of pathological dependency, I have emphasized this perspective.

Some Historical Background

Traumatic etiology for perversion has been emphasized by most psychoanalysts. Freud's (1905, 1910) theory of etiology in male homosexuality was one of infantile sexual seduction by the mother. Unlike his theory of neurosis, he never revised this theory into one of intrapsychic conflict resolution in fantasy. Freud's early description of the childhood of the male homosexual is similar to what later investigators (Socarides, 1968, 1978; Bieber et al., 1962) were to report. In the absence of an emotionally strong father, the son is seduced by the mother into precocious sexual overstimulation. The homosexual remains emotionally attached to the mother and remains faithful to her. He transfers his sexual arousal from women onto men. His sexual object is not simply a man, but someone who combines the sexuality of both sexes while possessing a penis. Identification with the mother as a woman and narcissistic object choice allows detachment from the actual relation to the mother. The homosexual escapes the dangers of his intense sexual response to the mother by his compulsive search for sexual contact with other men. Precocious sexual arousal leads to the "impulsive" quality of the male homosexual's sexuality, which is not then able to be suitably tamed and integrated during development with the rest of psychic functioning.

By 1910 Freud had modified his view of perversion to include defensive functions. Male homosexuality was regarded as a defense against intense attachment to the mother, and the fetish as a substitute for the missed penis of the mother. By 1919, Freud saw perverse fantasy as defense against oedipal conflict. Freud's 1919 revisions have not been sufficiently acknowledged, and some of these have been credited to Sachs's (1923) paper, which has been especially influential in the past 30 years. Freud (1919) wrote:

> The perversion is no longer an isolated fact in the child's sexual life, but falls into its place among the typical, not to say normal, processes of development which are familiar to us. . .[the]

Oedipus complex. It first comes into prominence in the sphere of this complex, and after the complex has broken down it remains over, often *quite by itself, the inheritor of the charge of libido* from that complex and weighed down by the sense of guilt that was attached to it. The abnormal sexual constitution, finally, has shown its strength by forcing the Oedipus complex into a particular direction, and by compelling it to *leave an unusual residue behind* [p. 192; italics added].

Sachs (1923) made this formulation more explicit, although Freud seems to have been saying the same thing—that the perverse component instinct after the oedipal phase represents the remainder of infantile sexuality which has become displaced onto the former, the rest having been repressed. Sachs emphasized that the perverse sexuality chosen relates to fixation at a given pregenital stage together with a special relation to the ego that allows this form of sex to escape repression.

The organizing focus of the Oedipus complex was sharpened around castration anxiety in perversion by Freud in 1927. The fetish, central hallmark of perversion, here was regarded as the symbolic substitute for the missing penis of the woman. Inconsistency and contradiction, faults in the synthetic function of the ego, and the concept of splitting of the ego in the service of defense (Freud, 1940) derive from the fetishist's oscillation between opposite ideas, one of which tends to be disavowed. Freud introduced hostile aggression into his view of perversion in 1922, with sexualized defense against jealousy and hostile rivalry explaining one aspect of homosexuality. "The hated rivals are transformed into love-objects," Freud wrote (p. 231). For our purposes in this book, we are less concerned with how important this mechanism is in the etiology of homosexuality than with this more general mechanism of attempting to transform hatred and destructiveness into excitement and seeming love.

Defense against hostile aggression as *central* to perversion was stressed by Deutsch (1932), Glover (1933), Nunberg (1938), Payne (1939), and others. Primitive drive aims (oral sadism) and anxieties (over introjection, projection, destruction, loss, and separation), as well as impairment of reality sense and magical imitative and appropriative wishes were described. Ego organization, ego function, and defense became the central focus of the literature of the 1950s. Gillespie (1952, 1956) differed from Greenacre (1953, 1955, 1960) and Bak (1953, 1956) in emphasizing regression rather than fixation as central to perversion. For Gillespie, intense castration anxiety leads to a partial regression to pregenital levels; thus regression includes the ego, its object relations, anxieties, and defenses. Drive regression leads to increased sadism.

The role of the superego in perversion was noted by both Gillespie (1952, 1956) and Glover (1933, 1964): intense sadism must be defended against; the pervert's superego is particularly tolerant of the form of pregenital rather than genital sexuality that has been selected. In this view, the pervert's superego is not simply a defective one that tolerates his perverse enactments. Rather, the superego participates actively in the construction and functioning of the perversion just as in neurosis. The relation between the superego and pregenital sexuality derives from Freud (1919) and Sachs (1923) and leaves open the question whether the perversion results from infantile sexual seduction (trauma) or is primarily the child's own construction.

Greenacre (1953, 1955, 1960) and Bak (1953, 1956), in contrast, emphasized early trauma, intense separation anxiety, and fears of destructiveness, together with the need to maintain the stability of the body image against primary identification with the mother and wishes to fuse with her. Rage, overstimulation, and damage to early ego functions, including ordinary defensive and integrative ones, lead to defensive narcissistic identifications and interference with libidinal development. Greenacre (1960, 1968, 1969) especially emphasized the role of infantile trauma in perversion. The mother-child relationship is disturbed so that separation-individuation is interfered with, as reflected in impaired object relations and faulty body and self-images. Phallic and oedipal phase progression is interfered with by this development, as well as by the castration anxiety and aggression then evoked, so that lust must be sacrificed to narcissistic needs, especially for maintaining the stability of the body (genital) image. The traumas noted by Greenacre include maternal deprivation and overstimulation, visual shocks such as frequent and prolonged exposure to the body of the opposite sex parent, and injuries involving bleeding and mutilation at crucial developmental stages. Greenacre (1960) argued that the concrete, ritualized quality of perversion testifies to "the actuality of the original traumas" (p. 169).

Bak (1968) subsequently reversed his earlier emphasis on separation anxiety in perversion. He organized castration anxiety as the primary danger and proposed that the symbolic construction of the phallic woman as fetish is the hallmark of perversion. Within this model, however, Bak, much like Gillespie, subsumed earlier developmental interferences as contributants rather than as central determinants of perversion. Bak's (1974) final paper on perversion clarified the point that earlier needs, for example for transitional or prosthetic objects, which in some psychoanalytic writings had become equated with an infantile fetish, should be sharply differentiated from the adult fetish. The adult fetish entails the symbolic construction of the female phallus, which is required for sexual performance. Perversion should be regarded as an adult psychopathological formation, consolidated only through adolescent development, without which adult sexual functioning cannot occur. A child's use of transitional or prosthetic objects for reassurance against separateness, destruction, body-self dissolution, instability, or inadequacy is different from adult fetishistic behavior, even if adult behavior does subsume some preoedipal factors. Given the recent interest in conflicts involving separation-individuation in psychoanalysis generally and in the study of perversion particularly, Bak's reminder is relevant.

The Ostow Report

In 1974 Ostow reported the deliberations of a distinguished study group on perversion (R. Bak, P. Blos, S. Furst, G. Gero, M. Kanzer, D. Silverman, R. Sterba, A. Valenstein, J. Arlow, E. Loomis, and E. Rappaport). The group defined perversion as a deviation in either the aim or the object of the sexual instinct (unlike Freud, 1905, who referred only to deviation of the sexual aim), as long as this deviation is exclusive and fixed (like Freud). The action orientation in the pervert is stressed throughout the volume and is a central issue considered. It is related to the action of masturbation. Connecting masturbation with perversion, Sterba notes that Freud's definition of perversion did not require the presence of another person; fetishism and transvestism performed alone are still perversions.

Ostow's group attempted to establish an ordered series of tendencies toward perversion, beginning with the persistence of pregenital influences in masturbation fantasy. Both Valenstein and Blos, however, differentiated pregenital tendencies in masturbation fantasies as the ordinary stuff of neurosis and as distinct from the pervert's need for behavioral enactment. This is an important disagreement among contemporary psychoanalysts. Some believe there is a continuum between perverse behavior and perverse, in contrast to erotic, fantasies while some differentiate perversion as requiring the enactment of fantasy and include perverse fantasy within the province of neurosis. Remember that, in large part, Freud's 1919 paper on perversion was based on perverse fantasies of neurotic patients. Freud tells us, if we read closely, that his theory of perversion derives primarily from neurotic patients (the six cases he refers to in his paper). When he then discusses male perversion, however, he refers to other persons, some of whom we might regard as perverts and others who merely used masochistic fantasies during masturbation. Ostow's group at times shows this tendency to regard "the perverse wish" as a thing in itself, which will be enacted given sufficient freedom from others' and one's own restraints.

Valenstein (cited in Ostow, 1974) recommended an approach to perversion that combined a developmental perspective with an emphasis on preoedipal and oedipal conflict. The developmental approach to perversion had seen it as relatively conflict free; the emphasis was on fixation, which prematurely established certain patterns of discharge in the wake of actual seduction and aggression. Valenstein preferred to modify the traumatic etiology of perversion; if there was not an actual traumatic event, then an event that could be misconstrued as one was experienced as real. Erotization may be used as a defense *because* seduction experiences were frightening especially because of the hostile-aggressive forcefulness and exhibitionism of a parent—rather than for the mere repetition of sexual pleasure. The pervert's action tendencies may represent identification with the aggressor, as in seductions, or with an aggressively demanding and humiliating mother. Gero cautioned, nevertheless, against the assumption that behind the pervert's action tendencies there has to be an identification with a parent. Central to the dynamics of perversion is the transformation of anxiety, anger, and wishes for revenge from childhood traumatic experiences into sexual excitement.

Valenstein's plea for an integration of developmental trauma with intrapsychic conflict is at times lost in the report. Thus Ostow, not unlike Stoller, defines perversion as "a repetitive reliving of the transformed expression of an infantile experience" (p. 27). Ostow is here contrasting perversion with neurosis: in the latter, unlike the former, there is a "symbolic compromise expression of conflict among id, ego, and superego forces" (p. 27). He then asserts that superego influence is less clear in perversion than in neurosis.

One (unnamed) contributor differentiates perversion from neurosis in terms of the superego's tolerance of perverse fantasy in perversion. He proceeds to get himself into a logical contradiction when he then acknowledges how restricted and impoverished is the pervert's fantasy life. We must ask, how can the superego be tolerant of perverse fantasy and yet the pervert's fantasy life be so constricted? The answer might be not that the pervert's superego is simply tolerant or absent, but that certain fantasy constellations are allowed while others are not. As it is in all patients with pathological dependency, superego functioning is uneven, immature, and unable to regulate drive and affect smoothly. In some respects the superego is very harsh and intolerant; in other respects it is entitled (see chapter 9) and permissive.

Although the instability of the superego's functioning is emphasized in the Ostow book, my guess is that a major difficulty the group had with the superego in perversion had to do with their reluctance to acknowledge superego forerunners derived from preoedipal conflict. More generally, many of the group seem to have had difficulty integrating developmental trauma and aspects of preoedipal fixation and conflict with oedipal level conflict. Not only traditional analysts, but many revisionists prefer to separate early developmental issues from what is considered to be involved in conflict. My own view is that whatever is troublesome to a person tends to be drawn into conflict and to be used for various adaptive and defensive purposes.

Action, it is suggested by Ostow's group, is used because fantasy is inadequate and is "favored if an actual event in childhood provides material for a magical replication through action (*doing makes it so*)" (p. 42; italics added). Arlow and Valenstein suggest that a seductionlike experience or actual seduction in childhood provides the framework for the perverse act and the pattern for discharge through action. They emphasize the magic of action in perversion. Magical events are especially needed to repair a severely impaired body image and a sense of gender inadequacy. Like McDougall (1980), Ostow's group relates the gender inadequacy to the child's humiliation at being inadequate to satisfy the sexually desired parent, usually a sexually provocative and seductive parent of the opposite sex, at a point where there has been a heightened instinctual thrust.

Ostow's group is not sufficiently circumspect about what they have established as specific to the pervert's ego. For example, they discuss at length (pp. 36–40) the pervert's "extraordinary capacity for visualization" (p. 38). They are referring to visual modes used in fantasy. When they then describe the homosexual's special ability to "incorporate" the penis through visual stimulation, this statement becomes tautological. It is unwarranted to assume special ego capacities for visual perceptivity. Better that we ask why and how vision is used.

Greenacre (1968), among others, has suggested that visual scanning and looking may be especially developed in the pervert to compensate for deficient close maternal contact, touching, and holding. Claims that certain male homosexuals are limited in their capacity for abstract thought and have, as a result, adapted vision as a substitute, are unsupported. Similarly, there is emphasis on the pervert's "tolerance for inconsistency," which the group focused on in fashioning a structural assessment as well as in estimating the therapeutic prognosis of the pervert. It is assumed that there is general understanding of this "developmental defect" in the pervert as relating to splitting of the ego. The pervert certainly may use defensive splitting, as well as denial, omnipotent manipulation, and contradictory attitudes. However, whether this defensive activity entails a particularly well-developed ego capacity for tolerance of inconsistency or a developmental defect in synthesis and integration is another story that needs to be clarified. And drivenness and defense need to be carefully distinguished from developmental defect and arrest.

Valenstein (see Ostow, 1974), in contrast to the conclusion drawn by Ostow's group, reminds us that Freud did not insist that the treatment of perversion must lead to its elimination but rather as with all psychoanalytic treatment, to better integration and adaptation. By contrast, Ostow's prognostic criteria and therapeutic aims seek to transform the pervert into a neurotic with an ego-dystonic symptom, one that then should be given up.

Stoller

Like Greenacre (1953, 1955, 1960), Stoller (1975) especially emphasizes the actuality of infantile trauma, although Stoller construes the trauma as much more specifically directed toward one's sex or gender identity. Precocious sexual arousal, according to Stoller, leads to perversion only when intense overstimulation and guilt are also present. Otherwise the pleasurable repetition that follows will not be contaminated by rage and revenge, and deviant, rather than perverse, sexuality will result. Perverse fantasy enactments are especially intended to prevent fear of repetition of the original trauma. This is accomplished by active mastery and repetition, reversing the original traumatic situation so that, just at the point of orgasm, the passive child victim triumphs over his infantile victimizer in the use of his sexuality and genitals.

Stoller explicates well the psychodynamics of the pervert's public fantasy, his particular pornography. For example, each detail in the transvestite's erotic script can be convincingly accounted for in Stoller's account. Stoller claims that transvestites were humiliated by women during childhood by being cross-dressed. The perversion then aims to undo and reverse this trauma. Other investigators (Person and Ovesey, 1974; Ovesey and Person, 1976; Person, 1978), however, have been unable to corroborate Stoller's hypthesis and suggest instead that transvestism involves dynamic conflict surrounding especially separation and castration. Stoller also contends that the degree of humiliation and sadism in one's pornography reflects the degree of cruel treatment actually experienced during childhood. Although Freud (1919) did not find a correlation between beating fantasies and actual experiences of having been beaten, this formulation remains appealing. A less specific traumatic etiology than Stoller's for transvestism offers greater variability in understanding the transvestite's rage. Stoller emphasizes a model of identification with the aggressor in transvestism, of becoming a stronger woman than the victimizer so as to protect against feared humiliation. The phallic woman fantasy here is used to make the dangerous woman more familiar and controllable (Coen and Bradlow, 1982). Only once in his exposition of transvestism does Stoller suggest an earlier background for understanding the traumatic effectiveness of cross-dressing, namely, that the boy must already have been damaged in his development. Those unfamiliar with Stoller's work might misunderstand this single disclaimer. Even the reference to identification with women and the fear of intimacy with a live woman does not sufficiently order the levels of danger and need for the transvestite.

Stoller suggests that the excitement in perversion is not primarily sexual. Hostility, revenge, power, and control take precedence over and subordinate sexual pleasure. Stoller relates the excitement in perverse enactments to rapid switching between anxiety about traumatic repetition and fantasied vengeful triumph. The original trauma relates to interference with the phases of separation-individuation. Stoller argues that perversion (for men) is a gender disorder based on rage, fear, and revenge in relation to differentiation from the mother: rage at having to be separate; fear that one cannot escape from the mother; and revenge on the mother as the cause of this conflict. Stoller argues for the traumatic role of the mother in perversion, with the result that the mother rather than the patient is seen as the creator of the perverse solution. The pervert's mother contributes to the son's perversion in two ways: by discouraging the son's full individuation from her and by interfering with his masculine identifications and pleasurable masculinity. This maternal impingement is compounded, Stoller claims, by the boy's beginning life in a protofeminine phase, a sense of being feminine like mother and her feminine body. The boy must then relinquish this protofeminine phase and forever after struggle against it in order to establish his masculine identity. In this model, gender and separateness for the male become virtually identical. Masculine gender development then requires gender disidentification from the mother's femininity.

Stoller's evidence for the existence of a protofeminine phase is based on his work on male transsexuals. The unconflicted and pleasurable femininity of the male transsexual, is said to entail primitive learning (of femininity) and unconflictual preservation of a focal symbiosis involving gender and sexuality and overly gratifying mother-infant bodily closeness. Once Stoller has established that a protofemine phase really does exist in the male transsexual, he then argues that it exists in every man, that is, every man begins with a primary identification with the mother's *femininity* toward which he yearns to regress while struggling toward separateness and masculinity. The critical issue is whether a protofeminine phase exists and whether primitive wishes for closeness with a maternal imago *necessarily* involve identification with mother's gender. In short, how are differentiation and the establishment of gender identity connected?

Stoller (1976a) focused the question of what determines sexual excitement in a paper in which he generalized the issue for the nonperverse as well. This important contribution was elaborated in his book *Sexual Excitement: The Dynamics of Erotic Life*. Stoller (1979), like Klein (1976a), Stolorow (1979), and me (see chapter 8), points out the contradiction that psychoanalysis, which began with an emphasis on sensuality, has ignored sexual pleasure and excitement, as if they were self-evident and self-determining, which they are not. Stoller extends the same dynamic explanation of sexual excitement from the perverse to everyone else; only the degree of hostility and fetishization differentiates one from the other. All sexual excitement, indeed all excitement, involves rapid oscillation among fantasied danger, repetition of prior trauma, and fantasied triumph and revenge. Sexual excitement involves "hostility, mystery, risk, illusion, revenge, reversal of trauma or frustration to triumph, safety factors, and dehumanization (fetishization)" (p. 6). The model of excitement begins to shift, however, when Stoller points out that it is the real occurrence of sexual arousal and genital tumescence that validates one's needed illusions (Nydes, 1950). Stoller then describes excitement as a defense against anxiety. The defensive functions of the sexual experience are emphasized as the excitement. The traditional model is that sensual pleasure, arousal, and gratification are sought because of the pleasure involved as well as the meanings that have become elaborated with such pleasure; defensive use of sexual pleasure is usually distinguished from the pleasure itself.

When Stoller emphasizes *the mechanisms of hostility* in sexual excitement, he may be misunderstood. He is not referring simply to discharge of drive derivatives of hostile aggression, nor merely to repetition, mastery, and revenge. Rather he implies that the hostile-aggressive drive component is involved in a complex defensive operation aimed at the temporary repair of narcissistic and object-related conflicts, especially involving one's psychological sense of maleness and femaleness. For example (p. 8), the perversely aggressive dehumanization in fantasy of one's object to a part-object relates to childhood experiences of feeling robbed of valuable, human qualities, usually related to gender worth and adequacy. This model of representation of an object intrapsychically as a part object explains certain aggressive and defensive functions, but it omits the contributions of developmental failure, as well as those deriving from an intense need for an object, with its associated dangers, in the representation of others as part objects. Partly this apparent omission owes to Stoller's concise style of exposition; elsewhere he does describe the dangers of intimacy as related to the need to dehumanize the object. Not only is hostililty a central component of sexual excitement, but so too is defense against this hostility insofar as a feeling of safety can be achieved through one's own and one's partner's sexual arousal.

McDougall

McDougall (1980) is optimistic about the psychoanalytic understanding and treatment of perverts. Her clinical descriptions are moving, appreciative of her analysands' struggles, and convincing. Perversion (except for female homosexuality, which we will consider later) contains a core of infantile sexual trauma, even though McDougall regards it as the child's own fantasy construction. The child has been sexually overstimulated by a mother who encourages the child's illusion that he, with his pregenital sexuality, is adequate and favored as mother's lover. Sexual reality is denied and the father's phallic function, together with his sexual and family role, is denigrated by the mother. The only phallic object esteemed by the mother is a distant and unavailable one such as God, or her own father or brother. The child is both encouraged in his illusion that mother desires only him and rejected doubly, for he does not receive adequate warm mothering and mother does not desire him sexually but, rather, his father.

The concurrence of highly seductive behavior with a denial of the child's sexuality is particularly conducive to perverse solutions, McDougall believes, because of the ambiguity in the sexual arousal when paired with this denial of sexuality. The child, unable to establish his own autonomy and dreading separation and disintegration, identifies and wishes to merge with the maternal imago. In fantasy alone he is unable to secure his differentiation from the maternal imago. McDougall offers two reasons for this failure. First, the ability of the pervert to symbolize and to resolve conflict in fantasy is impaired. This limitation is a central determinant of the action tendencies of the pervert—what cannot be established securely in fantasy must be endlessly enacted. Second, the actual object relation with the father, intrapsychic identification with him, and elaboration of his "true" phallic function have been deficient. In McDougall's view, this deficiency exposes the future pervert to the dangers of a psychotic loss of delimitation from the maternal imago. A phallic object, or "barrier" (a person or an identification), is required to validate the distinction between mother and oneself—and just this is a central function of perverse behavior. So, too, is this phallic object appealed to for protection against the dangerous destructiveness associated with one's rage at the overwhelming or depriving "oral" mother and the overcontrolling "anal" mother.

Some of McDougall's genetic hypotheses may be too specific to be generally applicable to perversion. For example, although the pervert's mother may seem to have had heterosexual and phallic, masculine conflicts, it may be unwarranted to assume that these conflicts stem from the mother's inability to love any man other than a distant and unavailable one (God, father, or brother). Similarly, insufficient attention is paid to the hierarchical organization of the pervert's psychodynamics that includes not only conflicts over earliest issues in separation-individuation, but also later, phallic-aggressive conflicts. Thus McDougall's concept of a "phallic barrier" should be expanded to include defense against phallic-aggressive and retaliatory castrative dangers. Then, too, there is relevancy in Bak's (1974) caution that we not regard the manifest content of the pervert's productions as only primitive, but seek to understand the contributions from all developmental phases and all levels of conflict to the latent meanings of the perversion. Here the disagreement among Gillespie (1952, 1956) and Greenacre (1953, 1955, 1960) and Bak (1953, 1956) in the 1950s about fixation versus defensive regression is central in sorting out psychodynamic meanings in perversion. The pervert, like the neurotic, may turn out in analysis to be screening developmentally later, higher level conflicts under seemingly more primitive ones, even when there is evidence of early fixation.

According to McDougall, the meaning of the primal scene—that the father's penis completes the mother's vagina—is denied and thus maintains the illusion that mother desires only oneself. McDougall considers this denial a magical act in which the differences, both between the sexes, and between the generations, are disavowed. She contrasts the neurotics's ability at just this point to elaborate the difference between the sexes in fantasy constructions with the pervert's magical and violent destruction of meaning in this disavowal, which will need to be repeated forever after in perverse magical acts. The future pervert's narcissism is too injured for him to tolerate the insult of a correct understanding of the primal scene. The castration trauma that is thereby warded off is fundamentally a narcissistic humiliation; the little boy with his little penis cannot satisfy the mother sexually. The pervert's deficiency in symbolization and fantasy construction results from the (violent) disavowal of the primal scene and repudiation of the paternal phallus.

McDougall does not implicate infantile sexual seduction in the etiology of female homosexuality. Much of the genetic background offered for male perversion fits McDougall's model of female homosexuality, except the seductive pregenital relationship between child and mother. Indeed, the infantile determinants for an erotized disorder in females go unclarified in McDougall's account. The mother is regarded as narcissistic, overpowering, or overcontrolling; as tending to use her daughter as a counterphobic object; and as discouraging her daughter's autonomous functioning and relationship and identification with the father. Splitting and projective identification defend against hatred of the mother; destructiveness is attributed to men rather than to women. The mother is experienced as rejecting of the daughter's body, sexuality, and independent existence, all of which the daughter seeks to reclaim in homosexual intimacy.

McDougall writes touchingly about the lesbian's search for acceptance of her body and her self from her partner, as for example, in the vignette of the lover who kisses her partner's vomitus to signify unconditional loving acceptance. The daughter has felt dominated, controlled, like a body part, and despised by her mother in a symbiotic relationship. Fearfully mistrustful, the lesbian seeks to dominate and control her lover as a part object. Like Deutsch (1932, 1944) earlier, McDougall focuses on the lesbian's need to erotize her intense destructiveness and to be reassured that she is loving rather than hating. McDougall regards the lesbian's phallic identification as protection against psychotic oneness with mother and as offering the path toward differentiation from the mother. The daughter has relinquished her relationship with the father to appease the jealous mother (Bacon, 1956). Anal-sadistic regression in the father imago protects against the loving, sexual wishes toward him that are prohibited by the maternal imago. The father is felt to have failed to protect the daughter from the dangerous mother.

The role of illusion, games, and fantasied exhibitionism in perversion elaborates earlier ideas of McDougall and Chasseguet-Smirgel (1974, 1978). The pervert's illusory anal phallus, which leaves him feeling inauthentic and an imposter, must be continually validated in his perverse enactments. Someone else in fantasy or reality must respond to this exhibitionistic demand. Panic and mistrust at genuinely being in need of another person are defended against by manic denial and omnipotent self-sufficiency—both actualized in game playing. McDougall here connects the "anonymous spectator" of the pervert's exhibitionism to the phallic imago, the wish that the father were watching and responding.

McDougall also elaborates a currently popular model of masturbation involving bisexuality. (Ostow, 1974, attributes the idea originally to Nunberg.) The hand functions as the sexual partner's genital in a fantasied sexual relationship. Exclusion from the primal scene, with its narcissistic hurt, the difference between the sexes, separateness, and dependency, all must be repudiated in masturbation. The ultimate wish in masturbation is total self-sufficiency and omnipotence. Although I agree with McDougall's view of masturbation as theatrical fantasy play, I think she does not offer a sufficiently balanced perspective on the multiple functions of masturbation but overdoes the emphasis on narcissism and omnipotence in the style of Ferenczi (1913) and Eidelberg (1945).

I am dissatisfied with McDougall's distinction between creativity and perversion. She highlights, as does Chasseguet-Smirgel (1974, 1978, 1981), the pervert's demand that his perverse creation be acknowledged as real by an imaginary audience. Unlike the creative artist, the pervert seeks to dupe his imaginary audience that his false creation, symbolic of a magical anal phallus, is better than the real thing. Yet to my mind it is not clear that, as McDougall asserts, the creative artist tends to be relatively uninvested in his esthetic object as compared with the act of creation. Nor is it necessarily true that the creative artist, unlike the perverse fabricator of erotic scripts, leaves his audience substantial imaginative space. Built into a novel, for example, may be a narrative style that allows the reader little room to exercise his own creative imagination. Moreover, if the author is a self-confessed pervert, say Jean Genet, who makes perversion central in his work, what distinction can be made between his art and his sexual life (Coen, 1984)? Although most contemporary psychoanalytic writers agree with McDougall about the impoverished fantasy life of the pervert and its repetitive, restricted, ritualized quality, there is evidence that this may not be true of certain perverts (cross-dressing effeminate homosexuals). The differences in the creative freedom to elaborate sexual fantasy in perversion remain to be explained. The restriction of the pervert's capacity for fantasy may apply only to his central conflict, the perversion leaving him free otherwise to be creative. Although the pervert, unlike the neurotic, may be relatively less successful at resolving internal conflict in fantasy so that action is required, this *per se* does not interfere with creative ability. Certainly many self-proclaimed perverts have made significant contributions to the arts and like Genet, are able to utilize "perverse" fantasy in the form and content of their art.

Certain writers (Freedman, 1978; Blum, 1978; Jucovy, 1976) have stressed a longitudinal life view of perversion, with particular emphasis on the contribution of each developmental phase. Bak's (1974) concept of perversion as an adult psychopathological formation, consolidated through adolescent development and obligatory for adult sexual functioning, is central to this perspective. Trauma, conflict, defense, and regression are emphasized not only at the preoedipal and oedipal phases, including separation-individuation, but throughout the life cycle, especially during latency, adolescence, and early adulthood. Sexual and nonsexual childhood traumata, particularly ones entailing intense aggression and destruction and the concomitant need for mastery, through repetition, of weakness, helplessness, aggression, anxiety, and guilt, are emphasized in Freedman's (1978) case. Blum's (1978) discussion of this case included the adolescent trauma of witnessing the holocaust and its validation of the patient's fantasies of destructiveness. This calamity led to traumatic regression and disorganization, for which the perverse solution integrated multiple functions and meanings related not only to typical preoedipal and oedipal phase conflicts, but also to issues of survival, guilt, and sacrifice.

Blum's (1973) model of erotized transference is relevant to perverse seductiveness. Blum connected his patient's seductive style of defense to a childhood history of parental seductiveness and denial of complicity, which formed a model for a seductive style and superego corruption. Childhood sexual seduction during the oedipal phase led to instinctual overstimulation without adequate protection. Feelings of omnipotence and confusion between fantasy and reality were augmented by the illusion of oedipal triumph and by the actual seduction. Thus, according to Blum, repetition in erotization expresses not only the pleasure of infantile love, but also an attempt at active mastery of hostility, homosexuality, loss, and narcissistic injury. Such patients struggle between feeling special as an exception and feelings of overstimulation, guilt over their transgression, and rage and helplessness because of their exploitation and neglect. Hunger, greed, contact, power, and control were emphasized by

Rappaport (1956, 1959) in his discussion of erotized transference. Shengold (1963, 1967, 1971, 1974) described patients who as children had been repeatedly seduced or subjected to exhibitionistic rape, leaving them needing to repeat the actual experiences of traumatic confrontation with another, often before a mirror. The affects to be mastered were pleasure, overstimulation, rage and terror, accompanied by castration shock. Myers (1973) related the pressure to engage in fantasied primal scenes (ménage à trois experiences, making pornographic films) to repeated traumatic primal-scene experiences during childhood. Peto (1975) also emphasized actual primal-scene observation in the etiology of perversion. Ego integration, sexual drive representation, and whole-object relations may be interfered with, and archaic, harsh superego structures may persist.

Notes on the Psychodynamics and Etiology of Perversion

Ostow's (1974) group assert that the realistic aspect of the perverse behavior yields excitement and gratification, whereas the make-believe aspects defend against anxiety. Stoller (1975, 1979), in contrast, understands the excitement and risk in perverse behavior to be an intrapsychic phenomenon related to the danger of recreation of the original infantile trauma. McDougall (1970, 1972, 1980), like Khan (1964, 1965a, b, 1969) believes that perverse behavior offers some opportunity for repair and change through actual behavior with another human being. McDougall asserts that the lesbian seeks a woman with whom she in contrast to the relationship with the mother, can have reciprocal loving acceptance of her body, femininity, and even masculinity—the introjected father and his penis.

I like and agree with McDougall's (1980) elaboration of the pervert's sexualized dramas. It extends contributions from Freud (1919), Nydes (1950), Smirnoff (1969), Khan (1964, 1965a, b, 1969), and Bach and Schwartz (1972). McDougall conceives of the intrapsychic dimension of the pervert's activities as involving the validation of essential illusions regarding not only sexual identity, but also subjective identity. She emphasizes the role of the public as anonymous spectator of the perverse scenario for authenticating it. I think she unnecessarily reduces this public to a symbol of the paternal phallus in line with her thesis that it is precisely this which protects the pervert from psychotic union with the maternal imago. Both she and Stoller (1975) nicely describe sadistic exhibitionism, the hostile aggression involved in forcing others to respond to and confirm the pervert's drama.

McDougall (1970, 1972, 1980) has stressed that in perverts, in contrast to neurotics, sexual fantasy tends to be rigid and impoverished. She suggests both an internal prohibition against fantasy and a breakdown or deficiency in the pervert's capacity to symbolize and to create an inner fantasy world to deal with intolerable reality. This may be confirmed also by Stoller's report about the specificity of pornography in exciting different groups of perverts. Ovesey and Person (1973) have reported similar findings from a large sample of perverts, although they note that their findings do not apply to cross-dressing, effeminate homosexuals (Person and Ovesey, 1978). McDougall (1970, 1972, 1980) and Khan (1964, 1965a, b, 1969) suggest that what is missing as suitable fantasy construction within the mind must be endlessly enacted in behavior by the pervert so as to validate his illusions. Ostow's (1974) group and Stoller (1975, 1979) tend to play down this distinction between rich sexual fantasy as the province of the neurotic and perverse behavior as the action mechanism in perversion. My own views are presented in chapter 14.

McDougall (1980) describes the pervert's mother as seductively suggesting that her son is her object of desire while simultaneously frustrating him and denying this game. McDougall emphasizes the pervert's continual defensive recreation of this illusion of "incestuous promise." Ostow's (1974) group and Blum (1973) have a similar view.

What do contemporary psychoanalysts say about the object relations history of the pervert? McDougall (1980) has emphasized maternal seductiveness and complicity together with paternal failure, a pattern by now well established in the literature, especially of male homosexual perversion (Litin, Giffin, and Johnson, 1956; Sperling, 1959; Bieber et al., 1962; Khan, 1965b, 1969; Socarides, 1968; and Stoller, 1975). Surprisingly, aside from McDougall's work and Khan's description of a lesbian experience enacted during analysis, the recent psychoanalytic literature in English contained no other detailed case reports of the psychoanalytic treatment of lesbians until Siegel's (1988) book. McDougall's lesbian seems to have had an impoverished relationship with a physically and emotionally rejecting mother, whom she idealized to protect from her hatred. Wishes for closeness and merger with the mother are protected against by phallic, father identifications and, indeed, by introjection of the father. The paternal imago is protected from the patient's anger at him for his failure to save her from the pathological mother. Sexual desire for the father as admirable and phallic is defended against by anal-sadistic regression in the paternal imago and by the patient's own masculine wishes (Jones, 1927). As others have written about the male homosexual, McDougall's lesbian offers up to the mother her relationship with the father and thus allows the preservation of the idealized maternal imago as feminine and desirable in contrast to the patient. McDougall stresses the role of erotization of defenses against depressive and persecutory anxieties stemming from intense rage and defensive splitting. Here we have a psychodynamic explanation for female homosexuality, without, however, understanding why the patient became homosexual instead of some other psychopathological entity. Thus, McDougall does not consider why and how sex has been adapted to cope with these early real and fantasy difficulties of her patients. McDougall does not apply her concept of the fictitious, rewritten script of the primal scene in perversion to women, including lesbians. That concept offers us clues about the role of early seductive experiences, of sexual feeling and sexual fantasy, in the development of the future male pervert.

Siegel's (1988) analytic cases of female homosexuality are rendered sensitively and optimistically. She focuses on early deficits and deformations of development related to significant narcissistic pathology in both parents. Central to her understanding of the female homosexual, however, is the contention that lesbians have never formed a mental representation of their genitalia. To my mind, Siegel presents insufficient analytic evidence for many of her theoretical claims, so that the reader must frequently wonder about alternative hypotheses. Her cases need to be described in much greater analytic detail, with much less insistence on interpretation of meanings, which seem to come before the data. Careful derivation of theory from analytic detail is especially important in this area of clinical theory, which needs so much clarification.

Masculinity and Femininity in Perversion: Developmental Considerations.

Current psychoanalytic writing argues that sex and gender need to be understood in relation to separation-individuation conflicts. The bedrock of sexual conflict has been shifted from anatomy to gender identity, the immutable core gender identity and the shifting psychological sense of masculinity and femininity. To a degree, a man's achievement of masculinity represents stable and satisfactory individuation. Feminine attitudes in men, for Stoller (1975,1976b), tend to represent the opposite, that is, failure of full differentiation from a maternal introject together with conflict about wishes for fusion with the mother. It is clearer to distinguish issues of masculinity-femininity from separation-individuation problems, to the degree that they are indeed differentiated. Stoller and Greenson (1966, 1968) make a popular but problematic assumption that feminine wishes and wishes for merger with a maternal introject are fundamentally the same. At the deepest level, they may be, but better that these be teased apart. We, as analysts, are certainly aware of manifold meanings to men's feminine wishes. Bisexuality remains an important explanatory concept even if we no longer assume it is biologically inevitable. Men's feminine wishes need to be understood on a developmental spectrum from wishes for merger with the mother; to preoedipal wishes for contact, dependency, protection, love, affirmation, and sexual gratification from father; to negative and positive triangular oedipal conflicts involving issues of dependency, power, aggression, lust, anxiety, and guilt. Even as we have become more aware of the nonsexual meanings of men's feminine wishes, the sexual charge attached to these should not then be dismissed as no longer relevant, but instead understood psychoanalytically. As we understand better the contributions of early developmental phases to later psychopathology, we may be led to unbalanced formulations of psychopathology that do not sufficiently integrate contributions from later developmental phases in favor of undue emphasis on our newer ideas.

Stoller's and Greenson's ideas about symbiosis anxiety and the need to disidentify with mother are interesting but do not clarify why some men with extensive primary identification with the mother are feminine while others are not. Although most investigators report that patients with more severe gender disorders are borderline (or psychotic) characters, not all borderlines have profound gender disorders. How does one identify in feminine, in contrast to nonfeminine, ways with the mother? Stoller's assumption of a protofeminine phase in boys leads him to the conclusion that extensive identification with mother must be feminine.

Stoller starts with the idea, currently questioned by child development researchers, that the infant begins in a primary state of merger with the mother. Merger fantasies may be the psychopathological products of a later age rather than neonatal intrapsychic reality. He buttresses his position that there is a protofeminine phase in boys by his theory of the etiology of male transsexualism, although there is no evidence of a protofeminine phase in boys. It is speculative to argue that since the boy must separate from a feminine mother with a female body, he must struggle against such perceptions of himself or such wishes for himself. He may, indeed, but such feminization is psychopathology rather than normal development, and we then want to understand the dynamic motivation for these ideas rather than treat them as self-evident.

Stoller's genetic and dynamic model of male transsexualism has been criticized by others (e.g., Ovesey and Person, 1973; Meyer, 1982; Person and Ovesey, 1983; Glasser, 1979). Only a few points are in order here for us to question Stoller's model of the bliss of the infant male transsexual's maternal symbiosis, a model related to his idea of a protofeminine phase in boys and the ever-present longing in every man to return to a *feminine* merger with the mother. I agree with those who find it inconceivable that a child whose mother cannot or will not conceive of him as an autonomous being, and, in fact, seeks to prevent his becoming one, does not experience rage, helplessness, despair, and terror. For example, Meyer (1982) noted, in a large sample of transsexual patients at The Johns Hopkins Hospital, instead of pleasurable symbiosis, "abandonment, disregard and psychological misusage" in the mother-child relationship. Thus, instead of Stoller's hypothesis of a nonconflictual etiology for male transsexualism, others emphasize conflict involving separation anxiety and intense aggression, uncompleted separation-individuation, impairments in ego functioning and object relations, and especially the defensive needs served by the feminine identification. Symbiotic bliss is, then, understood as a defensive fiction, and aggression and distance are viewed, in part, as efforts to protect against maternal impingement and intrusiveness. Person and Ovesey (1983) criticize Stoller for formulating a model of primary femininity for both sexes and deriving his data for femininity from male transsexuals. They remind us of Kleeman's (1971) basic question, still insufficiently answered, as to how a three-year-old boy becomes so clearly masculine even when his contact is predominantly with an adult woman. A model of primary identification does not answer the question.

This question leads to the parallel problem: how femininity is established. Stoller's model is an important synthesis among biological, interpersonal, cognitive and learned, intrapsychic, and bodily and genital experience. Stoller uses female transsexualism, for which he posits a conflictual etiology, to argue that interruption of the normal maternal symbiosis, together with masculine identification with the father, leads to masculinity in girls. It would be more accurate to say that premature interruption of maternal symbiosis interferes with femininity in girls. Stoller claims that wishes for merger in women promote or at least preserve femininity. Thus, wishes for closeness and heterosexual and homosexual intimacy do not pose dangers as grave for women and their femininity as for men and their masculinity. McDougall (1980) takes the opposite view, and I agree; for women to become fully heterosexually feminine requires psychic independence. Individuation is required together with selective, partial identification with the mother in her role as heterosexual. Thus the female homosexual, for McDougall, struggles to resolve conflict about a separate identity primarily and about a sexual identity secondarily. The female homosexual is not simply feminine, nor do her wishes for merger with a maternal introject make her more feminine.

We do not know what role gender and sexuality play in normal separation-individuation. We used to take for granted that men rely on their phallic, masculine identity, their penis and sex, when they feel unable to maintain differentiation from a maternal introject and from a woman sexual partner. It is no longer self-evident that this is the preferred form for maintaining such differentiation. Again, the question is why sex and gender are chosen to preserve identity and how this preservation is accomplished. We can no longer assume that all men preserve their identity by exploiting sexuality rather than by other modes. In contrast to Stoller's assumption of a protofeminine phase in boys is Jacobson's (1964) model, similar to what McDougall has adopted, in which the acquisition of sexual identity becomes a powerful motivator and vector to differentiate oneself from mother and to relinquish the omnipotentiality of infantile wishes. Similarly, I agree with Person and Ovesey (1983), who stress the important organizing role played by core gender, especially for object choice and sexual fantasy. Those who have written most usefully about separation-individuation (Mahler's group) have so far devoted relatively little attention to gender and sexuality. There has been some acknowledgment of Roiphe and Galenson's (1981) contention that preoedipal castration reactions are significant organizing experiences for sexual identity and sexuality. Roiphe and Galenson's work needs further clarification of whether young children's "castration" reactions relate more to a genital or a general difference from the mother, as in the typical rapprochement crisis. Although Roiphe and Galenson acknowledge the anlage of fears of object loss and of body-image disorganization, what the child's fear is and what his rage is about need further sorting out.

Parens et al. (1976) disagree with Galenson and Roiphe that the castration complex must lead the girl into the oedipal phase. Parens disagrees with Stoller about the time of emergence of primary heterosexuality; unlike Stoller, Parens does not refer to core gender identity but to a biological thrust to heterosexuality. As in Jacobson's (1964) model, this heterosexual thrust aids in further individuation.

Note also that Parens's group differs from Stoller in attributing the young girl's interest in babies to early self-object differentiation during the differentiation and rapprochement subphases. According to Stoller, wishes for pregnancy and mothering derive from oedipal phase conflict alone, without preoedipal contributants. Preoedipal conflict resolution is not part of Stoller's model of femininity. Although Stoller does not consider disidentification from mother in his female transsexuals as an imperative to see themselves as different from their deficient, pathological mothers, the concept might apply here.

Friedman (1988) suggests that male homosexuals had more difficulty with their masculine identity and self-esteem during childhood and adolescence than did heterosexuals; the extent of this difficulty is not yet clear. He claims that once homosexual identity and homosexual object choice are consolidated, the underlying conflicts are closed. I do not see why that should be the case for homosexuals since it certainly is not for heterosexuals. Although most adult homosexual men did not have marked gender identity disorder as children, we do not know whether many had a milder version. Of significance is that many boys with gender identity disorder will develop a homosexual object choice as adults (Coates and Person, 1985). Gender identity disorder in boys refers to ongoing distress about being a boy along with an intense desire to be a girl. This disorder is enacted in repetitive, obligatory (Coates, 1990) play at female activities, including cross-dressing. Such boys want to be rid of their male genitalia. Coates, Friedman, and Wolfe's (1991) formulation of the etiology of gender identity disorder in boys implicates a phase-specific vulnerability during ages two to three, before a stable internalized and differentiated sense of gender is developed (see also Coates, 1985; Coates and Person, 1985; Coates, 1990). Their case report, however, emphasizes multiple interferences by both parents with the development of the boy's masculinity and encouragement that he become, at least in part, female. Without such active attack on a boy's masculinity, activity, aggression, and destructiveness, is gender identity disorder likely to develop? That is, how do we differentiate gender identity disorder from other cases of significant interference with separation-individuation in which there is no gender identity disorder? Many boys want to cling to a symbiotic attachment with the mother, to imitate her, play at being her, feel connected to her, and thus ward off fears of loss and destruction; or they emphasize their passivity, helplessness, and unmasculine stance to ward off their own anger, wishes to separate from mother, competitiveness, and feared retaliation and punishment from both parents. And yet this latter group do not feel strongly that they are feminine, although clearly they are in conflict about being masculine.

Perhaps they wish less strongly to be a woman than to remain connected with mother.

Multiple determinants are offered as contributing to the etiology of gender identity disorder in boys: temperament, including predisposition to anxiety, depression, or both, and timidity with a sense of bodily fragility and vulnerability (the role of androgenization of the brain on stereotypic masculine sex role activities, especially rough and tumble play, is left unclear); severe separation anxiety, with wishes to fuse with the mother, who is depressed, needy, angry and envious and has difficulty being nurturant; the mother's hostility toward men; absence of a healthy father-son relationship; and a pathological mother-son relationship (Coates, 1990). Defense against destruction of the mother is sought through idealization of women and denigration of men. I would expect that such fears of destructiveness are expressed in the sense of bodily fragility and vulnerability in oneself and other.

McDougall's (1980) starting point in her discussion of perversion, and, to a degree, in her views about everyone else, is the need to maintain differentiation from a maternal introject that threatens, beckons, welcomes self-dissolution. Wishes for fusion require defense by efforts to detach oneself from the maternal imago and the establishment of a "phallic barrier." As in Stoller's (1975) hypothesis, differentiation from the mother is maintained by a phallic, masculine defense. However, in McDougall's view, this mechanism applies to both sexes. The male deals with this threat by an object relationship with an idealized phallic man (male homosexual solution), whereas the woman uses phallic, masculine identifications (ultimately the father appealed to for intervention between daughter and mother) and the creation of substitute maternal objects in an effort to detach from the maternal imago (female homosexual solution). McDougall, like Stoller, too quickly reduces bisexuality to archaic narcissism and omnipotence, to fusion wishes. The defensive, narcissistic requirements of adult perversion are overly stressed in her developmental model of masturbation, at the expense of playful fantasy whose aim is further identification with the parent of the same sex so as to consolidate gender identity and enhance one's gender and sexual value in relation to the parent of the opposite sex (See Edgcumbe and Burgner, 1975, on the phallic-narcissistic phase).

A BRIEF NOTE ON HOMOSEXUALITY IN THE CONTEMPORARY STUDY OF PERVERSION

The same criteria should apply in assessing perversion in homosexuals as in heterosexuals. That psychoanalysts are beginning to consider studying healthy adaptation in homosexuals is a welcome trend. Much remains to be clarified, in an unbiased way, about similarities in and differences between heterosexuals and homosexuals, in health as well as in psychopathology. The related issue of when to attempt to analyze *perverse* homosexuality as a defense against heterosexual incestuous fears is complex and not to be decided a priori. Isay (1985, 1986, 1987) has helped to heighten our awareness of countertransference tendencies to overemphasize heterosexuality in homosexuals. Friedman (1988) also challenges our bias against "homosexual psychopathology" when indeed we mean structural psychopathology, which would be similar in heterosexuals. Both Isay and Friedman clarify differences between homosexuality and bisexuality: bisexuals, not homosexuals, can sometimes be helped toward a more comfortable heterosexuality; *or* they may become more comfortable with their homosexuality or remain bisexual. In Isay's and Friedman's view, homosexuals cannot be transformed into heterosexuals; homosexual object choice must be respected.

With any patient, homosexual or heterosexual, we need to assess collaboratively within an ongoing analysis what is conflictual and what is potentially modifiable, in sexual orientation, as in any significant aspect of life. Isay (1985, 1986, 1987, 1989) focuses conflict in male homosexuals primarily in relation to external reality and its internalization within the superego, leading to shame and guilt about homosexual desire, which initially represented the desire for the father's love. Isay restricts the sense of "difference" in gay men to homoerotic desire; he omits the usual contributants of feeling unloved, unwanted, and inadequate. Feminine identification with the mother aims to attract the desired father, as mother does. Isay omits other contributants to feminine identification, such as the need to defend against feared loss or destruction of the mother. I find it inconceivable that the search for paternal love does not become contaminated by rage, destructiveness, envy, and jealousy. We would expect varied conflicts in relation to aggression, power, and competition between father and future homosexual son, akin to the heterosexual oedipal struggle, as well as rage and destructiveness from earlier conflict. For example, the heterosexual oedipal rivalry is not just for access to women (mother) but involves envy and rivalry about father's power, magical penis, authority, and position. Homosexual wishes in the future heterosexual involve varied wishes for contact, love, and dependency, together with rage, destructiveness, and competitiveness, including wished-for appropriation of the envied penis and power of the loved and hated rival. How could this conflict be so different for the future homosexual?

Friedman (1988) suggests that unless the patient is bisexual, that is, is excited *overtly* both homosexually and heterosexually, the concept of unconscious homosexuality is not useful. Friedman also suggests that other than in bisexuals, once erotic object choice has crystallized, unconscious erotic wishes do not persist toward persons of the gender opposite to such choice. In my experience, Friedman's position creates a dichotomy that is not true clinically. Heterosexual analysands who are not bisexual and have not previously been homosexually aroused regularly do experience and work through homosexual longings, with some excitement toward the analyst. Such excitement, which is new for these patients, is an expression of the patient's multiple desires toward the analyst: to seduce and cling to the analyst, to love and be loved, to rob and destroy the analyst of his powerful, magical penis, and so on. One could argue that earlier homoerotic excitement has been repressed or that it has been minimally and transiently experienced. In either event, these patients are not bisexuals.

My concern here is that the "blood and guts" of homosexual love, hatred, and destructiveness not be missed during the analysis of either heterosexuals or homosexuals. I would say exactly the same about analyzing the passions of heterosexual love! I am tempted to apply to homosexuals the analogy from analytic work with heterosexuals: that part of what underlies such homosexual transference love is envy, rage, destructiveness, and hatred; thus homosexual submission and surrender may protect against wishes to dominate, rob, and destroy the other. We do not know how far such analogies apply in nonperverse homosexuals who have made a stable and loving homosexual object choice. Psychoanalysts and other psychological researchers will need to assess these issues in nonperverse homosexuals, especially in nonpatients. My view is that Isay's and Friedman's approaches tend to divide homosexuals and heterosexuals too sharply. For example, Isay, 1989, attributing such desires only to gay men, ignores passive dependent longings in heterosexual men's homosexual wishes. Even as he gives clinical examples (pp. 75–76) that indicate heterosexual men's envy and wishes to be the cared-for child and the pregnant woman, he attributes these desires exclusively to defense against phallic oedipal rivalry. Later Isay claims that heterosexual men, unlike gay men, cannot shift psychologically between active and passive desires during sex (p. 91).

PERVERSE OBJECT RELATIONS

Perverse object relations is a less familiar concept than perversion. It refers to the object relations aspect of perversion, especially the quality of perversity in one person's misuse of another (Coen, 1985a). I want to emphasize the links between such sexualized or perverse use of others and the other varieties of pathologically dependent object relations considered in this book. It is a central tenet of this book that pathologically dependent patients misuse others to avoid responsibility for their own internal conflicts. They may do so in sexual, sexualized, or in relatively nonsexual ways. Exploitation of another person so as to avoid what one dreads within oneself involves mechanisms, attitudes, and rights that can be regarded as perverse, whether or not the relationship is sexualized. I regard perversion as a form of pathological dependency (see chapter 13). But more importantly, I want to highlight perverse object relations, because they characterize pathological dependency and because they have not been described in the literature outside of sadomasochism and perversion specifically.

Pathological object relations has been most often described in relation to sadomasochism, where multiple needs of the object have been reported. Dependence related to fear of abandonment leads to the turning of rage inward (Rado, 1945–1955; Loewenstein, 1957). Attenuation of aggression and hatred in the object is sought through seduction and surrender (Berliner, 1947, 1958; Brenman, 1952; Menaker, 1953; Loewenstein, 1957; Asch, 1976; Novick and Novick, 1987).

The Novicks (1987), discussing the genetic background for masochism, have described a kind of sadomasochistic parent-child relationship in which parental badness and failure is *externalized* onto the child, who accepts the role of the bad one so as to preserve and protect the tie to a troubled parent. Although the Novicks's focus is on sadomasochism, their descriptions of object relations in childhood and in adulthood are applicable to the broader group of patients with pathological dependency. Hence these descriptions deserve our attention. I agree with the Novicks that sadomasochistic object relations is remarkably akin to perversion (see chapter 12), at least to perverse misuse of others. Novick (1990) argues that perversion is the enactment of a sadomasochistic fantasy; I disagree (see chapter 13). Glover (1933, 1964) wrote that sadism is *the* perversion and is embedded in every perversion. Glover was emphasizing the role of sadism as the central determinant of all perverse sexual behavior. The Novicks's (1991) further elaboration on masochism describes a patient, Mr. M, who turned "his analysis into a masochistic perversion" (p. 30). By masochistic perversion, they seem to mean figuratively the patient's attempt to live out a sadomasochistic relationship with the analyst. Without the obligatory need for perverse sexual behavior in order to achieve orgasm, which defines perversion, I would not regard this patient's behavior as perversion but as a kind of perverse object relations, which is especially important to us in the study of pathological dependency.

I fully agree that focusing attention on the many similarities between perversion and such sadomasochistic object relations is valuable. When the latter is sufficiently sexualized, it may even approach sadomasochistic perversion. The similarities between perversion and sadomasochistic object relations include destructive omnipotence as a defense against multiple negative feelings in and negative representations of self and object, including helplessness, rejection/abandonment/neglect, rage, and destructiveness. Sexualized, or at least seductive, illusory attempts at transformation of rage and hatred into excitement and arousal occur in both perversion and in sadomasochistic object relations. The other person is, to a degree, to be used for the patient's imperative needs. A partial denial of his separate identity allows his illusory transformation into a needed fantasy object. Dehumanization, degradation to the status of part-object, extensive use of projective identification, omnipotent manipulation, and exploitation occur in both perversion and sadomasochistic object relations. The other person is to be controlled within one's own subjective world, denied his separateness and autonomy. Patients for whom sadomasochistic excitement becomes irresistible tend to resemble perverts in what they need from their partners, in the illusory games they play, and in their relatively perverse misuse of others.

REFERENCES

Abelin, E. (1971), The role of the father in the separation-individuation process. In: *Separation-Individuation: Essays in Honor of Margaret S. Mahler*, ed. J. B. McDevitt & C. F. Settlage. New York: International Universities Press, pp. 229–252.

———— (1975), Some further observations and comments on the earliest role of the father. *Internat. J. Psycho-Anal.*, 56:293–302.

Abraham, K. (1919), A particular form of neurotic resistance against the psychoanalytic method. In: *Selected Papers of Karl Abraham, M.D.*, trans. D. Bryan & A. Strachey. London: Hogarth Press, 1968, pp. 303–311.

———— (1920), Manifestations of the female castration complex. In: *Selected Papers of Karl Abraham, M.D.* trans. D. Bryan & A. Strachey. London: Hogarth Press, 1968, pp. 338–369.

Adler, G. (1985), *Borderline Psychopathology and Its Treatment*. New York: Aronson.

Asch, S. (1976), Varieties of negative therapeutic reaction and problems of technique. *J. Amer. Psychoanal. Assn.*, 24:383–407.

Atkins, N. B. (1968), Acting out and psychosomatic illness as related regressive trends. *Internat. J. Psycho-Anal.*, 49:165–167.

Bach, S. & Schwartz, L. (1972), A dream of the Marquis de Sade: Psychoanalytic reflections on narcissistic trauma, decompensation, and the reconstitution of a delusional self. *J. Amer. Psychoanal. Assn.*, 20:451–475.

Bacon, C. L. (1956), A developmental theory of female homosexuality. In: *Perversions: Psychodynamics and Therapy*, ed. S. Lorand & M. Balint. New York: Random House, pp. 131–159.

Bak, R. C. (1946), Masochism in paranoia. *Psychoanal. Quart.*, 15:285–301.

———— (1953), Fetishism. *J. Amer. Psychoanal. Assn.*, 1:285–298.

———— (1956), Aggression and perversion. In: *Perversions: Psychodynamics and Therapy*, ed. S. Lorand & M. Balint. New York: Random House, pp. 231–240.

———— (1968), The phallic woman: The ubiquitous fantasy in perversions. *The Psychoanalytic Study of the Child*, 23:15–36. New York: International Universities Press.

———— (1974), Distortions of the concept of fetishism. *The Psychoanalytic Study of the Child*, 29:191–214. New Haven, CT: Yale University Press.

309

Balint, M. (1950), Changing therapeutic aims and techniques in psychoanalysis. *Internat. J. Psycho-Anal.*, 31:117–124.

Barag, G. (1949), A case of pathological jealousy. *Psychoanal. Quart.*, 18:1–18.

Barsky, A. J. & Klerman, G. L. (1983), Overview: Hypochondriasis, bodily complaints, and somatic styles. *Amer. J. Psychiat.*, 140:273–283.

Bergler, E. (1961), The crucial question in psychoanalytic therapy: "Neurotic" or "malignant" psychic masochism? In: *Curable and Incurable Neurotics*. New York: Liveright, pp. 23–55.

Berliner, B. (1947), On some psychodynamics of masochism. *Psychoanal. Quart.*. 16:459–471.

―――― (1958), The role of object relations in moral masochism. *Psychoanal. Quart.*, 27:38–56.

Bibring, E. (1943), The conception of the repetition compulsion. *Psychoanal. Quart.*, 12:486–519.

Bieber, I., Dain, H. J., Dince, P. R., Drellich, M. G., Grand, H. G., Gundlach, R. H., Kremer, M. W., Rifkin, A. H., Wilbur, C. B. & Bieber, T. B. (1962), *Homosexuality*. New York: Basic Books.

Bird, B. (1972), Notes on transference: Universal phenomenon and hardest part of analysis. *J. Amer. Psychoanal. Assn.*, 20:267–301.

Blos, P. (1960), Comments on the psychological consequences of cryptorchidism. *The Psychoanalytic Study of the Child*, 15:395–429. New York: International Universities Press.

―――― (1984), Son and father. *J. Amer. Psychoanal. Assn.*, 32:35–61.

Blum, H. P. (1973), The concept of erotized transference. *J. Amer. Psychoanal. Assn.*, 21:61–76.

―――― (1978), Discussion of Freedman (1978). *J. Amer. Psychoanal. Assn.*, 26:785–792.

―――― (1980), Paranoia and beating fantasy: An inquiry into the psychoanalytic theory of paranoia. *J. Amer. Psychoanal. Assn.*, 28:331–361.

―――― (1981), Object inconstancy and paranoid conspiracy. *J. Amer. Psychoanal. Assn.*, 29:789–813.

Bollas, C. (1984–1985), Loving hate. *The Annual of Psychoanalysis*, 12/13:221–237. New York: International Universities Press.

Bornstein, M. (1977), Analysis of a congenitally blind musician. *Psychoanal. Quart.*, 46:23–37.

Bradlow, P. A. & Coen, S. J. (1975), The analyst undisguised in the initial dream in psychoanalysis. *Internat. J. Psycho-Anal.*, 56:415–425.

―――― & ―――― (1984), Mirror masturbation. *Psychoanal. Quart.*, 53:267–285.

Brenman, M. (1952), On teasing and being teased: The problem of moral masochism. *The Psychoanalytic Study of the Child*, 7:264–285. New York: International Universities Press.

Brenner, C. (1979), Working alliance, therapeutic alliance, and transference. *J. Amer. Psychoanal Assn.*, 27:137–157.

―――― (1982), *The Mind in Conflict*. New York: International Universities Press.

Broden, A. R. & Myers, W. A. (1981), Hypochondriacal symptoms as derivatives of unconscious fantasies of being beaten or tortured. *J. Amer. Psychoanal. Assn.*, 29:535–557.

Brody, S. (1960), Self-rocking in infancy. *J. Amer. Psychoanal. Assn.*, 8:464–491.

Brunswick, R. M. (1929), The analysis of a case of delusion. *J. Nerv. Ment. Dis.*, 70:1–22, 155–178.

Castelnuovo-Tedesco, P. (1978), Ego vicissitudes in response to replacement or loss of body parts. Certain analogies to events during psychoanalytic treatment. *Psychoanal. Quart.*, 47:381–397.

_____ (1981), Psychological consequences of physical defects: A psychoanalytic perspective. *Internat. Rev. Psycho-Anal.*, 8:145–154.

Chasseguet-Smirgel, J. (1974), Perversion, idealization, and sublimation. *Internat. J. Psycho-Anal.*, 55:349–357.

_____ (1978), Reflections on the connections between perversion and sadism. *Internat. J. Psycho-Anal.*, 59:27–35.

_____ (1981), Loss of reality in perversions—with special reference to fetishism. *Internat. J. Psycho-Anal.*, 29:511–534.

_____ (1983), Perversion and the universal law. *Internat. Rev. Psycho-Anal.*, 10:293–301.

Coates, S. (1985), Extreme boyhood femininity: Overview and new research findings. In: *Sexuality: New Perspectives*, ed. Z. DeFries, R. Friedman & R. Corn. Westport, CT: Greenwood Press, pp. 101–124.

_____ (1990), Ontogenesis of boyhood gender identity disorder. *J. Amer. Acad. Psychoanal.* 18:414–438.

_____ & Person, E. S. (1985), Extreme boyhood femininity: Isolated behavior or pervasive disorder? *J. Amer. Acad. Child Psychiat.*, 24:702–709.

_____ Friedman, R. & Wolfe, S. (1991), The etiology of boyhood gender identity disorders: A model for integrating psychodynamics, treatment and development. *Psychoanal. Dial.*, 1:481–523.

Coen, S. J. (1981), Sexualization as a predominant mode of defense. *J. Amer. Psychoanal. Assn.*, 29:893–920.

_____ (1984), The author and his audience: Jean Genet's early work. In: *The Psychoanalytic Study of Society*, 10:301–320. Hillsdale, NJ: The Analytic Press.

_____ (1985a), Perversion as a solution to intrapsychic conflict. *J. Amer. Psychoanal. Assn.*, 33 (supple.):17–57.

_____ (1985b), Freud and Fliess: A supportive literary relationship. *Amer. Imago*, 42:385–412.

_____ (1986), The sense of defect. *J. Amer. Psychoanal. Assn.*, 34:47–67.

_____ (1987a), Pathological jealousy. *Internat. J. Psycho- Anal.*, 68:99–108.

_____ (1987b), Sadomasochistic excitement: Character disorder and perversion. In: *Masochism: Current Psychoanalytic Perspectives*, ed. R. A. Glick & D. I. Meyers. Hillsdale, NJ: The Analytic Press, pp. 43–59.

_____ (1987c), Reply to Jennifer Downey. *J. Amer. Psychoanal. Assn.*, 35:1014.

_____ (1987d), Discussion of "Negative oedipal transference in the termination phase of a male patient with a female analyst" by J. Chertoff. Presented to American Psychoanalytic Association, New York City.

_____ (1988a), Superego aspects of entitlement. *J. Amer. Psychoanal. Assn.*, 36:409–427.

_____ (1988b), How to read Freud: A critique of recent Freud scholarship. *J. Amer. Psychoanal. Assn.*, 36:483–515.

_____ (1989), Intolerance of responsibility for internal conflict. *J. Amer. Psychoanal. Assn.*, 37:943–964.

_____ & Bradlow, P. A. (1982), Twin transference as a compromise formation. *J. Amer. Psychoanal. Assn.*, 30:599–620.

_____ (1985), The common mirror dream, dreamer, and the dream mirror. *J. Amer. Psychoanal. Assn.*, 33:797–820.

_____ & Sarno, J. E. (1989), Psychosomatic avoidance of conflict in back pain. *J. Amer. Acad. Psychoanal.*, 17:359–376.

Cooper, A. M. (1973), The narcissistic-masochistic character. In: *Masochism: Current Psychoanalytic Perspectives*, ed. R. A. Glick & D. I. Meyers. Hillsdale, NJ: The Analytic Press, 1988, pp. 117–138.

Deutsch, H. (1932), On female homosexuality. *Psychoanal. Quart.*, 1:484–510.

————— (1944), Homosexuality. In: *The Psychology of Women*, Vol. 1. New York: Grune & Stratton, pp. 325–353.

Dorpat, T. L. (1985), *Denial and Defense in the Therapeutic Situation*. New York: Aronson.

————— (1987), A new look at denial and defense. *The Annual of Psychoanalysis*, 15:23–47. New York: International Universities Press.

Downey, J. (1987), On the sense of defect. *J. Amer. Psychoanal. Assn.*, 35:1013–1014.

Dubovsky, S. L. & Groban, S. E. (1975), Congenital absence of sensation. *The Psychoanalytic Study of the Child*, 30:49–73. New Haven, CT: Yale University Press.

Earle, E. (1979), The psychological effects of mutilating surgery in children and adolescents. *The Psychoanalytic Study of the Child*, 34:527–546. New Haven, CT: Yale University Press.

Edgcumbe, R. & Burgner, M. (1975), The phallic-narcissistic phase. A differentiation between preoedipal and oedipal aspects of development. *The Psychoanalytic Study of the Child*, 30:161–180. New Haven, CT: Yale University Press.

Eidelberg, L. (1945), A contribution to the study of the masturbation fantasy. *Internat. J. Psycho-Anal.*, 26:127–137.

Eissler, K. R. (1958), Notes on problems of technique in the psychoanalytic treatment of adolescents: With some remarks on perversions. *The Psychoanalytic Study of the Child*, 13:223–254. New York: International Universities Press.

Epstein, L. (1977), The therapeutic function of hate in the countertransference. *Contemp. Psychoanal.*, 13:442–461.

Escalona, S. (1963), Patterns of infantile experience and the developmental process. *The Psychoanalytic Study of the Child*, 18:197–244. New York: International Universities Press.

Fairbairn, W. R. D. (1940), Schizoid factors in the personality. In: *Psychoanalytic Studies of the Personality*. London: Henley, 1952, pp. 3–27.

————— (1941), A revised psychopathology of the psychoses and psychoneuroses. In: *Psychoanalytic Studies of the Personality*. London: Routledge & Kegan Paul, 1952, pp. 28–58.

————— (1943), The repression and the return of bad objects (with special reference to the "war neuroses"). In: *Psychoanalytic Studies of the Personality*. London: Routledge & Kegan Paul, 1952, pp. 59–81.

————— (1944), Endopsychic structure considered in terms of object-relationships. In: *Psychoanalytic Studies of the Personality*. London: Routledge & Kegan Paul, 1952, pp. 82–132.

Feiner, A. H. (1977), Discussion of Epstein (1977). *Contemp. Psychoanal.*, 13:461–468.

Feldman, A. B. (1952), Othello's obsessions. *Amer. Imago*, 9:147–164.

Feldman, S. (1945), Interpretation of a typical and stereotyped dream met with only during psychoanalysis. *Psychoanal. Quart.*, 14:511–515.

Fenichel, O. (1935), A contribution to the psychology of jealousy. In: *The Collected Papers of Otto Fenichel*, New York: Norton, 1953, pp. 349–362.

————— (1941), *Problems of Psychoanalytic Technique*. Albany: Psychoanalytic Quarterly.

————— (1945), *The Psychoanalytic Theory of Neurosis*. New York: Norton.

Ferber, L. & Gray, P. (1966), Beating fantasies—clinical and theoretical considerations. *Bull. Phil. Assn. Psychoanal.*, 16:186–206.

Ferenczi, S. (1913), Stages in the development of the sense of reality. In: *Sex in Psychoanalysis*, Vol. 1. New York: Basic Books, 1950, pp. 213–239.

Freedman, A. (1978), Psychoanalytic study of an unusual perversion. *J. Amer. Psychoanal. Assn.*, 26:749–777.

Freedman, D. A. (1972), On the limits of the effectiveness of psychoanalysis: Early ego and somatic disturbances. *Internat. J. Psycho-Anal.*, 53:363–370.

Freud, A. (1952), The role of bodily illness in the mental life of children. *The Psychoanalytic Study of the Child*, 7:69–81. New York: International Universities Press.

_____ (1956), Comments on "A mother's observations on the tonsillectomy of her four-year-old daughter" by J. Robertson. *The Psychoanalytic Study of the Child*, 11:428–433. New York: International Universities Press.

_____ (1966), Obsessional neurosis: A summary of psychoanalytic views as presented at the Congress. *Internat. J. Psycho-Anal.*, 47:116–122.

Freud, S. (1900), The interpretation of dreams. *Standard Edition*, 4 & 5. London: Hogarth Press, 1953.

_____ (1905), Three essays on the theory of sexuality. *Standard Edition*, 7:123–243. London: Hogarth Press, 1953.

_____ (1909), Notes upon a case of obsessional neurosis. *Standard Edition*, 10:153–250. London: Hogarth Press, 1955.

_____ (1910), Leonardo da Vinci and a memory of his childhood. *Standard Edition*, 11:59–138. London: Hogarth Press, 1957.

_____ (1911), Psychoanalytic notes on an autobiographical account of a case of paranoia. *Standard Edition*, 12:3–84. London: Hogarth Press, 1958.

_____ (1914), On narcissism: An introduction. *Standard Edition*, 14:73–102. London: Hogarth Press, 1957.

_____ (1915), Observations on transference love (further recommendations on the technique of psychoanalysis, III). *Standard Edition*, 12:157–171. London: Hogarth Press, 1958.

_____ (1916), Some character-types met with in psychoanalytic work. *Standard Edition*, 14:309–333. London: Hogarth Press, 1957.

_____ (1919), A child is being beaten: A contribution to the study of the origins of sexual perversion. *Standard Edition*, 17:175–204. London: Hogarth Press, 1955.

_____ (1920), Beyond the pleasure principle. *Standard Edition*, 18:3–66. London: Hogarth Press, 1955.

_____ (1922), Some neurotic mechanisms in jealousy, paranoia and homosexuality. *Standard Edition*, 18:221–232. London: Hogarth Press, 1955.

_____ (1923), The ego and the id. *Standard Edition*, 19:3–67. London: Hogarth Press, 1961.

_____ (1927), Fetishism. *Standard Edition*, 21:147–157. London: Hogarth Press, 1961.

_____ (1933), New introductory lectures. *Standard Edition*, 22:1–182. London: Hogarth Press, 1964.

_____ (1939), Moses and monotheism: Three essays. *Standard Edition*, 23:1–137. London: Hogarth Press, 1964.

_____ (1940), Splitting of the ego in the process of defense. *Standard Edition*, 23:271–278. London: Hogarth Press, 1964.

_____ (1954), The origins of psychoanalysis. *Letters to Wilhelm Fliess, Drafts and Notes, 1887–1902*, ed. M. Bonaparte, A. Freud & E. Kris. New York: Basic Books.

_____ (1985), *The Complete Letters of Sigmund Freud to Wilhelm Fliess, 1887–1904*, trans. & ed. J. M. Masson. Cambridge,MA: Harvard University Press.

Friedman, L. (1969), The therapeutic alliance. *Internat. J. Psycho-Anal.*, 50:139–153.

Friedman, R. C. (1988), *Male Homosexuality: A Contemporary Psychoanalytic Perspective*. New Haven, CT: Yale University Press.

Frosch, J. (1981), The role of unconscious homosexuality in the paranoid constellation. *Psychoanal. Quart.*, 50:587–613.

Furer, M. (1972), The history of the superego concept: A review of the literature. In:

Moral Values and the Superego Concept in Psychoanalysis, ed. S. C. Post. New York: International Universities Press, pp. 11–62.

Furman, E. (1985), On fusion, integration, and feeling good. *The Psychoanalytic Study of the Child*, 40:81–110.

Gedo, J. E. (1979), *Beyond Interpretation: Toward a Revised Theory of Psychoanalysis*. New York: International Universities Press.

Gentry, W. D., Shows, W. D. & Thomas, M. (1975), Chronic low back pain: A psychological profile. *Jour. Occ. Med.*, 15:174–177.

Gill, M. M. (1963), Topography and systems in psychoanalytic theory. *Psychological Issues*, Monogr. 18. New York: International Universities Press.

Gillespie, W. (1952), Notes on the analysis of sexual perversion. *Internat. J. Psycho-Anal.*, 33:397–402.

_____ (1956), The general theory of sexual perversion. *Internat. J. Psycho-Anal.*, 37:396–403.

Giovacchini, P. (1967), Frustration and externalization. *Psychoanal. Quart.*, 36:571–583.

Gitelson, M. (1962), On the curative factors in the first phase of analysis. In: *Psychoanalysis: Science and Profession*. New York: International Universities Press, 1973, pp. 311–341.

Glasser, M. (1979), Some aspects of the role of aggression in the perversions. In *Sexual Deviations*, 2nd ed., ed. I. Rosen. London: Oxford University Press, pp. 278–305.

Glover, E. (1933), The relation of perversion formation to the development of reality sense. *Internat. J. Psycho-Anal.*, 14:486–504.

_____ (1964), Aggression and sado-masochism. In: *Pathology and Treatment of Sexual Deviation*, ed. I. Rosen. London: Oxford University Press, pp. 146–162.

Goldberg, A. (1975), A fresh look at perverse behavior. *Internat. J. Psycho-Anal.*, 56:335–342.

Gray, P. (1987), On the technique of analysis of the superego—an introduction. *Psychoanal. Quart.*, 56:130–154.

Greenacre, P. (1952), Pregenital patterning. *Internat. J. Psycho-Anal.*, 33:410–415.

_____ (1953), Certain relationships between fetishism and the faulty development of the body image. In: *Emotional Growth, Vol. 1*. New York: International Universities Press, 1971, pp. 9–30.

_____ (1955), Further considerations regarding fetishism. In: *Emotional Growth, Vol. 1*. New York: International Universities Press, 1971, pp. 58–66.

_____ (1956), Reevaluation of the process of working through. *Internat. J. Psycho-Anal.*, 37:439–444.

_____ (1958a), Early physical determinants in the development of the sense of identity. *J. Amer. Psychoanal. Assn.*, 6:612–627.

_____ (1958b), The impostor. In: *Emotional Growth, Vol. 1*. New York: International Universities Press, 1971, pp. 93–112.

_____ (1960), Regression and fixation: Considerations concerning the development of the ego. In: *Emotional Growth, Vol. 1*. New York: International Universities Press, 1971, pp. 162–181.

_____ (1968), Perversions: General considerations concerning their genetic and dynamic background. In: *Emotional Growth, Vol. 1*. New York: International Universities Press, 1971, pp. 300–314.

_____ (1969), The fetish and the transitional object. In: *Emotional Growth, Vol. 1*. New York: International Universities Press, 1971, pp. 315–334.

Greenson, R. R. (1966), A transvestite boy and a hypothesis. *Internat. J. Psycho-Anal.*, 47:396–403.

_____ (1968), Dis-identifying from mother. *Internat. J. Psycho-Anal.*, 49:370–374.

_____ (1971), The "real" relationship between the patient and the psychoanalyst. In: *The Unconscious Today*, ed. M. Kanzer. New York: International Universities Press, pp. 213–232.

_____ (1972), Beyond transference and interpretation. *Internat. J. Psycho-Anal.*, 53:213–217.

Grossman, W. I. (1982), The self as fantasy: Fantasy as theory. *J. Amer. Psychoanal. Assn.*, 30:919–937.

_____ (1986), Notes on masochism: A discussion of the history and development of a psychoanalytic concept. *Psychoanal. Quart.*, 55:379–413.

Grotstein, J. (1982), The spectrum of aggression. *Psychoanal. Inq.*, 2:193–211.

Hartmann, H. (1950), Comments on the psychoanalytic theory of the ego. In: *Essays on Ego Psychology*. New York: International Universities Press, 1964, pp. 113–141.

_____ (1952), The mutual influences in the development of ego and id. In: *Essays on Ego Psychology*. New York: Interna tional Universities Press, 1964, pp. 155–181.

_____ (1955), Notes on the theory of sublimation. In: *Essays on Ego Psychology*. New York: International Universities Press, 1964, pp. 215–240.

Hill, L. B. (1938), The use of hostility as defense. *Psychoanal. Quart.*, 7:254–264.

Isay, R. (1985), On the analytic therapy of homosexual men. *The Psychoanalytic Study of the Child*, 40:235–254. New Haven, CT: Yale University Press.

_____ (1986), The development of sexual identity in homosexual men. *The Psychoanalytic Study of the Child*, 41:467–489. New Haven, CT: Yale University Press.

_____ (1987), Fathers and their homosexually inclined sons in childhood. *The Psychoanalytic Study of the Child*, 42:275–294. New Haven, CT: Yale University Press.

_____ (1989), *Being Homosexual: Gay Men and Their Development*. New York: Avon Books.

Jacobson, E. (1959), The "exceptions": an elaboration of Freud's character study. *The Psychoanalytic Study of the Child*, 14:135–154. New York: International Universities Press.

_____ (1964), *The Self and the Object World*. New York: International Universities Press.

Jessner, L., Blom, G. E. & Waldfogel, S. (1952), Emotional implications of tonsillectomy and adenoidectomy on children. *The Psychoanalytic Study of the Child*, 7:126–169. New York: International Universities Press.

Joffe, W. G. (1969), A critical review of the status of the envy concept. *Internat. J. Psycho-Anal.*, 50:533–545.

Jones, E. (1927), The early development of female sexuality. *Internat. J. Psychoanal.*, 8:459–472.

_____ (1929), Jealousy. In: *Papers on Psychoanalysis*. Boston: Beacon, 1961, pp. 325–340.

Joseph, E., ed. (1967), *Indications for Psychoanalysis*. New York: International Universities Press.

Jucovy, M. (1976), Initiation fantasies and transvestism. *J. Amer. Psychoanal. Assn.*, 24:525–546.

Kanzer, M. (1952), The transference neurosis of the Rat Man. *Psychoanal. Quart.*, 21:81–189.

Kavka, J. (1962), Ego synthesis of a life-threatening illness in childhood. *The Psychoanalytic Study of the Child*, 17:344–362. New York: International Universities Press.

Kernberg, O. F. (1974), Barriers to falling and remaining in love. *J. Amer. Psychoanal. Assn.*, 22: 486–511.

_____ (1975), *Borderline Conditions and Pathological Narcissism*. New York: Aronson.

_____ (1984), Clinical aspects of severe superego pathology. In: *Severe Personality*

Disorders: Psychotherapeutic Strategies. New Haven, CT: Yale University Press, pp. 275–289.

_____ (1988), Clinical dimensions of masochism. In: *Masochism: Current Psychoanalytic Perspectives*, ed. R. A. Glick & D. I. Meyers. Hillsdale, NJ: The Analytic Press, pp. 61–79.

Kernberg, P. (1984), Reflections in the mirror: Mother-child interactions, self-awareness, and self-recognition. Presented to the Association for Psychoanalytic Medicine, New York City.

Khan, M.M.R. (1962), The role of polymorph-perverse body experiences and object-relations in ego-integration. *Brit. J. Med. Psychol.*, 35:245–261.

_____ (1964), The role of infantile sexuality and early object relations in female homosexuality. In: *Pathology and Treatment of Sexual Deviations*, ed. I. Rosen. London: Oxford University Press, pp. 221–292.

_____ (1965a), The function of intimacy and acting out in perversions. In: *Sexual Behavior and the Law*, ed. R. Slovenko. Springfield, IL: Thomas, pp. 397–412.

_____ (1965b), Foreskin fetishism and its relation to ego-pathology in a male homosexual. *Internat. J. Psycho-Anal.*, 46:64–80.

_____ (1969), Role of the "collated internal object" in perversion-formations. *Internat. J. Psycho-Anal.*, 50:555–565.

_____ (1979), *Alienation in Perversions.* New York: International Universities Press.

Kleeman, J. (1971), The establishment of core gender identity in normal girls. *Arch. Sex. Behav.*, 1:103–129.

Klein, G. S. (1976a), Freud's two theories of sexuality. In: *Psychoanalytic Theory: An Exploration of Essentials.* New York: International Universities Press, pp. 72–102.

_____ (1976b), The resolution of experienced incompatibility in psychological development. In: *Psychoanalytic Theory: An Exploration of Essentials.* New York: International Universities Press, pp. 163–209.

Kohut, H. (1971), *The Analysis of the Self.* New York: International Universities Press.

_____ (1972), Thoughts on narcissism and narcissistic rage. *The Psychoanalytic Study of the Child*, 27:360–400. New Haven, CT: Yale University Press.

_____ (1977), *The Restoration of the Self.* New York: International Universities Press.

_____ (1979), The two analyses of Mr. Z. *Internat. J. Psycho-Anal.*, 60:3–27.

Kornfeld, D. S. (1985), Psychiatric factors in the management of pain. In: *Pain Research and Treatment*, ed. S. J. Levitan & H. L. Berkowitz. Washington, DC: American Psychiatric Press, pp. 50–77.

Kris, E. (1956a), On some vicissitudes of insight in psychoanalysis. In: *Selected Papers of Ernst Kris.* New Haven, CT: Yale University Press, 1975, pp. 252–271.

_____ (1956b), The personal myth: A problem in psychoanalytic technique. In: *Selected Papers of Ernst Kris.* New Haven, CT: Yale University Press, 1975, pp. 272–300.

_____ (1956c), The recovery of childhood memories in psychoanalysis. In: *Selected Papers of Ernst Kris.* New Haven, CT: Yale University Press, 1975, pp. 301–340.

Kubie, L. (1939), A critical analysis of the concept of a repetition compulsion. *Internat. J. Psycho-Anal.*, 20:390–402.

Laforgue, R. (1930), On the eroticization of anxiety. *Internat. J. Psycho-Anal.*, 11:312–321.

Lagache, D. (1950), Homosexuality and jealousy. *Internat. J. Psycho-Anal.*, 31:24–31.

Langs, R. (1980), The misalliance dimension in the case of the Rat Man. In: *Freud and His Patients, Vol. 2.*, ed. M. Kanzer & J. Glenn. New York: Aronson, pp. 215–231.

Lax, R. (1972), Some aspects of the interaction between mother and impaired child: Mother's narcissistic trauma. *Internat. J. Psycho-Anal.*, 53:339–344.

_____ (1975), Some comments on the narcissistic aspects of self-righteousness:

Defensive and structural considerations. *Internat. J. Psycho-Anal.*, 56:283–292.

Levin, S. (1970), On the psychoanalysis of attitudes of entitlement. *Bull. Phila. Assn. Psychoanal.*, 20:1–10.

Levine, H. (1979), The sustaining object relationship. *The Annual of Psychoanalysis*, 7:203–231. New York: International Universities Press.

Lichtenstein, H. (1961), Identity and sexuality: A study of their interrelationship in man. *J. Amer. Psychoanal Assn.*, 9:179–260.

_____ (1970), Changing implications of the concept of psychosexual development. *J. Amer. Psychoanal. Assn.*, 18:300–318.

Lipton, S. (1962), On the psychology of childhood tonsillectomy. *The Psychoanalytic Study of the Child*, 17:363–417. New York: International Universities Press.

Litin, E., Giffin, M. & Johnson, A. (1956), Parental influences in unusual sexual behavior in children. *Psychoanal. Quart.*, 25:37–55.

Loewald, H. W. (1952), The problem of defense and the neurotic interpretation of reality. *Internat. J. Psycho-Anal.*, 33:444–449.

_____ (1960), On the therapeutic action of psychoanalysis. In: *Papers on Psychoanalysis*. New Haven, CT: Yale University Press, 1980, pp. 221–256.

_____ (1970), Psychoanalytic theory and the psychoanalytic process. In: *Papers on Psychoanalysis*. New Haven, CT: Yale University Press, 1980, pp. 277–301.

_____ (1971a), The transference neurosis: Comments on the concept and the phenomenon. In: *Papers on Psychoanalysis*. New Haven, CT: Yale University Press, 1980, pp. 302–314.

_____ (1971b), Some considerations on repetition and repetitioncompulsion. *Internat. J. Psycho-Anal.*, 52:59–66.

_____ (1975), Psychoanalysis as an art and the fantasy character of the psychoanalytic situation. In: *Papers on Psychoanalysis*. New Haven, CT: Yale University Press, 1980, pp. 352–371.

_____ (1979), The waning of the oedipus complex. *J. Amer. Psychoanal. Assn.*, 27:751–775.

Loewenstein, R. M. (1957), A contribution to the psychoanalytic theory of masochism. *J. Amer. Psychoanal. Assn.*, 5:197–234.

Lorenz, K. (1935), Companionship in bird life. In: *Instinctive Behavior*, ed. & trans. C. H. Schiller. New York: International Universities Press, 1957, pp. 83–128.

_____ (1937), The nature of instinct. In: *Instinctive Behavior*, ed. & trans. C. H. Schiller. New York: International Universities Press, 1957, pp. 129–175.

Lussier, A. (1960), The analysis of a boy with a congenital deformity. *The Psychoanalytic Study of the Child*, 15:430–453. New York: International Universities Press.

_____ (1980), The physical handicap and the body ego. *Internat. J. Psycho-Anal.*, 61:179–185.

Mahler, M. S. & McDevitt, J. B. (1982), Thoughts on the emergence of the sense of self, with particular emphasis on the body self. *J. Amer. Psychoanal. Assn.*, 30:827–848.

Mahony, P. (1986), *Freud and the Rat Man*. New Haven, CT: Yale University Press.

Maleson, F. G. (1984), The multiple meanings of masochism in psychoanalytic discourse. *J. Amer. Psychoanal. Assn.*, 32:325–356.

Margolis, M. (1977), A preliminary report of a case of consummated mother-son incest. *The Annual of Psychoanalysis*, 5:267–293. New York: International Universities Press.

McDougall, J. (1970), Homosexuality in women. In: *Female Sexuality: New Psychoanalytic Views*, ed. J. Chasseguet-Smirgel. Ann Arbor: University of Michigan Press, pp. 94–134.

_____ (1972), Primal scene and sexual perversion. *Internat. J. Psycho-Anal.*, 53:371–384.

_____ (1980), *Plea for a Measure of Abnormality*. New York: International Universities Press.

Menaker, E. (1953), Masochism: A defense reaction of the ego. *Psychoanal. Quart.*, 22:205–220.

Meyer, J. (1982), The theory of gender identity disorders. *J. Amer. Psychoanal. Assn.*, 30:381–418.

Modell, A. H. (1961), Denial and the sense of separateness. *J. Amer. Psychoanal. Assn.*, 9:533–547.

_____ (1965), On having the right to a life: An aspect of the superego's development. *Internat. J. Psycho-Anal.*, 45:323–331.

_____ (1971), The origin of certain forms of preoedipal guilt and their implications for a psychoanalytic theory of affects. *Internat. J. Psycho-Anal.*, 52:337–346.

_____ (1976), The "holding environment" and the therapeutic action of psychoanalysis. *J. Amer. Psychoanal. Assn.*, 24:285–307.

_____ (1984), *Psychoanalysis in a New Context*. New York: International Universities Press.

Moore, W. T. (1975), The impact of surgery on boys. *The Psychoanalytic Study of the Child*, 30:529–548. New Haven, CT: Yale University Press.

Murray, J. (1964), Narcissism and the ego ideal. *J. Amer. Psychoanal. Assn.*, 12:477–511. New Haven, CT: Yale University Press.

Muslin, H. (1979), Transference in the Rat Man case: Transference in transition. *J. Amer. Psychoanal. Assn.*, 27:561–578.

Myers, W. (1973), Split self-representation and the primal scene. *Psychoanal. Quart.*, 42:525–538.

Nacht, S. (1948), Aggression and its role in psychoanalytic treatment. *Internat. J. Psycho-Anal.*, 29: 201–223.

Niederland, W. G. (1956), Clinical observation on the "little man" phenomenon. *The Psychoanalytic Study of the Child*, 11:381–395. New York: International Universities Press.

_____ (1965), Narcissistic ego impairment in patients with early physical malformations. *The Psychoanalytic Study of the Child*, 20:518–534. New Haven, CT: Yale University Press.

_____ (1975), Scarred: A contribution to the study of facial disfigurement. *Psychoanal. Quart.*, 44:450–459.

Novick, J. (1990), Discussion of "Sexual addiction" by S. Coen. Presented to the Symposium on Perversion, Michigan Psychoanalytic Society, Dearborn, MI.

_____ & Novick, K. K. (1991), Some comments on masochism and the delusion of omnipotence from a developmental perspective. *J. Amer. Psychoanal. Assn.*, 39:307–331.

Novick, K. K. & Novick, J. (1987), The essence of masochism. *The Psychoanalytic Study of the Child*, 42:353–384. New Haven, CT: Yale University Press.

Nunberg, H. (1932), *Principles of Psychoanalysis*. New York: International Universities Press, 1955.

_____ (1938), Homosexuality, magic and aggression. *Internat. J. Psycho-Anal.*, 19:1–16.

Nydes, J. (1950), The magical experience of the masturbation fantasy. *Amer. J. Psychother.*, 4:303–310.

Ogden, T. H. (1979), On projective identification. *Internat. J. Psycho-Anal.*, 60:367–373.

_____ (1983), The concept of internal object relations. *Internat. J. Psycho-Anal.*, 64:227–241.

Oremland, J. D., Blacker, K. H. & Norman, H. F. (1975), Incompleteness in "successful" psychoanalysis: A follow-up study. *J. Amer. Psychoanal. Assn.*, 23:819–844.

Ostow, M.. ed. (1974), *Sexual Deviation: Psychoanalytic Insights.* New York: Quadrangle.

Ovesey, L. & Person, E. (1973), Gender identity and sexual psychopathology in men: A psychodynamic analysis of homosexuality, transsexualism, and transvestism. *J. Amer. Acad. Psychoanal.*, 1:53–72.

_____ (1976), Transvestism: A disorder of the sense of self. *Internat. J. Psychoanal. Psychother.*, 5:219–236.

Panel (1979), The infantile neurosis in child and adult analysis, reporter J. S. Malkin. *J. Amer. Psychoanal. Assn.*, 27:643–654.

Panel (1991), Hate in the analytic setting. Presented at meeting of the American Psychoanalytic Association, New Orleans.

Pao, P.-N. (1965), The role of hatred in the ego. *Psychoanal. Quart.*, 34:257–264.

_____ (1969), Pathological jealousy. *Psychoanal. Quart.*, 38:616–638.

Parens, H., Pollock, L., Stern, J. & Kramer, S. (1976), On the girl's entry into the Oedipus complex. *J. Amer. Psychoanal. Assn.*, 24 (suppl.):79–107.

_____ & Saul, L. J. (1971), *Dependence in Man: A Psychoanalytic Study.* New York: International Universities Press.

Parkin, A. (1980), On masochistic enthralment. A contribution to the study of moral masochism. *Internat. J. Psycho-Anal.*, 61:307–314.

Payne, S. M. (1939), The fetishist and his ego. In: *The Psychoanalytic Reader*, ed. R. Fliess. New York: International Universities Press, 1948, pp. 21–30.

Person, E. (1976), Discussion of Jucovy (1976). *J. Amer. Psychoanal. Assn.*, 24:547–551.

_____ & Ovesey, L. (1974), The transsexual syndrome in males. *Amer. J. Psychother.*, 28:4–20, 174–193.

_____ (1978), Transvestism: New perspectives. *J. Amer. Acad. Psychoanal.*, 6:301–323.

_____ (1983), Psychoanalytic theories of gender identity. *J. Amer. Acad. Psychoanal.*, 11:203–227.

Peto, A. (1975), The etiological significance of the primal scene in perversions. *Psychoanal. Quart.*, 44:177–190.

Plank, E. N. & Horwood, C. (1961), Leg amputation in a four-year-old: Reactions of the child, her family, and the staff. *The Psychoanalytic Study of the Child*, 16:405–422. New York: International Universities Press.

Porder, M. S. (1987), Projective identification: An alternative hypothesis. *Psychoanal. Quart.*, 56:431–451.

Rado, S. (1945–1955), In: *Adaptational Psychodynamics: Motivation and Control*, ed. J. Jameson & H. Klein. New York: Science House, 1969.

Räkköläinen, V. & Alanen, V. O. (1982), On the transactionality of defensive processes. *Internat. Rev. Psycho-Anal.*, 9:263–272.

Rapaport, D. (1953), Some metapsychological considerations concerning activity and passivity. In: *The Collected Papers of David Rapaport*, ed. M. M. Gill. New York: Basic Books, 1967, pp. 530–568.

_____ (1957), A theoretical analysis of the superego concept. In: *The Collected Papers of David Rapaport*, ed. M. M. Gill. New York: Basic Books, 1967, pp. 685–709.

Rappaport, E. (1956), The management of an erotized transference. *Psychoanal. Quart.*, 25:515–529.

_____ (1959), The first dream in an erotized transference. *Internat. J. Psycho-Anal.*, 40:240–245.

Raskin, M., Talbott, J. A. & Meyerson, A. T. (1966), Diagnosis of conversion reactions: Predictive value of psychiatric criteria. *J. Amer. Med. Assn.*, 197:102–106.

Richards, A. (1981), Self theory, conflict theory, and the problem of hypochondriasis. *The Psychoanalytic Study of the Child*, 36:319–337. New Haven, CT: Yale University Press.

Riviere, J. (1932), Jealousy as a mechanism of defense. *Internat. J. Psycho-Anal.*, 13:414–424.

Robertson, J. (1956), A mother's observations on the tonsillectomy of her four-year-old daughter. *The Psychoanalytic Study of the Child*, 11:410–433. New York: International Universities Press.

Roiphe, H. & Galenson, E. (1981), *Infantile Origins of Sexual Identity*. New York: International Universities Press.

Rosen, I., ed. (1979), *Sexual Deviation*, 2d ed. Oxford: Oxford University Press.

Rosenberg, E. (1949), Anxiety and the capacity to bear it. *Internat. J. Psycho-Anal.*, 30:1–12.

Rothstein, A. (1977), The ego attitude of entitlement. *Internat. J. Psycho-Anal.*, 4:409–417.

Rubinfine, D. L. (1965), On beating fantasies. *Internat. J. Psycho-Anal.*, 46:315–322.

Sacher-Masoch, L. von (1870), *Sacher-Masoch, An Interpretation by Gilles Deleuze, Together with the Entire Text of "Venus in Furs,"* trans. J. M. McNeil. London: Faber & Faber, 1971.

Sachs, H. (1923), On the genesis of perversions. Appendix to C. Socarides, *Homosexuality*. New York: Aronson, 1978, pp. 531–546.

Sade, D. A. F. de (1785), The 120 days of Sodom. In: *The 120 Days of Sodom and Other Writings*, comp. & trans. A. Wainhouse & R. Seaver. New York: Grove Press, 1966, pp. 189–674.

————— (1791), Justine, or good conduct well chastised. In: *The Complete Justine, Philosophy in the Bedroom and Other Writings*. comp. & trans. R. Seaver & A. Wainhouse. New York: Grove Press, 1965, pp. 453–743.

Sander, F. (1989), Marital conflict and psychoanalytic theory. In: *The Middle Years: New Psychoanalytic Perspectives*, ed. R. Liebert & J. Oldham. New Haven, CT: Yale University Press, pp. 160–176.

Sandler, J. (1960), On the concept of superego. *The Psychoanalytic Study of the Child*, 15:128–162. New York: International Universities Press.

—————Holder, A. & Meers, D. (1963), The ego ideal and the ideal self. *The Psychoanalytic Study of the Child*, 18:139–158. New York: International Universities Press.

————— & Sandler, A. M. (1978), On the development of object relationships and affects. *Internat. J. Psycho-Anal.*, 58:285–296.

—————with A. Freud (1985), *The Analysis of Defense: The Ego and the Mechanisms of Defense Revisited*. New York: International Universities Press.

Sargent, M. (1946), Psychosomatic backache. *New Eng. J. Med.*, 234:427–430.

Sarno, J. E. (1974), Psychogenic backache: The missing dimension. *J. Fam. Practice*, 1:8–12.

————— (1976), Chronic back pain and psychic conflict. *Scand. J. Rehab. Med.*, 8:143–153.

————— (1977), Psychosomatic backache. *J. Fam. Practice*, 5:353–357.

————— (1981), Etiology of neck and back pain: An autonomic myoneuralgia? *J. Nerv. Ment. Dis.*, 169:55–59.

————— (1984a), *Mind Over Back Pain*. New York: Morrow.

————— (1984b), Therapeutic exercise for back pain. In: *Therapeutic Exercise*, 4th ed., ed. J. V. Basmajian. Baltimore, MD: Williams & Wilkins, pp. 441–463.

Savitt, R. A. (1969), Transference, somatization, and symbiotic need. *J. Amer. Psychoanal. Assn.*, 17:1030–1054.

Schacht, L. (1981), The mirroring function of the child analyst. *J. Child Psychother.*, 7:79–88.

Schafer, R. (1960), The loving and beloved superego in Freud's structural theory. *The*

Psychoanalytic Study of the Child, 15:163–188. New York: International Universities Press.
_____ (1983), The psychoanalyst's empathic activity. In: *The Analytic Attitude*. New York: Basic Books, pp. 34–57.
Schmideberg, M. (1953), Some aspects of jealousy and of feeling hurt. *Psychoanal. Rev.*, 40:1–16.
Schur, M. (1955), Comments on the metapsychology of somatization. *The Psychoanalytic Study of the Child*, 10:119–164. New York: International Universities Press.
Seeman, M. V. (1979), Pathological jealousy. *Psychiat.*, 42:351–361.
Segel, N. F. (1969), Repetition compulsion, acting out, and identification with the doer. *J. Amer. Psychoanal. Assn.*, 17:474–488.
Seidenberg, R. (1952), Jealousy: The wish. *Psychoanal. Rev.*, 39:345–353.
Shapiro, D. (1976), The analyst's own analysis. *J. Amer. Psychoanal. Assn.*, 24:5–42.
Shapiro, D. (1981), *Autonomy and Rigid Character*. New York: Basic Books.
Shapiro, R. (1985), Separation-individuation and the compulsion to repeat. *Contemp. Psychoanal.*, 21:297–308.
Shengold, L. (1963), The parent as sphinx. *J. Amer. Psycho-Anal. Assn.*, 11:725–741.
_____ (1967), The effects of overstimulation: Rat people. *Internat. J. Psycho-Anal.*, 48:403–415.
_____ (1971), More about rats and rat people. *Internat. J. Psycho-Anal.*, 52:277–288.
_____ (1974), The metaphor of the mirror. *J. Amer. Psychoanal. Assn.*, 22:97–115.
_____ (1988), *Halo in the Sky*. New York: Guilford Press.
Siegel, E. V. (1988), *Female Homosexuality: Choice Without Volition*. Hillsdale, NJ: The Analytic Press.
Sifneos, P. (1974), Reconsideration of psychodynamic mechanisms in psychosomatic symptom formation. *Psychother. Psychosom.*, 24:151–155.
Smirnoff, V. N. (1969), The masochistic contract. *Internat. J. Psychoanal.*, 50:665–671.
Smith, G. R. (1959), Iago the paranoiac. *Amer. Imago*, 16:155–167.
Socarides, C. W. (1968), *The Overt Homosexual*. New York: Jason Aronson.
_____ (1978), *Homosexuality*. New York: Aronson.
Solnit, A. J. & Stark, M. H. (1961), Mourning and the birth of a defective child. *The Psychoanalytic Study of the Child*, 16:523–537. New York: International Universities Press.
Sperling, M. (1959), A study of deviant sexual behavior in children by the method of simultaneous analysis of mother and child. In: *Dynamic Psychopathology in Childhood*, ed. L. Jessner & E. Pavenstedt. New York: Grune & Stratton, pp. 221–243.
_____ (1968), Acting-out behavior and psychosomatic symptoms: Clinical and theoretical aspects. *Internat. J. Psycho-Anal.*, 49:250–253.
Spielman, P. M. (1971), Envy and jealousy: An attempt at clarification. *Psychoanal. Quart.*, 40:59–82.
Stein, M. (1981), The unobjectionable part of the transference. *J. Amer. Psychoanal. Assn.*, 29:869–892.
Stern, D. (1982), The early development of schemas of self, of other, and of various experiences of "self with other." In: *Reflections on Self Psychology*, ed. D. A. Berkowitz. New York: International Universities Press, pp. 49–84.
Sternbach, R. A., Wolf, S. R., Murphy, R. W. & Akeson, W. H. (1973), Aspects of chronic low back pain. *Psychosom.*, 14:52–56.
Stoller, R. (1968), *Sex and Gender*. New York: Science House.
_____ (1975), *Perversion: The Erotic Form of Hatred*. New York: Pantheon.
_____ (1976a), Sexual excitement. *Arch. Gen. Psychiat.*, 33:899–909.
_____ (1976b), Primary feminity. *J. Amer. Psychoanal. Assn.*, 24 (supple.):59–78.
_____ (1979), *Sexual Excitement: Dynamics of Erotic Life*. New York: Pantheon.

Stolorow, R. (1975a), Addendum to a partial analysis of a perversion involving bugs. *Internat. J. Psycho-Anal.*, 56:361–364.

_____ (1975b), The narcissistic function of masochism (and sadism). *Internat. J. Psycho-Anal.*, 56:441–448.

_____ (1979), Psychosexuality and the representational world. *Internat. J. Psycho-Anal.*, 60:39–45.

Strachey, J. (1934), The nature of the therapeutic action of psychoanalysis. In: *The Evolution of Psychoanalytic Technique*, ed. M. S. Bergmann & F. R. Hartman. New York: Basic Books, pp. 331–360.

Szalita, A. (1982), Further thoughts on reanalysis. *Contemp. Psychoanal.*, 18:327–348.

Valenstein, A. F. (1971), The defense mechanisms and activities of the ego: Some aspects of a classificatory approach. In: *The Unconscious Today*, ed. M. Kanzer. New York: International Universities Press, pp. 127–136.

_____ (1973), On attachment to painful feelings and the negative therapeutic reaction. *The Psychoanalytic Study of the Child*, 28:365–392. New Haven, CT: Yale University Press.

_____ (1979), The concept of "classical" psychoanalysis. *J. Amer. Psychoanal. Assn.*, 27:113–136.

Waelder, R. (1930), The principle of multiple function: Observations on overdetermination. In: *Psychoanalysis: Observation, Theory, Application. Selected Papers of Robert Waelder*, ed. S. A. Guttman. New York: International Universities Press, 1976, pp. 68–83.

Walters, A. (1961), Psychogenic regional pain alias hysterical pain. *Brain*, 84:1–18.

Wangh, M. (1952), Othello: The tragedy of Iago. *Psychoanal. Quart.*, 19:202–212.

Weil, A. (1970), The basic core. *The Psychoanalytic Study of the Child*, 25:442–460.

_____ (1978), Maturational variations and genetic-dynamic issues. *J. Amer. Psychoanal. Assn.*, 26:461–491.

Willick, M. S. (1987), Review of *Borderline Psychopathology and Its Treatment* by G. Adler. *Psychoanal. Quart.*, 56:553–558.

Wilson, A. & Malatesta, C. (1989), Affect and the compulsion to repeat: Freud's repetition compulsion revisited. *Psychoanal. & Contemp. Thought*, 12:243–290.

Winnicott, D. W. (1948), Reparation in respect of mother's organized defense against depression. In: *Through Paediatrics to Psychoanalysis*. New York: Basic Books, 1975, pp. 91–96.

_____ (1956), The antisocial tendency. In: *Through Paediatrics to Psychoanalysis*. New York: Basic Books, 1975, pp. 306–315.

_____ (1967), Mirror role of mother and family in child development. In: *Playing and Reality*. New York: Basic Books, 1980, pp. 111–118.

Wisdom, J. O. (1959), On a differentiating mechanism of psychosomatic disorder. *Internat. J. Psycho-Anal.*, 40:134–144.

Yorke, C. (1980), Some comments on the psychoanalytic treatment of patients with physical disabilities. *Internat. J. Psycho-Anal.*, 61:187–193.

Ziegler, F. J., Imboden, J. B. & Meyer, E. (1960), Contemporary conversion reactions: A clinical study. *Amer. J. Psychiat.*, 116:901–910.

INDEX